Jo Draper's parents were from two long-established Hampshire families, one small-holders from near Wickham, the other blacksmiths at Droxford. She went to schools at West Meon, Portchester and Fareham, and started her archaeological career on Ports Down in the snows of Christmas 1964. She now lives in Dorset and has written several books including *Thomas Hardy's England* (with John Fowles), *Dorset: The Complete Guide, Dorset Food* and *Hampshire Curiosities*.

FRONTISPIECE *Selborne*

JO DRAPER

HAMPSHIRE

The Complete Guide

THE DOVECOTE PRESS

For my mother, Betty Margaret Draper, 1922-1990
She loved Hampshire

First published in 1990 by the Dovecote Press Ltd,
Stanbridge, Wimborne, Dorset BH21 4JD
ISBN 0 -946159 -82 -3
© Jo Draper 1990

Designed by Humphrey Stone
Photoset by The Typesetting Bureau Ltd,
Wimborne, Dorset
Origination by Chroma Graphics
(Overseas) Pte Ltd, Singapore
Printed by Kim Hup Lee Printing Co Pte Ltd, Singapore

British Library Catalogue in Publication Data
Jo Draper
Hampshire, the complete guide
1. Hampshire – Visitors' guides
1. Title
914.22704859

Contents

The main MAP *and six pages of colour plates
fall between pages 96/97*

Using this Book

I have tried to include every village (and as many interesting hamlets as I could find) in the Gazetteer, and all the places open to the public.

The main map, which forms the centre of the colour section in the middle of the book, shows the position of virtually all the entries in the alphabetical Gazetteer, and really forms the index. The letter bracketed after the entry gives the relevant square on which it can be found on the map. In addition, each of the towns has its own map, showing car parks and tourist information offices as well as features of interest.

The introductory Glorious Hampshire gives brief descriptions of each main area in the county and lists all the most interesting places in it. The sections on museums, walking, houses and so on list all the best of those categories, hopefully forming another sort of index.

The Lists at the back of the book given opening times and other information, including as a rough price guide all those places which charge admission, indicated in the Gazetteer by 'fee'.

For getting about the county the Ordnance Survey's 1:50,000 (which used to be the one inch) map is vital. Most of Hampshire falls within sheets 185, 186, 195 and 196, but there are fringes of the county on 174, 175, 184 and 197. For walking the larger 1:25,000 (the old 2½ inch) is better, especially as it looks as though one has walked further, and all the rights of way are shown. There is a useful, especially extensive sheet for the New Forest (Outdoor Leisure Map) which is a must. Modern editions of the 1:50,000 (and the New Forest 1:25,000) give useful 'tourist' information in blue – viewpoints, houses, gardens and monuments open to the public, information centres and so on.

The ★ system of grading used here is bound to be a problem, and I will be the only person to agree with all the ratings. The top is fairly obvious and straightforward: most people would agree that Winchester Cathedral is ★ ★ ★ ★ (if not more) and that many of the 19th century churches are not of great interest. It is the middle, the ★ ★ and ★ ★ ★, which are more controversial, and inevitably rather arbitrary. Broadly I have tried to reserve ★ ★ ★ ★ for those places which are worth travelling to see, and these, along with the ★ ★ ★ are listed both in the sections on areas and on subjects, so that they cannot be missed. Allowance has been made for quantity as well as quality, so that although Greatham Mill or Spinners, Boldre are first class gardens, they rate ★ ★ ★, behind all the larger gardens, where there is more to see.

19th century churches are dealt with in their own right, not dismissed as second-rate imitations, which may be regarded as heresy by some entrenched medievalists, but Hampshire does have some good specimens.

I have had to confine myself strictly to Hampshire, using blinkers when necessary – there are all sorts of interesting places just over the borders which are completely ignored.

I will be glad to hear of omissions and mistakes in this Guide, and they should be addressed to me via the publisher: Dovecote Press Ltd, Stanbridge, Wimborne, Dorset BH21 4JD.

Glorious Hampshire

A small province it is, fruitfull in corne, furnished in some places with pleasant woods standing thicke, and well growne; rich in plenteous pasture, and for all commodities of sea most wealthy, and happie

WILLIAM CAMDEN *Britannia 1586*

THE NEW FOREST

Towns Brockenhurst, Lymington, Lyndhurst, Ringwood.
Villages ★ Beaulieu; Breamore; Buckler's Hard; Damerham; Martin; Rockbourne. ★ ★ ★ Eling.
Houses ★ ★ ★ Beaulieu; Breamore.
Forts ★ ★ Calshot Castle; Hurst Castle.
Gardens ★ ★ ★ Exbury. ★ ★ ★ Furzey Gardens, Minstead; MacPenny's, Bransgore; Spinners, Boldre.
Walking The whole of the New Forest but particularly: ★ ★ ★ Beaulieu estuary; Bolderwood Ornamental Drive; Burley; Knightwood Oak; Lymington area; Lyndhurst area; Rhinefield Ornamental Drive; Ringwood area. ★ ★ ★ Fritham, Hatchett Pond, and East Boldre.
Other areas: ★ ★ ★ Downland: Martin Down. Shore: Lepe Country Park.
Churches ★ ★ ★ Beaulieu; Breamore; Milford on Sea; Minstead. 19th century Lyndhurst; 18th century Hale; Ringwood Chapel.
Museums ★ ★ ★ Breamore Countryside and Carriage Museum, Buckler's Hard; National Motor Museum, Beaulieu; Sammy Miller (Motorcycles) Museum, New Milton. ★ ★ ★ New Forest Museum, Lyndhurst.
Animals ★ ★ ★ Longdown Dairy Farm; Longdown Butterfly Farm; New Forest Owl Sanctuary.
Other ★ ★ ★ Eling Tide Mill; Woodgreen Village Hall.

Camden emphasises Hampshire's agricultural riches, and its sea harvests, but surprises by calling the county small. It is the ninth largest English county, and very varied, changing from coastal clays to chalk and back to heathy sands and clays in the north. This diversity impressed Britton and Bayley in 1800: 'The surface of Hampshire is beautifully varied with gently rising hills, and fruitful vallies, adorned with numerous seats and villages, and interspersed with extensive woodlands. Its southern parts were the first peopled, and there the population is still the greatest; the mildness of the seasons, and the convenience of the ports, operating as strong inducements to continued residence.'

There are still extensive woodlands, and still the southern parts have the greatest population. Hampshire's diversity makes it a fascinating county to explore and a good one for continued residence.

The heart of this area is the New Forest, the largest wild area in lowland Britain, covering 145 square miles (more than 90,000 acres). The soils are poor and acid, and almost half the area is grassland or heath, much of the heathland being covered with heather. There are lots of bogs, and peaty brown streams. The woods vary from old oak, beech and holly to modern plantations of conifer, but happily the native trees still dominate and the conifer plantations are only a small area. There are a few fences apart from those keeping animals off the main roads – the bulk of the forest is not enclosed.

The landscape is undulating, and with the great variety of vegetation, provides frequently changing views. The whole area is superb for walking, and even a short stroll from the car parks gives a feeling of remoteness, of being in a wilderness. The south and east of the Forest are the most popular areas, so that in summer it is best to head north and west to escape the crowds.

There is hardly any arable in the New Forest, but lots of animals running wild. All the ponies belong to someone, as do the pigs, donkeys and cattle, but they fend for themselves and are very hardy. The five different species of deer are less likely to be seen, although there are a goodly number of them.

Most of the inhabitants of the New Forest were not farmers but commoners, living by their rights to graze animals, cut turves, gather firewood and so on. *The Children of the New Forest* gives a rather romantic view of forest life, but the New Forest Museum in Lyndhurst illustrates the reality well. There are only a few older cottages surviving in the Forest because many of them were flimsily built of cob and thatch. Most of the houses date from late Victorian or Edwardian times when it changed from a remote backwater to a fashionable place for both living in and holidays.

On all except the main roads the Forest boundary is clear because of the cattle grids across the road to prevent animals from straying. Until these were put in ponies grazed road verges as far as Christchurch and Totton.

The southern part of the forest, now mostly outside the boundary, is flatter, better land which has more agriculture, and so there are more villages and many more old farmhouses. The area from Lymington to the Beaulieu river is still rural, but from Lymington eastwards there is much development, although the area is still woody. The shore is sandy, particularly in the west, and Milford on Sea and Barton on Sea have developed as small resorts.

TOP *New Forest heathland*
ABOVE *Cottage at Martin*
RIGHT *Mark Ash beeches, New Forest*

On the west the Forest is bounded by the wide flat valley of the Avon, with a distinct steep short slope up to the Forest. The big river wanders about the valley, which has arable fields and watermeadows, rich in contrast to the Forest.

To the north-west of the Forest is a little corner of chalk, very like adjoining Wiltshire. This part is low, rolling and agricultural, mostly still pasture but with some woods. Right on the country boundary is preserved a large area of downland, Martin Down.

The eastern side of the Forest is bounded by Southampton Water, and here there is much modern development and industry, including the massive oil refinery at Fawley and Fawley Power Station.

The long tongue of Southampton Water and the wide estuaries of the Hamble and Itchen rivers offer sheltered anchorages and deep water, advantages which made the development of the port at Southampton and ship building industries inevitable. Whereas Portsmouth is the Royal Navy, Southampton is a commercial port, for both cargoes and passengers. The land around Southampton was poor, not useful for much agriculturally and now covered by development.

Southampton is Hampshire's largest city, with a vast shopping centre, big new office blocks around the railway station and lots of suburbs. The Docks for container ships expand up Southampton Water, but the older town end of the docks has been converted to housing. The modern developments, the docks and

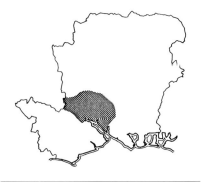

SOUTHAMPTON EASTLEIGH ROMSEY

Towns Eastleigh, Romsey, Southampton.
Villages ★ ★ ★ ★ Botley; Hamble.
Houses ★ ★ ★ ★ Broadlands. ★ ★ ★
Medieval Merchant's House, Southampton.
Archaeology ★ ★ ★ ★ Southampton Town Walls. ★ ★ ★ Netley Abbey.
Walking ★ ★ ★ ★ Brownwich and Chilling, Hill Head; Holly Hill Park Sarisbury; Lower Test Nature Reserve, Southampton; Royal Victoria Country Park, Netley; Upper Hamble Country Park; Warsash shore. ★ ★ ★ Itchen Valley Country Park.
Churches ★ ★ ★ ★ Romsey Abbey ★ ★ ★ East Wellow, North Stoneham; and St Michael, Southampton.
Museums ★ ★ ★ ★ God's House Tower, Southampton; Hampshire Farm Museum, Upper Hamble Country Park; Maritime Museum, Southampton; Southampton Art Gallery; Tudor House, Southampton.
★ ★ ★ Bargate, Southampton; Southampton Hall of Aviation.
Other ★ ★ ★ ★ Paulton's Park.

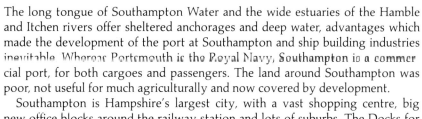

RIGHT *St Michael's church, Southampton*

The Hamble at Warsash

industry, tend to obscure the old town. Although this was damaged by war-time bombing and is affected by modern development, much remains. Visitors can see several medieval buildings now housing museums, and a surprising amount of the medieval town wall survives.

The outskirts of Southampton spread for miles, and nearly join up with Eastleigh in the north. Eastleigh is a famous railway centre, still with vast works and sidings. Romsey retains its independence, and is still a market town, with one of the finest churches in the county.

The rest of the Test valley is rural, as is the area to the west, but along the eastern shore of Southampton Water development is almost continuous. Netley Abbey and the Royal Victoria Country Park are two of the few rural spots. The Hamble river's estuary is a famous yachting centre, offering good walking as well. Upper Hamble Country Park has part of the estuary, and the superb Hampshire Farm Museum. Hamble and Botley are the best villages. The old centre of Hamble is small, but Botley is larger, one of the handsome small towns/large villages which seem to be a Hampshire speciality. Other villages have interesting churches, but generally this is an area of dispersed settlement, without big old village centres. East Wellow is a good example, with the church standing alone and the older houses and cottages spread over a wide area.

Southampton Docks

PORTSMOUTH
FAREHAM
GOSPORT
EMSWORTH

Towns: Emsworth, Fareham, Gosport, Portsmouth.
Villages ★ ★ ★ ★ Langstone, Portchester, Titchfield, Wickham.
Archaeology ★ ★ ★ Titchfield Abbey
Forts and Castles ★ ★ ★ ★ Fort Brockhurst, Gosport; Portchester Castle. **★ ★ ★** Fort Nelson; Portsmouth Point and Defences; Southsea Castle; Spitbank Fort, Southsea.
Walking and Views ★ ★ ★ ★ Curbridge; Farlington Marshes, Forest of Bere; Titchfield area **★ ★ ★** Emsworth; Portsdown; Southwick area.
Churches ★ ★ ★ Portchester; Portsmouth Cathedral; Southwick; 20th century St Philip Cosham.
Museums ★ ★ ★ ★ D-Day Museum ; HMS Victory; HMS Warrior Portsmouth; Mary Rose and Museum; Royal Naval Museum. (All in Portsmouth) **★ ★ ★** Fareham Museum; Royal Marines Museum Portsmouth; Royal Navy Submarine Museum Gosport.
Country Parks ★ ★ ★ ★ Country Park, garden, farm and conservatory, George Staunton Country Park, Leigh Park.

The sea has been (and indeed remains) of great importance to the Portsmouth area, with Portsmouth itself only established as a town because of the sheltered harbour, exploited by Navys since the Roman period when Portchester castle was built at the head of the harbour. Portsmouth is inevitably coupled with the Royal Navy: the growth of the Navy caused the development of the town. The regular visits of navy ships caused the town of Portsmouth (or Pompey as sailors call it) to grow as a sort of shore depot, with dozens of pubs for vital supplies. Although the Dockyard has closed, the harbour is still full of shipping, and the narrow harbour mouth must be one of the best places in the country to watch ships passing.

All the coastal or near-coastal towns were ports: even Titchfield where the river was large enough for small medieval ships. Emsworth, Portchester, Fareham and Gosport are the older towns, with other coastal settlements like Southsea, Lee-on-Solent, Hill Head and Hayling developing from the 19th century as holiday resorts rather than useful ports. Hayling boasts most of Hampshire's sandy beaches; all the shoreline inside the two harbours consists of unalluring mud. The harbours are however yachting centres, and rich in many types of birds. Everywhere the coast is low.

Recent development means that the southern part of the area is virtually solidly built up, with another wide wedge of modern housing and industry along the main road from Portsmouth to London. Hayling, and the area between Hill Head and the Hamble river are the only large undeveloped coastal areas.

Portsmouth Guildhall

South Parade Pier, Southsea

Over Ports Down (known locally as The Hill), is a different country, far more sparsely settled and still rural. Remnants of the medieval Forest of Bere offer good walking, as does much of this hinterland. Ports Down, a chalk outlier, is high in contrast to the flat lands of the coast, giving panoramic views.

There is a great deal to explore. Much of Portsmouth consists of later 19th century or even more recent development but the old town, the dockyard with its historic ships, and the resort of Southsea are all well worth seeing. Gosport, just across the harbour mouth, offers the unusual opportunity to explore a submarine at the Submarine Museum, and the Gosport area has several of the big mid-19th century forts known as Palmerston's follies, one of which (Brockhurst) is open to the public. There are more along Ports Down, and even in the sea off Portsmouth, again with two open (Nelson and Spitbank).

A much earlier fort survives at Portchester with Roman outer walls and a medieval castle inside, one of the best English castles. The village of Portchester is one of several small towns/large villages in this area, all of which have interesting Georgian buildings and are worth walking. Emsworth, Titchfield and Wickham are as fine in their different ways, all tiny scale urban, the latter two with good countryside around.

Fareham is a larger town in the same mould: the High Street is one of the finest Georgian streets in the country. Many small villages are interesting, and several contain churches which should be seen.

The east is heavily built up, but surviving in the middle is the garden of the old house of Leigh Park, still with some of its follies and now a country park with a children's farm and tropical conservatory.

The entrance to Portsmouth Harbour

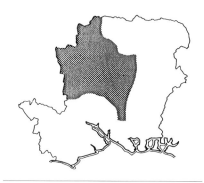

THE CENTRAL CHALK WINCHESTER

Towns: Andover; Bishop's Waltham; New Alresford; Stockbridge; Whitchurch; Winchester.

Villages ★ ★ ★ ★: Hurstbourne Tarrant. ★ ★ ★: Abbotts Ann; Ashmansworth; Broughton; Crawley; Micheldever; Ovington; Titchborne; Wherwell. **Houses ★ ★ ★ ★:** Highclere; Hinton Ampner. ★ ★ ★: Avington; The Grange; Old Alresford House.

Other buildings ★ ★ ★: The Great Hall, Winchester; Winchester College.

Archaeology ★ ★ ★ ★: Danebury ★ ★ ★: Bishops Waltham Palace (ruin).

Gardens ★ ★ ★ ★: Hillier's Garden and Arboretum; Longstock Water Gardens; Mottisfont. ★ ★ ★: Houghton Lodge (see also Highclere and Hinton Ampner)

Walking ★ ★ ★ ★: Abbotstone Down; Beacon Hill; Farley Mount County Park; The Grange area; St Catherine's Hill Winchester; Stockbridge Down. ★ ★ ★: Farley Chamberlayne; New Alresford; Ovington area.

Churches ★ ★ ★ ★: St Cross Winchester; Winchester Cathedral (Winchester Cathedral) ★ ★ ★: Ashmansworth; Farley Chamberlayne; Stoke Charity; Titchborne. 18th century: Abbotts Ann; Avington. 19th century: Andover; Itchen Stoke; Micheldever.

Museums ★ ★ ★ ★: Museum of Army Flying, Middle Wallop; Museum of the Iron Age Andover. ★ ★ ★: Andover Museum; City Museum Winchester; Royal Greenjackets Museum, Winchester; West Gate Winchester; Winchester Heritage Centre.

Animals ★ ★ ★ ★: Finkley Down Farm Park; Andover Hawk,Conservancy Weyhill; Marwell.

Other ★ ★ ★ ★: Whitchurch Silk Mill

RIGHT *On the Test in spring*

The chalk is classic Hampshire, the wide rolling hills empty and devoid of buildings because virtually all the villages are down in the valleys. Gilpin of Boldre (the exponent of the picturesque) disliked the chalk, describing the hills around Winchester in 1798 as 'heavy, uninteresting swells of ground', admiring only 'some of the intersections of their vast heaving forms'. When he saw them they were virtually all downland, unenclosed and covered with short turf cropped by sheep.

Today most of the downland has gone, ploughed up for corn growing, but a few areas have been preserved, complete with their rich flora. the chalk makes good walking, even with the downland gone, because of the wide views and simple emptiness. It is also the best area of the county for archaeology, with many hillforts.

The valleys are much lusher, well-wooded and threaded by the clear chalk streams and rivers which are world famous for their fishing. The Itchen and the Test are classic trout rivers, all their upper reaches carefully managed. Some of the villages cluster closely in the valleys, others are spread out, but all are surrounded by rich green water meadows. Many have classic thatched cottages, Georgian houses and old churches. Several of the village churches are unrestored and of great interest.

There are several small market towns: Bishop's Waltham, New Alresford, Stockbridge, and Whitchurch are all picturesque and interesting to visit. Andover was the same sort of size, but has expanded enormously.

Woodlands are present, even on the chalk, particularly in the areas covered with clay. these clay patches are also the sites of the few villages high on the chalk, like Sparsholt. Harewood Forest is a remnant of a much larger area, but is still good walking. Farley Mount Country Park has downland and woods.

TOP *St Catherine's Hill, Winchester*
ABOVE *St Swithuns, Kingsgate, Winchester*
RIGHT *Bishop Waynflete's chantry,*
Winchester Cathedral

Winchester is still the capital and heart of the county, as once it was the capital of England. The city has much to offer the visitor – not just supremely beautiful large historic buildings like the cathedral or Great Hall, but also the intermingling of fine urban and rural landscapes. Winchester is not a museum: almost all the historic buildings are used for their original purpose, and are still involved with the life of the city. Small buildings make picturesque corners everywhere, so that walking the paths and streets is a constant pleasure. If a visitor could see only one place in Hampshire it should be Winchester, and he should walk around the cathedral, through the Close to the College and then out to St Cross through the watermeadows. Adding on the urban High Street and the Great Hall of the Castle would complete the mixture, giving a perfect section of historic England.

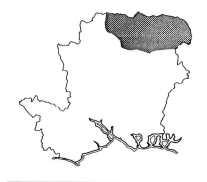

BASINGSTOKE
ALDERSHOT
THE HEATHLANDS

Towns: Aldershot, Basingstoke, Farnborough and Odiham.
Villages ★ ★ ★ ★: Eversley; Steventon (Jane Austen) **★ ★ ★**: Crondall; Upton Grey.
Houses ★ ★ ★: Stratfield Saye; The Vyne.
Archaeology ★ ★ ★: Silchester Roman Walls; Old Basing House ruins.
Gardens ★ ★ ★: Spring Wood, Hackwood Park, Basingstoke.
Walking ★ ★ ★ ★: Yateley **★ ★ ★**: Greywell.
Churches ★ ★ ★ ★: Burghclere Memorial Chapel (20th Century). **★ ★ ★**: Bramley; Eversley; Hartley Wespall; Odiham; Old Basing; Pamber Priory; Sherborne St John; Upton Grey; Winchfield. 18th century; Wolverton. 19th century: Farnborough Abbey; Fleet.
Museums ★ ★ ★: Airborne Forces Museum Aldershot; Aldershot Military Museum; and Royal Corps of Transport Museum Aldershot.
Birds ★ ★ ★ ★: Birdworld.

RIGHT *The Roman Town walls and medieval church, Silchester*

This north-east corner of the county is sometimes thought of as less interesting than the rest, and so not a good area to visit. The prejudice is easily dispelled – the area is heathy and woody, with many areas open for walking, and although the landscape is not dramatic, it is charmingly rural, and there are many varied places to visit.

The south and west fringes are chalk, but most of the area is contrasting gravels, sands and clays. When the Driver brothers surveyed Hampshire's agriculture in 1794 they were 'sorry to observe much immense tracts of open heath and uncultivated land, which strongly indicate the want of means or inclination to improve it, and often reminds the traveller of uncivilised nations, where nature persues her own course, without the assistance of human art'. Many of these tracts of heath were in the north-east of the county, and our attitudes towards them have changed completely since the 18th century, with wild natural areas now appreciated as a considerable asset.

Yately is one of the larger heathy commons, but there are many others still open to the public, despite the Army moving to Aldershot in the 19th century and taking over some of them. Aldershot is a surprisingly interesting town, unexpectedly woody and with many military museums. Farnborough and Fleet developed as commuting areas because of the railway to London, but Odiham is a market town, full of Georgian (and earlier) houses. All three towns have interesting churches, and there are many more worth seeing in the villages. Eversley is associated with Charles Kingsley and Steventon with the young Jane Austen.

Two of the biggest and best large houses are here: The Vyne and Stratfield Saye. The Basingstoke Canal provides a good footpath through interesting countryside.

ALTON
PETERSFIELD
THE HANGARS

Towns Alton and Petersfield.
Villages ★ ★ ★ ★: Buriton; Chawton; East Meon; Hambledon; Selborne. **★ ★ ★:** Chalton; Droxford; Froyle; Meonstoke; Priors Dean.
Houses ★ ★ ★: Rotherfield Park, East Tisted, house and garden.
Archaeology ★ ★ ★ ★: Butser Ancient Farm.
Gardens ★ ★ ★ ★: Jenkyn Place, Bentley **★ ★ ★:** Bohunt Manor, Liphook; Bramdean House; Greatham Mill; Wyck Place, East Worldham.
Walking ★ ★ ★ ★: Alice Holt Forest; Empshott; Hawkley; Old Winchester Hill; Queen Elizabeth Country Park; Selborne; Steep; Waggoner's Wells, Bramshott **★ ★ ★:** Droxford; Bramdean; Chalton; Meonstoke; Woolmer Forest.
Churches ★ ★ ★ ★: East Meon **★ ★ ★:** Empshott; Hambledon; Idsworth; Petersfield; Warnford.
Museums ★ ★ ★ ★: Jane Austen's House, Chawton. **★ ★ ★:** The Curtis and Allen Museums, Alton; Romany Museum, Shelborne; the Wakes, Shelborne.
Other ★ ★ ★ ★: The Watercress Line.

ABOVE *Oakhanger, with radar 'ball'*
RIGHT *The hanger at Selborne*

The east of the county is the most diverse part, with striking scenery of several different kinds. The greensand, the start of the Weald, has abrupt short hills and deeply cut roads, a very distinctive landscape. The adjacent rolling heathlands like Bramshott are much more like Surrey than any other part of Hampshire. Woolmer and Alice Holt Forests are remnants of larger areas, but still offer good walking.

The chalklands vary from the gentle to the steep and high. The famous Meon Valley has a string of villages along the river, and gentle hills either side, a couple still with large areas of preserved downland. Butser and the hills around it are much bigger, giving panoramic views. The Queen Elizabeth Country Park encompasses Butser and great areas of forest as well.

The chalk scarp running north-south is dramatic, and parts of it have the renowned hangars, the woods which cling to the steep slope. Gilbert White's book on the natural history of Selborne celebrates the hangars and all the variety of this area, and has brought pilgrims to Selborne for two centuries, including William Cobbett in 1823, who thought that nothing could surpass the beauty of the area with its 'dells, hillocks and hangers' luxuriant trees and (Cobbett would notice) good agricultural land.

Jane Austen's house at Chawton is another famous shrine, visited by her readers in their thousands. Chawton and several other villages in the area are as interesting as any in the county. The area is rich in good gardens open to the public, and has the county's only steam railway – the Watercress Line between Alton and Alresford.

The only towns are Alton and Petersfield, both worth visiting, but it is the varied countryside and its fine villages which makes this small part of the county so attractive.

Gazetteer

ABBOTTS ANN (D) Big, dense and pretty village, lots of thatched cottages, some with flint panels surrounded by brick. The church of St Mary the Virgin is on the north-east, looking out over meadows. The (ex) vicarage, by the church car park, is a handsome brick house of the early 18th century, a reminder of how rich vicars then were.

The church was totally rebuilt in 1718, and was paid for by Thomas Pitt, once Governor of Madras and usually known as 'Diamond' Pitt because of the huge Indian diamond he sold to the Regent of France, making a fortune in the process. His church is charming, brick and stone with a handsome tower (neat Victorian pinnacles with a wind vane each). Inside it is a period piece: the Victorians put in stained glass, and in most of the windows 'just enough tracery to make an honest church of Abbotts Ann' (Pevsner). The western windows remain as they were built. Little else is altered and apart from the organ (Victorian) all the fittings are 1718. Tiny wooden font, pulpit, squire's pew (and all the others); west gallery on thick columns, and perhaps best of all, the fittings of the chancel. Here the panelling and communion rails are especially fine. Hanging just under the ceiling in the nave are more than 40 Maiden's Garlands. These crowns or garlands were carried at the funerals of those who were born, baptised and confirmed in the parish, and died unmarried. They are made of hazel,

ABOVE *Maiden's garlands, Abbotts Ann*
OPPOSITE *Winchester Cathedral (see page 204)*

decorated with paper flowers and have five gloves hanging from them. A nameplate behind gives the person's name and date of death. The earliest is dated 1811, the latest 1973. Abbotts Ann is the only place where this ancient tradition still survives.

Little Ann, to the east, is not really part of the village, although it seems like it. Varied thatched cottages mix in with modern houses.

★ ★ ★ *Church and village*

ABBOTSTONE DOWN (E) (south east of Northington). Car parks here give access to many footpaths, several of them incorporated into waymarked circular paths. Some lead to the Grange or New Alresford and vary in length from 1-6 miles. Abbotstone deserted medieval village can also be seen off one walk. The car parks and picnic site are on either side of an oval single-banked enclosure, probably Iron Age, which is cut through by the road. Like several other Hampshire earthworks this is inaccurately called Oliver's Battery. Lots of trees including birch and stunted oak. Good views.

★ ★ ★ ★ *For walking.*

ABBOTS WORTHY see **KING'S WORTHY**

ALDERMOOR see **SOUTHAMPTON WEST**

ALDERSHOT (F) Before the Army came, Aldershot was a small village set in a large area of heathland. In 1851 the population was 875, in 1861 16,750 – and half of that number were civilians. In the middle of the 19th century the Army realised that land was needed where large numbers of troops would be trained together, and where exercises or mock battles could take place. When these were carried out in areas that did not belong to the Army, huge sums had to be paid out in compensation to landowners for damage done to crops and buildings.

Aldershot offered the needed open area of cheap land, and in 1854, after a

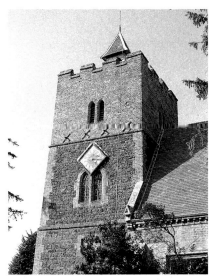

St Michael's church, Aldershot; heathstone with brick edges and top

successful exercise in the area when the troops were accommodated in tents, 6,000 acres were purchased. A permanent barracks was started immediately, and also a large area of wooden huts which were intended to be temporary but which were only replaced in the 1890s by brick buildings. Generally the 1850s buildings are yellow brick, the 1890s red brick.

The town grew up outside the camp both to supply the soldiers and to house the thousands of workers employed building the barracks. Today the town consists of rather plain terraces and houses of the later 19th century, mixed with modern. The shopping parts are the same – there is little evidence of building between about 1900 and the 1960s. The only area with between-the-wars houses is around the old parish church, now to the south-east of the town.

Today the slight hills and large quantities of trees (many planted just after the Second World War) make the camp and town an attractive place. The camp has tree-lined roads and many playing fields. Soldiers are everywhere, and occasionally the military police on horseback are seen.

The church of St Michael is a real parish church, having grown over the centuries.

Most prominent is the 17th century brick and brown heathstone tower: the church seems to have every possible sort of material – red and white brick, stone, flint and rendering. The flint parts are 1910 and there is much early 20th century woodwork inside. 15th century south chapel and south aisle, originally the chancel and nave. Two good wall memorials with figures, both women, 1606 and 1620 one near the altar, the other in the south chapel. Many of the graves in the graveyard are covered by brick vaults, constructed to stop graves being robbed of the bodies.

★ *Church.*

The town centre landmark is a stone church and tower of 1874, built as a Methodist chapel, uncharacteristically Gothic.

The only town building in the area which became the Camp is still there – the Union or Workhouse (still called Union Building) in Hospital Hill Road, adapted from a 17th century house. The front still has three gables of this date. The Army Camp is now a mixture of 1960s and 70s buildings both small and large (none of which look military) and remains of the brick barracks of the 1890s. Most of the 19th century buildings have been demolished to make way for the new ones. Hospital Road is the best place to see the old camp. At the west end is Maida Gym, large and redbrick 1890s. Further along the Sebastopol Bell sits under a little roof, with a small cannon beside it, outside a modern officers' mess. The Bell was brought back from the Crimean War, which broke out soon after the Army came to Aldershot. Until 1914 the gun was fired at one o'clock as a time signal and at 9.30 in the evening as a curfew signal for all troops to return to their quarters. The Cambridge Military

The Prince Consort's Library, Aldershot

Hospital, built in 1873, is a little further along the road: a huge yellowy brick building. The central block has a big dome and clock turret. A few recent wooden buildings around the hospital are the only reminders of the hundreds of wooden barrack blocks which accommodated troops until the 1890s. At the end of the road is the military cemetery and the artificial ski slope (open to the public: fees).

Queen's Avenue runs through the centre of the Camp, lined with trees. In the middle two redbrick churches: the one with a spire is Roman Catholic of 1912, the other 1927. Opposite, easily found because of the Dakota airplane parked outside is **The Airborne Forces Museum** (fee: lists) which details the history of this regiment, formed in 1940. Interesting, crammed with objects including the cockpits of two wartime gliders, a jeep framed up for dropping by parachutes, briefing models used during the War, and material from the Falklands.

★ ★ ★ *Museum*

The south-western part of the camp also preserves some earlier buildings. The Prince Consort's library in Knolles Road is a handsome building of 1859. Beside it

the Royal Coat of Arms from Willems Barracks, saved when the building was demolished.

The original yellow brick entrance gates to Willems Barracks remain, part of the 1850s permanent camp, but now with modern buildings behind. South along Farnham road is the big yellow brick wall which enclosed the Cavalry Barracks, and again the entrance survives. On the opposite side of the road, behind iron railings, is a smallish wooden building with a verandah, the guard-house to the now demolished Royal Pavilion built in 1855 for Queen Victoria to stay in when she visited Aldershot. Behind is the Riding School also of 1859, a handsome heavy building. Winston Churchill endured his initial training here, 'jumping a high bar without stirrups or even saddle, sometimes with hands clasped behind one's back'.

In one of the most park-like areas close by is the Royal Garrison church of 1863, plain brick with a big tower. On a hump to the north-west stands the massive (40 tons) statue of Wellington, originally on top of Constitution Arch, Hyde Park, but moved here in 1883.

Two of the 1890s barrack blocks in red brick are preserved towards the far end of Queen's Avenue as the **Aldershot Military Museum** (fee: lists) the best place to see the history and development of Aldershot. Fine displays, including many photographs, plans and models,

The Duke of Wellington's statue, Aldershot

Dakota outside the Airborne Forces Museum, Aldershot

The Royal Garrison Church, Aldershot

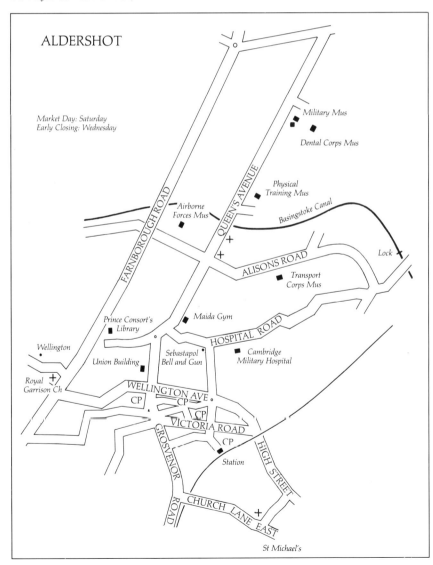

ALDERSHOT

Market Day: Saturday
Early Closing: Wednesday

Military Mus

Dental Corps Mus

Physical
Training Mus

Basingstoke Canal

FARNBOROUGH ROAD

Airborne
Forces Mus

QUEEN'S AVENUE

Lock

ALISONS ROAD

Transport
Corps Mus

Prince Consort's
Library

Maida Gym

HOSPITAL ROAD

Wellington

Union Building

Sebastapol
Bell and Gun

Cambridge
Military Hospital

Royal
Garrison Ch

WELLINGTON AVE

CP

CP

CP

GROSVENOR ROAD

VICTORIA ROAD

CP

Station

HIGH STREET

CHURCH LANE EAST

St Michael's

with a reconstructed Victorian barrack room. The Canadian forces in Aldershot are included, and the displays continue the story to the present. Outside armoured cars, guns, a tank etc.

★ ★ ★ *Museum.*

The Army term 'Glasshouse' for military prison comes from the Detention Barracks at Aldershot, which had a glass roof and were away to the north of the museum, but are now demolished.

Apart from the Aldershot Military Museum and the Airborne Forces Museum, which are open even at weekends, there are other military museums which are inside barracks. All are open to the public on weekdays, although some of the sentries at the barracks gates may not even know there is a museum there. To the constant query 'Can I see your pass please?' Simply reply that you have no pass, are a member of the general public who wishes to see the museum. Expect security precautions like having to sign in and giving your car number. These are all Regimental museums, and are very welcoming when you finally get there, and worth the effort.

Royal Army Dental Corps Museum Evelyn Woods Road, a new block just behind (to the south-east) of the Aldershot Military Museum. Within the RADC building: apply to reception. One large room crammed with material showing the history of dentistry in the Army from the time soldiers needed front teeth to bite through the paper cartridge when loading flintlock muskets. The Dental Corps was founded in 1921. Lots of tools, chairs (both field and surgery), photographs, medals and campaigns up to the Falklands. In fact a comprehensive history of dentistry and dental equipment, with Army history as well.

★ ★ *Museum.*

Royal Corps of Transport Buller Barracks, Alison's Road. The history of this vital part of the Army from 1794 when it was called the Royal Waggoners. Transport by horse, ship, train, air, or lorry of all the army's needs – food, ammunition, tanks, etc. Well displayed, one large room, laid out chronologically with sections on different periods and methods. Good series of uniforms, medals, models, smaller equipment like a folding bicycle, etc.

★ ★ ★ *Museum.*

Army Physical Training Corps Queen's Avenue. Entry off Queen's Avenue end of Prince's Avenue. Traces the history of the Corps from its beginnings in 1860, and demonstrates the transformation of puny recruit into superman. Early equipment, and photographs. Many mementoes of more recent athletes, including Olympic participants. One large room. ★ ★

Queen Alexandra's Royal Nursing Corps (free:lists), Royal Pavilion, Farnborough Road. Not unfortunately the original pavilion, but a new building on the site. Good displays trace the history of Army Nursing from its earliest days, with much about Florence Nightingale and the Crimea, including a Russian carriage she used there.

★ ★ *Museum.*

Two of the military museums are just over the border into Surrey, and so outside the scope of this book. For completeness the Royal Army Medical Corps Museum is at Keogh Barracks, Ash Vale, north of the Ash Vale Railway Station; and the Royal Army Ordnance Corps Museum is at Blackdown Barracks, Deepcut, Camberley.

St. Michael's Church ★, *Aldershot Military Museum* ★ ★ ★, *Airborne Forces Museum* ★ ★ ★, *Royal Corps of Transport* ★ ★ ★, *Army Physical Training Corps* ★ ★, *Royal Army Dental Corps Museum* ★ ★, *Queen Alexandra's Nursing Corps Museum* ★ ★

ALICE HOLT FOREST (F) (south of Farnham and just east of Bentley). This area was part of a Saxon hunting forest, which extended southwards to Liss, incorporating what is now Woolmer Forest. From the 16th century oak for shipbuilding became more important than hunting. In 1815 the deer were all removed and over the next twenty years 16,000 acres of oaks planted. At the same time the main road, now the A325 was constructed through the middle of the forest, with a convenient pub in the middle called Halfway House. Car Parks in many parts of the Forest, which still extends to 2,000 acres.

Areas of the early 19th century oaks still survive in the south of the forest, in Goose Green enclosure and Abbots Wood although there are also conifers of various sizes. In Goose Green are the sites of many Roman pottery kilns, and a reconstruction of one. There are waymarked paths in several parts of the forest, with an introductory path running from the Visitor Centre with its displays on the history and natural history of the Forest, including reproduction Roman pots made in the experimental kiln. In the

north-west is a big pond, and in the north-east an arboretum of forestry trees, plots of various trees with labels, explaining when they were planted, and their types.

★ ★ ★ ★ *Walking.*

ALRESFORD see OLD ALRESFORD and NEW ALRESFORD

ALTON (F) A large market town, which grew up on the main road from London to Gosport and Southampton. Low chalk hills around, and the river Wey runs through the town. Alton manufactured cloth from medieval times into the 19th century, but by 1840 the trade was reduced to supplying bags for another local industry – hops. Brewing as well as hop-growing was carried on here from the 18th century, as was fulling, paper-making and tanning. Only brewing survives as a large local industry today. The town is large but friendly, with many good Georgian buildings, a pleasant church and two fine museums.

The main road through, High Street and its continuation Normandy Street, has an interesting mixture of buildings, and the road curves slightly uphill, giving variety to the views. At the west end the town starts from the railway line (part of the Watercress Line : see entry) with a triangular green known as The Butts because archery was once practiced there. All Saints church of 1874 has a pretty steeple. The church and several other Victorian buildings close by are of an unusual building stone, laid like vertical

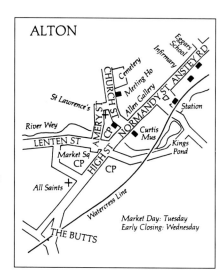

crazy paving. Prominent redevelopment at this end of the High Street, but there are still many earlier buildings, mostly Georgian brick, but including tile-hanging. The Swan Hotel, an old coaching Inn, and the Midland Bank are particularly good.

To the north Lenten Street, Amery Street and Church Street also have attractive houses, on a rather smaller scale than the High Street. The Market Square (market on Tuesdays) has the plain Town Hall of 1813 now filled in underneath with shops. The Market Hotel is plain, but on the far corner of the square is a very elaborate late 19th century building. Just off the market square, down Amery Street, is a large house refronted in the Georgian period with a plaque recording that Edmund Spenser the Elizabethan poet lived there in 1590. To the west of the market square is Cross and Pillory House, a good new development with, inside, figures carved into the bricks. The brewery can be glimpsed on the other side of the High Street.

ABOVE *The lodge by the railway, Alton*
LEFT *Victorian cottages in Alton*

The Curtis Museum, in the High Street, is part of a courtyard of buildings, dating from 1880, originally built as a cottage hospital, assembly rooms and mechanics institute. The latter is now the museum, not large but with good displays of toys and local history including hop growing, Fanny Adams, and so on. Another describes and illustrates the work of William Curtis on fossils and botany. Very effective new display on the history of the area from the Ice Age to the Civil War. One of the best modern displays in Hants (free:lists). Fine Georgian brick buildings opposite the museum, one with Venetian windows.

Church Street over the road has Geales Almshouses, founded, as the inscription on the front confirms by Thomas Geale, a captain in Cromwell's army in 1653. Comely brick building. **The Allen Gallery** opposite (free:lists) has a huge collection of ceramics from the 16th century to the present; a small display of silver including the Tichborne spoons, made in 1592 with figures on the knobs including Queen Elizabeth; display of W. Herbert Allen (1863-1943) paintings; and a small exhibition gallery with temporary exhibitions. Outside is a charming garden, with many herbs.

The eastern end of the main street, Anstey Road, has the railway station (part of the Watercress Line: see entry), then further east the vast infirmary, a classical building set back from the road and built in 1793. On the same side is Eggars Grammar School, founded in 1638. The low part of the brick and stone building

Kings Pond, Alton

dates from the foundation, the higher from 1880s. Down Paper Mill Lane is King's Pond, large with lots of different ducks and trees. An odd lodge built from massive flints sits on the bank by the railway.

Along Church Street, almost to the cemetery, is the plain 1670s Quaker Meeting House, with a cottage attached. In the town cemetery off the second path parallel with the road is the grave of Fanny Adams, whose murder in 1867 shocked Alton and gave the language a new phrase.

The main church (St Lawrence) is prominent and the surrounding old cedar trees are visible from much of the town. This good defensive position led to its being the scene of a battle in the Civil War: the Royalists held Alton, but in December 1643 they were assaulted by the Parliamentarians. The King's Cavalry fled leaving 500 foot soldiers to defend themselves. They fell back on the churchyard, and finally the church. Here they made a final stand: Captain John Bowles, their leader 'there fought six or seven hours, and then the Rebell Breaking in upon him he slew with his sword six or seven of them and then was Slayne himself, with sixty of his men about him'. All this is recorded on his memorial brass in Winchester Cathedral, reproduced inside the church on the pillar by the door.

The church is large enough to have a decent battle in: internally the building is

unchanged, but almost all the fittings are different. Outside it seems sprawling with a pretty Victorian spire and a huge clockface below. Inside the porch the door's bashes and slashes are supposed to date from the battle. The building is odd inside: it seems to have two parallel naves – one is really the south aisle and at its head is the original part of the church, the base of a Norman tower, with finely carved capitals including birds and animals to the four arches, originally central to the church. The wooden ceiling and the bells are supported on supplementary wooden posts – not an elegant solution. The rest of the church is 15th century, all high and rather barn-like with a simple roof and no chancel arch.

Good fittings include the fine and unusual mid 17th century wooden pulpit with detached decorated columns and pretty arches over them. Plain 15th century choir stalls in the back row in the chancel, and a wall painting of the same date on one pillar in the nave showing saints. Above the Victorian font under the tower a fine two-tier brass chandelier dated 1780. 17th century alms box to the right of the altar on a pillar. Nice early 20th century mosaic memorials up by the altar, and a large, perhaps Saxon font set on a millstone at the west end.

★ ★ ★ ★ *Town well worth visiting,* ★ ★ *Church,* ★ ★ ★ *Museums, not large but worth seeing.*

ALTON ABBEY see **MEDSTEAD**

Fanny Adams' grave, Alton

Geology and Scenery

Hampshire's geology is basically quite simple. A broad band of chalk fills the middle half of the county, producing rolling downland, most of it high. To the north east are clays and gravels, a great contrast to the adjoining downlands. The east of the county from Petersfield northwards has the start of the Weald which continues eastwards. In Hampshire this is Greensand and Gault clays. The south of the county, all along the coast, has a mixture of gravels and clays, with Ports Down an outlying chalk ridge.

The Chalk Uplands are classic downland, smooth rolling rounded hills, with many dry valleys created when the water-table was higher than it is now. On the north side there is a steep escarpment. Patches of clay-with-flints on top of the chalk are often wooded as they are better suited for trees than the thin soil on the chalk. The chalk did originally support woodlands, but was cleared in prehistoric times. Ever since the chalk has been downland, fine permanent turf on which animals, particularly sheep, were grazed. Small parts were broken up for arable for the late 17th century as the newly-invented water meadows provided earlier and better grazing, but now most of it has been ploughed and is used to grow cereals because modern fertilisers make it possible for the thin soils to support the growth of corn. A few large areas of downland are preserved (see Walking and Nature Reserves), but in general farming on the chalk has changed to arable this century, altering the whole appearance of the

The chalk between Hambledon and Soberton

landscape. Even on surviving downs the lack of rabbits and less frequent grazing by sheep has allowed scrub to grow.

Only a tiny part of *The Weald* is in eastern Hampshire, but it produces a dramatic and distinct landscape, generally small scale but very varied with small deep valleys and short steep slopes. Towards Hindhead the Greensand rises to 800 ft very dramatically.

The clays and sands and gravels of the north-east are poor soils, with many heaths and wastes, and unsuitable for agriculture, but perfect for military manoeuvres, which explains the vast Army settlement at Aldershot.

The south-west is filled by the New Forest, also on poor gravels or clays and again not rich agriculturally. Although undulating, there is no very high land. Many areas are boggy, even on the higher ground which only reaches 400 ft. The Avon Valley has large deposits of gravel, now being quarried.

Apart from Ports Down, a long ridge of chalk, the south-east is also clays with some sand, but this area is much more fertile than the New Forest, mostly being good farming or even market gardening country. The clays are eminently suitable for brickmaking, and there used to be many kilns in this area.

The *coast* is formed entirely from clays, sands and gravels, protected from erosion by the Isle of Wight. There are no high cliffs, and the less exposed areas like Portsmouth and Langstone harbours are fringed with mud and salt marsh. The present shore was created perhaps only 15,000 years ago when sea levels rose and drowned a river which ran between the county and the Isle of Wight. Southampton Water, and Portsmouth and Langstone Harbours are all drowned river valleys.

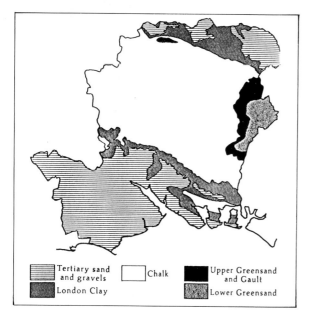

Tertiary sand and gravels

London Clay

Chalk

Upper Greensand and Gault

Lower Greensand

ALVERSTOKE (N) The mother parish of Gosport, right at the head of the Haslar Creek. Its daughter has out-grown it, although Alverstoke itself now covers a large area with later 19th century and modern development. The medieval Church of St Mary was totally rebuilt in the later 19th century. Big stone church, with inside an unusually decorated chancel arch and reredos. East of the church a big rectory, stone with brick detailing, partly dating from the medieval period. To the west of the church is the middle of the village, with a thatched cottage and other nice small scale rural houses. The head of Haslar Creek, dammed off from the sea is attractive, with a few Regency houses at the north-east end. Good view of the church.

In 1826 the Marquis of Anglesea tried to establish a seaside resort here, named after him. One grand terrace was built, but the scheme failed. The Crescent survives (left off Anglesea Road, south from the church, the Crescent is parallel with shore, but one road back) large, slightly curved with a colonnade. It is surrounded by later development.

South of the village are several car parks on the shore. Good views of the Isle of Wight opposite, especially Ryde, and ships passing by. Gilkicker Point has a small 1850s fort and one of the forts actually in the sea is visible (see Palmerston's follies).

About ½ mile north of Alverstoke church are several Georgian houses, including Bury House, a handsome large redbrick building. They are the remains of a hamlet, now enclosed with more recent development.

ABOVE *Alverstoke church.* BELOW *Anglesey Crescent, Alverstoke*

Ampfield church

AMPFIELD (H) So woody it looks like a forest. Oak and beech mostly, with large houses set back from the busy road. The middle is more open. Good Victorian school. The church is also enclosed by woods. It was built in 1841, and as with Otterborne (see entry), the architect was Charlotte Yonge's father, helped by Owen Carter, a Winchester architect. The effect is similar to Otterborne, being of also of brick, but the style is Decorated with another odd narrow bellcote, this one twisted on its base. Ampfield House is redbrick and of c. 1760, and there are a few old timber-framed cottages.

A street leads off by the school to Knapp, a hamlet backing into the woods with many thatched cottages, some with lattice windows.

★ *Church for its oddness.*

AMPORT (D) A big informal green, with a wide selection of handsome houses and cottages facing it along one side. From the 18th century there were unusually large quantities of charity cottages here, one set called Quality Square. The church of St Mary is to the east of the main village, past one of the lodges to Amport House (house best seen from the road between Monxton and Grately – large 1857 Elizabethan in yellow brick). The church is Decorated style, early 14th century, which is rare in Hampshire. It was restored in the 1860s, but much is original. Not very elaborate: cruciform with a central tower. Attractive sedilia and piscina in chancel, and on the wall a little 15th century alabaster showing the head of John the Baptist surrounded by saints, found locally in a cottage. Good monuments all round, and huge 1865 font and cover at west end. Notable 1860s and 70s stained glass in most windows.

★ ★ *Village and church.*

ANDOVER (D) An important medieval town, already quite large by Norman times, but until the 1960s when it was selected to increase by taking some of London's population, it grew little. Today it is ringed by modern housing estates and industry, and bypasses remove all the through traffic.

The town centre has lost quite a few of its older buildings, and there are many large modern ones close to the middle, hemming in the old. There is still the feeling of a market town, especially around the High Street, where the wide street is still used as a market place on Saturdays. At the south end the Danebury Hotel is a fine example of a large Regency inn, and the other

The Town Mill, Andover

buildings are an attractive urban mixture, with several alleyways leading off. The prominent Guildhall is of 1825, classical and good stone, originally open in the lower storey. The iron supports inside came from the nearby Taskers Waterloo Iron Works.

The High Street continues past the Guildhall, and on the right is a reset Norman arch saved from the old parish church. Chantry Street, curving opposite the church, has a few jettied houses. **The Church of St Mary** is prominent, with its big tower. It was totally rebuilt in the 1840s, in imitation of Salisbury cathedral, and the end result is both impressive and pretty. The interior is not so good, but has a high nave, rather flat plaster vaults, and an odd east end with three arches, and a five-sided apse beyond. The 1840s patterned glass survives in the apse. The two long columns in the chancel are cast iron from Tasker's Waterloo Iron Works. Some monuments were moved from the old church: to the left of the altar Richard Kentish (died 1611) has small figures, the man himself seated, and list of gifts below, while on the right Richard Venables (1621) monument has two of the more usual kneeling figures and a painted panel on the adjacent wall recording his benefactions. Victorian pulpit of many marbles.

To the east of the church is Church Close with **Andover Museum and the Museum of the Iron Age** in the same building. Andover Museum is free (lists) and has displays on Tasker's Iron Works, Weyhill Fair, local geology, natural

history, glass, local history and temporary exhibitions. Several tanks with live fish, varieties found in chalk streams.

★ ★ ★ *Museum.*

The Museum of the Iron Age (fee:lists) has superb displays explaining this last phase of our prehistory, mostly based on excavations at Danebury hillfort (see entry). Reconstructions of the rampart and a hut, mix with models and finds to give a clear picture of life in the Iron Age. Well worth seeing.

★ ★ ★ *Museum.*

Newbury Street close by has a handsome Georgian Old Vicarage and around the corner in East Street is the classical United Reform church of 1830, and more Georgian houses and cottages.

The old town also survives to the south of High Street, in the old London Road (London Street) with the handsome Regency Savoy Chambers particularly fine, and along Bridge Street. Town Mill Road leads down to the brick mill and millhouse, dated 1764, now used for other purposes, and overshadowed by big modern developments behind. The mill stream is picturesque. The flint building beyond it is the Victorian Methodist Church. At the far end of Bridge Street is the Station Hotel a reminder that Andover had two railway stations, one close to this Hotel, which was next to the Andover-Redbridge canal when originally built in 1790.

Junction Road, leading north from the end of Bridge Street, is lined with Victorian villas and has the Workhouse of 1836, now used as part of a college.

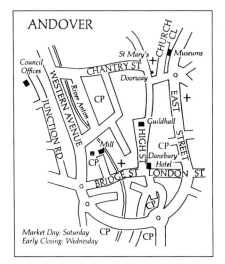

ANDOVER

Council Offices
St Mary's
CHURCH CL
Museums
CHANTRY ST
Doorway
River Anton
WESTERN AVENUE
CP
EAST STREET
JUNCTION RD
Guildhall
CP
Mill
HIGH ST
Danebury Hotel
CP
BRIDGE ST
LONDON ST
Market Day: Saturday
Early Closing: Wednesday
CP
CP

The iron bridge over Micheldever Road, Andover

Andover workhouse had a bad reputation for mistreating paupers.

To the east, along Micheldever Road, the road cuts picturesquely and deeply through a hill, and one of Tasker's shapely iron bridges was erected to carry a footpath across it. The footpath called Ladies Mile, was laid out in 1863 as a local celebration of the marriage of the Prince of Wales.

Finkley Down Farm Park (fee:lists) is two miles east of Andover, on a minor road heading towards Whitchurch. All types of farm animals, often with young ones, many varieties of bantams and other decorative fowl, and tractors for climbing on make this a good place to visit with small children. Gypsy caravans and farming bygones are on display, but it is the animals, many of which can be handled, which are the main attraction.

★ ★ *Town* ★ ★ ★ ★ *Museum of the Iron Age* ★ ★ ★ *Andover Museum* ★ ★ ★ *St Mary's Church* ★ ★ ★ ★ *Finkley Down Farm Park for young children.*

ANDOVER AND REDBRIDGE CANAL

The canal from Andover to the sea, 22 miles long, opened in 1794, with wharves at Andover, Stockbridge and Romsey. It was never a success: even in 1838 before the railways came to the county its traffic was described as 'very trifling' and it was sold to a railway company in 1857. They re-used part of the route for the railway line. Links to extend the canal to Southampton and Salisbury about 1800 failed.

See **HORSEBRIDGE, LEE, REDBRIDGE,** and **ROMSEY** for the surviving parts of the canal.

ANNA VALLEY (D). Not really a village, and now mostly modern houses running alongside the river. The Waterloo Iron Works were established here early in 1813 (named a little later) and part of the ironmaster's house, Clatford Lodge still survives at the eastern end. Big arched entrance with heavy flint window surrounds: these were the schoolhouse and schoolmistress's dwelling, built in 1830s. The main house has been demolished and replaced by modern housing. Further along the road is the Waterloo Free Church, with a cast iron plaque identifying it as the 'Waterloo

Workmen's Hall 1867'. The iron bridge at Upper Clatford nearby was cast at these iron works in 1843 as were the columns in Andover Guildhall and church, and another bridge in London Road Andover. The firm lasted until 1968, latterly mostly producing trailers. During the Second World War 900 people were employed here. A display about the firm can be seen in Andover Museum.

Bury Hill to the south is an Iron Age Hillfort. A footpath leads right round the triple banks.

APPLESHAW (D) One long village street, so wide that it seems to have a long thin green beside it. Lots of thatched cottages, many of them rendered, and several farms in the village. In the middle of the street a clock put up to celebrate Victoria's jubilee sticks out from a barn wall – a more useful memorial than many. Close by is the big Georgian ex Vicarage, with a Venetian window. There are other larger Georgian houses about the village, and on the outskirts two with their own parks. From at least as early as the 17th century, until 1910, a huge sheep fair was held here.

The church is towards the north end, forming a picturesque group with a little verandahed lodge. The church was rebuilt in 1830 in smoothed-out Gothic. Inside is plain and austere. 1831 Royal Coat of Arms.

All around the village are parks and woods, with hamlets at Redenham to the north rather sparse but with some thatch, and Ragged Appleshaw to the east, mostly later houses and cottages but a fine name. **Clanville** is almost a separate village, with thatched cottages, a grand

The entrance to Taskers' Iron Works, Anna Valley

Georgian farmhouse and a big early 18th century house and park. Even further to the south the foursquare Remenhan House, large, square and 1830ish, sitting in its park.

ASHE (E) A tiny hamlet right at the head of the River Test. The source of the river is usually just to the south of the church, but in wet weather can be further up the valley. Ashe House, close to the valley road, is a handsome Georgian brick building often visited by Jane Austen. It was then the Rectory, and the Rector's wife was one of her closest friends. At Ashe House Jane met Tom Lefroy to whom she seems to have been briefly engaged.

The church of Holy Trinity and St Andrew is not that of Jane Austen's time, having been totally rebuilt in 1877. Memorials to the Lefroy family were replaced at the west end. To the right of the 1877 screen is a small iron door, and inside is a carving of a robin on a nest of shavings, commemorating the bird which nested on the top of the screen while it was being made.

ASHFORD HILL see KINGSCLERE WOODLANDS

ASHLEY (H) (just west of Farley Mount). A hamlet running up the hill to Farley Mount Country Park, with several Victorian houses. Beside the small church is the ringwork of a medieval castle, quite prominent but too big and shallow to be called a motte. The church and part of the village are inside the outer earthwork or bailey, which is much less prominent. All can be seen on a good model inside the church.

St Mary's church is interesting as a survivor: it is a tiny Norman church, without aisles or transepts. Many Hampshire churches have grown from just this sort of beginning, but it is difficult to appreciate their small origins after additions. Here the church remains small and simple. Brick porch dated 1701, and some later medieval windows have been inserted, but the shape and size of the church are original. Tiny entrance and tiny chancel arch, with later openings each side. Distinct slope up to the altar. Several small Norman windows survive. Faint 13th century wall painting in one of the chancel windows. The memorials are on a larger scale than the building. By the door a poor box, cut from a re-used post.

★ ★ *Church, as an interesting survival.*

ASHMANSWORTH (A) A long village, running up a dry valley on the northern chalk, and the highest medieval village on chalk in England at 235m. Mostly older cottages, well-spaced, and the occasional house, brick with some flint. Very rural with the cottages well spaced out. The church of St James is to the south, with thatched walls all around. Unusually it escaped severe Victorian restoration and alteration. Gerald Finzi (1901-1956), the composer best known for his settings of poetry, lived in Ashmansworth from 1937, building himself a house and cultivating rare apple trees in his large orchard. He is buried beside the porch, with a finely lettered tombstone by Reynolds Stone. The tiny brick porch is dated 1694, and inside is a small superb engraved glass window dedicated to English music. The names of English composers are painted on the wall, while their initials make the roots of the engraved tree.

Inside the Norman chancel arch is tiny. Remains of wall paintings ranging in date from Norman to 17th century all around, with not enough surviving to give their proper effect. Small windows. The east wall must have given trouble in the 18th century: it was rebuilt in brick, dated 1745 outside.

★ ★ ★ For association with Finzi, for the fine countryside around, and for the unrestored state of the church.

ASHURST (H) This is the closest the railway comes to Lyndhurst, some 2½ miles from the town, and it has a station called Lyndhurst Road. A big late Victorian-Edwardian 'suburb' grew up, presumably because of the railway, and there is a large hospital, converted from the New Forest Workhouse.

AVINGTON (E) A small village with much brick and flint. One long terrace of seven cottages, with an open well-house in front. From the 17th century this was the village to Avington Park. Between the village and big house, and reached from either, is the church of St Mary. There are several 18th century churches in Hampshire, most of them brick but none is so complete as Avington which retains all its original fittings. It was built in 1770, and all the pews and other woodwork are of mahogany, rarely used in churches. The pews are so high that one cannot see out of them when sitting down, and the hat pegs are preserved all along the side walls. Clear glass in the windows. The pulpit with a large tester over, brass chandelier, garden ornament type font and in the gallery front the Royal coat of arms, are all of about 1770, if a little old-fashioned in style for that date. In the gallery an elaborate barrel organ, early 19th century, which can play 31 hymns and 6 chants. The east end is classical, with a Venetian window, panelling with testament boards and fine wrought-iron communion rail. Here is the memorial to the Marchioness of Carnarvon who died in 1768 but left the money to pay for the church. Her epitaph is worth reading 'Religious without Enthusiasm, Just without Severity, Charitable without Ostentation, Generous with Profusion'. A set of Georgian virtues: enthusiasm was not a

LEFT *Memorial window to Gerald Finzi by Laurence Whistler, in Ashmansworth church*
BELOW *A roof boss in Ashmansworth church*

Avington Park

good thing then. In a glass case beside the squire's pew are an 18th century bible and prayer book with decorated velvet covers.

Avington Park, the mansion in the park next to the church, is open weekends in summer (fee: lists). There was a house here from about 1600, but this was encased in a new and larger building about 1710. The new house has big brick wings and a large wooden portico in the recessed centre. The lead statues on top were added later in the 18th century. Inside, the hall has wooden pillars painted to look like marble, and painted walls and ceiling imitating trelliswork and the sky. This, like most of the painted (and plaster) decoration was added later in the 18th century, when the Duke of Chandos lived here. Unusually the intricate decoration in the support for the bannisters of the stairs is of lead. The Great Saloon upstairs has fine plasterwork and some of the original furniture. The red drawing room has unusual decoration including medieval figures probably based on Sir Walter Scott's Waverley novels, which were so popular in the early 19th century.

The library downstairs (a late 18th century addition) has Roman style decoration, designs based on scenes excavated at Pompeii and Herculaneum. Handsome 1850s conservatories, joined by a colonnade. Attractive wooded park, with a skinny and elegant cast iron bridge

of 1800 over the river.

★ ★ ★*Church, one of the best* 18th century churches in the county ★ ★ ★ *Avington Park.*

AVON see **BISTERNE**

AWBRIDGE (H) is so spread about that the church of All Saints (stone, 1875) is in a separate hamlet called Upper Ratley. The whole parish is well-wooded, wet in the lower parts and with many small hills.

AXFORD (E) A small village at the head of the Candover valley, with a couple of thatched cottages and a big Victorian House. The church was to the north at **Nutley**, but has been demolished. Only the graveyard remains.

BADDESLEY see **NORTH & SOUTH BADDESLEY**

BANISTER'S PARK see **SOUTHAMPTON NORTH**

BARTLEY (H) A scattered hamlet right on the edge of the New Forest and mostly modern with the occasional older cottage. Difficult to distinguish from its neighbours Netley Marsh or Cadnam.

BARTON-ON-SEA (L/M) Now a border village, because Highcliffe etc have been taken into Dorset. Although nothing in

Barton-on-Sea seems to predate the 1920s, there was originally a small hamlet inland called Barton. This has been swamped by the scale of the modern development: seas of bungalows give way to houses (and increasingly, small blocks of flats) by the sea. All is set back from the shore, leaving a wide strip of green behind the low cliffs. Strangely the only buildings on the green are the main shops, with a rare survival – a 1930s style garage.

The cliffs are orange gravels and sands, crumbling away. Fine shingle beach, with lots of groynes presumably to try and check erosion. Wonderful views: Hengistbury Head and Christchurch Harbour to the west, with Purbeck beyond; ahead the Isle of Wight, with the Needles apparently close enough to throw a stone over. Eastwards the rest of the Isle of Wight, with Hurst Castle on its spit looking part of the Island although really attached to the mainland.

Fine shingle beach, with lots of groynes to check erosion. Wonderful views: Hengistbury Head and Christchurch Harbour to the west, with Purbeck beyond; ahead the Isle of Wight, with the Needles. Eastwards the rest of the Isle of Wight, with Hurst Castle on its spit looking like part of the Island although really attached to the mainland.

Just to the east, wild heathland leading down to the sea, a good bit for walking.

A gravestone at Barton Stacey

BARTON STACEY (D)

Quite a large village, with lots of Georgian houses and cottages, many of them brick. Rural, but with a big Army estate to the north of the village. The church of All Saints has many fine 18th century gravestones and table-tombs in the graveyard around, and the good stonework of the tower (c. 1500) contrasts with the flint of the rest, which is mostly Victorian externally. Internally it is 12th and 13th century, with an odd chancel arch, two pillars supporting four arches, tree-like. Lots of good monuments and big funeral hatchments.

★ ★ *Church.*

BASING see OLD BASING

BASINGSTOKE CANAL

The canal from the river Wey in Surrey to Basingstoke opened in 1794, having cost almost twice the estimate. Although Basingstoke had been pressing for a canal for twenty years so that agricultural goods could be taken to London cheaply, canals which did not carry industrial materials were rarely profitable. The Basingstoke canal never made money, and the shareholders never received a dividend. About half the 37 miles of the canal was in Hampshire, and most of the 29 locks were in Surrey, but the 1,200 yard tunnel is at Greywell, Hants.

One of the few prosperous periods for the canal was the later 1830s, when materials for the London-Southampton railway were carried by canal. Competition from the completed railway made the canal company bankrupt, but under new ownership it struggled on, bringing materials to the new Army camp at Aldershot from 1854. In 1914 the last barge passed through the whole route to Basingstoke, and in 1932 part of the Greywell Tunnel collapsed. Commercial traffic continued as far as Aldershot until 1921: the last cargo was 22 barge loads of aeroplane parts.

The canal gradually became derelict, but from the mid 1970s it has been restored, and is now navigable from the Greywell tunnel to the Wey. The western end has disappeared, the dry channel is visible in places (eg Basing House), but is built over closer to Basingstoke.

From North Warnborough to the county boundary the canal towpath passes through woody or heathy countryside, providing good rural walks. A canal narrowboat offers trips, and rowing boats can be hired at Odiham. The best places to see the canal are listed below, but all of it is attractive.

See especially: **GREYWELL, ODIHAM & UP NATELY,** and also **ALDERSHOT, CROOKHAM VILLAGE & DOGMERSFIELD.**

BASINGSTOKE (J/B)

Until the 1960s Basingstoke was a proper market town, still much the same as it had been in 1805 when it was described as 'a large ancient and populous town, situated in a pleasant and well-wooded part of the county, and commanding a considerable trade from its standing at the junction of five great roads ... '

The Basingstoke canal (see entry) opened in 1794, improving communications still more, and with the railway from London opening in 1839, the population increased from 2,500 in 1801 to nearly 11,000 in 1901. Good communications are still important – the town has extensive ring roads and the M3 motorway.

From 1952 Basingstoke was expanded to take London overspill, and the population is estimated to have quadrupled from the 25,000 of 1961. The town centre was virtually demolished in the mid 1960s to make way for an entirely new elevated pedestrian centre, then a novelty. The elevation is still unusual – roads actually pass under the town centre.

Part of the south of the town centre escaped demolition. Winchester Street

The chapel of the Holy Ghost, Basingstoke

Mountbatten House, Basingstoke

and its continuation London Street have most of the town's surviving older buildings, with a few more in the streets to the north of the Town Hall. At the western end of London Street is Deane's Almshouses, dating from 1608 and still in use. The 1832 Town Hall is now the **Willis Museum** (free;lists) with displays on local history and archaeology, the canal, clocks etc. Temporary exhibitions too.

Museum, only ★ ★ as it is not large.

The church of St Michael is basically 16th century, but very restored. At the west end are the Royal Arms of Elizabeth, 1596, and there are two other later ones as well. A few older cottages survive around the church.

The most striking part of Basingstoke is the range of gigantic office buildings to the east of the town centre along Churchill Way. Mountbatten House (1976) towards the east end was specifically designed to take the tiers of trees and plants, a modern hanging garden. Lots of industry and housing estates around the ring roads. The railway station is to the north of the centre, and just above it are the ruins of the Holy Ghost Chapel, set in a big graveyard with a twirly Victorian lodge. Holy Ghost Chapel was a fine building, but little now remains.

★ ★ *Willis Museum*

BASSETT see **SOUTHAMPTON NORTH**

BAUGHURST (B) The northern part merges with Heath End in modern development, but the south is more rural, with older brick houses and cottages along the main road. The church of St Stephen is in the south, and dates from 1845, although it could be taken for a much later Victorian church, as it is historically accurate. Odd tower and spire.

BEACON HILL (B), between Whitchurch and Newbury, on the A34). An Iron Age hillfort on the highest part (872 ft) of the northern chalk, with wonderful views. Car park at the bottom, and a long haul up, cheered in late spring by hundreds of cowslips. The ditches and banks seem hardly needed, the slopes are so steep. Inside, flat platforms indicate the positions of huts. On the far side, just inside the defences, is the grave of the 5th Earl of Carnarvon, the discoverer of Tutenkhamun, who died in 1923. Wide views over what seems like the whole of Hampshire, and to the north Highclere Castle in its extensive woods. The horses of the Highclere stud look like toys from this height.

★ ★ ★ ★ *Downland, hillfort views.*

Grave of the Earl of Carnarvon on Beacon Hill

Building Materials

Hampshire has no good building stone, so that virtually all the stone buildings in the county were built of imported material, brought from the Isle of Wight where good limestone was quarried extensively, or from Caen in France. Only the very best medieval buildings, like Winchester Cathedral, Portchester Castle or rich merchant's houses in Southampton were stone built. Humbler builders had to use flint.

'England has perhaps no more curious [building] material than flint, a stone of obscure origin quite unlike any other in colour and texture, and not used for building in any other country on so extensive a scale' Alec Clifton Taylor.

The flint occurs as nodules or narrow bands in the chalk, and although durable, is difficult to use for corners of buildings, or window and door surrounds. Until early Victorian times it was regarded as cheap substitute for stone, and often rendered over to disguise it, but from then onwards it was considered ornamental and 'rustic' and left exposed. Flint can be used in several different ways, varying from irregular nodules laid as they are found, to neat squares cut from the nodules. Occasionally slivers of flint are pressed into the mortar between the larger flints: this is called galetting and is usually Victorian.

A contrast in flint: left, carefully squared blocks (with pebbles in the middle) and the smaller pier (right) natural flints. At Warnford.

ABOVE *Natural flint at Itchen Stoke, with huge flints unusually used for the window arch.*
BELOW *Flushwork at Curdridge – faced flints cut into patterns.*

BELOW *Some of the earliest brickwork in Hampshire – around 1439 at Bishop's Waltham Palace, with a diaper pattern in darker bricks. Lower right is English Bond, alternate rows of long sides and short sides.*

All Hampshire's building materials together at Littleton – stone corners, brick flints and stone chequering, and timber framing with flint infill.

The Post Office, Southampton, built from terracotta made at Blanchard's works, Bishops Waltham.

Hampshire has many deposits of clay suitable for brick making, and from the 15th century some were produced, with the industry expanding greatly in the 18th century. Many colours of brick were produced, with red being popular in the 18th century, and yellow from the early 19th. Fareham reds were famous well beyond the county boundaries, being used for the Albert Hall, London and The Town Hall, Cape Town, as well as numerous local buildings. Fareham High Street is one of the best places to see the variety of colours, and different methods of bricklaying. It also has an example of mathematical tiles – tiles made to look like bricks, which were attached to the front of buildings to 'modernise' them when timber framing and so on seemed unfashionable. In the later 19th century, Bishop's Waltham produced terracotta, with elaborate moulded decoration.

Chalk was also used for building, in the form of cob. Most of the New Forest cottages were built of this muddy mixture, and thatched, but only very few survive because cob, (not being baked like bricks to make it durable), is very vulnerable to the weather. There are still examples of cob garden walls in many parts of the county, with footings of brick or flint and a thatch 'hat' to keep the weather out. In a few places harder chalk was used in buildings, but it is too soft to be satisfactory externally.

In the east of the county the pale and rather soft malmstone was used for many buildings, but it was not durable enough to be worth moving far. The dark brown heathstone is also used in a few areas such as Aldershot, Greatham and Selborne.

ABOVE *A cob wall at Broughton, with brick and flint lower part and a thatched top.*
BELOW *The pale malmstone at Buriton, with brick corners. The garden wall is the dark brown heathstone.*

Hampshire Houses

Only the houses open to the public are considered here.

Hampshire does not have any of the largest mansions: the Vyne was regarded as very large when it was built in the 16th century, and remains the most impressive house in the county, but it is not on the biggest scale. There were medieval palaces, both of the King and the bishop of Winchester, but none survives with its roof on, except Castle Hall Winchester, only a fragment, but still seeming like a habitation, a regal room. At Winchester as well are two institutions which preserve the medieval way of life in their original medieval buildings. St Cross and Winchester College both still have all the appendages of medieval households, a church, great hall and so on, and in the College they are still used for their original purposes: the hall still being used to eat in. On a smaller scale, the Medieval Merchant's House, Southampton gives a good idea of 'normal' sized houses, as it is furnished with reproduction medieval furniture. The much larger

ABOVE *The Medieval Merchant's House, Southampton*
BELOW *The Vyne*

Tudor House, Southampton is a museum, but is also interesting simply as a building.

The other four star houses range in date from the 16th to the 19th centuries, but none are so interesting architecturally as The Vyne. They do all have added attractions. The 18th century Broadlands has a lovely riverside setting, and exhibition of the life of Mountbatten. Hinton Ampner is a superb reconstruction of a Georgian house, with gorgeous fittings and furniture, and good gardens. Stratfield Saye has many relics of the first Duke of Wellington, a fine exhibition, with superb grounds and gardens. Highclere is the one other house which has claims to be on the largest scale, having been rebuilt in the 1830s, and also has a perfect park. The three star houses are simply smaller, or are less open. Breamore is Elizabethan (although restored after a fire). Palace House, Beaulieu is a Victorian adaptation of a medieval gatehouse. Avington is a handsome 18th century house, and The Grange very interesting architecturally as it is Greek in style, but since it is a shell with a roof on only offers a quick visit. The two rooms opened at Mottisfont are of the highest quality – one a medieval undercroft, and the other decorated by Rex Whistler.

The Grange

There are many 18th and earlier 19th century moderate sized 'big' houses around Southampton and in the Portsmouth hinterland built by successful naval officers, and one of them (Alresford House) is open to the public.

Many of the big houses are associated with famous people – Broadlands with Palmerston and Mountbatten for example, and there are three ordinary sized houses which have particular people linked to them. Charles Dickens' birthplace in Portsmouth did not house him for long, but is an ordinary early 19th century terraced house interestingly furnished and decorated in period style. Jane Austen's House at Chawton has many relics, and part of The Wakes, Gilbert White's house at Selborne, is furnished as it was in his day.

All these are homes of more normal size, and there even are a few cottages which can be visited.

★ ★ ★ ★ *Broadlands, Romsey; Castle Hall Winchester; Highclere Castle (with perfect park); Hinton Ampner (with garden); Stratfield Saye (with grounds); Winchester College; The Vyne. Smaller houses: Jane Austen's House, Chawton; Tudor House, Southampton (with museum).*

★ ★ ★ *Alresford House, Old Alresford; Avington Park; Palace House, Beaulieu; Breamore House; The Grange; The Medieval Merchant's House, Southampton; Rotherfield Park, East Tisted (with gardens); The Wakes, Selborne.*

See also: *King John's House, Romsey (the museum but also a small medieval house); Pilgrim Hall (a small medieval hall) Winchester; Charles Dickens birthplace, Portsmouth (a little townhouse); Fareham Museum (an 18th century town house); Hampshire Farm Museum, Upper Hamble Country Park (a furnished traditional farmhouse); Mottisfont Abbey (only a couple of rooms open); and for cottages Furzey Gardens and Buckler's Hard.*

LEFT *The hall at Highclere*

Palace House, Beaulieu

BEAULIEU (M) Literally Bellus Locus, or beautiful place. A Cistercian abbey was founded here in 1204 by King John, at the head of the navigable tidal estuary of the Beaulieu river. The village grew up outside the abbey, and at the dissolution of the monasteries in 1538 parts of the abbey buildings were converted for other uses, while many (including the abbey church) were demolished and the stone used to build Hurst and Calshot castles. With alterations and additions the abbey gatehouse continues in use as a house, but from 1972 it has shared the grounds with the large modern building of the National Motor Museum. The museum, house, grounds and abbey buildings are all open to the public (fee:lists).

The National Motor Museum contains over 200 cars and lorries dating from the 1890s to the 1960s, including racing cars and speed record cars besides normal production models. 1930s street scene with many commercial vehicles. Motorcycles from 1902-1975, and displays of tyres, lighting etc. Many slide shows and videos. 'Wheels' is a display of motoring history, where the visitor is taken through the exhibition in a seat which moves through the display on a fixed track. A monorail goes through the building and around the site.

Close by are Railway World in miniature, and Transportarama.

The Abbey ruins vary wildly in their state of preservation, because so much stone was robbed. The large church has gone completely, and is only marked out on the ground. Enough of the cloisters survive to give a good idea of how they looked. The best buildings are the lay brothers' dormitory and the abbey refectory. The Lay brothers' quarters now house a display on monastic life, and the original vaulted roof survives.

The 13th century abbey refectory became the parish church after the abbey was dissolved in 1538. The orientation is entirely wrong: the altar is in the south instead of east. The church is a single space, with no chancel arch, and gives a good idea of the scale of the abbey. The finest feature is the original 13th century reading pulpit on the east wall. A flight of stairs inside the wall is lit by elegant arches on Purbeck marble columns, and a larger arch gives access to the pulpit itself (the upper part is modern, the triangular lower part original). From here one monk would read to all the others as they ate their meals. Good 14th century roof with lots of bosses.

Palace House An odd name: it should really be gatehouse house as it was converted from the large 14th century inner gatehouse of the abbey. Although the original building was large, it was nothing like the size of the present house, because it was enlarged in 1872. The fine vaulted ceilings in the downstairs rooms are original: the rooms were the roads entering the abbey. The heavy stone fireplaces are additions of 1872. Upstairs, the upper drawing room was originally a chapel. All the rooms are interestingly furnished with many fine paintings. The series of portraits is especially interesting, ranging from Thomas Wriothesley who bought the abbey in 1538 to the present Lord Montagu. Fine views over the garden and lake from the house, particularly from the upper floor which has super Victorian wallpapers.

The gardens around the house are pretty: to the south is the small 13th century outer gatehouse, a simple building with a 19th century clock tower on top.

Beaulieu village is also worth visiting: small but crammed with handsome brick

The Cloisters, Beaulieu

houses and cottages, with good tiled roofs. One is 17th century, timber framed with herringbone brickwork, but they mostly date from the 18th or 19th centuries. The quantities of brick contrast with the stone of the monastic buildings. Going out of the village towards Palace House, the last building on the left a simple brick structure, is a tide mill, and the road is on a causeway which is also the dam for the reed-fringed mill pond. The estuary itself is picturesque, especially at high tide, when mud is covered and the close-cropped grass runs right down to the water. Lots of birds.

★ ★ ★ ★ *Beaulieu as a whole offers a good day out, riveting to those interested in cars or the history of transport. Good monastic remains and an interesting house. Beautiful landscape.*

BEAUWORTH (J) A remote hamlet, with some plain brick thatched cottages, and one larger house. The church of St James dates from 1838, rendered with a slated bellcote. Inside it is very austere and chapel-like, but with bright 1989 glass in the east window which includes local scenes. Above the church is the tiniest redbrick schoolhouse and a big timber framed cottage.

BEDHAMPTON (O) Now enclosed on three sides by modern suburbs and (apart from the village centre) seeming like part of Havant. The village street still survives and is rural. The church of St Thomas Becket is at the south end, with only open ground beyond it (and the noisy Havant bypass and the railway). Facing the fields is Bidbury House, late 18th century, and opposite the church is the large Old Rectory, also Georgian but with a huge Victorian porch. Pretty flint coachhouse. These and other smaller Georgian houses of the village are all brick, but the oddest house is not. The Elms at the west end of the old village is rendered, with delicate Georgian Gothic detailing to the main house and a fantastic single storey addition with a tower attached, also Gothic in style but coarser with decoration dotted about. This was added by Sir Theophilus Lee as a large room to entertain the Duke of Wellington in after the Battle of Waterloo in 1815.

In 1819 the poet Keats visited Bedhampton to stay with the miller in The Old Mill House which still survives close to the bypass. Here he wrote most of 'The Eve of St Agnes' a popular poem in the 19th century.

The church is simple, of flint, and was heavily restored in the 1870s. Inside a good chancel arch of about 1140 survives and there are some fine wall memorials in the chancel.

The road to the right beyond the church leads over a very long brick bridge, constructed over the railway when it was built in 1848 by the special request of the landowner. The 21 arches can be seen from a footpath beneath the bridge. Over the bridge is The Old Mill where Keats stayed in 1819, a picturesque building with the river on both sides. The motorway immediately behind detracts from this part of Bedhampton, which must have been very peaceful and pretty. Over the motorway the footpath continues along the creek and shore, and is a good place to see the birds of Langstone Harbour. Car park by the shore.

West of Bedhampton the B2177 climbs Portsdown Hill and crosses the motorway on a high bridge and just over the bridge is Belmont Castle, a gothic fantasy of about 1800, brick with castellations and odd windows. In the grounds a tiny mock temple of the same date.

BEECH (F) An area which was split up into small-holdings in the 1920s, with small wooden or galvanised iron bungalows being built on each plot. Compton Mackenzies' novel *Buttercups and Daisies* (1931) is based on Beech (called Oaktown) and has a lot of fun with the would-be rural inhabitants. Virtually all the bungalows have gone, the plots now having big new houses, but a few can be seen, set back in the trees. Just off

the main road is the original village, a few thatched houses. The church of St Peter is still corrugated iron. The whole village is well wooded.

BENTLEY (F) divides into two parts – Bentley Station in the south, surprisingly with several old cottages, and the village proper. There are Georgian houses and cottages along the main road, and close to the cross-roads, by the village hall, an elaborate roofed village sign of 1923, with a map showing places of interest and a brief history of the village. The area off the main road was described in 1760 as 'a very pretty, cheerful, well-built village, the houses scattered, and all with neat well-planted gardens before them'. With the addition of more modern houses, this is still true.

The church of St Mary is in the northern part, well sited with extensive views to the east. The top of the tower is 18th century diapered brick, and inside is rather cold 19th century reconstruction apart from the tower arch and the east end. The chancel is Norman, with big pillars. 15th century glass in one high window, and 17th century communion rail. The Bentley churchwardens agreed in 1774 that 'no relief be given to any of the poor of this parish who drink tea or frequent the public house'. Presumably drinking beer at home was acceptable.

A group of four elderly yews by the church path must have been planted at much the same time – all are now ill, but one has its branches held up by a substantial pergola.

Close to the road to the church is

The tin church at Beech

Jenkyn Place with its famous garden. Created from the 1940s with a superb selection of plants and trees wonderfully arranged, this garden is well worth seeing. Many small gardens and courtyards in different styles, many specimen trees (some ancient) and good vistas. Unusual plants, trees and shrubs. Large, and good at any season. Heartily recommended.

⭐ ⭐ *Village and church.*

⭐ ⭐ ⭐ *Garden at Jenkyn Place.*

BENTWORTH (E) A sizeable village along one curving street with several thatched cottages, and farms with barns. Hall farm in the middle has a 14th century porch. There is a big pond. On the green an oak planted in 1919.

George Wither (1588-1667) the poet was born in the village: his satire on the government got him imprisoned.

The church of St Mary has a flourishing thorn by the gate grown from the Glastonbury thorn which is supposed to have been planted by Joseph of Arimathea. The church is virtually all of the early 13th century, characteristically with thick Norman style pillars but the later pointed arches. Lots of good memorials. The medieval font has a pyramidal wooden cover dated 1605, a charming rustic piece. Behind the church a large early 19th century rectory.

⭐ ⭐ *Church, interesting as all of one date.*

BERE FOREST see FOREST OF BERE

BEVOIS VALLEY see SOUTHAMPTON NORTH

BIGHTON (E) Lots of good buildings, brick, flint, plastered or timber framed. Some thatched cottages. Big farmyard with a large thatched farmhouse opposite. Lots of trees and garden walls. Lovely wide views from the roads around, particularly the one to Medstead.

The church of All Saints is up a little side road, with the Manor House beyond. The house is handsome and brick, of about 1675, and the church is tiny and charming. Everything about it is small-scale. Basically Norman, with fat pillars and an original tiny chapel at the east end of the north aisle. The overwhelming impression is of painted decoration: the ceilings were painted and the screen built in 1904 by Ninian Comper, a fine church architect. Tiers of pews under the tower, with a facetted ceiling. Simple Norman windows in the

side walls of the chancel. The pews, doors and east window must date from a restoration of the 1840s or 50s and add to the charm of the church. 12th century table-type font. Top of the tower weatherboarded. Just below a huge ex-rectory, perhaps bigger than the church.

The superbly named hamlet of **Gundleton** to the south is mostly modern, with lots of trees.

⭐ ⭐ *Church*

BINSTEAD (F) Very rural, with an interesting medieval church, and the burial place of Viscount Montgomery of Alamein. To the west of the village oast houses, and in the north part a big set of malthouses. Several timber framed cottages, including up by the church a 16th century jettied one; an attractive row together with plain old farm buildings, some (and parts of cottages) in Malmstone.

The church of Holy Cross is a puzzle: records make it clear that it was built from about 1322, but in style it is much earlier. Simple lancet windows, and inside fat Norman pillars with transitional pointed arches – which should date from around 1160. The chancel with its round arches should be even earlier. All very odd, but a fine medieval church. The east window of stained and painted glass is impressive: it came from Brussels in the 1870s. 1896 alabaster font. Big flag hanging at the back of the church – Montgomery's banner. Very plain tower, and fine wide views from the churchyard. Montgomery's grave is at the west end of the graveyard; the gravel path leads to the plain slab. He died in 1976, having lived at Isington Mill in the parish from 1958.

⭐ ⭐ *Church*

BIRDWORLD (F) at Holt Pound on the A325, south of Farnham, but just in Hampshire). A superb place, with an enormous variety of birds, ranging from huge ostriches, emus and rheas to native birds like stone curlews. Cranes, flamingoes, owls, spoonbills, cockatoos, macaws, pelicans, storks, kookaburras, and even a condor. The African Royal Starlings and the Red Billed Blue Magpie are unbelievably bright, and the penguin pool has a glass side so that one can see them diving and swimming underwater. All well laid out with lots of flower borders. Fascinating. Underwater World next door has a selection of tropical fish,

some brightly coloured.

⭐ ⭐ ⭐ *For Birdworld.*

BISHOPSTOKE (J) The village is down by the river, off the main road, and most of the older buildings are where the wide river Itchen fills one side of the road. Large early 19th century villas on the other side, well set back, some now flats. A small park where the road turns up the hill and leaves the river marks the site of the old parish church, now just footings. Itchen House towards the river is of about 1840, with fantastic decoration around the eaves and complex chimneys. A path leads through from the old graveyard to the river, and then to the second waterway which is the Itchen Navigation (see entry). One of the few surviving Navigation locks is here, relined with brick. The tow path leads northwards with views of big gardens of the villas running down on the opposite side, and gradually becomes more rural.

The village has grown up the hill, with a mixture of Victorian, Edwardian and the odd earlier house leading up to the church of St Mary, flint and stone of the 1890s with a wrought iron screen of high quality.

The village was quite large before about 1960, but has grown enormously since, both by infill and with new estates. To the south of the old village is a completely new area, with its own shopping centre.

Stoke Park Wood to the east of Bishopstoke has many footpaths. Good woodland walking.

BISHOP'S SUTTON (E) At least part of the parish was granted to Winchester by King Ine in 701, and the Bishop of Winchester's hunting dogs were kept here in medieval times. The Bishop's palace was to the north of the church with fishponds where the watercress beds are now, and there was also a park for hunting. The palace was demolished in the 18th century. The manor house next to the church is a large brick house of 1700 which developed from a farmhouse.

The church of St Nicholas dates from the 12th and 13th centuries, and is larger and more lavish than one would expect a village church to be because of the association with the bishop. Inside the Georgian brick porch is a fine Norman doorway decorated with stylised heads of birds. The arch is of hard chalk, not hard enough to prevent the many graffiti scratched into it. The nave is high, with small Norman windows surviving and a wide chancel arch. Open bell frame at the west end. The chancel is 13th century with lancet windows surviving all round. Fine 1630 communion rail. Two brasses of about 1500 in the chancel. Big and rather ugly 18th century font.

★ ★ *As an austere early medieval church.*

BISHOP'S WALTHAM (J) A charming small town, with many 18th century (and earlier) buildings in the handsome local red brick, and full of pretty roofs made from small clay tiles. The centre is a tight grid of streets, disturbed in the 1960s when one whole block was removed to make way for car parks, destroying large numbers of humble but historic Georgian cottages. The village lies between the medieval bishop's palace which gives the place its name and the parish church.

St George's Square on the south of the old town shows a good selection of buildings. The 18th century Crown adjoins a 17th century house with three gables to the street, while next to that is a very pretty Georgian house in the local grey and red brick with a 1960s building making the corner and blending well. A very plain redbrick Georgian house stands alone on the other side. The Square was on the main road, at the entrance to the palace, but a new road has altered all this, so that the relationship between the palace and the town which grew up beside it is destroyed.

High Street is the central one leading from the Square, with most of the shops. Barclays Bank, the first building on the left has an unusual textured finish to the walls of the two Victorian wings and the middle Georgian block has a nice plain doorway. This was a private house until early this century. The Oddfellows Hall of 1895 (now a shop) displays patterned terracotta, presumably from Blanchard's works in Bishop's Waltham. There are several simple 19th century shopfronts surviving in High Street, perhaps the best in the north-east corner.

Houchin Street and Basingwell Street to the east of High Street have suffered because the area between them was cleared in the 1960s for car parks. What survives is small-scale and attractive. Brook Street, parallel on the west, has mostly modern development on one side but gives an impression of the denseness of old Bishop's Waltham, which can be best appreciated in photographs displayed in **Bishop's Waltham Museum**, in Brook Street (fee:lists). ★ ★

ABOVE *St Peter's church, Bishops Waltham.* BELOW *St Peter's Street, Bishops Waltham*

The ruins of the Bishop's Palace, Bishops Waltham

Towards Bank Street Southfield House was saved from demolition, and has been restored to its 17th century form as part of the recent development. Beyond is Duke's Mill, still grinding corn.

Bank Street runs across the north, starting with the big Victorian granary (now shops and workshops) and continuing for quite a way westwards, with big timber-framed cottages and many Georgian brick buildings. One of the larger plain houses on the north (east of the new flats) side was Gunner's Bank, founded in 1809 a time when many small banks started, but surviving until 1953, one of the last private banks to close. It had only the one office, and like many small banks issued its own banknotes in the first half of the 19th century. At the corner with Free Street and along that road leading back to the church are more Georgian brick houses.

The church is to the north-east of the town, along St Peter's Street, narrow, picturesque and lined with Georgian houses and cottages The church is of varied building materials – flint for the tower, good stone for the side walls of the aisles, and chequered work at the east end of the aisles. The plain tower is of 1589, an unusual date for church building. The parish register records 'the steeple and tower of the church fell down the 31st day of December 1582', so a new tower had to be built. On top is an odd little circular structure, perhaps 17th century but adapted in the 19th century restorations.

The aisles were rebuilt in 1637 (north) and 1652 to enlarge the church, plain with domestic looking windows. 17th century door inside the porch. The inside is large and wide, much altered by 19th century restorations. Gallery of 1733 at the back, and good memorials all around including one of 1629 with a bust of a man in ruff high on the north wall. The wooden pulpit – dated 1626 – must be the most elaborate one of its date in Hampshire. The tester over it is Victorian but matches well. The ex Rectory beyond the church is plain Georgian with an unusually large fanlight over the door.

★ ★ *Church for the unusual date of tower and aisles.*

Bishop's Waltham Palace. This area belonged to the Bishops of Winchester before the Norman Conquest, and there was probably a Bishop's house here then, and certainly a hunting park as Domesday Book records one here in 1086. The Bishop of Winchester had the second richest see in Europe in the middle ages, and were often important officials of the King as well, so their palaces were impressive. The surviving palace was built in the later 12th century, but much modified later. Bishop's Waltham was a favourite with several Bishops, especially William of Wickham (Bishop 1367-1404) and Cardinal Beaufort (Bishop 1404-47). William of Wickham remodelled much of the place, and spent the last three years of his life here, and Beaufort also remodelled some of the buildings. It was taken by Parliamentarians in 1644, and although restored to the bishop in 1660 it was never used as a palace again. but was robbed for building materials.

The entrance is across the moat, and the end of the brick building by the moat has some original diapered brickwork (with a pattern in darker brick). This is the remnant of a range which extended for 240 ft all along this side of the inner enclosure, built in 1439 to provide lodgings for guests. The brickwork is some of the earliest in the county, and the bricks were probably made on site. This corner of the lodgings survived because it became a farmhouse in the later 17th century, after the Bishops ceased using the palace. The lower floors are furnished as a farmhouse, but the upper ones have been restored to their medieval appearance. The finest carved stones from the site are displayed, and an exhibition explains the history of the palace.

The stone and flint building next to the farmhouse was built in 1378 as a bakehouse and brewhouse. The footings to the south are of the chapel, with the sunken part overhung by trees, the chapel crypt which dates from the Norman palace. The long range and tower on the far side with some of the walls surviving are Norman too, but greatly altered in the 15th century with the large windows in the outer wall. This was the hall, with to the left the kitchen and storage rooms.

The tower in the corner probably provided the Bishop's private accommodation. Many fireplace and window details survive here. The range around the corner included on the first floor, the Bishop's Great Chamber, with storage rooms underneath.

Cloisters and other buildings filled the angle between the two ranges, but only footings remain. The original entrance with gatehouse was in the west corner, at the end of the long lodging block.

The inner court with the surviving buildings is moated, and to the south a larger area is enclosed by a redbrick wall of about 1500 beside which run the roads. On two corners, one to the east of the main buildings, are charming little turrets, brick with stone dressings. The wall originally enclosed the garden or pleasure grounds. There is now an 18th century house inside part of it.

To the north-west are the remains of the huge fish pond which belonged to the palace, cut in two when the new road was built. Below it are the big buildings of Abbey Mill. The deer or hunting park covered 1,000 acres to the west of the palace on either side of the Hamble river and was not abolished until 1663.

★ ★ ★ ★ *Small town,* ★ ★ *Museum*
★ ★ ★ *Palace, some of the buildings only footings, but others more complete.*

BISTERNE (L) one of the straggly settlements on the western side of the New Forest, bounded by the wide valley of the Avon. Only a few cottages and the small yellow brick church of St Paul (1842) set in trees. Just to the south of the church is a big Elizabethan house, now rendered. **Avon** further south is again only a hamlet along the road, but with a good selection of brick buildings – big barn, farm and farmyard and cottages. Many large oaks in the area.

BLACKMOOR (F) Close to Bordon, and so heathy although with many trees. A variety of building materials including malmstone. Next to the church a three-sided timber and stone cloister, an unusual war memorial. The school next door is now the village hall, a solid stone building. The church of St Matthew is large, with a pretty tower and dates from 1868. Stone lined inside, and with some original pastel patterned glass surviving. Open treey heath next to the church.
  ★ *Church.*

BLACKWATER see HAWLEY

BLENDWORTH (K) On a hill just outside Horndean. The church of Holy Trinity was rebuilt in 1851 on the highest point, and is an attractive flint building with a distinctive spire. This is the parish church of Horndean as well as Blendworth. Several Victorian flint and brick cottages around the church, and some older ones, one timber framed, a little to the east, mark the old village centre where the church used to be. All very rural.

BLISSFORD see HYDE

BOARHUNT (J/N) The main part of the village is North Boarhunt, along the main road and running north. Typical scattered village with a few older houses between bungalows and modern infill. Lots of trees, especially oak.
  The church is away to the south, on the side of Portsdown Hill. No village here, only a single cottage and a huge farm. The brick and flint farm buildings have pretty tile roofs. The church of St Nicholas sits on a shelf on the hillside, with an old churchyard yew at its eastern end. Hollow and perhaps dying. This one could be a thousand years old.
  All the walls of the simple church are Saxon - very late Saxon since it is believed to date from about 1064. The

west wall and the chancel walls outside have been decorated with little slivers of flint, charming but not original. The only Saxon window surviving is on the north side of the chancel, only visible externally as it is blocked. Inside the chancel arch is the main original feature, the windows and doors are later. Up by the altar is a monument of 1577, still being added to. The pine fittings are of the restoration of 1853, but are old-fashioned for that date, with a squire's pew, three-decker pulpit, gallery and so on. The extra-large font may be Saxon. On the south nave wall a monument to Robert Eddowes Esq (d.1765) 'late Store-keeper of the Ordnance at Portsmouth' partly obscures a Saxon round-headed doorway. Nice later medieval painted decoration on one side. The church is of interest as a complete example of a small late Saxon church, and the countryside is good.
  ★ ★ *Church*

BOKERLEY DYKE see MARTIN DOWN

Boarhunt church

BOLDERWOOD ORNAMENTAL DRIVE (H/M) leads north from the Christchurch/Lyndhurst road (A35), a couple of miles from Lyndhurst and is the easiest place to see the ancient woodland of the New Forest. At the south end of the drive is the Knightwood Oak (see entry). The road was originally a private drive to Bolderwood Lodge, first a hunting lodge, but in the later 18th century the home of Lord Delwar. Gilpin, in his *Forest Scenery* (1791) admired it as 'one of the finest situations of the forest' and the area was already famous for 'rich forest-scenery, composed chiefly of beech'. Deer and hogs were common, because they fed on the beech mast. The drive to the house, now demolished, was made into a public road by the Forestry Commission in 1964, and runs through Mark Ash Wood, with its ancient beech pollards (some of the oldest trees in the Forest) as well as more modern plantations of oak and conifers.
  At the north end of the drive is Bolderwood Arboretum (car park: toilets).

Several walks of different lengths are marked out from the car park through the arboretum and beyond. The trees here were planted from 1860, and include exotics like monkey puzzle, giant redwood and swamp cypress with Rhododendron underneath. A list identifying the trees is available at the entrance. On the borders of the woods are two deer observation platforms: the fields beyond are a deer reserve, and the animals are often to be seen. The longest marked walk leads down to a river and into Mark Ash wood with its ancient beech. Varied topography, and good walking.

Half a mile to the north, by the side of the road, is a simple cross, a memorial to the 3rd Canadian Division RCASC who held services there up to D day 1944.

Bolderwood Drive ★ ★ ★ ★ best place to see the old trees of the New Forest.

BOLDRE (M) Too scattered to be called a village: the different parts even have different names. Mostly now technically outside the New Forest, but it still seems forest edge in character, with most of the fields pasture, and lots of trees. The constituent hamlets – Portmore, Pilley and Sandy Down are pleasantly rural with a little thatch surviving, especially in Pilley, which also has a pond. The church stands all alone on top of a small hill, and although it is in a charming position and is an interesting medieval church, it is most likely to be visited for its association with the Reverend William Gilpin. He

Boldre church

was rector of Boldre from 1777-1804 during which time he wrote his five 'Tours', expounding the different qualities of landscapes in Scotland and Wales, as well as England. He was an exponent of the picturesque – those parts of the landscape suitable for painting – which became a cult in his lifetime, referred to in Jane Austen's *Sense & Sensibility*. He was satirised in a long and very successful poem of 1809: *Dr Syntax in search of the picturesque*. Being short of money Dr Syntax decides:

> "I'll make a TOUR – and then I'll WRITE IT
> You well know what my pen can do,
> And I'll employ my pencil too:-
> I'll ride and write, and sketch and print,
> And thus create a real mint;
> I'll prose it here, I'll verse it there,
> And picturesque it ev'ry where"

Locally Gilpin is best known for *Remarks on Forest Scenery ...... illustrated by the scenes of New-Forest (1791)*

In the north chapel is his memorial stone recalling 'his Munificence as the founder of the School in this parish, for the Education of children of the Day Labourers' The school is at the west end of Pilley, rebuilt in the Victorian period, but still bearing his name. Opposite, on the corner of School Lane is Gilpin's Cottage, built by him in 1791. Gilpin lived to the south in the appropriately named Vicar's Hill, a treey hamlet. His rectory is now called Gilpin's, and is off a tiny triangle with a big tree in the centre.

The oldest part of St John's church is the late 12th century south arcade: very primitive, not pillars but blocks of wall holding up the arches. Most of the rest is 13th century, apart from the top of the tower, brick and dated 1697 and the chancel 1855. Fine stained glass in the east window of 1967, strong and modern in style. On the north wall of the nave a good bust, a memorial to John Kempe, MP for Lymington in the Civil War who died in 1652. There are reminders of the loss of *HMS Hood*, which blew up and sank in 1941 with the loss of 1,416 lives, in the north chapel and the porch. A memorial service is held annually in May. A brass on the pillar just inside the door commemorates Richard Johnson, a curate here who went as chaplain with the first fleet taking convicts to Australia in 1788 and he built the first church in Australia.

Spinners (fee:lists – in the south between Boldre village and Vicar's Hill) is an interesting woodland garden, with many choice plants, trees and shrubs. Winding pathways with something interesting around each corner.

★ ★ For landscape, church and association with Gilpin.

★ ★ ★ For Spinners, a superb woodland garden.

BORDON (F) Until 1903 when the Army Camp was built there was nothing here except a few poor farms on the sandy soil. The area was surrounded by the woodlands of Woolmer Forest (see entry). The Army had used the area since the 1860s for training, but in 1903 the camp was established by moving 68 big huts five miles from Longmoor Camp on a 22ft wide railway especially constructed through the woodlands. It took two years to move them. Today Bordon has grown virtually to the size of a town, still with a large Army presence. Lots of trees.

BOSSINGTON (D/H) (south of Houghton). A deserted medieval village, whose humps and bumps are visible in the meadows around the church. In the 1830s a large yellow brick mansion was built, and the church rebuilt in flint and stone. They are the only buildings in the meadows. Elaborate Victorian lodges to the big house on the main road. The small church of St James is down a grass track. The road west from Bossington is on the track of a Roman road, and is lined with beeches, leading up to the downs with splendid views.

★ Church for setting.

BOTLEY (J) Village sized, but somehow a small town, with the market hall in the middle looking like a town hall. Architecturally it is one of the best villages in Hampshire, although the scale of its square is too small for its traffic.

William Cobbett the well-known reformer and writer bought Fairthorne Farm, nearby in 1805. He thought Botley 'the most delightful village in the world ... the soil was rich, set with woods; the farms were small, the cottages neat; it had neither workhouse, nor barber, nor attourney, nor justice of the peace'. Here Cobbett practiced the farming reforms he preached, but he was imprisoned in 1810, and on his release in 1812 sold the farm. The house he lived in has since been demolished. From the later 19th century Botley was one of the main centres for strawberry growing, and a basket-making industry grew up here to supply the containers.

All ways of laying bricks seem to be present in Botley: many different bonds, and colours in bands, spots or panels. The red or grey brick can be any date from the 17th century, but the yellow, as used in the church, was introduced about 1800.

The market hall of 1848 is the only stone building, with big pillars and a little clock tower of 1897. It was built by the local Farmer's Club. On one side is The Dolphin a handsome 18th century building, and on the other an earlier timber framed house. All around the square are good buildings, many Georgian or re-fronted then. The Bugle

Botley Mill

opposite is perhaps the most perfect, with its porch and carriage entrance and everything in hot red Georgian brick. The east end of the Square is closed by early 18th century cottages in red brick spotted with grey ones, with nice leaded windows. The road leads down towards the mill with several Georgian houses including one with a good doorcase, and by the side of the road is a granite memorial to William Cobbett, erected in 1957.

The mill is large, and still functioning. The mill house is 18th century, but the

central block of the mill building is classical and early 19th century. Inside the large timbers are supplemented by iron columns. The river is tidal to Botley. Cobbett pointed out that the mill worked by fresh-water power, while here, immediately below the mill, is salt water. Until about 1900 there were wharfs for small ships bringing timber up to be cut at one of the mills. Cobbett lived for a short while in the large house Shorecroft House, beyond the mill, and is supposed to have written in the summer house on the wall by the road.

Back up to the Square, where Church Lane leads south. Good Georgian cottages and houses along here too, and a large two storey malthouse, built by the local brewery. The lane leads on to Hampshire Farm Museum (see entry Upper Hamble Country Park) accessible only on foot from this direction. Winchester Street, from the opposite corner of the square has 17th century jettied houses and a good mixture from the 18th century onwards. ¾mile along the road is an octagonal mid 19th century toll house, yellow and red brick.

Towards the church there are more Edwardian houses and cottages. The church of All Saints was rebuilt here in the 19th century: the remains of the medieval church are a mile to the south, and are now in the Hampshire Farm Museum. The tower and nave of All Saints church are of yellow brick, dating from 1836. In the 1890s a north aisle was added, and the domestic looking dormers

The Bugle Inn, Botley

Botley church

added to the roof. Inside the 1836 nave is bare and simple, but the new roof and aisle have heavy and complex timbering. The 12th century font has simple decoration, and towards the chancel is a reset 14th century wall-tomb with a fine effigy of a man. In the north aisle a stained glass window of 1970, commemorating a doctor, with contemporary scenes.

★ ★ ★ ★ *Botley village*

BRADLEY (E) A small village with a very tidy pond. Some thatch but also modern houses. The church of All Saints sits rather apart from the village, with good rural views. It is mostly of 1877, with big carved heads holding up the chancel arch. Unusual Art Nouveau and rustic style pulpit of the 1930s.

BRAISHFIELD (H) has a pond, some thatched cottages and is generally attractive. The church of All Saints is 1885, by Butterfield the Victorian architect famous for his use of coloured bricks, as here. Decorative spirelet, and elaborately fitted chancel inside with wall painting.

BRAMDEAN (J) Some good cottages, and opposite the turning to the church a large handsome early 18th century house, grey and red brick with good iron gates. Up beyond the church Bramdean Manor,

redbrick, large and Georgian. On the other side of the church a large farmyard. The church of St Simon and St Jude is small and rendered. Inside a handsome late 12th century chancel arch. The building is lop-sided because of the big south transept, added in 1877.

Bramdean House, an early 18th century brick house with a big doorway has good gardens which are opened to the public (fee:lists). One acre walled garden, still partly kitchen garden but with roses through the middle, with a wider orchard beyond. Fine trees, good early bulbs and many unusual plants.

★ ★ ★ To the north of the village is Bramdean Common, an area of woods and more open grazing, good for walking. To the east of the open common, close to the road, is a little corrugated iron church, known as the Iron church, built in 1883 for the gypsies who use the common as a camping place. Minute spire, and even stained glass in the east window. A very peaceful place, a clearing in the woods.

★ ★ ★ *Good walking country, lots of footpaths.*

★ ★ ★ *Garden at Bramdean House.*

BRAMLEY (B) 'A well-built and picturesque little place' according to VCH in 1912, 'the cottages, which are dotted about at irregular intervals, being excellent and far above the average in comfort and appearance'. The good

Bramdean church

cottages survive, now interspersed with modern houses. Most of the older ones are around the church, several with latticed windows and some thatched. Many farm buildings, including a small barn on steddle stones. The eastern part by the railway is more modern and to the south of this was the Army's Central Ammunition Depot which closed in 1978. **Bramley Green** further east has a few older cottages around the green.

The church of St James was described by Pevsner as 'one of the most fully furnished churches in Hampshire'. Externally the 1636 brick tower and the big south transept are interesting features, but the interior is best. The big south transept was designed in 1802 by the classical architect Sir John Soane, well known for his secular urban buildings. The plaster ceiling is in an attractive but fanciful Gothic style. The later window has panels of early 16th century Swiss glass, and in the middle of the transept is the monument to Bernard Brocas, white marble of superb quality 'a fat, stately man expiring in the arms of a kneeling young woman' (Pevsner). Carved panels on the sides. Funeral hatchments for the same family around the walls, and two Royal coats of arms, one unusually to the Prince of Wales, probably the one who became Charles I. In the floor two brasses, both 16th century and with figures.

The chancel is the most fully furnished

In Bramley church

part, with 15th century screen, Victorian rood beam, 1539 panelling on the ceiling, and more of much the same date on the walls. The wall paintings are 13th century, mostly scrolls and imitation masonry. On the nave wall a big 15th century St Christopher is painted, and opposite a much clearer representation of the martyrdom of St Thomas a Becket painted in the early 13th century, only fifty years or so after it happened. The plain bench ends are known from accounts to date from 1535, but the attractive Priest's chair and stall are 1970. Small purbeck marble font, Norman.

The west end has a gallery of 1728 with the organ aloft, placed here in Victorian times. Under the tower is panelling from the Army Camp chapel, including a roll of honour commemorating those trained at Bramley and killed on bomb disposal duties.

★ ★ ★ *Church for the tower, transept and fittings.*

BRAMSHAW (H)

BRAMSHAW (H) A spread-out village, with wide verges merging into small greens, all cropped by the ponies as the village is within the New Forest despite lots of small pasture fields. Many brick houses ranging from the 17th century to the present. Big hedgerow oaks everywhere. The church of St Peter right at the north end of the village on a large hump, has a good view with woods all around in the middle distance. All brick and 1829, apart from the stone medieval nave. Nice wooden top to the tower. Until the boundaries were re-arranged in 1895 the church straddled two counties with its chancel in Hampshire and its nave in Wiltshire. Beyond the church the road runs through a fine mixed wood, with big oaks and beeches (car park).

BRAMSHOTT (F)

BRAMSHOTT (F) (and Grayshott) Part of a different type of heathland to most of Hampshire, on the Lower Greensand, with lots of short steep ridges. Good (if exhausting) walking country, far more like Surrey than Hampshire. In 1795 Bramshott was described as 'nearly enclosed on three sides by extensive heaths which though apparently barren, are of great benefit, feeding considerable flocks of sheep, whose fleeces are of very fine texture, and the flesh equal in flavour to the Bagshot mutton. The turf, being pared off and dried, is a good fuel, and in the forest there are extensive peat-moors. Of the heaths, great quantities of brooms are made, which affords employ to the

Thorney Hill church, Bransgore

poor; and in the summer the women and children gather large quantities of hurts, or whortleberries.' The whortleberries or bilberries are still common, occurring in patches on the hillsides. They are short bushes, looking more like a herb. Bramshott Common to the east is a good walking area.

Lots of trees in Bramshott, which hide most of the houses. The roads have all cut down into the Greensand, the one running eastwards to Waggoner's Wells so deep that it is in a tiny gorge.

Occasional oast houses, and some cottages built of the greensand (actually very pale) with brick door and window surrounds, others are all brick. The church of St Mary is greensand too, a mixture of dates. 13th century chancel, most of the rest 1872, but attractive – especially inside. Brasses in the north transept of 1430, with scrolls coming from the mouths of the people. Many Canadian graves from the First and Second World Wars in the graveyard, a reminder of how close Bordon is.

Waggoner's Wells to the east is a series of three large ponds, dammed down the valley. Well wooded, and surrounded by short steep ridges, two of which have to be crossed from the Bramshott car park to reach the ponds. The dams and ponds were created in 1615 to supply water power for the local iron industry. Flora Thompson (see Grayshott) visited the lakes often, admiring the strange scenery and describing the natural history.

★ ★ ★ ★ *Waggoner's Wells for walking.*

BRANSGORE (L)

BRANSGORE (L) Technically just outside the New Forest, but with many trees and still feeling foresty on the eastern side despite quantities of modern development. The older church of St Mary is to the south, a simple brick building mostly of 1822, but away to the north in **Thorney Hill** is a curious little church (Christ Church) built in 1906 in an individual classical style and designed by Detmar Blow for the owners of the big house nearby. Combined with the pine tree grove along the path it looks distinctly foreign, even Greek. Inside it is vaulted, and has wall paintings of 1922. Good memorials.

Towards the centre of Bransgore, east of the road from Thorney Hill is **MacPennys**, a superb garden of lime-hating plants set in an old gravel pit. Rhododendrons, azaleas and camellias abound, but there is much more variety than that. Big forest trees too. Superfine paths and very hilly. Recommended.

★ ★ ★ *Not* ★ ★ ★ ★ *simply because of its moderate size.*

★ ★ *For Thorney Hill, a very unusual little church in a fine setting.*

BREAMORE (G)

BREAMORE (G) The best of the pretty villages in this attractive corner of Hampshire, with a little Saxon church, a large Elizabethan house and two good museums.

The village spreads over a large area, starting down in the valley of the Avon with a large picturesque brick mill on an island with its mill house. This road to

Breamore church

have glass flush with the wall. A west chamber, part of the original church, has disappeared. Up under the tower, on the right, is an original arch, round-headed tall and thin, with an inscription. This is contemporary with the building of the church, and translates 'here is manifested the Covenant to thee'. The text was probably continued on the chancel arch (where a tiny bit survives) and on the doorway to the north chapel, now gone.

The south chapel, through the inscribed arch, is original, but is difficult to see into because the arch is so small. The Saxon chancel arch (now replaced by a 15th century one) was only two feet wider than this surviving one.

The chancel is 14th century, and at the west end, with the organ, is an early 19th century gallery. Outside, the typical

Woodgreen from Breamore has eight river bridges because the river splits into so many streams, and yet another bridge (closest to Breamore) for the Salisbury/ Ringwood railway.

Along the main road are mixed modern, Victorian and earlier houses and cottages, but off the main road are many early brick cottages, mostly thatched and some timber-framed. The middle of the village has a huge, partly boggy, green, and there are groups of cottages up by Breamore House, at Upper Street, North Street, Outwick and Flood Street.

The church of St Mary, close to Breamore House, is a rare and important survival – a Saxon building. Despite later alterations and a new chancel, the church preserves the shape and size of a late Saxon village church. The porch is a Norman addition, but inside, on the wall of the nave, is a large (but defaced) rood – Christ on the Cross. This is contemporary with the church, (although it has been moved) and like others at Romsey and Headbourne Worthy. The Hand of God appears from the clouds above. Large sculpture of this early date is very rare, and Hampshire has more than anywhere else in Europe. Recently the 16th century painted plaster background has been revealed, showing a wooded landscape.

Inside, the nave and crossing are all of the original church of about 1,000 A.D., although with several later windows. The Saxon windows which survive are small, simple, round arched, and have the glass of the windows in the middle of the wall (double-splayed). This is more obvious from outside, where the later windows

ABOVE *Breamore Mill.*   BELOW *The Green, Breamore*

The Countryside Museum, Breamore

Saxon long and short work is clear on the corners, and there are pilaster strips (vertical lines of stone) in the middle of the walls, also characteristic. The flint walls were originally plastered externally. The original stone tower barely rises above the roof, but was continued up in timber in the 19th century.

Breamore House (fee: lists) is Elizabethan. The south front seen from the drive is the original, E shaped with short wings. Handsome red bricks with stone dressings. The back wings are Victorian added after the fire of 1856 gutted the house. They imitate the original house, apart from the rather more fanciful water tower with clock over.

Inside, most of the fittings date from after the fire: three very elaborate Elizabethan fireplaces survived, one in the Dining Room and two in the Great Hall. Much 17th and 18th century furniture throughout the house, and a fine series of portraits including Mary Queen of Scots. Other important pictures as well. Guided tours of the house take about an hour.

Breamore Countryside Museum is in new buildings close to the car-park, and is large with comprehensive displays of both hand tools and machinery, alongside good reconstructions of a farm-worker's cottage, a village shop, saddlemaker's workshop, a laundry, a blacksmith's shop, a dairy, a bootmaker's shop and so on. There are more than twenty tractors ranging in date from 1917 to the 1950s, a huge threshing machine, a traction engine, ploughs, carts, and masses of farm equipment. Thoroughly recommended. Also the new maze, prizewinner in *The Sunday Times* competition in 1983, laid out in brick inside the countryside museum.

Breamore Carriage Museum is behind the house, in the 18th century stables. There are more than fifteen different types of carriage on display, ranging from the Red Rover stagecoach which was built in 1800 and ran between London and Southampton until 1843 to the tiny cart pulled by a dog. Also fire-fighting equipment and harness. A good display.

Up in the hills, about a mile north of Breamore House is the **Mizmaze**, not accessible by road but with footpaths to it from many directions The usual route to it is the footpath past Breamore House, through the woods, but a footpath from Castle Ditches, Whitsbury is almost as direct and no longer. The Mizmaze is a circle full of winding paths all of which lead to the central mound, the paths cut through the turf to the chalk. The whole thing is about 85 feet across, and surrounded by a grove of yews. Its purpose and date are uncertain.

About a mile north is part of Grims Ditch, built as a defence against the Saxons in the late Roman period, and here still the county boundary. It is wooded, but the bank and ditch with a couple of barrows behind is clear.

★ ★ ★ ★ *Breamore House and the museums.*

★ ★ ★ ★ *Village, best appreciated on foot.*

★ ★ ★ *The church as a rare survival and for the inscribed Saxon arch.*

BROADLANDS (H) (fee:lists). Once the home of Lord Palmerston, Prime Minister 1855-61, and Lord Mountbatten, this handsome 18th century house sits in the flat Test valley just south of Romsey. Guided tours of the house take about an hour. The drive goes through part of the park, laid out by Capability Brown. Many clumps of trees and attractive despite the flatness of the ground. The ticket office is in the 18th century ornamental dairy, where the ladies of the house entertained themselves by pretending to be dairymaids. The yellow brick house sits on a slight eminence, overlooking the river. Encased in this 18th century house is the 17th century manor house of the St Barbe family: the redbrick stables were built by them. Capability Brown was the architect for the transformation of the house from 1767, but his son-in-law Henry Holland also worked here from 1788. The giant portico on the river front is Brown's and the loggia on the far side is Holland's, as is the strange little domed hall the house is entered by. Beyond is the sculpture hall, built to house sculpture brought back from Rome in 1765. Much of the rest of the house retains its original 18th century furniture. The Dining Room, Library, Drawing room and one of the bedrooms have recently been redecorated, some in rather startling colours.

The Saloon is the finest room, the delicate plasterwork on the walls and ceiling painted white and gold. All the rooms have fine furniture and good paintings. Upstairs is the oak room, with 17th century panelling, and several sumptuous bedrooms.

Downstairs again the Palmerston Room contains portraits of the 3rd Viscount Palmerston (1784-1865) and some of his possessions. He was an MP for nearly 60 years and a minister for almost 50. A lively man, known to the public as 'Old Pam', he was born at Broadlands and lived here all his life.

In the 17th century stables is an exhibition on the life of Lord and Lady Mountbatten, ranging from his extensive Royal connections through service in the Navy: as Supreme Allied Commander in South-East Asia, to being the last Viceroy of India. A short film complements the exhibitions.

A footpath south off the A31 just west of its junction with the A27 (signposted Test Way) leads down alongside a drainage ditch and gives a good view of the house and park.

★ ★ ★ ★ *For the house, its furnishings and exhibitions.* (see also page 152)

BROCKENHURST (M) Brockenhurst had less than a thousand inhabitants in its whole 7,000 acres until 1851, and this is reflected in the small number of early houses. The centre is dominated by buildings of 1890s-1920s, brick or brick with half-timbering. The latter can be exuberant. The opening of the railway in 1849 caused all this expansion. The same mixture, but more sparse, is found on the outskirts, with a few thatched cottages to the north set attractively around open pieces of forest which look like village greens. Everywhere there is recent infilling. The name means thick badger wood.

South of the railway line (with the crossing keeper's house of the 1850s) are only a few houses and the original parish church. St Nicholas is set in a vast graveyard with lots of trees, including an ancient yew which smothers the tower. Very isolated. In the graveyard, on the north side by a large memorial, are buried more than 110 New Zealand soldiers (and 3 Indians and one Canadian) of the First World War, who died in hospital near Brockenhurst. Just in front of their graves is that of Brusher Mills, the famous late

Brockenhurst church

Brusher Mill's grave, Brockenhurst

19th century New Forest snake catcher. His tombstone shows his simple hut as well as his portrait with snakes.

The church of St Peter is a medley of dates and materials. Wise, in 1883 was not impressed: 'a wretched brick tower has been patched on at the west end; and on the north side a new staring red brick aisle, which surpasses even the unusual standard of ugliness of a dissenting chapel'. The tower of 1761 and the aisle of 1832 are plain, and were unlikely to find favour with a Victorian, although the

tower is certainly handsome, with its small spire. Norman arch inside the porch, plain inside, with 13th century chancel. The Victorian monuments look odd here because the walls have been stripped of their plaster. Highly coloured Victorian stained glass in the side windows of flowers. Deeply carved Royal coat of arms for Queen Anne. 12th century Purbeck Marble font, table-type. Photographs of the First World War Hospital on display. (The church is open 2.30-5.00 p.m. April-Sept., otherwise locked).

By the watersplash, west of the centre, is St Saviours, built from 1895-1903. This

is totally different and rather alien, being large, regular and built from proper limestone. The lack of tower gives it an odd look. Internally none of the decorative carving was done, so the capitals are fat and blank. Pretty galleries to the chancel.

Balmer Lawn to the north of Brockenhurst is a large hotel and a few houses. The word 'lawn' is the New Forest name for these open areas of grazing, and this is one of the largest. It ised to be used for pony races. Car park by the river, crowded in summer. To south-east New Forest Waggons take visitors through the forest in horsedrawn wagons (summer, fee).

★ ★ *Town*

★ ★ *Church of St Peter, good mixture and fine setting.*

BROOK (H) is a tiny forest hamlet, with some thatched cottages.

BROUGHTON (D) On the nicely named Wallop Brook, low-lying with many pollarded willows down by the river. The outskirts have thick hedges, many trees and good cottages, but the middle is the best. A big village, with Georgian brick houses, thatch and timber framing, and several cob walls with little thatch 'roofs'. Two chapels, one in classical style, both 19th century. The church of St Mary is 12th and 13th century, with short pillars and wide high pointed arches. In the south aisle, in the middle of the triptych, a fine 16th century Dutch painting of the descent from the cross. The chancel is

Broughton

Broughton dovecote

Broughton church

19th century, but has an elaborate 15th century pillar piscina (for washing the vessels used for the Mass). The base of the tower is Norman, with a pretty doorway.

In the churchyard, originally presumably in a field, is a 17th century circular brick dovecote, with 482 nest boxes, a door at the bottom and a lantern on top for the pigeons to enter through. The revolving ladder inside and huge post to support it were reconstructed in 1984. Dovecotes were used to supply young pigeons (squabs) as fresh meat all the year round.

Church Farm, opposite the church, is handsome Georgian brick and tile, with outbuildings, and further along are the brick and flint school and schoolhouse 1864. On the main street north of the church is a heavy timber framed building surrounding a well. Inscriptions record that the well was dug in the drought of 1921.

★ ★ ★ *Village.*

BROWN CANDOVER (E) The southernmost of the Candover villages, small, with brick and flint estate cottages, some large, and farmyards right in the middle. Lots of trees, and a village green in front of the church of St Peter. This was rebuilt on a large scale in 1845, in flint with a pretty broach spire. Rather blank and cold inside, but with a handsome elaborate carved wooden Flemish communion rail.   Figures of husband and wife of brass on the west wall, small and of about 1520. By the pond in the middle a couple of small sarsens, once common in this valley.

BUCKLER'S HARD (M) On the winding Beaulieu River, a picturesque wide village street laid out in the first half of the 18th century by the 2nd Duke of Montagu who intended to build a complete new town here to import and refine sugar grown on his West Indian estate. This failed, but the single street is 80ft wide, the width he intended all the roads in his new town to be. From the 1740s Buckler's Hard became a ship-building centre, one of many in Hampshire but now the only one to survive looking just as it did then. (fee:lists) The village is still lived in, and there is a shop and garage.

Traffic has been banned from the village, and the entrance for visitors is via the Maritime Museum, with displays on ship-building and models of some of the ships built here. One of Nelson's favourite ships, the *Agamemnon* was built at Buckler's Hard. A large model shows Buckler's Hard in 1803, with ships under construction and materials stored all around. The route through the museum leads into one of the rows of houses, with superbly reconstructed interiors of the inn

Buckler's Hard

49

ABOVE *The Beaulieu estuary*

BELOW *A model of Buckler's Hard in the 18th century.* BOTTOM *Part of the displays at Buckler's Hard*

and different cottages in the 1790s. The life size models of the people and the complete furnishing of the rooms are very effective.

The single street leads down to the river, supremely picturesque: just two rows of brick cottages, far apart, with the river at the bottom. One of the 18th century brick cottages is furnished as a shipright's cottage in the 1790s, and next door the cottage was converted to a chapel in the late 19th century, with 17th century panelling added this century. The large house at the bottom of the street was the Master Shipbuilder's house, and a reconstructed interior can be seen from outside. The building is now an hotel.

At the riverside are the remains of small inlets where the ships were built. Boat trips up the river are available, or one can walk up river for 2½ miles to Beaulieu. Lots of birds. Upstream is a yacht marina, and tucked up on the bank a little deliberately picturesque cottage, built in the later 18th century.

★ ★ ★ *Well worth seeing.*

BULLINGTON (D/E) divides into two parts, both tiny. **Lower Bullington** is a farming hamlet, and the old farm buildings are bigger than the church of St Michael which has a little pollarded avenue leading to its porch. Tiny Victorian tower of brick and flint, the rest basically Norman. Crossing the valley are lots of little iron bridges, and then watercress beds. **Upper Bullington** has a few more cottages, some thatched. The eastern part around Norton is picturesque, with a small lake. The whole area has charming small-scale landscapes, especially along the river.

BURGATES (K) Almost part of Liss, but with its own church. Several buildings of the local darker malmstone, and some lower parts of buildings in the dark brown heathstone. The church of St Peter is mostly 13th century, with a good entrance doorway of that date. The tower is of the dark brown heathstone.

BURGHCLERE (B) Older cottages are scattered about the parish, but the centre is mostly recent, with the church of the Ascension dating from 1875. Opposite is an elaborate brick hall.

The area has gentle hills and lots of trees, especially at Burghclere Common to the north.

Old Burghclere is two miles south of the village, and has the old church and manor house. The house has a Georgian brick front to the church side of very squat proportions: presumably a refronting of an earlier timber-framed house. The church of All Saints is large and medieval, although restored. Long plain nave with 16th century benches and many memorials.

At the south-western end of the main village, just beyond the railway bridge, is **Sandham Memorial Chapel** built in the 1920s specifically to house Stanley Spencer's powerful paintings of the First World War. These were based on his service in a British War Hospital and in Macedonia, and concentrate on the life of the ordinary soldier. They fill the small chapel, and have to be seen in this, their intended position, to be properly appreciated. (fee:lists).

★ ★ ★ *For the Sandham Memorial Chapel.*

BURITON (K) Just off the chalk and into the greensand which wears away leaving the roads in cuttings, and which supplies the local building stone, the dark cream-coloured malmstone. The village is set in a wide valley, and at the church end is extremely picturesque, with a large pond, pasture in the bottom of the valley and trees above. Lots of malmstone cottages ranging from the 17th to the 20th centuries, and a little flint. The malmstone is not the best quality building stone, so doors, windows and often corners have to be surrounded with bricks. Some thatch, and a few Victorian flint cottages. Many of the retaining walls in the village have oddly curved faces.

Next to the church is the Manor House, which was rebuilt early in the 18th century by the father of Edward Gibbon, the historian (*Decline and Fall of the Roman Empire* etc) who lived there until he went to Oxford in 1752 at the age of 15. Edward Gibbon recalled the house: 'an old mansion in a state of decay has been converted into the fashion and convenience of a modern house, of which I occupied the most agreeable apartment; and if strangers had nothing to see, the inhabitants had little to desire'. Strangers

ABOVE *The Sandham Memorial Chapel, Burghclere*
BELOW *Buriton Manor House.* BOTTOM *Buriton church and pond*

still see the malmstone outbuildings rather than the main brick house because the house is tucked round the corner of the courtyard. Gibbon thought 'the spot was not happily chosen – at the end of the village and the bottom of the hill' but 'the Downs commanded the prospect of the sea, and the long hanging woods in sight of the house could not perhaps have been improved by art or expense'.

The church of St Mary has a very plain tower built of dark ironstone facing the pond, with thin classical windows, one inscribed JOHN BONE CHURCHWARDEN. The early tower burnt down and this is the replacement of 1715.

The interior is largely Norman, with fat pillars. The 13th century arch through from tower to nave is unusual because it has large bases of unknown purpose either side, narrowing the entrance. The late 13th century chancel is also fine, with its original east window, sedilla and piscina. Good Victorian stained glass. Many interesting memorials around the church. In the chancel a polished black marble one which looks like a brass to Thomas Hanbury who died in 1617, with his wife, two daughters and six apparently identical sons. Purbeck Marble table-type font.

The road southwards to Chalton is deeply cut and well-wooded, running through part of Queen Elizabeth Country Park (see entry).

★ ★ ★ ★ *Very picturesque village, and the church worth seeing too.*

Looking from Castle Hill, Burley

BURLEY (L) Small, and with forest trees coming right down into the village. Lots of Edwardian houses, a little thatch, and many shops catering for visitors including 'witchcraft' shops, here because for some time into the 1960s a prominent 'white' witch lived in Burley. She dressed in black and had a crow as her familiar. In the 1920s it was described as having 'a vogue as a place of residence for the leisured who have also the hunger for that peace of soul to which trees and natural growth secretly minister' (Stevens), which accounts for many of the newer houses. To the north, opposite the church Burley Castle, 1850s Elizabethan, now a hotel, sits in a park-like clearing. The church of St John the Baptist is small, of brick, 1839 and chancel 1886. **Burley Street** is very spread out with lots of stables. The forest to the west is good walking country: small sharp hills, bogs and many trees, although not solidly wooded.

Castle Hill on the west of Burley Street is a simple single-banked enclosure sitting on top of the short steep ridge which is so marked on this western side of the New Forest. (Car park off the road to Crow from Burley Street). The enclosure is probably Iron Age. From the car-park side it is difficult to distinguish from the natural slumping of the hill, but the far side is much clearer. From the top there are superb wide views west and south, over this side of the Forest and the Avon valley.

★ ★ ★ *Landscape and walking.*

BURSLEDON (J) The Hamble river was not bridged here until 1798, when the bridge and new straight roads either side were built by a Turnpike Trust (a private road company). Tolls had to be paid on the bridge until the 1930s, when it was rebuilt by the County Council. Bursledon's prosperity did not depend on the road, but on the river. With good supplies of timber from the area around and sheltered water, the Hamble river is an eminently suitable area for shipbuilding. Bursledon has built ships since medieval times, and continues to do so.

The old village was scattered about the short steep hills on the bank of the river, and although modern development has filled some of the gaps there are still lots of trees and wooded footpaths. The main road has much modern housing. A car park by the railway station is the best place to park and explore, as the roads are narrow. The railway line (1888) on the heathland around encouraged strawberry growing but cuts off most of the village from the river.

Up the hill from the station are several 18th century cottages, and on top a rather larger Georgian house, all of brick. There are a few more along High Street (straight on) and scattered over the whole parish.

The road leads left over the railway, and down by the shore is the Elephant Boatyard, named after one of Nelson's ships which was built here in 1786.

Steep paths lead down to the river, most of them dead ends at high tide. The Jolly Sailor pub is right on the river at the bottom of the cliff, a picturesque Georgian brick building. The road leads on to a dead end at the river's edge with Brooklands, a big regency villa, visible on the far side. The best views of the river are from above the Jolly Roger.

The church of St Leonard can be approached from the higher road through the village, or by footpath from Station Hill. The church was basically 13th century, but was remodelled in 1828 and again in 1888. The complex wooden porch at the west end is 1888, but the little tower and external arch under it predate those alterations. Inside is mostly 1888, with the 13th century chancel arch (cheerful head corbels) surviving and simple lancet windows. Over the west doorway a wallpainting of 1888. Big 12th century font with interlocking arcading. In the west transept a memorial to Mr Philomen Ewer, a Bursledon shipbuilder who died in 1750. He 'built seven large ships-of-war ... gaining the reputation of

The Hamble River at Bursledon

an ingenious artist, an excellent workman, and an honest man, dying with a fair character and a plentiful fortune'. Under the inscription is a model of a ship-of-war in the state it would have left Bursledon to be fitted out at Portsmouth, a carcase with no masts. Outside, on the north wall is the gravestone of John Tayler who died in 1691, with on the lower part pick axes and spades representing his trade as a brickmaker. Bursledon was a brickmaking centre from the 17th into the 20th centuries, and the older houses of the village must be of local bricks. The main later works were over the river at Swanwick, big chimmney stack dated 1897.

On one of the highest points in the parish, just to the south-east of the huge roundabout on the Southampton road, is Bursledon windmill, built in 1814 of local bricks. It cost £800, and worked into the 1880s when strawberry growing started to dominate the area. After that its top was removed and replaced by a flat viewing platform, used to watch the Solent from. All the wooden machinery survived, and recently the mill has been restored and is occasionally open to the public (fee:lists). The cap has been restored, and close by is a granary on steddle stones.

★ ★ *An interesting and picturesque village, with good views of the Hamble river.*

BUTSER ANCIENT FARM (K) in Queen Elizabeth Country Park, or a couple of miles down the road at Windmill Hill on the A3) An interesting full-scale re-creation of Iron Age farming and houses. Many types of early sheep are kept and a few cows. The small fields are cultivated with replica Iron Age tools and sowed with primitive corn. Grain is stored in pits, as we know it was in the Iron Age, and demonstrations of iron smelting, pottery making, spinning and weaving are given occasionally. The circular huts, one very large, and the smaller square buildings, have been reconstructed from archaeological evidence. Fascinating, very atmospheric on quiet days so that one can wander through the deserted settlement which seems as though the occupants have just left.

★ ★ ★ ★ *A unique opportunity to see our prehistoric past reconstructed.*

BUTSER HILL see **QUEEN ELIZABETH COUNTRY PARK**

CADNAM (H) Once a New Forest hamlet, but now right on the edge of the Forest and affected by being so close to Southampton. The motorway has removed most of the through traffic. Some market gardening, and a few older thatched cottages, but 20th century development lines the roads.

Winsor to the north is in the middle of a more rural area.

CALMORE see **COPYTHORNE**

Bursledon windmill

Butser Ancient Farm

Walking and Nature Reserves

Hampshire's great variety of countryside offers many different types of walking. The coast, the chalk, the heathlands and the clays differ enormously from one another. Every village has its favourite walks and only a small selection are listed here, hopefully including some of the most characteristic places for each type of landscape.

As a county Hampshire has double the average area of woods, and even outside the forests trees are an important part of the landscape. The chalk downs are mostly an exception to this, with wide rolling hills, no longer turf downland but arable. A few large areas of down are preserved, with their distinctive short turf, rich in flowers, and several of them have archaeological interest as well. Even on the chalk some areas are covered with clay, and these support woodlands. Farley Mount Country Park has both open downland and woods.

The commons in the north have marshy woods, and also heathland ones with lots of birch. The New Forest (see entry) is the best area for walking, with heaths and woodlands of all descriptions.

Hampshire's rivers vary from the small brown streams in the New Forest to the sparkling fishermen's paradises of the Itchen and Test. The fishing rivers are rather short of footpaths, but there are some, and the other rivers and estuaries give wonderful walking. The Itchen Navigation and the Basingstoke Canal are also good, as both pass through superb countryside.

Hampshire's coastline is more than 100 miles long, and although much of it is muddy rather than dramatic, there are many walks with good views. The mud is rich in birds.

The Itchen at Itchen Abbas

Another characteristic of the Hampshire landscape is the hangers, the woods which hang onto the steep chalk slope running north from Petersfield. Gilbert White and Edward Thomas both describe this distinctive landscape, which makes interesting walking with extensive views. Selborne, Steep, Hawkley and Empshott are some of the best places, and a long distance footpath – The Hangers Way – is waymarked from Petersfield to Alton.

There are four other long distance footpaths in the county. The Test Way follows the valley and then the chalk downs from Totton for 46 miles right across the county to Inkpen Beacon (Wiltshire). The Clarendon Way starts at Winchester and heads west across the chalk to Salisbury, 24 miles in all. The Wayfarer's Walk is the longest, 70 miles from Emsworth to Inkpen. The Solent Way runs right along the coast. All these are well marked with signposts, and of course can be enjoyed in small portions.

The county is rich in Country Parks, which offer visitors way-marked paths, often exhibitions about the area, guided walks and so on. They are only a small part of the vast area available for walking, but do often offer particularly good countryside.

Heathland in the New Forest

The Test Valley near Romsey

Nature Reserves are usually rich in birds, animals and plants, and while their first object is the preservation of this flora and fauna, they often have footpaths from which the riches can be seen. Some of the Country Parks incorporate Nature Reserves.

Downland and the Chalk
★ ★ ★ ★ *Abbotstone Down; Beacon Hill; Butser (Queen Elizabeth Country Park); Farley Mount Country Park; Martin Down; Old Winchester Hill; Stockbridge Down; St Catherine's Hill, Winchester.*
★ ★ ★ *Chalton; Farley Chamberlayne; Portsdown.*

Woods and Forests
NEW FOREST all good but see particularly:
★ ★ ★ ★ *Bolderwood Ornamental Drive; Burley; Knightwood Oak; Lyndhurst area; Ringwood area; Rhinefield Ornamental Drive.* ★ ★ ★ *Fritham; East Boldre.*

OTHER FORESTS
★ ★ ★ ★ *Alice Holt Forest; Farley Mount Country Park; Forest of Bere; Queen Elizabeth Country Park; Waggoners Wells, Bramshott. The hangers at Empshott; Hawkley; Selborne, Steep and Yateley.* ★ ★ ★ *Woolmer Forest*

River walks
★ ★ ★ ★ *Beaulieu – Bucklers Hard; Curbridge; Holly Hill Woodland Park; New Alresford; Sarisbury; Titchfield; Upper Hamble Country Park.* ★ ★ ★ *Ovington*

Marshes
★ ★ ★ ★ *Lower Test Nature Reserve; Lymington*
★ ★ ★ *Farlington Marshes; Hurst/Keyhaven*

Seaside and Shore
★ ★ ★ ★ *Lepe Country Park; Royal Victoria Country Park, Netley; Warsash shore.* ★ ★ ★ *Emsworth.*

Mixtures
★ ★ ★ *Bramdean; Brownwich & Chilling, Hillhead; Droxford area; The Grange area; Greywell; Itchen Valley Country Park; Meonstoke area; Sir George Staunton Country Park, Leigh Park; Southwick area.*

Gardens

Hampshire has a rich variety of gardens open to the public. Only the larger ones which open regularly are listed here.

The New Forest has several specialising in lime-haters, with azaleas, rhododendrons and so on in great profusion, tormenting those who do not have the right soil for growing them. Exbury is the largest and most popular, giving its name to a whole race of azaleas and rhododendron hybrids. MacPenny's at

Jenkyn Place, Bentley

Bransgore and Spinners at Boldre are also good for rhododendrons and azaleas, and like Exbury are set in woodlands. All three have much to offer alongside the rhododendrons, and are worth seeing at all seasons. Furzey Gardens at Minstead is slightly less woody, but just as interesting.

The best garden in the rest of the county is Hillier's Garden and Arboretum at Ampfield, housing the biggest collection of ornamental trees and shrubs in the world, all beautifully laid out, with herbaceous borders, bulbs, a peat garden and many other features. It is impossible to decide the best time to visit, because all seasons are good here.

Mottisfont must be one of the best places in the whole country to see roses, with its National Collection of old fashioned types. Jenkyn Place, Bentley, is well known both for its interesting plants and effective layout, repaying repeated visits.

Hampshire has several small reproduction historic gardens – a medieval one behind the Great Hall at Winchester; the Tudor Garden at Southampton; and a 17th century Physic Garden at Petersfield.

★ ★ ★ ★ *Exbury; Hillier Gardens and Arboretum, Ampfield; Jenkyn Place, Bentley; Longstock Water Gardens (only occasionally open); Mottisfont (when the roses are out); Sir George Staunton Country Park, garden, conservatory, and farm.*
★ ★ ★ *Bohunt Manor, Liphook (with wildfowl); Bramdean House; Furzey Gardens, Minstead; Greatham Mill; Houghton Lodge; MacPennys, Bransgore; Spinners, Boldre; Spring Woods, Hackwood Park; Wyck Place, East Worldham.*
See also: *Queen Eleanor's Garden, The Castle, Winchester; Petersfield Physic Garden; Tudor House garden, Southampton; Jane Austen's garden at Chawton; and Gilbert White's garden at Selborne. The following big houses also have gardens: Beaulieu; Highclere Castle; Hinton Ampner; Rotherfield Park; Stratfield Saye.*

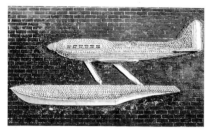

ABOVE *A flying boat making a brief visit to Calshot.* BELOW *Pebble flying boat on a wall of Houston House.* RIGHT *Calshot Castle*

CALSHOT (N) A shingle spit which sticks out into the mouth of Southampton Water, with a 16th century fort on the end. Difficult to see the fort from the land, because there are so many other buildings on the head of the spit. An odd place altogether, lined on the thin bit with more than a hundred small beach huts, all painted different colours. Marshes on the landward side, but dominating everything is Fawley Power station, so large it is difficult to work out its size – the chimney is 670 ft high.

Wonderful long, low sea views from the spit: Cowes straight ahead and much of the Isle of Wight visible. The Solent is clear both ways with Hill Head, Lee-on-Solent etc on the east skyline. North is Southampton Water with Fawley oil refinery. The concrete enclosure close to the shore is an outfall from the power station.

On the wider head of the spit are huge hangars, some from the First World War. A Naval Air Station was established here in 1913 and became the most important training establishment for RAF flying boats and sea-planes, because Southampton Water is relatively calm and was suitable for these early planes. The station was transferred to the RAF, and continued in use until the 1950s. All the buildings on the spit (apart from the castle and the new coastguard tower) were part of the base, and back in the village the Flying Boat pub was originally the officer's mess. A narrow guage railway ran from the spit to the village. The modern tower is part of the radar system of Southampton Water. The Air Station

buildings have since 1965 been the Calshot Activities Centre, used by Hampshire schoolchildren.

The castle looks low and small, moated and of neat grey stonework. Henry the VIIIth constructed a series of these castles around the south coast from 1539, because Catholic Europe was threatening to invade England to restore the Catholic Church here, recently abolished by Henry. Calshot is small compared to some of the others: nearby Hurst is much larger. Due to its useful position at the head of Southampton Water the castle has been in military or coastguard use ever since it was built, until the coastguards moved out to their new tower next door. Originally the outer defences were much higher, with gun ports cut through them, and the buildings on this ground floor are additions of the 18th and 19th centuries. The stone keep is original, although adapted inside as a barracks in the 1890s. There are superb views from the top of the keep.

The castle's most famous time was the late 1920s, when it was the base for the competitors in the Schneider Trophy air races, a popular competition held over Southampton Water with the prize going to the fastest plane. In 1931 a locally built Supermarine won, reaching 340 mph.

Good displays on the very varied history of the castle can be found inside · the castle, and much about the local aircraft industry: some of the planes are at the Southampton Hall of Aviation, Southampton (see entry).

★ ★ ★ *The castle is small, but worth seeing.*

CANADA (H) not a country, but a long, thin New Forest edge settlement, leading onto West Wellow Common, a northwards extension of the New Forest. Originally squatter's cottages on Common ground, all small holdings. Now prosperous.

CANDOVERS see **BROWN CANDOVER, CHILTON CANDOVER, PRESTON CANDOVER**

CATHERINGTON (K) Totally rural, despite the proximity of Horndean and Clanfield. The village is scattered along the one road, brick or flint cottages of the 18th or 19th centuries and lots of flint walls. In the middle one earlier timber-framed jettied cottage. Catherington House towards the south, a redbrick Georgian mansion, is where

Catherington

Queen Charlotte, the estranged wife of George IV stayed before the trial set up to try to divorce them in 1820.

The church of All Saints has some of the best views from this village, looking southwards across Havant to Langstone Harbour, and from the corner of the graveyard north-east to the chalk hills. The church is mostly later 12th century, with a pretty entrance doorway and a complex plan. The brick top of the tower is Georgian, and many of the windows date from a restoration of 1883. Inside, opposite the entrance is a fine 1350ish wall-painting of St Michael, the archangel, weighing souls to see if they shall go to heaven. A demon is trying to weigh down one side of the scale, but the Virgin Mary holds up the other end. The round arches to the arcades have unusually deep mouldings. Fine 14th century wooden roof.

The windows at the east end are medieval, and especially good in the north chapel behind the big memorial, with wall paintings around. The memorial is quite restrained for its date (1631) with big effigies, ten children below, little figures of Time and Death in the back and much larger ones of Justice and Wisdom on top.

Catherington Down to the west of the village has part of the downland preserved as a nature reserve. Several footpaths lead through the area.

★ ★ *Catherington village and church*

CHALTON (K)

Sited on the slope of a big chalk down, and originally the centre of a vast parish which was split up in the late 19th century when Idsworth, Blendworth and Rowlands Castle became separate parishes, the village is probably smaller than in medieval times. Although the area seems all rolling chalk, there is clay over some of the chalk and the area was once well-wooded, at least in the valleys. In the 13th century Chalton supplied 350 oaks for the building of Portchester Castle.

The village is mostly around a sloping triangular green, with the Red Lion pub prominent. This timber-framed, thatched building, is probably 16th century, and was built as an inn. Manor Farm up beyond the church and The Priory next to it are also medieval buildings which have been added to and altered over the years. The village pond is at the bottom of the hill, and there are a few more houses there. Even the 19th century brick and flint cottages are on ancient sites.

ABOVE *Windmill Hill, Chalton*
BELOW *The Red Lion, Chalton*

The church of St Michael is much larger than one would expect for such a small village, but it was the mother church for a wide area. The Victorian porch has medieval woodwork incorporated. Inside the building the height is surprising and the 13th century chancel particularly impressive. Tall thin lancets in the side windows and a fine east window. Up by the altar a memorial to a vicar who died in 1632, with a kneeling effigy in an Oxford gown. Small north chapel, also medieval, and even all the windows in the nave are of the 13th and 14th centuries. Lots of classical memorials, many to the owners of Idsworth.

A footpath alongside the church leads up onto Chalton Down, and links up with a network of paths there.

Right away from the village, to the west close to the A3 is Windmill Hill, only accessible by footpath but retaining its prominent windmill. One of only three remaining in Hampshire the present building dates from 1785, although there has been a windmill here from at least 1289.

★ ★ ★ *Village, and good walking area.*

CHANDLER'S FORD (H/J)

A very recent settlement. In the 1890s there were only a few houses to the south of the railway line and several large brickworks. Chandler's Ford brick was used for much of the late 19th and early 20th century development at adjacent Eastleigh, including the railway works. Bricks were also sent to London, with the largest order being 35 million for the Courts of Justice in the Strand. Chandler's Ford's development followed that of Eastleigh, expanding from the 1890s. In 1931 there were only 3,148 people, but now there are 23,000. Today it is a huge area of houses, many of them large, but all in a wooded setting. Despite the population there is no real town centre, but several different areas with shops. Chandler's Ford Lake is really only a large pond, presumably one of the claypits left by the brick makers. It is off Hiltingbury road, towards the centre of Chandler's Ford, well wooded and with lots of ducks.

CHARLTON (D)

Originally a small village, but now part of Andover. Some cottages survive, and the church of St Thomas in the middle is the village church. Most of Foxcote church, built 1830, was moved here in Victorian times. Attractive chequering externally of light and dark flint. **Foxcote** to the west is still only a hamlet. The small tower of the church of 1830 survives, now in domestic use.

CHAWTON (F)

Known and revered internationally as the village where Jane Austen lived for the last eight years of her life. Here she wrote three of her novels and revised her earlier ones. The large cottage where she lived with her widowed mother, sister and friend is preserved in much the same state as when she lived there, and is open to the public (fee:lists). Standing on the corner of the road through the village, it looks like a respectable tradesman's residence. It belonged to one of Jane's brothers who had inherited the estate at Chawton and who lived partly at Chawton House.

The cottage he offered his widowed mother and sisters has six bedrooms (which they considered ideal because they could house visitors) and two good room downstairs. Whilst one might wish that displays of documents and so on were limited to certain rooms and others shown furnished, instead of the current mixture, it is wonderful to go into the second sitting room, where she wrote,

ABOVE *Jane Austen's House, Chawton*
RIGHT *Chawton House in 1745*

and to see her bedroom. Here is a
venerable relic: a patchwork made by Jane
and her mother. Some of her jewellery is
also to be seen amidst many letters and
her hand-written music books. Much
material about the rest of the family. Here
she wrote *Mansfield Park, Emma,* and
Persuasion and revised the early novels.
While she was living here her first book
Sense and Sensibility was published,
followed by three more in her lifetime, all
printed anonymously. She was delighted
at the money she earnt by them.

The church is along what was the
Meon Valley road, now a cul-de-sac. The
shallow valley is pasture with old trees, a
row of thatched cottages on one side
completing the classic English scene. The
view along the drive to the church, up a
short hill to Chawton House is equally
picturesque. Sadly the church was rebuilt
in 1871, and although it has a pretty
tower, one regrets the loss of the church
where she worshipped. Only the early
18th century communion rail survives
from her time, and some monuments
including the big one to Sir Richard
Knight (an earlier occupier of Chawton
House) up by the altar. He died in 1679,
and his effigy is dressed in armour. In the
south-east corner of the graveyard are the
graves of two Cassandra Austens, Jane's
mother and sister who lived at the
cottage until their deaths.

The rest of the village consists of a
single street of mostly brick houses and
cottages, with a little of the pale local
malmstone and some timber framing. In
the middle is a gap with a larger Georgian
house set back from the road. Even
without Jane Austen this would be a
village worth exploring, as all the
buildings seem Georgian or earlier.

The north of Chawton was part of

Edward's estates, now noticeable because
of the very high fencing around its fields,
needed because it is now a deer farm. The
animals are usually visible from the A339.
(See also Four Marks for Chawton Park
Wood).

★ ★ ★ *Village and Jane Austen's home.*

CHEESEFOOT HEAD (J) (just over 2
miles east of Winchester on the A272).
Car parks 500 ft up on the chalk give
extensive views, and footpaths run off in
all directions. Clumps of beech on the top.
From 1829 there was a telegraph station
here, one of a chain from London to
Plymouth run by the Admiralty. Good
walking country.

CHERITON (J) A neat village, with
ducks on the river running through. Quite
big, with a variety of houses and cottages,
some thatch and flint. Best houses and
cottages off the main road. Early in the
19th century the village was famous for
truffle hunting: six families supported
themselves by finding this fungus. To the
east of the village is the site of the battle
of Cheriton, one of the most important
battles of the Civil War. On 29th March
1644 more than 8,000 footsoldiers and
cavalry on each side fought all day, with
the Parliamentarians emerging the
winners. This was the first time they had
defeated the Royalists in pitched battle.
The battlefield is marked by a commem-
orative stone, erected in 1975, which can
be found by taking the minor road east
from North End, Cheriton for a little over
a mile, until the junction with the road
south from Bishop's Sutton. The memorial
is at the junction. The battle spread over a
large area, including Cheriton wood,
remnants of which can still be seen to the
south.

The church of St Michael and All
Angels, in the middle of the village, sits
on a large mound which has been thought

to be a prehistoric barrow. Much of the
church is 13th century, including the
porch, which has been rebuilt and
incorporates on either side two
decorative 14th century carvings whose
original use is uncertain. The tower was
refaced after a fire in 1744. The church
register records 'a sudden and very
terrible fire broke out ... the church which
being shingled was immediately all in
flames, the roof and seats entirely
destroyed, the bells melted, the windows
demolished and nothing left standing but
the walls'. Inside simple fat pillars and
15th century chancel. The fittings are
Victorian, but the interesting stained glass
in the short nave windows was given in
memory of four men killed in the First
World War. Knights represent Honour,
Loyalty, Duty and Courage.

★ ★ *For battlefield, village and church.*

CHILBOLTON (D) A big village, still
with a lot of thatched cottages and many
trees. The Norman church of St Mary has
a pretty Victorian tower and spire. Good
Jacobean pulpit.

West Down, just south of the village, is
a public open space with a small car park.
Downland with scrub and woods.

To the south-east is the Chilbolton
Observatory, with a prominent radar dish.
This research station was set up in the
1960s on a Second World War airfield,
and the observatory investigates radio
engineering and meteorology.

CHILCOMB (J) Less than a mile and a
half from Winchester cathedral, yet
totally rustic. Only a hamlet with a large
brick and flint farmyard, brick farmhouse
and a thatched cottage. Neat fences
everywhere. The church of St Andrew is
up under the downs, away from the
houses. Many trees and much scrub on
the downs, forming a perfect backdrop to
the little church. Basically Norman, with
two plain doorways of that date and a
miniature chancel arch complete with later
wooden screen. A good example of the
smallest type of parish church, superbly
sited with wide views.

★ ★ *Church.*

CHILLAND see MARTYR WORTHY

CHILTON CANDOVER (E) Very small
village. The church was demolished in
1878, but the churchyard survives, with
the Norman crypt, which was excavated
out in the 1920s. Strange semi- subter-
ranean room, apsidal end, with a font.

CHILWORTH (H) Until recently just a tiny village, a large house and a church. The hamlet survives in a hollow behind the church, still picturesque with several thatched cottages, although some cottages have been tiled and a few new ones built. Most of Chilworth is to the south-east, huge modern houses set in trees.

The church of St Denys was totally rebuilt in 1812, an unusual date for a rural church. As commemorated by an inscription in the tower porch, Peter Serle, the local landowner and philanthropist, paid for the new building. Externally it is plain except for the porch. Inside it is much livelier because of the plaster vaulting. Not a close medieval imitation. Most of the fittings are 1812, including the pews and communion rail. The font is Norman, a survivor from the earlier church. The monument to the local sculptor, R.C. Lucas (1800-1883) has a portrait medallion he carved himself in 1840. He also produced the statue of Watts in the park behind the Civic Centre, Southampton. He built himself a house at Chilworth called the Tower of the Winds, since demolished.

★ ★ *More for those interested in churches, as although small, it is a complete example of an unusual date.*

Chilworth church

CLANFIELD (K) Described in 1900 as being 'grouped round the cross-roads' and consisting of 'a collection of half-timbered thatched farm-houses and cottages, which, although somewhat out of repair, are of a picturesque appearance' (VCH). Surprisingly this hamlet still survives to the north-west of the large area which developed since the Second World War. There are shops elsewhere in the village, but the old centre is close to the church. Outside the church is a big thatched well-head, once the village's water supply. The church of St James was rebuilt in 1875, and although small the interior is impressive, lined with stripes of red, black and yellow bricks, and with a dark timber roof. The neat and tiny 14th century font can be matched at nearby Chalton and Idsworth.·

The streets leading to the cross-roads by the church still have farm buildings, the odd timber framed cottage, Georgian brick, and brick and flint cottages. There is even a pond, but the absolute centre has an extraordinary building – a prefabricated single-storied pub erected in 1960. With its flat roof and 'modern' appearance it would look more at home in the middle of a city, and is totally out of place here.

CLIDDESDEN (E) A surprisingly rural village, considering how close it is to Basingstoke. Around the pond is a big farm and a thatched cottage with timber frame and herring-bone brick. More thatched cottages spread around, and a big Georgian Rectory. At the south end a handsome Regency farmhouse. The church of St Leonard is mostly 1889, with a reset Norman doorway.

COLBURY (M) A hamlet on the edge of the New Forest, just into farming country. There are several large and intricate Victorian estate cottages, and the little flint church of Christ Church (1870) has a

ABOVE *Clanfield.* BELOW *Timber framing with flint infill at Clanfield*

modern hexagonal hall attached. All rural despite the proximity of the main road.

COLEMORE (K) A rural hamlet, with a few cottages and the little church of St Peter ad Vincula, now redundant. The simple building is Norman, and unusually for such a small church it had transepts. Only the northern one survives, with a simple Norman arch to the body of the church, and a squint through to the main altar. Small original windows. No chancel arch, but a wooden screen partly medieval. At the west end is a ladder of 1694, and the bells are exposed because they now hang below the tower. One dates from 1380: the founder's mark is still visible, the other is of 1627. Norman Purbeck Marble font. 1866 wooden turret and spire.

★ ★ *Church, for its early date and for the serene interior.*

COLDEN COMMON (J) was only made a parish in 1843, and the flint and stone church built a year afterwards right on the boundary. Later Victorian school next door. The village is spread out along the main road, with no real centre. Big, partly timber, mill and pond at Fishers Pond to the south.

COMPTON (J) The old part of the village is a single street leading nowhere, with the odd thatched cottage. The whole settlement is small, rural and prosperous, with a row of mostly Edwardian houses along the top of the hill overlooking the village. The church is in the lower part, very small until a big aisle was added in Victorian times. The original part is mostly Norman, with an elaborate entrance door. Up by the altar a seat made of carved wood, very rustic in style, of about 1500. Above is a wall painting of a bishop.

★ *Church.*

COPYTHORNE (H) The sparse village is now one-sided because the motorway runs parallel to its main street. Still rural, if noisy from the motorway, with redbrick smallholder's cottages and a big Victorian school. The church of St Mary is surprisingly large, brick and dates from 1834. Attractive tower, plain inside and out, but interesting as a pre-Victorian church. Tall thin rather industrial looking pillars. The chancel was added in 1891 and the church refitted then. **Calmore** to the east is also rural, with the odd thatched cottage and a Victorian school. Tatchbury Mount Hospital to the west. The village is now called Old Calmore because of the large housing estates recently built to the Totton side along with an industrial estate.

CORHAMPTON (J) A small village, right on the Meon river. This part of the valley is amazingly densely villaged: Meonstoke church is only 200 yds to the south and Exton church ½ mile to the north. The mill is only a stone's throw from the church, which sits on a probably artificial mound, with a yew of great antiquity beside it. With all these indicators of ancient settlement, it is no surprise that the church is Saxon. Apart from the east wall, which fell out in 1885 and was replaced in brick, and the porch, all the walls are early 11th century. Externally the side opposite the entrance is the best, with an elaborate surround to an original doorway, now blocked. Characteristic long and short work on the corners. To the right of the porch a sundial, probably contemporary with the church, with a leaf pattern.

Inside the bold chancel arch dominates: typical late Saxon. In the chancel wall, paintings of the 12th century, with enough preserved to appreciate the whole scheme. Band of figures above, possibly

Corhampton church

the life of St Swithin, with drapery below.

The huge yew tree was described in 1890 as filling half the church yard: it now fills two-thirds.

★ ★ *Worth seeing as a good example of a pre-Conquest church.*

COWPLAIN (K) Like its neighbours, Cowplain developed because of the main road from London to Portsmouth. It is supposed to have been named from The Spotted Cow pub, but the name is probably earlier, meaning a clearing for cows, which would be appropriate as it was within the Forest of Bere. The shops are modern, but lots of oak trees are a reminder of the Forest, and there is the odd Edwardian villa. The tramway from Portsmouth reached out through Cowplain in 1903, bringing trippers for country walks. **Lovedean** is to the north west, and has a few more older houses amongst many modern ones.

Edwardian cottages at Crawley

CRANBURY PARK see HURSLEY

CRAWLEY (D/H) A prosperous looking village, consisting of a single dense street of houses and cottages. The simpler ones are old, the more complex ones like the Fox and Hounds pub date from 1900-1920s and were built by the Philippi family who bought the estate in 1900 and turned it into a model village with even a bath house and roller skating rink. Opposite the Fox and Hounds and a little up the street is Orchard Cottages, rather Germanic in style. Oak Cottages opposite are also 1900s. The village pond survives at the east end, surrounded by cottages, and the church is at the other end. Opposite the church is the Dower House, 1911, with a big water tower behind and the street frontage like cottages.

The church of St Mary has some good carved heads on the windows externally dating from the 15th century, but the

surprise is inside. Instead of conventional stone pillars, the roof is held up by simple squared posts of wood, an arrangement common in barns but unusual in churches, especially churches where the outside walls are flint like this one. The posts contrast with the smooth walls and neat windows. Partly Norman chancel arch, but the chancel itself is of 1887.

★ ★ ★ *An interesting village both for the original cottages and the early 20th century fakes.*

★ *Church.*

CRONDALL (F)

A large village, just back from the edge of the heathlands of north east Hampshire and bordered to the south by the chalk North Downs. The village is on a band of clay, a classic geographical siting exploiting three different environments. Lots of brick and timber framed cottages ranging from the 16th to the 18th century, and some Georgian brick houses. 16th century jettied pub in the middle. Glazed headers in some buildings, giving a spotted effect to the brickwork. A little flint. Church Street and the roads around it are all good, with lots of tile hanging particularly in Dippenhall Street. A wonderfully named hamlet to the east: Dora's Green.

The church of All Saints looks distinctly odd from the path. The flat roof makes the nave look incomplete, and huge buttresses run up to support nothing. They used to hold up the Norman tower, removed in the mid-17th century because it was unsafe. It was replaced by a brick tower of about 1655, in a different position. Nice detailing, especially the doorway. Economically the stair turret of the original tower was re-used, with two timber bridges giving access to the new tower.

The porch is a hotch-potch of dates and building materials, but the neat doorway inside is 1840s, as are many of the lower windows. The interior is powerful: the nave all Norman with stout pillars and the chancel even prettier. The eastern part of the nave is the earliest, rather altered by attempts in the 17th century to improve support for the tower above. The chancel of two bays is wonderful: Norman decoration, but with a pointed arch. Either side of the altar a tomb chest, the darker one Purbeck Marble of 1563, the other 1532. Small and heavily iron-bound chest in the chancel: it cost 2s (10p) in 1546. Good memorials all about the church. By the altar in the south chapel a brass of

Heywood Sumner's sgraffito in Church Crookham church

1641 with a gruesome skeleton and verse. Under the carpet in the chancel a big brass to a rector who died in 1381 (rubbing in north transept). Close by on display a small font of 1688. The main font is large, featureless and difficult to date.

To the south Powderham Castle (not the famous one – in Devon) a motte and bailey just visible through the trees. The big plain redbrick house close to it is Wimble Hall, built as an orphanage.

★ ★ *Church*

★ ★ *Village*

COVE see FARNBOROUGH

CROOKHAM (F)

Divided into Crookham Village which is in the country, and Church Crookham which seems like part of Fleet. Crookham Village is on the edge of the large area of heathland which was not enclosed until 1829, and there are only a few 17th and 18th century commoner's cottages scattered about the parish along with many modern houses. The Basingstoke Canal runs to the south, and there is a car park at Crookham Wharf, south of Crookham Village. Tobacco was grown in the village from 1911-1937, and there are a couple of oast houses, now converted to houses.

Christ church is to the south-east of Church Crookham, close to the Ghurka Barracks. It was built in 1841, plain brick with lancet windows, and extended in 1876. Heywood Sumner (see Gorley) decorated the new chancel with sgraffito (incised and painted plaster) showing the

Adoration, and angels. Delicately coloured stained glass in two western lancets. Monster pulpit. Fine gravestone by the entrance to the graveyard of 1936 to William Eggleton, by F. Martin with roundels and a compressed figure.

★ ★ *Church for Heywood Sumner plasterwork.*

CRUX EASTON (A)

High on the chalk, with the mostly modern village down a cul-de-sac. The big house at the end of the road, once the Rectory, was used in the Second World War to house Sir Oswald Mosley, the interned leader of the British Fascists.

The small church of St Michael is a replacement of 1775, a simple brick building. Inside it is like a nonconformist chapel. Fine brickwork in arches over windows and wrought iron gates to the churchyard apart from the eastern apse which has a radial pattern marble floor and fine panelling. 1775 pulpit, lectern with eagle and stone font, probably Italian.

★ ★ *Church for date.*

CURBRIDGE (J) (between Curdridge and Swanwick)

A hamlet stretching along the road, with a variety of brick houses and cottages. Fairthorne Grange at the northern end has a great variety of farm buildings including a granary on steddle stones right by the road. The tiny neat brick church dates from 1892.

The bridge is barely noticeable on the road, but from the car park of the big pub by the river a footpath leads through

National Trust woodland along the small tidal river to the wider Hamble. The path winds through the woods, with small enclosed views of the best sort of river scenery. Some reed-beds, and both rivers mud edged except at high tide. The path continues down the Hamble.

Burridge to the south is slightly more developed.

★ ★ *For river walks.*

CURDRIDGE (J) (just north of Curbridge) A dispersed village, with no real centre. The church of St Peter is 1880s and 90s replacing the first church here built in the 1830s. The tower has flushwork, that is, flints knapped and cut into shapes, set in stone borders, an East Anglian tradition.

Behind the church are several brick and thatch cottages, and large late Victorian or Edwardian houses. There are more of these large houses to the north-east: presumably they grew up here because of the proximity of Botley station. Still much market gardening in the area, and lots of trees.

★ *Church for flintwork.*

DAMERHAM (G) Very different from its neighbour Martin, but just as pretty. It was also part of Wiltshire until 1895. The village is so scattered that areas have their own names: North End, East End and so on. The handsome, mostly brick, cottages and farmhouses spread over the sides of the valley, with many trees and small woods. Lots of thatch and some timber framing. A good village for walking. Several larger Georgian houses of brick. The most spectacular is Court Farm, north-east of the church, by the road to Sandleheath. Big brick front, with re-set 14th century greensand windows. Very unusual: the stonework came from an earlier building on the site, which belonged to Glastonbury Abbey. A 14th century tithe barn also survives from the monastic buildings.

Close to the picturesque river, and opposite a pub is The Terrace, originally called The Barracks, built in 1863 as temporary accommodation after a bad fire destroyed many houses in the village. It is a three-sided square, alternating houses and bungalows all joined together. Many 'rustic' porches made from branches with the bark left on can be seen around Damerham.

The church stands alone, just up the slope from the river. Outside, the large squat tower dominates. Basically Norman,

ABOVE *Damerham church.* RIGHT *Norman carving of St George in Damerham church* BELOW *Rustic porch at Damerham*

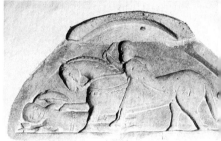

it looks more like a bit of a castle. The wooden thing on top houses the bells, one of which is inscribed: 'I WAS CAST IN THE YEARE OF PLAGUE WARRE AND FIRE 1666' (ie the Great Plague, the Fire of London & war with the Dutch). Nice 15th century porch, with an earlier defaced carving of Christ in Majesty on the outside. Inside another carving in good condition – St George (the patron of the church) slaying a Saracen, perhaps at the battle of Antioch 1098. Good 15th century roof in the porch, and others inside.

The rounded Norman tower arch inside is of three different coloured stones – greenish, white and brown. Later Norman

north aisle, and originally chapels on either side of the chancel, now gone, but the arches can be seen in the walls. The big 15th century windows at either end make the building very light. 1925 glass east window. Remnants of wall painting behind the organ.

★ ★ *Church.*

★ ★ *Village, good for walking.*

DANEBURY (D) (2½ miles north west of Stockbridge) A large hillfort, and the one which we know most about because it has steadily been excavated over the last twenty years. There is a car park at the bottom of the hill, and the natural route to the hillfort leads past a Bronze Age round barrow, outside the area of the fort and pre-dating it. The earliest hillfort consisted of only the inner bank, and was built about 550 B.C. The middle and outer banks were added later, along with the complicated gateways with their outworks, designed to make the best use of the defenders' long distance weapon – slingstones.

Under excavation, the interior of the fort showed pits and post holes, and it is estimated that the whole interior contains 5,000 pits and 18,000 post-holes. These are the remnants of almost 500 years of occupation, the pits used for grain storage, and the post-holes the remains of the timber houses and granaries. The houses were mostly circular, 20-30 ft across. A road ran across the fort from the main entrance to the blocked one, and in the centre by the road were some unusual buildings which may have been temples. Excavation has shown the interior of Danebury to be highly organised, looking much more like a town than one would expect.

About 100 B.C. intensive occupation of the hillfort ceased, but a few people continued to live there until around the time of the Roman Conquest in A.D. 43. From that time the hill was abandoned, used for sheep grazing and in medieval times a fair. A few of the beech trees planted in 1850ish remain on the western side of the defences.

Walking around the inner rampart is the best way to appreciate the hillfort and the trees, but the outer rampart gives extensive views. Explanatory boards around the fort help to understand the site in the Iron Age, especially the entrance.

The fine Museum of the Iron Age at Andover (see entry) is based around the excavations at Danebury and should be visited in conjunction with the hillfort.

The slopes leading up to the fort still have downland plants.

★ ★ *For the hillfort.*

DEANE (E) A little rural hamlet, often visited from nearby Steventon by Jane Austen. The cluster of cottages and pub on the valley road was known as Deane Gate, and it was here that the Austen family caught the coach to Basingstoke or London.

The path to the church runs past the lawn of Deane House, Georgian brick of several blocks giving an irregular look. Jane visited the house for dances, and Henry Fielding is supposed to have based the rumbustious Squire Weston in *Tom Jones* (1749) on one of the owners of the house (Jane admired Fielding's fiction but deplored his morals).

The church of All Saints has been rebuilt since her time, but is interesting in its own right as a pre-Victorian Gothic church, unfettered by Victorian ideas of what was correct for church building (see Hursley). The walls are rendered, and many of the details (eg pinnacles, some window tracery) are Coade stone, an artificial stone. The east window has iron

tracery. The whole effect is pretty, romantic and unserious. Most of the 1818 fittings survive, and earlier memorials.

The village is tiny, with several thatched cottages. Away to the south, standing high above the road is Ashe Park, another Georgian house visited by Jane Austen.

★ ★ *Church for its odd date.*

DENMEAD (J/K) Now built up, but until the 1930s a scattered little village. A few Victorian villas and even one thatched cottage, with lots of 1930s on the main road and modern housing estates behind. Close to the brick and flint church of 1880 are the school and shops, rather suburban feeling.*World's End* to the west of Denmead is undeveloped, wet but attractive countryside with lots of hedgerow trees. Denmead must have been like this. Towards the north end of the one street of World's End is an early pillar box, perhaps the oldest still in use. It is dated 1859, and has a flap like a domestic letterbox and an odd-shaped top.

DIBDEN (M) A rural part of the otherwise industrial east side of the New Forest. Scattered village, with many trees. The church of All Saints was bombed in 1940, and the stonework of the late 13th century chancel still shows the effects of bombs and weather. The building was re-opened in 1955 with a new nave. The tower of 1884 survived, but the 12th century font had to be reconstructed from hundreds of fragments. Superb stained glass of 1955 in east window.

From the churchyard, and intermittently from the road, the towers and docks of Southampton just across the

ABOVE *Deane House.* BELOW *Deane church*

water fill the sky-line. The Dibden shore has been extended by land reclamation since the early 19th century. ★ *Church.*

DOGMERSFIELD (F/C) Several oast houses, all now converted into houses, are a reminder that hops were grown here. Tiny green in the middle, now partly filled by the pub. Very rustic. The church of All Saints is all stone, unusual in this area, and was rebuilt on a new site in 1843 in Early English style. Some earlier memorials inside were moved from the old church.

The Basingstoke Canal makes a big loop through the parish, and from the

southern canal bridge is a good view of Dogmersfield House in the distance, large, redbrick and 1720s. Further south is a group of cottages, farmhouse and large stables, almost a little village, at the back of which is the old church, rebuilt in 1806 in brick and now a house. Tower visible through the trees.

DROXFORD (J) One of the largest and most attractive of the Meon Valley villages. The main road (which carries far too much traffic) runs up and down slight hills through the village, parallel with the river Meon but a little way up the side of the valley. There are many Georgian houses, mostly brick with flint relegated to the garden walls. On the outskirts are a few rather larger Georgian houses. The middle of the village is a triangular green, now tarmaced, with the Manor House (17th century onwards) to the north, and south (down a short drive) the Old Georgian Rectory. Izaac Walton (1593-1683), the author of *The Compleat Angler* lived partly at Droxford rectory in the latter part of his life because his daughter married the rector.

Mill Lane, running off the main road to the north of the Green, has old cottages, including a timber-framed house, and a modern estate which fits in well. The 18th century mill has been converted to a house, but the water still rushes beside it, and a path leads on beside the mill-stream. The horse chestnut close to the mill was planted in 1911 to mark the Coronation.

The church of St Mary and All Saints is on the edge of the meadows: a path leads from the north-east corner of the graveyard to the mill, and another alongside the south of the churchyard leads down to the river.

ABOVE *Droxford.* BELOW *Droxford church*

The church tower is of a very unusual date: 1599. The rest is a typical Hampshire village church, although the south side has a rather domestic look because of the 19th century dormers in the roof. Inside the porch is a reset and pretty Norman doorway, matched by another on the north side (visible externally only). Inside the church is basically Norman (eg chancel arch) and 13th century (south aisles etc) with a few later additions such as the fine 14th century head corbels which hold up the arch to the south chapel. Fittings mostly 19th century. In the south chapel a smooth 13th century Purbeck Marble effigy of a lady, popularly supposed to be the mother of John of Drokensford, Chancellor to Edward I and then Bishop of Bath and Wells 1310-1329. Behind the effigy is an elaborate 14th century niche. In the north corner of the church an

effective small stained glass window, 1960.

To the north-east, over the river, is a hamlet called **Brockbridge**, which grew up around the railway station. The Meon Valley line was one of the last to be built, only opening in 1903. The station has been carefully converted to a house. In 1944 Churchill, de Gaulle, Eisenhower and Smuts met here in a railway carriage to discuss the invasion of France. The security was tight, with troops and military police, but the local Home Guard (including the author's father) formed a significant part of the guard.

The Railway Hotel (now The Hurdles) is redbrick Edwardian like most of the houses, and has extensive stabling at the back (now a motel) put up to accommodate horses who travelled here by train to attend the Hambledon Hunt.

★ ★ *Village for its buildings, setting and walks.*

DUMMER (E) Has recently found fame as the home of the Duchess of York before her marriage. The village has several thatched cottages, one with a long cat-slide roof. Proper village pond. Huge Victorian 'Tudor' Old Rectory, flint and stone. Behind the church Dummer House, stuccoed and classical.

The church of All Saints is basically 13th century, and is odd inside because the bell tower and then the gallery make much of the nave low. Narrow chancel arch, and above is a small area of Wooden Ceiling, a canopy over the rood. The wooden pulpit is 15th century and the heavy twisted balustered communion rail 17th century. Up by the altar brasses of 1508 with male and female figures.

★ ★ *Church.*

DURLEY (J) Described by William Cobbett, who lived at Botley, as 'certainly one of the most obscure villages in the whole kingdom'. In a lush, wet area, where every field seems to be pasture bounded by oaks if not woods, the village itself is mostly old and straggly, along one long street and another running down to the mill. The church of the Holy Cross stands alone at the western end of the village, and is a typical small village church, mostly 13th century. Ancient hollow yew tree. The roof continues over the transepts in an odd way inside. Good fittings include the pulpit (dated 1630) and the panelling etc at the back adapted as a War Memorial.

★ *Church*

EAST BOLDRE (M) A separate parish from Boldre, and well to the east of it. From East End (actually in the south) it runs for more than two and a half miles on the edge of open heathland. The houses are virtually all on one side of the road, creating a lop-sided as well as very long settlement. Mixture of houses, from the occasional old cob and thatch to modern. Pond towards the middle, and a simple red brick church of 1839, with a spirelet. The pub is called the Turfcutters Arms, recalling the old fuel of the area. **Hatchet Pond** to the north was created to feed Hatchett Mill, below the road causeway which is also the dam. It is now a popular spot, with a large car park.

★ ★ *For Hatchet pond area.*

EAST DEAN (H) A small scattered village. To the south is Deane Hill, an outlying wooded chalk ridge which dominates the landscape. East Dean has good farmyards and a handsome Georgian brick house. The little church is entered through an unusual doorway of big timbers with an old wooden door. Inside seems little restored, with open beams in the roof and a simple 18th century west gallery. The origins of the church are Norman, but much is later. Tiny Norman window on the south side of the chancel. Three-quarters of picturesque West Dean are in Wiltshire as the county boundary unusually passes through the village.

★ *Church for the doorway and unrestored interior.*

EASTLEIGH (H/J) Nothing but a farm before the London-Southampton railway was laid through the area in 1839. Winchester was too hilly for east-west railways, so Eastleigh developed as a junction when branches to Gosport and Salisbury followed in the 1840s, and a small village grew up at the junction, named after the farm. In 1861 the population was 250, but huge growth followed the transfer here of the Nine Elms (London) carriage works in 1891, and by 1901 there was a population of nearly 8,000. More railway workshops were set up here in 1903 and 1910, so that a complete railway town was needed to house the workers. This is still there, south of the town centre, a tight grid of streets filled with redbrick terraced houses. Most of these have simple classical detailing on the doorways indicating their late date.

The original railway station of 1839

survives. It was designed (like the surviving early stations at Gosport and Terminus, Southampton) by the eminent railway architect Sir William Tite. Towards Bishopstoke (the parent parish) over the railway bridge was a large cheese market founded in 1852. To the east of the railway line are the railway works, now much smaller and only used for repairs. They open once every two years for a popular weekend. Their extent can be appreciated from the lower bridge over the railway which leads to more railway housing and the classical redbrick works buildings. Sidings and trains everywhere.

The centre of Eastleigh is The Park, given to the town by the railway

company in 1896, with a bandstand in the middle. At the west end are the (ex) municipal buildings, 1898 and later and the eastern end has a market on Thursdays. Around the north side of the park are large houses of the 1890s, now mostly offices but presumably originally housing the railway managers. The church of the Resurrection is one of the few stone buildings in the town, beyond the north-east corner of the park. It was built in 1868, with later additions as the population grew, but was gutted by fire in 1985 and its future is uncertain.

In High Street is **Eastleigh Museum**, housed in an ex Salvation Army Citadel. Smallish, with displays in the main hall on the history of Eastleigh and of the

ABOVE *In Eastleigh High Street*
BELOW *Eastleigh railway works*

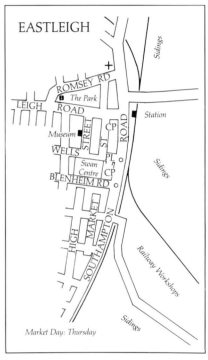

Market Day: Thursday

railways, and a smaller room with temporary exhibitions (free:lists)

Eastleigh now has many different industries, and has expanded well beyond the area of the railway town. The shopping centre is large and extends down High Street, and the roads parallel with it. A new shopping precinct spreads to the main road to Southampton, having faintly castle-like arches.

To the south of Eastleigh is Southampton Airport, founded in the First World War, and by 1934 the third busiest airport in the country, after Croydon and Portsmouth. Regular flights to the Continent still take off from the airport, but its importance has waned.

The new municipal offices are to the west, close to the motorway and incorporate the old buildings of the Home Farm, now enclosed in modern buildings.
★ ★ *Eastleigh Museum.*

EAST MEON (K/J) The highest village in the Meon Valley, and the one which is not on the main road. Until the end of the 19th century the parish covered more than 11,000 acres, and in medieval times it was the administrative centre for an area several times larger. The village is large and picturesque, much visited for its fine Norman church and village street. A car park at the west end of the village, off the main street, is useful for visitors.

The church of All Saints sits slightly apart from the village, sidling up under a steep chalk down. Externally the big central tower dominates, emphatically Norman with its rounded arches and zig-zag decoration. It dates from about 1150, and the spire was added in later medieval times. The entrance doorway is Norman too, but reset. Inside the church is lop-sided because there is only an aisle on one side, with octagonal pillars and pointed arches. This is 13th century. At the back of the north side a deep small Norman window survives. Under the tower the crossing has four rounded Norman arches, and two more Norman windows survive in the south transept.

The pulpit has simple inlay, dates from 1706 and was brought here from a London church. The finest fitting is the Tournai marble font, one of four in the county, of about 1130. Vigorously carved with Adam and Eve, their creation, the temptation, expulsion and Adam learning to dig.

East Meon belonged to the Bishops of Winchester which accounts for the village having such a large Norman church. Just

ABOVE *East Meon.* BELOW *Adam & Eve on the font at East Meon*

to the east of the church (and best seen from the path up to the church) is a rare medieval survival, Court House, dating from about 1400. The long windows show the position of the hall, the main room where the manor courts were held.

Church Street leads from opposite the church, and has a wide selection of buildings including flint almshouses of 1863, a Regency stuccoed house with fancy glazing, and several plainish Georgian houses. At the end is the High Street, with the Meon running along one side, tidied into a lined channel but still picturesque. Handsome houses and cottages line both sides of the street. The most elegant building is Glenthorne, with a big two-storied porch, red and grey brick dating from about 1690. At the far end the little green is called Washer's Triangle, and has several timber-framed cottages, probably 16th century. Another timber-framed cottage on the south side of High Street is still thatched.

Westwards is Tudor House, which really is of that date, and beyond, in

Workhouse Lane two long sets of cottages, still thatched. The Cross, leading back to the main road has more Georgian houses and some timber-framing. Narrow street, with a small stream one side.
★ ★ *A deservedly popular village, well worth seeing with a fine church.*

EASTON (E/J) Beautifully sited on the slope just above the river Itchen, and off the main road. A big village, with largish Georgian houses on the road to the church, a few timber-framed cottages, a long row of thatched brick cottages, with a thatched Georgian house at one end, and a mixture of more modern buildings. Footpaths lead across the river to Martyr Worthy or downstream.

The church of St Mary is basically Norman, but the tower was severely altered in a restoration of 1870. The entrance doorway is mostly 1870, but inside the rather deformed chancel arch, the vaulting in the chancel and the arch to the apse are all of c. 1200. The elaborate chancel windows are 1870. Two windows in the north wall of the nave are Norman, with tiny areas of glass, but a big opening inside the church. 1870 font, Jacobean pulpit. Deeply carved Royal coat of arms for William III. Early classical revival monument in the chancel, dated 1595, for Agnes Barlow, a nun released by the Reformation who married a monk who became Bishop of Chichester. Their five daughters all married bishops.

★ ★ *Church, impressive Norman chancel.*

EAST STRATTON (E) A proper rural village, with many thatched cottages, especially down the cul-de-sac behind the church. The church of All Saints is big and of 1885, with a timber porch and a spire. Along the main street are five pairs of plain brick thatched cottages with side porches designed by the distinguished Regency architect George Dance, very different from his usual Greek revival style buildings. He also designed Stratton Park (1803) to the north of the village, where his portico survives, now attached to a new house (see also Micheldever). The park, mostly ploughed but with many trees, and the house can be seen from the road north.

EAST TISTED (F) The estate cottages and the big house with its long park are prominent on the Alton Road. All these, and the church are 19th century, but there was a medieval village here, remnants of which (a few thatched cottages and the village pond) can be seen along the road to Selborne. Decorative estate cottages along the main road range from the 1820s to the end of the 19th century.

Rotherfield Park, sits up on the hillside, with little (and pretty) lodges of 1820 on the main road. The house is open to the public (fee:lists) as are the gardens. Magnificently sited, 500 ft up with wide views, the house is a sham castle of around 1820, but much altered in later Victorian times. On the entrance side are a collection of picturesque flint towers, the slim ones originally used as chimneys. The house is densely furnished, the best room being the big hall and staircase, perhaps part of the 1820 house but dominated by the stencilled decoration of the 1880s. The gardens are varied, with fine trees despite the elevation, and more formal parts include a rose garden and yew hedges.

The church of St James was rebuilt in 1846 in rather heavy imitation Gothic. The arches inside are of cement and the

George Dance's cottages at East Stratton

bench-ends (except in the chancel) are cast iron. Only a few years later these imitative materials would not have been acceptable. 1846 woodwork – tower screen and font lid.

Many monuments were preserved from the old church. In the left hand aisle is an early Elizabethan monument with John Norton and his wife, both kneeling, rather rustic, and at the end of the same aisle Sir John Norton, a strong Royalist who died in 1686. A big reclining figure, in armour, badly sculpted. In the other aisle, at the end, the memorial to Richard Norton and his wife (1540), a medieval style tomb-chest with Renaissance decoration.

Close to the church is a stone imitation medieval shed, a Victorian well-head.

Pelham Place on the main road to the north has a park which joins up with that of Rotherfield Park. The house is a pretty villa of the 1820s, with verandahs.

★ ★ *Rotherfield Park, House and gardens.*
★ ★ *Church for early Victoriana and monuments.*

EAST TYTHERLEY (H) On the road south from the village the huge Victorian lodges for Lockerly Hall are very prominent, and so are the farm buildings, including an odd octagonal building, perhaps a dairy. Many neat estate cottages in the village, which is spread out along the main road. The fine old trees which ornament the fields around the centre of the village were part of the park of the manor house, which was close to the church and demolished in 1903.

Outside the church of St Peter is an immense Wellingtonia, planted in 1887 to commemorate Victoria's Jubilee. The chancel and nave of the church are later

12th century, but it was very thoroughly restored from the middle of the 19th century, and the south transept added. The pretty tower is 1897. The result of the alterations and additions is a compact, pleasing building. The fittings are mostly 19th century, including finely carved corbels in the chancel with plants and birds. Here also set in otherwise plain windows, are three 13th century stained glass figures of saints, rare survivals, and attractive. At the west end, set much too low, a monument of 1568, with figures. Powerful and large painting of St Peter on the nave wall, 1983.

★ ★ *Church*

EAST WELLOW see WELLOWS

EAST WOODHAY (A) On the boundary with Berkshire, and in the Greensand lowland with the chalk scarp rising behind. The small rural village is on a little hilltop, with good views. This was an important stopping place on the drovers' route from Wales or the west country to London and hundreds of sheep were temporarily penned here and then shod with tiny iron shoes to protect their feet from the hard roads which they had to take from here onwards.

St Margaret's church is brick of 1823 (datestone on tower), not a common date for a rural church. The Victorians added tracery to the windows and a flint chancel and porch. An odd wide nave with an unusual timber roof made of thin timbers carefully braced to span the whole width. Plain memorial up by the altar to Edward Goddard (who died in 1724) and his wife, with big figures of them in their usual clothes. Painted George IV coat of arms at

ABOVE *Eling Tide Mill.* BELOW *The pond at Eling Tide Mill*

ELING (H) Surprisingly, Eling, the main medieval settlement to the west of the head of Southampton Water, still survives as a rural village. All the villages around, including Totton, Netley Marsh and Copythorne, were originally in the parish of Eling. Totton is now a separate settlement, much larger than Eling. The north part of Eling seems like a bit of Totton, with dense housing and industrial works on the shore, but over the Bartley Water River estuary all is rural.

The estuary, a branch off Southampton Water, is bridged by a causeway (toll bridge) which pens water for the tide mill, the low brick buildings sitting on the causeway.

The tide mill is open to visitors (fee: lists: car park on the far side of the toll bridge). The tide fills the mill pool behind the causeway, and the water is trapped by automatic sluices. There has been a tide mill here since at least the 14th century, but the present buildings are 18th century and the machinery mostly dates from a refitting of 1898. The mill worked until 1941, and was restored to working order and opened as a museum in 1980. The milling process and history of the mill are well-displayed, and a good video also details the processes. Shop, flour for sale, and further displays. Worth seeing.

One advantage of tide mills was being able to have grain delivered by boat, which happened here. The main quay is just to the north, with the old Anchor Inn and the lower parts of the stone walls of a steam mill (directly opposite the tide mill) being the only older buildings surviving on this side.

Over the causeway it is another world. The church of St Mary sits on top of the small hill, with pleasant smaller Georgian houses opposite, and a path leads down through the churchyard to the back of Goatee Beach, Southampton Water. Opposite are the complexities of Southampton container dock, usually with ships in, but back up the slope is the church, flanked by a large, handsome yellow brick Old Rectory, and Grove House with a pretty Georgian verandah. The path leads on back round to the mill causeway.

The church, despite its complex plan, looks Victorian outside because it was heavily restored in the 1860s. Inside is totally different, virtually all medieval. The most impressive part is the 13th century chancel arch, high and wide. The rest 13th and 14th centuries, except the north chapel, where the restorer put in

the west end, contemporary with the rebuilding.

★ ★ *Unusual date for a church. Good countryside.*

EAST WORLDHAM (F) A large village, with oast houses on the road to Wyck, a reminder that hops were grown here. Some thatched cottages and lots of good brick buildings. The church of St Mary is unusual because it is virtually all of one date – early 13th century. The characteristic lancet windows are deeply set and high in the walls. No chancel arch and so rather barn-like. A fine arrangement of lancets at the west end, and another at the east, perhaps prettied up in Victorian times. Pretty doorways, and a rather horrid Victorian font.

Binswood to the south-east has the now uncommon tree-pasture in its central part, ie a combination of trees and grazing. This was much commoner in the medieval period. Wyck Place to the north has a good late winter/early spring

garden which is opened to the public (fee:lists). Drifts of early bulbs – crocuses, aconites, snowdrops and so on, and winter flowering shrubs. Wonderful setting in the steep valley with old trees and good views.

★ ★ *Church, interesting as all of one date.*

★ ★ *Wyck Place gardens, fine winter gardens.*

ECCHINSWELL (B) Rural and flat, lots of trees and hedgerows. Complicated Victorian school and schoolhouse. The best part is on the road to Kingsclere, where the wide river, cottages and farm buildings make a pretty picture. The church of St Laurence is of 1886, small but high and impressive inside.

ELDON (H) (south of King's Somborne) Now only two small hamlets in the middle of an empty and attractive rural area. **Upper Eldon** has a tiny Norman church, now redundant and incorporated into a farm garden.

some decidedly French styled windows, and was sharply criticised for doing so. There are two tiny remnants of the Saxon church: a minute window high up on the south wall of the west end of the nave and a larger one on the left hand side of the chancel.

Behind the altar is a painting of the Last Supper, Venetian and mid 16th century. Many good memorials about the church, ranging from the sophisticated one to Elizabeth Serle over the pulpit, 1741 with a portrait medallion by Rysbrack, to the homely ones like the one at the end of the north aisle to Mary and George Bartlett of 1765, with simple portraits, a heart and a sailing ship. The church is normally open 1-5 p.m.

★ ★ *For the mill, the rural/urban contrast, and the church.*

ELLINGHAM (L)

ELLINGHAM (L) Tiny village, tucked away on its own road, which goes no further. Vicarage, big house, a farm and not much more. The church of St Mary is homely: mostly brown heathstone but with a redbrick porch dated 1720 made gaudy by an over-sized blue sundial above. Little timber spire. Inside the church is unusual because the chancel arch was not opened up by the Victorians: most of the space is filled by a plastered wall with 17th century texts, so that the altar is only seen through the 15th century wooden screen of the lower part. Attached to the screen, an hour glass. The

The porch of Ellingham church

squire's private pew survives, and the fine 17th century pulpit has very domestic legs. Good wooden reredos of 1700, now at west end, classically carved with theatrical curtains, swags of fruit etc. The high quality modern needlework on the altar, seats and so on is most attractive. Outside, just east of the porch is the grave of Dame Alice Lisle, beheaded in Winchester marketplace in 1685 for harbouring fugitives who took part in the Monmouth rebellion. Her husband was deeply involved in the trial of Charles I which led to his execution, and himself administered the oath to Cromwell which made him Protector. Dame Alice may have been present at the execution of Charles I – the usual image of her as an elderly lady (she was probably 70 when executed) rather ignores her robust earlier days. The west end of the church outside is brick 1746 with heavy classical details.

★ ★ *Church.*

ELLISFIELD (E) Small and scattered village, with lots of woods. The little Victorian church of St Martin is a late Victorian replacement. It has a weathervane in the form of a louse.

EMERY DOWN (M) was originally part of Lyndhurst, but gained its own church in 1864. Small and simple, in several different coloured bricks designed by Butterfield who also designed the almshouses opposite. Mixed houses and cottages, mostly brick, some thatched, and with oak trees everywhere: the whole village foresty and pretty. The New Forest Inn is supposed to have been built around a caravan which comprised the original pub in 1800. Conan Doyle lived here while writing *The White Company* (1891), partly set in the New Forest.

EMPSHOTT (F/K) A tiny village close to Selborne, and well worth visiting for its hilly wooded countryside and the church. The lanes around are deep, and the few cottages malmstone and brick. The church of the Holy Rood is virtually all of one date – early 13th century, transitional between Norman and Early English with the tower and spire added in 1884. Inside the pillars are alternately round and octagonal, and above all the arches is dog-tooth decoration. The arches, along with the complex wooden roof (1884 based on a 15th century original) make the interior very pretty. The aisles are ludicrously narrow – the original outer walls must have given

trouble and were replaced probably in the 17th century. The eastern window is three simple lancets, and the pulpit is 13th century too, Purbeck Marble table type. Reset in the tower is part of a screen dated 1624, and the font cover is 1626. Jacobean pulpit and communion rails, and very solid and plain earlier benches.

Next to the church a pleasant malmstone and brick cottage, and some more complicated Victorian ones at Empshott Green to the west. The chalk escarpment is yet further west, heavily wooded and with footpaths running through it. Good walking there and all around the village.

★ ★ *Church, interesting as basically one date, and with pretty fittings.*

★ ★ *Walking country.*

EMSWORTH (O) A picturesque, much-visited small town at the head of one of the arms of Chichester Harbour, now a busy yachting centre but originally a small port and fishing village. The boundary between Hampshire and Sussex runs along the east side of the town. In the 19th century its oyster industry grew large, and since the town was on the main road between Chichester and Portsmouth, coaching also made it prosperous. As with all seaside places smuggling was carried on.

William Daniel, whose epic *Voyage round Great Britain* was published in the 1820s, was not impressed with Emsworth. 'The inhabitants subsist by boat-building, rope-making, and other occupations connected with navigation, which are not likely to be interrupted, as the place has no attraction for sea-bathers, and is void of any pretension to the picturesque'.

Daniel avoided referring to the mud which lines the shores, but presumably that was why he thought bathers would avoid it. At low tide mud stretches for more than three miles south of the town, with only the channels still holding water. Fashionable sea-bathing came only briefly to Emsworth: one of George III's daughters came to bathe in 1805, and Bath Road on the far side of the Mill Pond is named after the bathing station then built on the shore.

Daniel did not find Emsworth picturesque, but we do today because of its many Georgian buildings, two big mill ponds, and seemingly every street and lane leading down to the shore.

The town has been bypassed, but can still be very busy in the summer. The Square is the centre, a small triangle with

Quay Millpond, Emsworth

some good buildings including Lloyd's bank, plain and about 1810. Tucked away on the west side is a brick building with a little bell cupola and clock, built as St Peter's Church in 1789, but now in secular use, having been a town hall and then a cinema.

South Street leads down to the shore, lined with simple Georgian cottages originally owned by fishermen. At the bottom several small flint, weather-boarded, or brick buildings survive, and out on the point Quay Mill, now used by the Sailing Club. This was a tide mill and the large sheet of water to the north was the tide-filled pond. The causeway enclosing the pond was converted to a walkway in the 1920s, and called the Promenade. The far side of the pond is lined with Edwardian to 1930s houses, but where the Promenade joins the land again are Georgian brick buildings. A path leads on along the shore to Warblington.

On the town side, above the mill, is another plain industrial-looking building by the side of the Mill Pond. This was a malthouse, presumably served by the smaller boats which could enter the mill-pond through the hatches at high tide. Close by are unusual houses of 1931, plain but with a band of decorative flints.

At low tide one can walk along the shore line from Quay Mill, past the garden walls of brick or pebbles with their varied stone footings. Presumably the stone was brought in by ship, as none of it is local. The stumps revealed at low tide are the remains of oyster ponds, used to store and fatten them. The industry suffered an awful set-back in 1902 when guests at Mayoral banquets in Winchester and Southampton were taken ill after eating Emsworth oysters. Some died. The oysters had been polluted by sewage. Some ship-builders' works survive at the eastern end, but many have disappeared. To the south is the entrance to Emsworth Marina, an enclosure built as the pond of another tide mill.

King Street leads back towards the Square, with many Georgian houses and cottages, mostly brick, but of a variety of styles and sizes. A little way along is a peculiar-looking one of flush wooden weather-boarding, supposed to have been built by a boat-builder. Opposite, a footpath leads past Wharf House, later Georgian with newly fashionable yellow bricks for the front and red everywhere else. The footpath leads down to a channel beside Emsworth's third tide-mill pond, half of which is in Sussex.

Queen Street runs from the pond

LEFT *The weather-boarded house in King Street, Emsworth*
BELOW *1931 flint banding in Emsworth*

towards the Square. Close to the pond is The Old Flour Mill, dated 1897 and a handsome industrial building with iron windows. Most of Queen Street is Georgian with Newnham House the best building, with more decoration than most in the town. Several nautical shops towards the town end and opposite the end of the road is Tower Street, a picturesque cul-de-sac with varied Georgian houses. A footpath leads on past modern development to the shore.

West Street, from the Square, also has some Georgian houses and cottages. North Street is crossed by the inner by-pass, and north of this is Victorian Emsworth. **The Museum** (fee:lists) is above part of the fire station in North Street, north of the bypass. It is crammed with photographs and other material relating to the history of the area. Only one large room, but with temporary exhibitions too. ★★

The parish church of St James is to the north, built in 1840 to replace the small brick church in the Square. Odd looking, with staircases (now glassed in) between turrets, all in Norman style. Inside is almost as odd, although mostly later Victorian.

★★★ *Town for walking around and admiring the Georgian houses, and the long low sea views.*

★★ *Museum.*

ENHAM ALAMEIN (D) A hamlet which was developed after the First World War to house disabled servicemen, with workshops to provide employment. After the Second World War it was greatly expanded and renamed after the battle of El Alamein in North Africa. A few old cottages survive in the middle, one timber framed one being particularly prominent. Close by is the modern church of St George, full of memorials to the units which took part in the battle.

EVERSLEY (C) Rural and scattered, a great contrast to the heavily developed Yateley to the east. Eversley Cross on the east is the largest part, but there are also Up Green, Eversley Centre, Eversley and Lower Common. All have 17th and 18th century brick houses and cottages, a few timber framed. Lots of trees. Scattered about in Longwater Road, (Eversley Cross), Lower Common, Up Green and Warbrook are four blocks of half-timbered cottages, all with inscriptions incised on the main beams. They were built for farm labourers by a friend of Charles Kingsley,

Kingsley memorial cottages at Up Green, Eversley

Exbury House

Eversley school gates with a chimney sweep from The Water Babies

in memory of the writer. Another memorial is the school, at the west end of Eversley Centre, towards the church. Half timbered with brick, the iron gates were put up in 1951 for the Festival of Britain, and include a sweep in the centre, in reference to *The Water Babies*. John James, the 18th century architect, lived in the village and built Warbrook house in 1724 for himself. It is close to the football pitch, between Eversley and Eversley Centre. Handsome, sophisticated brick.

Charles Kingsley was curate and then rector here from 1844-1875. Most of his books, including *The Water Babies* were written here, in the rectory just below the church. The rectory is a 17th century house (the timber framed bit) refronted in the 18th century: not formal, all very homely. Very rural, with a tiny ha-ha in front, and small scale landscape beyond.

The clipped yews which line the church path were planted by Kingsley, and the huge Wellingtonia grew from a seed he brought back from America. He and his wife are buried to the left of the path, beneath a white cross with passion flowers, the graves being right up against the garden wall of the Rectory.

The church is mostly brick, grey and red. The porch is dated 1724 and 'this tower was built 1735'. It is assumed that John James was the architect and what may well be his architect's drawing table survives in the church, looking like a plain side-table, in the north chapel. The only medieval surviving is the chancel. When Charles Kingsley was here the church was smaller: the north aisle was added in 1876 to his memory. Inside the screen dominates, looking Byzantine and exotic. It is of 1730, but was painted in the 1860s. Above it a small pretty wallpainting of two angels with an inscribed scroll, dating from about 1810, a rare date for church paintings. Good reredos, and the reclining figure of woman in alabaster, Dame Marriane Cope who died in 1892. The 18th century triple-decker pulpit was cut down to a single decker in the 1860s. In the north aisle a relief portrait of Kingsley, and a tablet to John James 'Architect to the Churches of St Paul London, St Peter Westminster, the fifty new Churches and the Royal Hospital for Seamen at Greenwich'. Lots of memorials all round the church and a late painted Royal Coat of Arms – George VI. Under the wooden boards by the font is a large sarsen, perhaps natural or perhaps part of a prehistoric monument.

★ ★ ★ ★ *Church, landscape and Kingsley association.*

EVERTON (M) has more 18th and 19th century houses than the other villages in the area, but to make up has a church of 1984. The thatched cottage just to the west of the church, beyond the large white Yeovilton House, is believed to be the original for the keeper's house in *Children of the New Forest* much of which was set in Everton when it was part of the New Forest. It still feels edge of the forest.

EWSHOTT (C) Close to Fleet, but still rural. The church of St Mary is 1873 and of brown heathstone.

EXBURY (M) Best known for the gorgeous gardens at Exbury House. The village has many yellowy ochre brick cottages and big oak trees. The odd redbrick water tower of Exbury House looks like a little church, but the real church is unassuming; stone and a replacement of 1907. The Forster chapel contains an unusual memorial: a bronze effigy of a First World War soldier with tall candlesticks at each corner, in memory of John and Alfred Forster, both killed by the war.

Exbury Gardens were started by Lionel de Rothschild, who bought Exbury House in 1919, extended the early 19th century house considerably, and then started establishing a huge woodland garden on the acid soil. The oak and Scots Pine which were already growing here make a perfect background for the huge collections of rhododendrons and other acid loving plants. Many hybrid rhododendrons and azaleas were created here. Now nearly 250 acres, the gardens are a delight from early spring with every colour of rhododendron and azalea blazing forth. It is the most complete collection of the different varieties and hybrids of that species in Great Britain. The gardens are so big that one should allow at least a couple of hours for a visit, and there are many other types of rare trees, shrubs and plants besides rhododendrons. Several spring-fed ponds, informal and more formal plantings, a two acre rockery, views across the Beaulieu river estuary. Open March-July, and again in the autumn. (Fee: lists). ★ ★ ★ *Garden.*

EXTON (J) The most rivery of the Meon Valley villages, right down in the watermeadows. Luckily mostly off the main road. Picturesque, with lots of old tile roofs, flint and brick garden walls. Winding lanes, with sparse scatters of houses, almost all brick, but some timber-framed and occasionally still thatched. Smallish church, St Peter & St Paul, mostly medieval but drastically restored in 1847. Flint with little timber spire. Surprising 1891 stained glass in the east window: leaves and abstract design in fabulous colours. Its design is reflected in the fabric on the screen at the west end.
  ★ ★ *Village.*

FACCOMBE (A) 750 ft high on the chalk downs of north Hampshire, with lots of estate cottages, and a Georgian house greatly extended in the 1930s. Lots of flint and brick garden walls. The church of St Barnabas was rebuilt in 1886 on a new site, but has the small zig-zag decorated Norman font from the original church at Netherton, and several 17th century memorials. The best is by the door, to Anne Reade who died in 1624. Her slate panel shows her kneeling with her children in contemporary dress.
  Netherton a mile to the west was the village, and has a huge thatched barn and a big ex Rectory of 1720.

FAIR OAK (J) Acres of modern development, with virtually nothing, even in the middle, dating from before 1960 except the plainish small church of St Thomas, 1863 and the central pubs. The fair oak in the middle (a replacement of 1843) looks rather sick.

FAREHAM (N) Described by Leland in the 1540s as 'a fiscar village', but by 1805 when Bayley and Britton saw it 'a respectable and populous town, chiefly inhabited by persons employed in maritime occupations; and, indeed, indebted for its whole importance to the naval establishment at Portsmouth'. Apart from the High Street (the finest street in the county) Fareham is now a modern shopping town, with little to do with the sea and much cut about by recent roads. The new museum in West Street, and the Quay area are worth seeing, and the High Street is a superb display of Georgian architecture.

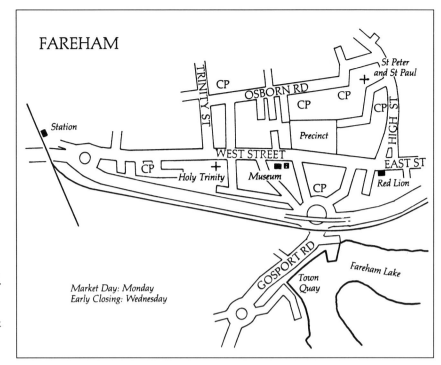

FAREHAM

Market Day: Monday
Early Closing: Wednesday

High Street was the main street of the town until the 19th century, when the commercial focus moved to West Street, leaving High Street unaffected by the growing prosperity of Fareham as a shopping centre. The junction of High Street and West Street and East Street is the start of the good buildings. The Red Lion in East Street was refronted about 1810, with a shallow semicircular porch. The building to the east is a warehouse of the 1860s, and like the Red Lion, is of Fareham Red bricks. Opposite, the start of High Street was wide to allow a market place, but the bottom part is now filled with a block of smallish scale buildings. Fairs were held in the street until 1871. Above this the wide street is lined with trees, and there is the first of the 1897 Jubilee electric lamp standards which are found at wide intervals all up the street. These are some of the earliest electric street lamps to survive, and are decorative with big swan necks. The range of houses on the right hand side going up from West Street are perhaps the best in this fine street. First is Kintyre House of 1767 of the typical grey brick with red brick dressings around the windows and doors, with a huge and splendid porch. Next door is its Georgian coach-house of the same materials, but

ABOVE *The Old Corn Exchange, West Street, Fareham.* BELOW *The County Club, High Street, Fareham*

the next house is a contrast in yellow, fashionable from the early 19th century. It uses mathematical tiles which look just like bricks unless one inspects the corners. The County Club (dated 1767) is of the hot red bricks known as Fareham Reds, with enormous two-storey bow windows, so large that they each have three windows. The next house is yellow brick, with a simple porch and little iron balconies, all Regency. Next door is

reproduction Georgian redbrick, followed by 1950s modern. The stuccoed one above is early Victorian, with fussier detailing than the Georgian houses, and an overhanging roof. The next house is of 1887, florid and complex but still classical in style. The street curves and goes uphill in a picturesque manner which adds to the charm of the buildings. The upper end has smaller scale houses, some still with original shop windows. Opposite the new road into the car parks is a house of the 1840s with a Greek style porch.

The other side of the road is as fine, with the same variety of styles and dates, including a pair of earlier houses with jettied first floors.

Over the top of the hill is a large new Georgian house on the right, and beyond the road junction the Old Manor House, early 18th century of red and grey bricks, with a big 19th century extension this side. Much further out, originally in open country, is St Christopher's, which was the workhouse.

The church of St Peter and St Paul is at the top of the High Street, tucked around the corner and farther hidden by yews. The path is partly made from grey ceramic paving stones, moulded to look like small squares, and there is one square inscribed FUNTLEY BRICKWORKS showing their origin in the local kilns. The plain flint and brick wall on two sides of the graveyard is inscribed 'Built 1830'. The church is complex. The flint and stone wall at the east end has long and short

Union Street, Fareham

work in the corner, showing that there was a Saxon church here, but most of the building is later. The heavy brick tower is of 1742, capped by a more elegant wooden cupola. The only medieval part of the church surviving is the north chapel, originally the chancel. Apart from the tower, most of the rest of the church is a rebuilding of 1930. Plain pillars inside. 1880s chancel with splendid mosaic reredos. Lots of memorials to naval officers, including one at the west end of the south aisle to the Captain of the ship *Hero* which was wrecked in 1811 and all her 600 crew drowned.

In the south-west corner of the graveyard, off Church Path, is a row of three charming early Victorian flint cottages, presumably built by the church.

LEFT *St Peter & St Paul church tower, Fareham*
BELOW *Church cottages, Fareham*

One is of little squares of flint. Looming over them is the largest building in Fareham, the ten storey Fareham Tower, built in the late 1970s to house the Civic offices. In the area to the south of the tower is the big new covered shopping precinct.

West Street was the main shopping area until the precinct was built behind it in the early 1980s. A mixture of buildings, a few Georgian but mostly ranging from the 19th century to the present. The street is a mile long, and still has shops virtually from one end to the other. In the middle on the corner with Portland Street is the former Town Hall (now a bank) with Greek style columns, built about 1835. The late Georgian Westbury Manor, further west, is now **Fareham Museum**. Superb local history displays covering Portchester and Titchfield as well as Fareham, the strawberry and brick industries etc. Superb house. Temporary exhibitions. One of the best town museums. ★ ★ ★ (and with a Draper gallery!)

Westwards again is *Holy Trinity Church*, built in the 1830s on the outskirts of the town, but now central. Although more substantial than most because more money was spent on it, the church is typical of its date: decorative imitation Gothic not trying too hard to look like real medieval. Inside it is high with thin iron pillars, and was originally galleried all round. Now only the west gallery

Fareham Creek

survives. The decoration with touches of blue is effective. Austere pews. The east end has modern stained glass, but at the west end, above the gallery is unusual painted glass of the later 18th century. Towards the chancel are two large memorials: on the south to Sir Charles Thompson who died commanding the Channel Fleet in 1799 has figures of sailors, one with a sextant. This is by Flaxman, and of much higher quality than the one opposite to his widow who died in 1833. Hers has children's figures.

★★ *Church.*

At the extreme west end of West Street is the railway station which opened in 1841. The stone part of the station is the original building.

Under the railway bridge on the corner of Redlands Lane to the south is Bishopswood, now the home of the Bishop of Portsmouth. The central part is an enchanting cottage orne of about 1780, with thatched roof, Gothic windows and rough tree trunk supports. Redlands Lane leads out to **West End** with its very modern style church of St John Evangelist (1964). Further out is Fort Fareham, another Palmerstonian fort, wooded around the outside but the middle an industrial estate. The western side of the town is filled with modern development, but further out, almost to Titchfield, is **Catisfield** an 18th century hamlet still distinct amongst the modern. It is a pleasant backwater with lots of

trees, plain Georgian brick cottages and some larger houses, all on top of a hill.

Beyond the modern road which bypasses the town to the south are **the quays**. Fareham has been a port since medieval times, and has also periodically had a shipbuilding industry. The silting up of the river gradually strangled the sea-borne trade, but a tiny amount still survives.

From East Street, Bath Lane leads south to the shore. The baths were built at the sea end of the road in 1838 and were filled with sea-water, rather a late manifestation of the craze for bathing in salt water. Beyond the Eastern Way is a recreation ground bordered by the estuary, here quite wide and wriggly, edged with mud except at high tide. To the west is Upper Quay, still functioning with ships bringing in sand and gravel. To the south, along the Gosport Road, is Lower Quay, which was also commercial but is now used by pleasure boats. Many of the buildings are preserved however, and the area makes an interesting walk. The preservation is happily unself-conscious and not at all twee. On the land side are first two originally industrial buildings. The first, gable end on to the road, was an electricity generating station built in 1897, and the next, set further back from the road, was Fareham Steam Flour Mill, built in 1830 and in use until 1960. Further on are several Georgian cottages and houses, the

first yellow brick of the early 19th century, the others redbrick. Behind the cottages is a long low building, built as part of the hospital for sailors in the 18th century and later used for sick French prisoners-of-war from the prison at Portchester Castle. The building was used as a rope walk (manufacturing rope) later in the 19th century.

On the waterside are Georgian brick warehouses, which were also part of the Hospital. Yachts are still built and repaired here, and the few shops are nautical.

Wallington to the east, over the river, is an ancient suburb, almost a separate settlement. There was a large tannery here until 1911. Wallington is now ringed by modern roads and industrial estates, but along the rivers are many small Georgian brick cottages, and many small fields still survive. On the highest point are the remnants of Fort Wallington, a Palmerstonian fort now used for industry.

Fareham has a lot more to offer than might be expected from driving along its recent roads, and the High Street should not be missed.

★★★★ *Town* ★★ *Holy Trinity Church* ★★★★ *The High Street* ★★★ *Fareham Museum.*

FARLEY CHAMBERLAYNE (H) (1½ miles south-west of Farley Mount). Miles from anywhere up on the chalk. The medieval village has gone, deserted perhaps for a more sheltered spot, and now only farms and the church are left. Deep roads around, with attractive hamlets like the Slacksteads. The church of St John is charming, especially inside. An avenue of limes planted as a memorial in 1922 leads up to the church, and the Norman doorway has two really odd heads attached to the arch. Inside the exposed roof and heavy framing for the bell-turret and the simple brick floor give a plain background for a wonderful selection of high quality monuments. The west end is stuffed with them, ranging from fine floor slabs to the large and handsome tomb of 1609 with a recumbent praying figure. The wall monument next to it is particularly sad: John St John died in 1627 aged 23, his wife died in 1628 also aged 23, and in a basket between them 'theire sonne: an infante; borne after his fathers death and dyed Befor his mother'. A wall monument of 1815 to Thrift Smith. One of the floor slabs is to Sir Paulet St John, who built Farley Mount just to the north (see entry).

Many of the fittings – the font, pulpit and so on are 18th century, as are many of the windows. Still gas lighting.

★ ★ ★ *For its position, surroundings, and its own small scale charm.*

FARLEY MOUNT COUNTRY PARK

(H) 1,000 acres of woods and downland, with many way-marked footpaths through them. Lots of free car parks. At the western end of the park is Farley Mount, a large barrow with a pyramid on top, all constructed as a memorial to a horse. As the inscription inside records the horse saved Paulet St John's life in 1733 when he successfully leapt into a chalk pit 25 ft deep. The views from the top of the hill are enormous, embracing the Isle of Wight to the south and what seems like the whole of Hampshire in other directions.

The path which leads to the memorial also leads on to a fine down with many yew trees. To the west are more woodlands, some ancient oak woods, others more recent. A superb walking area.

★ ★ ★ *For walking, and for the views.*

FARLEIGH WALLOP (E) divides into two parts. The upper has substantial 1930s estate cottages, some around a pond, and the church of St Andrew at the end of the lane, with a wide view of Basingstoke in the distance. The plain church sits high, surrounded by parkland and is mostly 1871. Inside are several 18th century monuments to the Earls of Portsmouth, whose estate this was.

The big house is to the south, set in trees. The front seen from the west is 1930s flint and stone, the other side 1731.

FARNBOROUGH (C) Now a large modern town, with many London commuters. Big modern office blocks and shops, all grown from two small settlements. One was close to the parish church, and the other (Farnborough

Concept 2000, Farnborough

Street) close to Farnborough North Railway station, where a few timber-framed or old brick cottages survive on the cross-roads. Elsewhere the earliest surviving buildings seem to be Edwardian. George Sturt's *A Farmer's Life* details the rural life of Farnborough in the later 19th century, when it was still small.

In 1906 His Majesty's Balloon Factory moved here from Chatham, and grew into the Royal Aircraft Establishment which now fills the area to the south of the town. Aeroplanes can be glimpsed from the roads which run around the perimeter. On even numbered years the famous Farnborough Air Show is held. On 16th October 1908 the first successful British powered flight happened here, piloted by Samuel Cody.

The church of St Peter has a 17th century wooden tower, and a fine 15th century timber porch over the Norman doorway. Super Jacobean west gallery, with chunky pillars, surprisingly swollen

The pyramid, Farley Mount

Farnborough Air Show

St Michael's Abbey, Farnborough

at the bottom. Screen of the same date now in the north transept. Painted Royal Coat of Arms of 1815. Just inside the door a wall painting of three female saints of about 1300: coincidentally one of them is St. Eugenia.

In 1881 the Empress Eugenie, widow of Napoleon III of France, bought Farnborough Hill (now a school) and lived there until her death in 1920. The house is a huge redbrick Swiss chalet, started in the 1860s but much added to, visible from many roads (north of the railway line, close to the A325). On a conical hill to the south, over the railway line, she built an abbey and church as a mausoleum for her husband and son.

St Michael's Abbey is opposite the railway station, across the main road. Footpaths lead up the wooded hill, and just below the summit are the abbey buildings – partly imitation medieval in stone of 1900, partly brick and French style of 1886. Right on the summit is the church, stone and French Flamboyant in style, very complex, whose dome is presumably, a reference to Les Invalides in Paris where the first and second Napoleons are buried, and the third would have been had he stayed in power. Simpler inside. The trees shield the abbey from the modern development all around: it is a magical place, very rural and French – a small scale, hilly, park. The church is only open at 3.30 Saturday afternoons.

The spread of modern development has made **Cove** 1½ miles to the west difficult to distinguish from Farnborough, but it was a village and has two churches. St John Baptist is in Norman style of 1844 and St Christopher is 1934 onwards.

★ ★ ★ *Abbey, the church and its hill.*

FARRINGDON (F) Divided into two parts – Lower Farringdon on the main road, Upper Farringdon to the east. Upper is a large village, with lots of colour-washed cottages and a few timber-framed ones. The church of All Saints has a 13th century tower and a homely classical brick porch of 1634. Inside fat Norman pillars. The chancel was rebuilt in 1856 and is a good example of the period, with an elaborate altar. Finely lettered war memorial in the church. Incredibly a certificate hanging in the church certifies that the big hollow yew by the tower is 3,000 years old – meaning that it started growing in the Bronze Age. This is crazy – it may well be 1,000 years old, but no more. Good row of cedars in the churchyard.

The church is not the dominating building: close by is Massey's folly, labelled Farringdon Village Hall. This redbrick beast was built over a period of thirty years by Reverend Thomas Massey, vicar here from 1857-1919. The huge building has three or four towers, odd round gables and incorporates lots of terra cotta panels. No one knows why he built it: suggestions include a theological college (there are 17 bedrooms) or tearooms for when the railway came (it didn't). Until recently part was used as the village school. A splendid folly.

FAWLEY (N) A surprising industrial area running along the eastern side of the New Forest. The village is insignificant compared with the vast oil refinery which covers more than 3,000 acres and is the largest in Britain. Close to, it is difficult to see because of the shelter belt of trees which surrounds it, but from any further away it is dominant. Refining started here in 1921, but was small scale until after the War. Southampton Water is suitably deep for ocean-going tankers and a large terminal for these ships has been built out in the estuary and handles 2,500 ships a year. Refined products are mostly distributed by pipeline.

The church of All Saints is right up by one of the entrances to the refinery. Basically Norman, with a very handsome west doorway of that date, protected by an imitation Norman porch of 1844. The east end was reconstructed after bombing.

The old village is just to the south, with much early Victorian building, including the Falcon and estate cottages. Small scale. Blackfield, Holbury and Langley are modern developments, built to house the influx working at Fawley.

Ashlett creek, on the shore of Southampton Water just to the east of the village, is remarkably rural, unless you look up stream to Fawley refinery and marine terminal, or downstream to Fawley Power Station. Large brick tide mill dated 1818 (now a club), a pub and two tiny cottages. Lots of small boats.

Dominating the south of the parish and Calshott is Fawley Power station, which started generating electricity from oil in 1971. The buildings are huge: the chimney is 670 ft high. Unfortunately the more attractive control buildings are masked from the landward side, and only really visible from ships in the Southampton Water. Oil is fed in from the

The Village Hall, Farringdon

Fawley oil terminal from Calshot

Fawley power station

adjacent Esso refinery and the generators can produce 2,000 kilowatts of electricity, enough for the whole of Southampton and Bournemouth. Electricity is carried away by pylon lines, and by a tunnel under Southampton Water to east Hampshire. The large machinery is well worth seeing, and booked parties of any size are welcomed for 2 hour tours. The power station has an open weekend each year at the end of July (list).

FINCHDEAN see ROWLANDS CASTLE

FLEET (C/F) When the London-Southampton railway was built in the late 1830s a station was put in at Fleet Pond because the railway thought it would make a good spot for excursions from London. There were no settlements closer than the small villages of Crookham and Crondall, but gradually those who came

as tourists decided to build houses in the wild heathland. Most of the earlier houses were large with big grounds, and have since been demolished to make way for more intensive development. In 1871 there were only 381 inhabitants, but by the First World War there were ten times that number. The main shopping street (Fleet Road) is a mixture from Victorian onwards, reflecting this growth. Today the population is about 26,000. The town is the home of a Ghurka battalion, a reminder of how close Aldershot is. The Basingstoke Canal runs right across the town.

Fleet Pond is a modest name for a fair-sized lake, tree fringed and rural despite the proximity of the railway,

Fleet church

industrial estate and houses. Access by car is from north of the railway line, about 1 mile east of the station, signposted Fleet Pond. The footpath round the north part can also be joined from the car park on the south side of the station. Lots of birds, especially ducks, waders and warblers, and walks through the woods. Until the 1920s special excursion trains from London were put on for skaters when the pond froze.

Unusually Fleet church pre-dates the growth of the town, because it was built as a memorial to Janet Lefroy, who died in 1857. Her husband, who commissioned it, died in 1861 before it was completed, but her father had it finished. It was designed by William Burges, an architect with an individual style and most famous for Cardiff Castle. All Saints is different from the familiar Gothic style of many mid Victorian churches. Outside it is robust and plainish, all brick, but inside lots of painted decoration, mostly bands in restrained colours. The boarded roof is painted too. Simple square pillars. Plain 'bottle' glass in most of the windows. It was extended westwards in the same style in 1934, and at the west end is the tomb of Mr and Mrs Lefroy, the founders. Good effigies, he holding a church and both with realistic dogs at their feet. Complex canopy over. Good carvings also outside over the doors.

★ ★ ★ *Church for anyone interested in 19th century architecture.*

The New Forest – history

Pigs in the New Forest

The history of the New Forest, as a forest, opens with a forgery. William the Conqueror, to give his afforestation an instant pedigree and to show precedent for the harsh forest laws, had forged a charter of 1018 (supposedly issued by King Canute). This was conveniently 'found' in the archives at Winchester. Although the charter was untrue, there probably was a Royal hunting ground here before the Norman Conquest, and William took over large Royal land holdings in what was to be the Forest, much of which remains Crown land today. Medieval chroniclers such as Henry of Huntingdon were hard on William. 'Beasts of the chase he cherished as if they were his children; so that to form the New Forest he caused churches and villages to be destroyed, and, driving out the people, made it a habitation for deer' (about 1135). Later writers claimed 35 churches had been beaten down, and it was not until the late 18th century that people realised that the poor soils of the New Forest could never have supported rich agriculture, and that the villages and churches supposedly destroyed by William were the invention of chroniclers trying to blacken him. A legal Forest in medieval times was not a wood, but an area reserved for hunting where forest law applied. The medieval (and even earlier) New Forest was probably similar to today's, with open grazing, woodland and heath.

William certainly made a huge area subject to Forest law, which was harsh. No land was to be enclosed to make new fields, no-one was to own bows and arrows, no-one could keep dogs unless they were lamed so they could not chase deer, and for unlawfully killing a deer the punishment was death or mutilation. These laws applied all over the area, whether the King owned the land or not. The death penalty was softened to fines or imprisonment from the 13th century, but the needs of the deer and hunting over-rode the needs of agriculture. Timber from the forest was felled for building, mostly for royal palaces and fortifications, but this was less important than hunting.

The wild animals – deer, boar and hare – hindered agriculture by eating anything not thoroughly fenced off, and competed with the cows and ponies of the foresters for grazing. This conflict between farming and animals of the hunt has always been a problem in the Forest, made worse because the grazing animals (both wild and domestic) prevent the regeneration of the trees by eating them while they are young. As the importance of the Forest shifted from hunting to providing timber the problem grew. To produce the oak needed for the Navy new plantings of trees had to

Deer in the New Forest

New Forest ponies

be enclosed from animals until the trees were large enough not to be browsed away. Thus the New Forest enclosures were the opposite to usual ones – they kept animals out, not in. From the late 15th century timber production dominated, and from 1698 the Crown had the legal power to enclosed large areas to protect young trees. The deer were still protected: from 1722 the second offence of killing or wounding a deer was punishable by seven years' transportation to America.

Huge quantities of timber were taken from the Forest in the 17th and 18th centuries for Naval shipbuilding followed by large-scale plantings of trees. Many of these trees still survive, as they became mature after shipbuilding stopped needing timber. Iron ships meant that the Forest was no longer important to the Crown, and although the Deer Removal Act of 1851 was intended to help protect the growing trees, it was soon followed by an attempt to abolish the forest.

The bill to disafforest in 1871 was defeated because the New Forest was already seen as a public asset. John Wise's book (1862) was centred on the beauty of the Forest, and urban man's need of it; 'Land has higher and nobler offices to perform than to support houses or grow corn – to nourish not so much the body as the mind of man, to gladden the eye with its loveliness, and to brace the soul with that strength which is alone to be gained in the solitude of the moors and the woods'.

Wise was heralding a new role for the Forest: recreation, first for the moderately well off, later for every-one. Visitors seem to have started coming in quantity from about 1870, as the increasing number of books about the Forest show. The huge increase in those visiting and camping in the Forest, and a greater concern with conservation of the environment, has led to great changes in management since the Second World War. To preserve the wildness the visitors come to see, all forest roads have been fenced or ditched since 1971, and cars confined to parking areas. Camping is also restricted to fixed sites, and the ancient woods and pastures are managed to conserve them.

The New Forest

ABOVE *Fordingbridge*
RIGHT *Augustus John at Fordingbridge*
BELOW *In Fordingbridge church*

hammer-beam roof with angels, unusual for Hampshire. Lovely embroidery of passion flowers on the altar, probably late 19th century. Vigorously carved wooden George I coat of arms over north door.

Augustus John (1878-1961) the painter, lived part of the year at Fryern Court, north of the town, from 1927-61. He is buried in the cemetery on the Stockton road. The grave is most easily found by taking the second gate on the way out from Stockbridge, and walking along that path until about 20 yards from the far hedge. The grave is on the left, a plain slab with fine lettering. John is also commemorated by a powerful bronze statue in the park just to the east of the main bridge over the river.

Fryern Court, a plain, yellow brick Georgian house, is visible from the road north to Breamore, about 1½ miles north of the town centre. A large Bohemian household lived here in John's time, and parties were common.

★ ★ *Museum.*

FOREST OF BERE (J) (just north of Wickham) A tiny remnant of a huge medieval forest which once stretched from Southampton to Rowlands Castle. This 'forest' was a Royal Hunting ground, not all wooded but subject to forest laws which preserved the deer, hares and wild boar, and even in 1800 the Forest of Bere still comprised 16,000 acres. It yielded oak for shipbuilding from the 13th century onwards, and was an important supplier to the dockyard at Portsmouth from the 17th century. The Forestry Commission now administer some 900 acres north-east of Wickham, and there are several car parks off the roads from Newtown to Boarhunt, and off the Soberton Heath road leading from the A32. West Wood and Woodend car parks have marked trails leading through the mixed woodlands. From close to West Wood car park is a stunningly extensive view north. Birch, sweet chestnut, oak and conifer woods are all to be found, and as the area is hilly views change constantly. Superb walking area, popular in summer, and in spring when the north-western part (Upperford Copse) has sheets of bluebells under beech.

★ ★ ★ ★ *For picnics and walking.*

FORDINGBRIDGE (G) The name was originally Forde – the fine medieval bridge added to the name makes it contradictory. The town was one of the centres of the 'Captain Swing' riots of 1830, when agricultural labourers smashed machinery in an attempt to preserve their jobs and increase wages. Many of the rioters were transported to Australia. The old town centre is small, having grown on the west of the bridge over the Avon. Most of the older buildings are in Bridge Street, High Street and Salisbury Street, with the brick Old Manor House, mostly 17th century at the north end of Salisbury Street. The Town Hall of 1877 is dull, but Church Street,

leading down to the parish church, has pleasant simple houses (even a little thatch), which group together well. Elsewhere the town seems to lack architectural unity. Off the east side of Church Street is Sherings Fordingbridge Museum (fee:lists), a good town museum ranging from archaeology to local photographs. ★ ★

St Mary's church is a little way south of the town centre, and is a large building, with an elaborate plan. Unusually, the tower is on the north. Mostly 13th century, with lancet windows. The big porch and south aisle were added in the 15th century. The north chapel has stunning 1970s stained glass, and a

FORT NELSON (N) 1 mile north of Portchester) is one of the chain of forts built around Gosport and Portsmouth in the 1860s to defend the Dockyard, and generally called Palmerston's Follies (see

The Forest of Bere

FRITHAM (H) An enclave of pasture fields within the New Forest. Mostly Edwardian and later cottages scattered about. The notable exception is Fritham Farm, severe Georgian. No church, only the United Reform Church of 1904. This, and several of the cottages were built for the workers at Schulze's Gunpowder factory. Car park at the west end of the village gives access to some of the more remote woods and Fritham plain.

Carry on down the hill on the tarred road to **Irons Well**, a large pond made for the gunpowder factory which existed here from 1865-1923, making smokeless gunpowder, originally from New Forest charcoal. There were over 100 workers at its heyday, and seventy buildings. The buildings have almost all gone, but a few survive off the track beyond the car park. The pond is surrounded by trees, and the water is brown, tea-like. There was a holy well here in medieval times, the water being believed to cure leprosy.

★ ★ ★ *Picturesque and remote place.*

FROXFIELD GREEN (K) A scattered village with lots of little hills, well-wooded, and with intricately winding lanes.

The centre is quite dense, with the church, a green 'several cottages and farms, a smithy, some old fashioned houses of the better sort, one of them a schoolhouse of 1733, a post-office and general shop and a reading room ' (VCH 1908). It is still the same, still with thatched cottages and no modern buildings on the green. The big redbrick ex-school house still survives, dated 1733. St Peter-on-the-Green is a small replacement church of 1887, with a rather pinched bell-turret. On a clear day the sea is supposed to be visible from the parish.

entry). Nelson is the westernmost one on Portsdown Hill, and is steadily being restored. The entrance arch has pseudo-Norman detailing, but all the rest of the buildings are plain. The tunnels bored into the chalk for access to magazines for storing ammunition are impressive, as are the complicated caponiers and galleries sited to deal with enemy forces who managed to get into the dry moats. The Royal Armouries are developing a museum of artillery here, and already there are a great many big guns on display ranging in date from the 15th century to the Second World War, and including both guns and mortars contemporary with the fort. Entrance is by guided tours only, and occasionally there are firings of some of the guns.

★ ★ ★ *Fort, more for those interested in guns.*

FOUR MARKS (E) The name comes from an old stone which marked the junction of four parishes – Chawton, Farringdon, Medstead and Ropley. The large village is almost entirely modern, and only became a parish in 1932. There are a few earlier cottages with the church in the south-west corner of the settlement. The church of the Good Shepherd dates from 1954, brick and rather domestic looking.

Along Telegraph Lane to the south west, close to the Ordnance Survey pillar, is Semaphore Farm, rendered, slate-roofed and with a central chimney, built in 1829 as part of the Admiralty Telegraph system for communicating from London to Plymouth.

Chawton Park Wood in the north-east is large and has several footpaths, one of which leads right through the woods to Chawton. This area was a favourite walk of Jane Austen and her sister when they lived at Chawton. A car park off the northern Medstead road offers easy access.

In the north-east of the village is a station on the Watercress Line (see entry). Steam trains stop here, and the Working Omnibus Museum Project has an exhibition at the station, and in summer runs veteran buses to Chawton and Selborne.

FOXCOTE see **CHARLTON**

FREEFOLK see **LAVERSTOKE**

FREEMANTLE see **SOUTHAMPTON WEST**

Fritham Pond

FROYLE (F) Upper Froyle is the main settlement, a pretty village, with several Georgian houses and some fine timber-framed cottages, a few still thatched. Mostly brick but there is a little malmstone, and some cottages are tile hung. A good mixture, with a proper farmyard and even a sawmill. Lord Mayor Treloar's College, founded in 1908 is a large school for physically handicapped children. Many of the houses and cottages have statues of saints in niches, placed there by a late 19th century lord of the manor, who brought them back from Italy. Oast houses around the parish attest to hop growing in the 18th and 19th centuries.

The church of the Assumption has a plain brick tower of 1722, but the nave looks odd externally because it has two tiers of windows. These have had tracery added, but otherwise the nave dates from 1812. Inside there are lots of funeral hatchments, a simple west gallery, and oddly for a church a plain flat ceiling. The chancel is very rich, of the late 13th century with a slightly later east window, a magnificent piece of net tracery, exactly the sort of medieval architecture admired by the Victorians. The upper part of the window has stained glass, heraldic in glowing colours, dating from around 1306. Jacobean communion rail, and a fine large chandelier in the nave dated 1716.

Lower Froyle is actually at the top of a hill, and also has older cottages and Georgian brick houses, mixed with more modern.

★ ★ ★ *Upper Froyle, the village.*
★ ★ *Church for the chancel.*

FUNTLEY (N/J) A rural hamlet north of Fareham, and surprisingly from the 17th century an industrial hamlet. The 3rd Earl of Southampton started the forge here, producing wrought iron, but in the 1770s Henry Cort succeeded in mechanising the production of wrought iron, and his patents changed England from being an importer of wrought iron to an exporter. The ironworks and water mill (for power) were at Funtley House Farm, off the road to Titchfield and just north of the motorway. A footpath leads past the site, which has a plaque commemorating Cort. The house is earlier than his time. Fareham Museum has a display on Cort and the ironworks.

There were also brickworks in the area now crossed by the motorway, and some pits remain. On the road into Fareham are small 19th century cottages which housed the kiln and claypit workers, now with modern development as well.

Despite these old industries most of the area is rural, with the River Meon running through, and some handsome timber-framed farmhouses. Great Funtley Farm in the north is the best, large and seen clearly from the road.

Knowle Hospital can be seen in the trees to the east, a large mental hospital. The area between the Meon and the Hamble, to the west of Funtley has no villages, but lots of woods with several footpaths giving access to them. Good walking country. (See also Curbridge).

FYFIELD (D) A small dense village, with many rendered Georgian cottages, and the occasional thatch. The church of St Nicholas stands on its own amongst old beeches, small, simple and mostly Victorian.

GODSFIELD (E) Two and a half miles north-north-east of Old Alresford, in the middle of the country, is a little chapel, once the centre of the estate of the Knights Hospitallers. The surviving flint and stone building is small, and looks domestic, but is in fact a 13th or 14th century chapel, with the two-roomed priest's house under the same roof. It is a rare survival, and not open to the public. However a footpath runs up the drive, right past the chapel, so it can be admired externally.

GODSHILL (G) The village runs up the hill leading into the New Forest east of Fordingbridge. Scattered, with some good cottages. **Godshill Wood** on the road to Woodgreen has a car park with a wide view to the south. All very New Foresty.

GOODWORTH CLATFORD (D) Superb name. Thatched cottages with later buildings in a variety of styles and materials on one side of the river, and the church of St Peter on the other, with a strange wooden tower in a field next to the church. Plain 14th century tower with a Victorian spire. Inside fat Norman pillars, others later including the north-east one which has very fine early 14th century large heads. 12th century table-type font.

★ *Church.*

GORLEY, north and south (G) Most of the villages north of Ringwood along the Avon valley are so dispersed that it is difficult to distinguish them.

Mockbeggar and the Gorleys are right on the New Forest boundary, with the higher, wooded land rising prominently on the east, and the flat Avon valley on the west. Wide verges and lots of small greens, cropped by the ponies. Scattered cottages and houses, varying in date from the 17th century onwards. The most interesting is at south Gorley on the west side of the road to Furzehill. Cuckoo Hill was designed by the artist, architect and archaeologist Heywood Sumner for himself in 1902, and it is tucked up in the trees under the low ridge. His *Cuckoo Hill, The Book of Gorley*, written in the early 1900s but only published in 1987, gives a wonderful picture of life on this side of the New Forest early in the 20th century. Many of the buildings, like the little thatched barn beside the drive to his house, can still be recognised. There are more stables in the area now, and perhaps more trees, but the small scale landscape is still the same.

GOSPORT (N) Now much larger than its adjacent parent, Alverstoke. The site of the town forms one side of the tight entrance to Portsmouth Harbour. Gosport started to develop from the mid 15th century, and when John Leland saw it in the 1540s it was only 'a little village of fisshar men by much hethy and feren [ferny] ground'. A blockhouse was built to defend it at that time, and from the early 17th century the town became a sort of overflow from Portsmouth, just across the harbour mouth, with store houses, timber yards, ironworks, ropewalks and a victualling station. In the 18th century with the growth of the Navy, Gosport also grew, and during the 17th and 18th centuries it was gradually enclosed by ramparts. The Navy's Victualling department was moved here in 1828, and the town expanded beyond the ramparts. From the 1850s a line of large forts was built to the west to defend the town (part of a much larger scheme). The town centre produced by all this development was severely damaged by bombing in the Second World War, and by planning since, making the centre, especially the shore around Haslar creek, empty except for blocks of flats.

Gosport was Portsmouth's poor relation, with many of the labourers for the 19th century dockyard at Portsmouth living in Gosport and travelling to work by the ferry across the narrow harbour mouth. In the later 18th century a visitor was not impressed: 'except for the

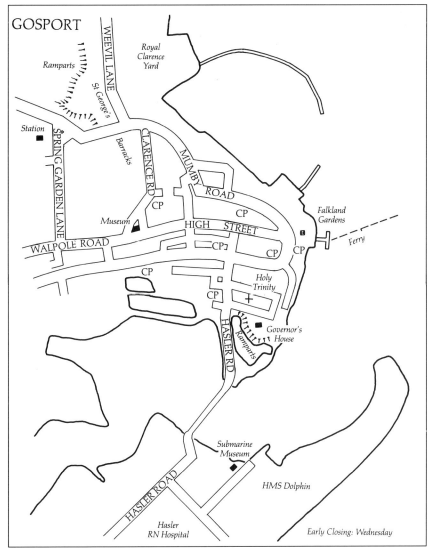

GOSPORT

Ramparts

Royal Clarence Yard

WEEVIL LANE

St George's

Station

SPRING GARDEN LANE

Barracks

CLARENCE RD

Museum

WALPOLE ROAD

MUMBY ROAD

CP

CP

HIGH STREET

CP

CP

CP

CP

CP

CP

Holy Trinity

HASLER RD

Ramparts

Governor's House

Falkland Gardens

Ferry

HASLER ROAD

Submarine Museum

HMS Dolphin

Hasler RN Hospital

Early Closing: Wednesday

1960s architecture, Gosport

The Governor's House, Gosport

vicinity of the sea, Gosport can claim little that is attractive for the town is not pleasant and the surrounding country has no particular charms. The town has the narrowness and slander of a small country town without its rural simplicity and with a full share of the vices of Portsmouth, polluted by the fortunes of sailors and the extravagances of harlots. To these evils are added the petty pride and sectarian bigotry of a fortified town'.

The High Street is largely modern and there are nearly as many shops in Stoke Road to the east. Beyond the western end, in Walpole Road, is Gosport Museum, smallish with good displays on the geology, archaeology and history of the area and a temporary exhibition gallery (free: lists). The museum building was constructed as the public library in 1902, and is unusual, in Art Nouveauish style. A little skinny lighthouse-like tower at one

end, and over the porch a big panel in low relief showing Bishop Henry of Blois landing at Gosport in 1158. The Town Hall is of 1964, and opposite are some of the few Georgian buildings surviving in the town. At the far end of the High Street are the jetty for the ferries to Portsmouth, and the Falkland Gardens. Interesting views of Portsmouth, with the Dockyard, the ships *Victory* and *Warrior* to the left, and Old Portsmouth and the tight mouth of Portsmouth harbour to the right, the latter seen more clearly from south of the ferry jetty. Ships are always passing, both naval and ferries, and there are boards along the outer fence explaining what they are. The small tug-like Portsmouth ferries cross and recross.

Two sixteen storey 1960s blocks of flats with jazzy murals on their thin sides dominate the area, and the only old

buildings surviving are the church and rectory to the south-west. The big grey brick house tucked into the rampart was the Governor's House, built in about 1800. Jane Austen's uncle was governor at one time and it is believed that she stayed here. The church of Holy Trinity looks 19th century, and the impressive detached bell tower dates from 1889. However the main church was only refaced in the 1880s, making it look like a north Italian church. The interior is of 1696, plain and light with big wooden pillars, an unusual date for a church. 1880s font, pulpit and reredos. The treasure of the church is the organ, installed here in 1744. It was played by George Frederick Handel when he was music-master to the Earl of Chandos in Surrey 1718-21, and although it has been altered since, much of the elaborate case is original. The high brick wall beside the church screens one

Gosport railway station

of the surviving bits of Gosport's ramparts. On the other side they are earthen, with a wide moat.

Gosport's Railway station opened in 1842, and originally also served Portsmouth. It is a handsome building with a long stone colonnade, now roofless after a fire in the 1950s. Decorative mid Victorian post-box nearby, with a Royal coat of arms. The station is at the corner of Mumby Road and Spring Garden Lane, and from the platform another line ran off, now covered by the road but visible passing through the small remnant of rampart to the east. This extension was made in 1845 so that Queen Victoria could take the train right down to the harbour, where she changed to the Royal Yacht for the trip to her holiday home at Osborne on the Isle of Wight. ★

The Royal station was within the Royal Clarence Yard, which fills the shoreline beyond Weevil Lane. The whole of the Navy's Victualling Depot was moved here in 1828, and a big handsome stuccoed gateway half way down Weevil Lane is the most easily seen part of it. Inside some of the 1830s and 40s large brick buildings survive, but many were bombed. It is now only a Naval store. To the north is Priddy's Hard, a big gunpowder store built from the 1760s with its own basin. The original powder magazine survives. Along the road to Fareham, Mumby Road, is a large yellow brick barracks of 1850s, St George Barracks, reputedly from a design which should have gone to the Far East, while

they built the barracks intended for Gosport. Two-storey verandas along the length of the buildings support this theory. Best seen from Clarence Road, where there are good original railings. Plainer blocks in Weevil Lane complete the barracks. Further out, on the north of the road (there called Forton Road) are St Vincent Barracks (1847) originally for the Royal Marines, but now a school.

A thin bridge leads from the centre of Gosport across Haslar Lake where there are many yachts. On this southern side are the naval hospital of Haslar, HMS *Dolphin* the submarine base and the submarine Museum. Haslar Naval Hospital was completed in 1754, and was then the largest hospital in Europe and the largest brick building in England. It was intended for 1,000 patients, but during the Crimean War more than 2,000 were here at one time. Many later additions including a big brick and stone water tower of 1885, seen clearly from

Haslar Hospital, Gosport

the town. The main entrance is now close to the water tower, but the hospital is best seen from the entrance on the north-east, where there is a large stone cornice with the Royal Coat of Arms flanked by figures representing Navigation and Commerce. The rest of the large building is plain, in brownish brick, looking rather industrial. High walls block the views of the hospital from most roads. Along the shore beside the Hospital are sea defences with a walkway along them, giving good views of Old Portsmouth and Southsea along the skyline, the three Palmerston forts actually in the sea, and the Isle of Wight. The walkway continues to Fort Monkton (one of the Palmerston forts still in use) where there is a large car-park. Gilkicker Point further along has another fort, also in use, with ponds on the landward side.

The Royal Navy Submarine Museum, Haslar (fee:lists) has several submarines on display. The largest, HMS *Alliance*, was completed in 1947, and the guided tour through her gives a good idea of life on these complex and cramped vessels. An introductory slide show explains the principles and history of submarines, further illustrated in the museum. The Navy's first submarine is also on display, with some midget class vessels.

★ ★ ★ *Museum.*

Gosport, as well as Portsmouth, was defended by Palmerston's forts. A line of them was constructed about 2 miles out of the town, running across the neck of the peninsula. **Fort Brockhurst**, off the Fareham road, has been preserved and is open to the public (fee:lists). The fort is monumental, surrounded by a moat, with the brick gun embrasures peeking out of the turn ramparts. Inside it seems even larger. Brockhurst was built in the 1850s, one of five which made the line cutting off the town from its hinterland. This Gosport Advanced Line was to stop an enemy landing a force and attacking Portsmouth Harbour from the side. Fort Brockhurst was equipped with 53 heavy guns, which could fire more than half-way to the forts next in line.

The entry is through the keep, which just like those in medieval castles, was self-contained, with its own moat and a place of last resort for the garrison. Mock-Norman detail on the outer door. The Parade ground beyond has a slightly later building in the middle, built in the late 19th century and now housing a fine display on the history of the defences of Portsmouth harbour.

Submarine leaving Portsmouth harbour, with Gosport behind

The grassy ramps were used to drag the guns up to the ramparts. The caponiers (tunnels protruding into the moat) were to allow the moats to be raked by gunfire from small guns. The garrison of 300 men lived in the rooms under the ramparts, or in the keep.

★ ★ ★ ★ *The best of the Palmerstonian forts.*

Brockhurst grew as a suburb after the forts came, and has several fine tiled pubs. Down Military Road to the south of Brockhurst are two more forts, part of the same line. Neither are open to the public. The first one is Fort Rowner, still moated and romantically overgrown with scrub. The other side of HMS *Sultan* (buildings for training marine engineers, not a ship) is Fort Grange, very similar to Rowner

but with the moat filled in and in use by the Navy.

Rowner was a small hamlet, developed since the 1950s with big housing states. In the middle of the park-like centre is the church of St Mary, with a big thatched cottage at the church gate. The stone part of the church is medieval, and the big modern addition is 1960s. When I saw it fire had gutted the extension and damaged the rest.

To the west of Gosport centre amongst much modern development is the remains of the hamlet of **Bury** which has several Georgian brick buildings including Bury House, large and impressive.

The Wildgrounds is an area of old oak forest preserved to the south of Rowner: admittance to guided walks on summer

evenings is by ticket (From Tourist Information Office, Falkland Gardens, Gosport). Entry otherwise is by permit only.

17th century Village is a reconstruction of a Civil War hamlet, opened occasional weekends and for ten days in August when crafts etc are all in 17th century costume (fee:lists).

Gosport as a whole has a surprising amount to offer the visitor.

★ ★ *Gosport Museum;* ★ ★ ★ *Royal Navy Submarine Museum;* ★ ★ ★ ★ *Fort Brockhurst.*

GRANGE, THE (E) (just south of Northington) An important house architecturally, a very early and pure example of the Greek revival. Until the late 18th century Greek buildings were not known, or copied, but with the publication of drawings of the early buildings around Athens, the severe Greek style became fashionable. Earlier classical revival buildings had been inspired by Roman buildings, and were much fussier.

The house was gutted in 1972, and it was planned to blow it up. Now under restoration by English Heritage. Many of the floors are missing inside, and there are no fittings. Therefore only the outside of the house is on view (lists). A long drive, with a flint lodge at the entrance, leads through the fine park, which runs along the valley. The river has been dammed to form a lake, and all the views, especially from the house, are supremely picturesque.

Fort Rowner, Gosport

The Grange

The house is startlingly plain, a large rectangle, with on the approach side, the centre brought forward with plain supports. By the car park is a redbrick facade, the only visible remains of the 17th century house which the architect Wilkins adapted in 1804-9 to make the Greek house. The main front is to the lake, a portico with monumental plain fluted pillars, no bases and very simple tops, like those on the Parthenon, Athens. The windows are all plain too, the only decoration being a frieze of wreaths under the cornice and studded decoration above. Coffered ceiling inside the portico.

The small building is probably contemporary, with more complex, but still Grecian, tops to the columns of the portico: it was originally an orangery, converted into a picture gallery in the 1880s. All the buildings are stuccoed brick, not stone as real Greek (and indeed many Greek revival) buildings were.

The house is strange now, structurally sound, but deserted; in a wonderful landscape but without any signs of occupation, its gardens all down to grass. Good display boards explaining the history of the house by the car park. Memorials to some of the Barings who lived here can be seen in Northington church.

★ ★ ★ ★ *For anyone interested in architecture, and good area for walking (see Abbotstone Down).*

GRATELEY (D) (east of Palestine). Bordering on Wiltshire, and with a railway station and little settlement on the Salisbury-London line, opened in 1854.

Palestine to the west has rectangular divisions to the small fields suggesting 20th century division, and a few earlier bungalows.

The village proper is to the north-east, with older cottages in the middle, a few of them timber-framed. Close to the church of St Leonard is a large barn with a huge tiled roof. The church is plain, mostly medieval (13th century tower and several 13th century lancet windows). In the last right hand window of the nave is stained glass from Salisbury cathedral dating from around 1225, superb quality in glowing blues and other bright colours. The panel with figures shows the stoning of St Stephen. No chancel arch, but unusually a rood beam with figures on, as it would have been in the medieval period.

GRAYSHOTT (F) See **BRAMSHOTT** for the surrounding heathland. All the housing is recent, and well screened by trees. Big church of 1901, with a spire. Waggoner's Wells (see Bramshott) is easily approached from the village, as is the adjacent woody Ludshott Common.

Waggoners Wells, Grayshott

Flora Thompson, the author of *Lark Rise to Candleford* lived here as a young woman from 1897-1901, working at the Post Office. She wrote about the village as Hatherley in a series of essays not published until 1979 (*A Country Calendar and Other Writings*) describing her life there and many of the inhabitants. Like her, many of them were newcomers, because this was on the fringe of the Surrey heathlands recently discovered by visitors. Many writers lived or visited including Conan Doyle and Bernard Shaw, and there were lots of week-enders and holiday makers.

Flora Thompson managed to find some of the few original inhabitants known as broom-squires who supplemented their small-scale farming by making besoms from the heather. She describes the natural history of the area with great affection.

GREATHAM (F/K) On the edge of Woolmer Forest, parts of which were enclosed in 1853 and a new road constructed east from Greatham to Liphook. Along this road Longmoor Army Camp was established in 1903 and is still there.

Greatham village is rather spoilt by the main road, but has older houses and cottages in the middle, some with the local dark brown heathstone used for the lower parts of the walls. The church of St John Baptist is prominent, 1875 and of the local malmstone. Next to it is a contrastingly dark heathstone cottage, still thatched. The farmhouse opposite is of the same material.

Just to the south, on the opposite side of the main road to the new church on a tiny triangular green, are the remains of the old church, really just the chancel surviving, with a big 1623 monument and a few other fittings.

Le Court, a big house to the west, was the first Cheshire Home. **Greatham Mill** to the west opens its gardens (fee:lists) and is well worth seeing. The mill building is partly 17th century and the gardens have winding paths over surprisingly undulating ground. Very lush, and with a good variety of plants and trees. Goleigh Farm just to the south is an impressive brick and ironstone building of the 17th century and earlier.

★ ★ ★ *Greatham Mill Gardens, not* ★ ★ ★ ★ *only because of its medium size.*

GREYWELL (F)

A handsome village, with lots of neat brick cottages and several quite large ones with timber framing, a few jettied. Occasional Georgian brick house. The main street is virtually one-sided, with the church and meadows on the other side. The land is gently rolling, too gentle one would think for the Basingstoke Canal to need a tunnel, but in fact the ¾ mile Greywell tunnel starts at the north end of the village. A footpath from just down the road to Odiham leads down to the canal, which is restored to this point. The entrance has been rebuilt, but the tunnel is not used for boats. A footpath along the canal leads to Odiham Castle (see Odiham).

By the path to the church is one of the larger timber-framed houses. The church of St Mary is medieval apart from the chancel of 1870. Norman entrance door. Unusually for Hampshire the wooden screen of about 1500 survives, with a loft above for the rood. Its height was raised in a Victorian restoration so that the original stair turret no longer fits. Above, instead of the rood, the Royal Coat of Arms for 1768.

★ ★ ★ *Walking along canal.* ★ ★ *Church.*

HACKWOOD PARK (E)

(just south of Basingstoke). The mansion is not open, but the **Spring Wood** is regularly opened in spring and autumn. 80 acres of formal woodland laid out in the 18th century with ponds, an avenue, a ruined temple, amphitheatre etc. Very good for bulbs and spring flowering shrubs.

★ ★ ★ *For an unusual garden.*

HALE (G)

has the wriggliest roads, and good views from its small hills north over the chalk of Wiltshire and west to the Avon valley. Most of the village is on top of the hill, with a large green and some nice cottages. A small Greek style lodge on the west side of the village marks the start of an avenue which shoots down the hill to Hale Park (footpath from where road crosses the avenue down to the church alongside avenue). The house was built by the architect Thomas Archer for himself early in the 18th century, although it was later altered. The house sits a little way up the steep slope from the Avon, and just below is the church of St Mary, which Archer rebuilt in 1717. The church looks like a house, tucked on a shelf in the hillside among laurels. The footpath up from the riverside road is so steep that brides must arrive breathless, and funerals don't bear thinking about.

Archer re-used parts of an earlier church and the Victorians altered most of the windows, but even so the building gives the impression Archer wanted, of a small Roman building, but with personal quirks like the doorways to the transepts which are not 'pure' Roman. The roof is Victorian, but still classical. Inside is plain, and less impressive apart from the monuments. Archer's own huge one shows him as a reclining Roman senator, with classical females either side. The monument was put up in his lifetime. His nephew, Henry Archer, who died in 1768 has a smaller memorial, a woman standing by an urn.

★ ★ ★ *Church, one of the best 18th century churches*

Hale church

HAMBLE (N)

The village at the mouth of the Hamble river, opposite Warsash. A ferry, runs across the river between the two. When John Leland visited Hampshire in the 1540s he considered Hamble 'a good fisshar toun': it is certainly not a town today, but a much-visited and picturesque yachting centre.

The riverside, the High Street running up the steep hill and the Square at the top are still mostly Georgian brick, and make the twisting street up the hill very pretty. The river is full of yachts and there seems to be constant movement of boats. At the bottom of the High Street, running seemingly into the water, is a row of brick cottages dated August 1818. Facing them a fine small Georgian house. Small scale but fine Georgian cottages, houses and pubs line the High Street right up to the Square, where there is a 17th century timber-framed house on the corner. The 'Square' is only built up on two sides, with Georgian cottages. Hamble Lane leads to the church, with the Gun House, 17th century brick with four guns outside, on the way.

The church of St Andrew was originally both a priory and parish church, and is basically Norman. A small priory, a French foundation, was established here in the 12th century. Slender Norman tower, and the entrance is through a reset elaborate Norman doorway. Inside the nave is barn-like, because it is tall and narrow, without aisles but with an open wooden roof and the 13th century lancet windows starting from high in the walls. The tower arch is high, with a Norman

window. Two Norman doorways on either side at the east end of the nave, the decorated one blocked, the other leading to a tiny 'corridor'. No chancel arch, but an impressive huge 13th century east window with simple but effective tracery. Good piscina of the same date. The chapel on the right was added in massive neo-Norman style in 1880, the only part of the church which is not medieval: unusually even all the windows in the rest of the church are medieval. Lots of naval memorials of the later 18th and earlier 19th centuries around the church, and one-third of the way down the nave on the right the memorial to Sir Edwin Alliot Vernon-Roe (1877-1958) the first Englishman to fly. There are two 18th century chandeliers hung conventionally in the nave, and the arms of another set along the walls as candle-holders.

The street along the shore leads up southwards to the Green, with a few Georgian and later cottages scattered around it. South again is Hamble Common, a Nature Reserve which runs between the Hamble river and Southampton Water. Parts are salt marshes. A car park on the Southampton Water shore gives wide views of Southampton Water with all its shipping and the enormous Fawley oil refinery opposite. The end of the point, at the mouth of the river was the site of the Fairey Aviation Company's works from 1916, producing seaplanes. Now speedboats are made there.

The oil storage tanks were first erected in 1924, but oil was stored in ships off-shore before that. In 1939 a pipeline for oil was built from here to London airport, the first in the country.

To the north of the village, between Hamble Lane and Satchell Lane, is an airfield, established in 1914 close to another aircraft factory started by A.E. Vernon-Roe. There are still aircraft firms in Hamble.

★ ★ ★ ★ *Village, but to be avoided at busy holiday times.*

★ ★ *Church.*

HAMBLEDON (J)
One of Hampshire's picturesque villages: the view up to the church must have starred in many calendars. However in the winter at least, it seems unselfconscious. Although now a village, it was a market town which declined from the 18th century. Cobbett saw it in 1826: 'formerly a considerable market-town, there is now not even the name of the market left, I believe; and the

ABOVE *Cricket at Hambledon*
BELOW *The church-like folly at Hambledon*

fairs amount to little more than a couple or three gingerbread stalls, with dolls and whistles for children. The church tells the same story: it is now a tumble-down rubbishy place'. The decline is what makes Hambledon interesting today, as it is full of plain, mostly Georgian houses, which fill the main street and spread up the hillside. The short street leading up to the church is especially good. The pubs all have signs which overhang high above the road.

The large church of St Peter and St Paul has a big 15th century porch with a two-storey vestry. On top of the vestry is an unusual stone chimney pot. The first part of the nave encloses a little Saxon church. Fat late 12th century pillars with slightly pointed arches were cut into what had been the outside walls of the Saxon

church, and on what was the outside face of these walls decorative vertical strips (pilaster strips) survive, parts of the original church. The first chancel arch is late 12th century, but further on is another one, needed when the church was enlarged eastward in the 13th century. Elaborate and heavy late medieval roofs throughout, late Royal coat of arms – 1953. Pretty tower, brick flint and stone. 1794, but with Victorian windows doors etc. Large churchyard, with straggly yews and many attractive tombs and gravestones. To the east, in the garden of Folly House, an imitation church, mostly brick.

Two miles north-east of the village is **Broadhalfpenny Down**, where the Hambledon Cricket Club played from about 1756-1787. A large stone opposite the Bat and Ball Inn commemorates this famous club, which in the 1760s could beat sides composed of the Rest of England. Cricket had been known since the 16th century, but only developed and became popular in the 18th century, and Hambledon Cricket Club was the fore-runner of the Marylebone Cricket Club (the M.C.C.). Booths for refreshments, and a lodge for spectators were not enough to make up for the bleakness, and so the club moved to a more sheltered ground in the 1780s. Even in 1810 cricket was regarded as a 'modern' game, 'of late years become exceedingly fashionable, being much countenanced by the nobility & gentlemen of fortune, who frequently join in the diversion' (John Strutt).

★ ★ ★ ★ *The village and the church together*

HAMPSHIRE FARM MUSEUM see **UPPER HAMBLE COUNTRY PARK**

HANNINGTON (B) High on the chalk, and unusually sited on the summit of a hill. Occasional thatched cottages, but rather dispersed except around the village green, which is a classic with a tiny spirelet covering the well head (1897 Jubilee), the church on one side with an avenue of trees beside it, farm buildings and cottages.

The church of All Saints is a proper mixture. The north-east corner of the nave, seen going up the path, has Saxon long and short work, and inside is an oversize Norman arcade. 15th century chancel and Victorian spire. There are two fine memorial windows engraved by Laurence Whistler, one in the chancel and another in the nave.

North Oakley is a hamlet to the south with a large farm and *Ibworth* another to the south-east, particularly remote with timber-framed houses and a pond, all set on a hill-top.

★ ★ *For good mixture of dates and Whistler glass.*

HARBRIDGE (G) Church, big house and a few cottages all cramped up together on the lip of the wide flat Avon valley. Picturesque, although the big church of All Saints dates only from 1838. The 'stone' windows are in fact moulded from artificial stone – very unusual. The many finely painted glass roundels are Netherlandish and 17th century.

★ *Church*

HARTFORD BRIDGE see **HARTLEY WINTNEY**

HARTLEY MAUDITT (F) (just south of West Worldham). A completely deserted medieval village, with just a large pond and the church standing in fields. The little church is basically Norman, with an elaborate entrance doorway decorated with motifs which look like horseshoes. Simple inside, with big colourful memorials in the chancel, and medieval tiles in the floor.

★ ★ *For its isolation and setting.*

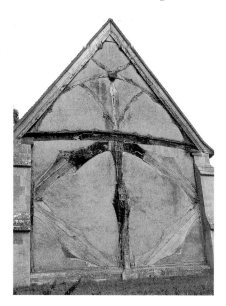

ABOVE *Hartley Wespall church*
RIGHT *The oaks in the middle of Hartley Wintney.* BELOW *Harbridge*

HARTLEY WESPALL (C) A farm and church, with the rest of the village to the south. The church is famous for its west wall, with huge cusped timbers forming large patterns. They are all structural braces to hold the 14th century timber framing of the church square. Originally this wall was blocked externally by a free-standing timber framed tower, demolished in 1868, shown in a drawing displayed inside. In 1868 the church was virtually rebuilt in flint, with a new tower. Originally it was all timber framed, and inside there are three big arches supporting the roof. The doorways and entrance door are original, all this woodwork being 14th century. Fine 16th century pulpit, and a huge memorial of 1692 just inside the door, which Pevsner describes as having 'a gruesomely pally demi skeleton' at the bottom.

★ ★ ★ *Church.*

HARTLEY WINTNEY (C) The original medieval settlement was to the south-east of the present town, where the old church is. In the 17th and 18th century it moved to its present position along the main road to London, and was an important coaching centre with many inns. The M3 has now relieved the town of the through traffic.

St Mary's church to the south-east now belongs to the Redundant Churches Commission. Before the Reformation of the 16th century there was a nunnery here, and the older parts of the church may have been built by them. Knapped flint tower of 1842, and brick transepts of

Hartley Wintney Old Church

1834. Inside almost all the fittings are 1834, surviving because a new church was built closer to the middle of the town in 1870. It is rare to see a complete set of early 19th century fittings as in most churches they have been replaced. Galleries to the nave and both transepts, with early 19th century funeral hatchments. In the north transept one of 1802 with contemporary figures. All the seating 1834, and the creed etc painted on the east walls. Remains of many late medieval wall paintings all round the church, and a fine late 12th century pillar piscina up by the altar, for washing the communion vessels. Plain wall cupboard close by. The altar table is dated 1636 on top. Big painted Royal coat of arms, 1705. An atmospheric church, worth seeing.

The middle of the town is a green filled with oaks planted in 1820, and set in rows like an orchard. The new church is amongst them, striped brick and stone of 1870. The main street has redbrick Georgian houses, one with two storey bow windows, and some timber framing. A pleasant street. To the north another green with oaks, and the well wooded road leads to **Hartford Bridge** a little roadside (or rather bridgeside) settlement with a Victorian church. To the south is **Phoenix Green**, also well wooded and with some older houses.

Elvetham to the east is a massive house of 1860, now a conference centre. Hot red brick striped with black, very complicated. Close to the house a Neo-Norman church of 1840, now part of the centre. Good parkland around.

★ ★ *St Mary's church.*

HATHERDEN (D) Lots of thatched cottages, a Georgian farmhouse, Victorian estate cottages and a little modern, all spread out in a park-like setting. The church of Christ Church is of 1857 by William White (see Lyndhurst), and rather startling looking as his churches usually are, with bright brick bands outside and brick lining inside. Odd bellcote. Next door is the school, partly a cottage with an inscription dating the founding of the school (for 24 poor children) to 1725.

Wildhern to the east is small and rural, again with thatched cottages.

★ *Church*

HAVANT (O) Now a large town, but until the 1950s just a small market town. The old centre is mostly still there, at the crossroads close to the parish church. The name now includes the huge housing estates of Leigh Park (see entry) and Havant itself has expanded greatly.

The parish church of St Faith looks old with its rubblestone walls, but in fact all this is a Victorian refacing, and only the stair turret to the tower (which looks smooth and bogus) is original. However the church is superbly placed right in the middle of the town, forming a prominent landmark. Inside, the nave is 1874, but the crossing, transepts and chancel are medieval. Pretty, but restored crossing capitals. Two features are unusual for a parish church: the transepts have aisles and the chancel has a stone vault. The latter is the more impressive, early 13th century. Up to the left of the altar is a big brass to Thomas Aylward, secretary to William of Wykeham and rector of

Havant who died in 1413. In the north transept hangs an ancient flag, the colour of the Havant Volunteers, formed in 1799 as part of the home defence in the Napoleonic wars, a rare survivor which was apparently painted by the ladies of Havant.

South Street and East Street have the best surviving buildings. Just below the church in South Street is The Old House at Home public house, a big 16th century timber-framed building with the first floor oversailing. Smaller Georgian brick houses beyond, and then Hall Place yellow brick in front and the less favoured redbrick behind, with a pillared porch, all of 1796 the time when yellow bricks were becoming fashionable.

The cross roads has two good buildings on the corner: one a late 19th century shop, the other an elaborate pub of the same sort of date. The Pallant, leading off North Street, has several Georgian brick buildings, including a nonconformist chapel of 1718, now offices. Just to the east, in Fairfield Road, is Fairfield Terrace, built in 1887 as a plaque at the far end records. A really odd terrace of ten houses, decorated with flint stone and (in the middle) over-fired brick. The brick gazebo of 1790 in the back garden of a house in East Street can be admired from this area.

In East Street is The Bear Hotel, Georgian brick, and further along Magnolia House, also grey and red brick. Opposite is another large town house, but this time all redbrick of about 1800. Towards the end of East Street is the Old Town Hall, now used as **Havant Museum** (free: lists). The Victorian buildings are of flint, most of it galetted – that is with tiny slivers of flint pressed into the mortar between the big flints. Recently

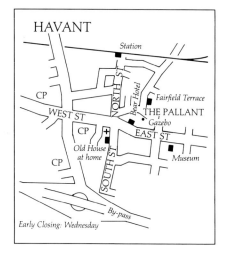

ABOVE *Jubilee Terrace, Havant*
BELOW *Plaque in Jubilee Terrace*

refurbished, with new displays on the local history of Havant, Hayling and Emsworth including wildfowling on Langstone Harbour and Scaletric, made at Leigh Park 1957-70. Upstairs the Vokes collection of guns is well exhibited. Temporary exhibitions too.

The railway line beyond the museum was the Hayling line, and is now a footpath. There are many narrow footpaths around the town centre, known locally as Twittens.

The growth of the town has overtaken several villages and hamlets. Warblington (see entry) has been absorbed in the south-east, and the hamlet of Brockhampton in the south-west is still distinguishable with a few Georgian cottages in the middle of an industrial area. See also Leigh Park and Bedhampton.

Havant is not an obvious place to visit, but there are rather more older buildings surviving than one might expect and the museum is worth seeing.

★ ★ *Museum.*

HAWK CONSERVANCY (D) (south of Weyhill, west of Andover). This would be worth visiting (fee:lists) simply to see all the birds – 29 species of owl including all the native ones, hawks, falcons, eagles, vultures and so on, but what makes a visit unforgettable is to see the birds being flown. Photographs do not do justice to the grace of their flight. To see this at close quarters is a delight. The ancient art of falcony has been practised in Britain since at least Saxon times, and in the medieval period they were flown both for sport and to get food.

The partnership between bird and man is surprising, and is demonstrated here several times a day. Avoid wet weather as the birds will not be flown.

★ ★ ★ ★ *Heartily recommended.*

HAWKLEY (K) The road from Priors Dean in the west is deeply cut through the chalk escarpment, a really romantic wooded ravine, and west of the village is a second little scarp, this time of green-sand, short and abrupt like a railway embankment. Footpaths lead through both of these woody hangers, one wriggling along the top through woods past Empshott and nearly to Selborne. The views, both close to of the woodlands and more distant ones, are unrivalled.

The village is around a green, with several brick and malmstone cottages, some with tile-hanging. The church of St Peter and St Paul is on the green too, Neo-Norman of 1865 with a Saxon style tower.

★ ★ ★ ★ *Walking country, both up on the woody chalk and down on the greensand.*

HAWLEY (C) Lots of trees and rhododendrons, over slight hills. Much recent development. The green in the middle is **Blackwater** surrounded by redbrick buildings – the almshouses with a clock tower, the timbered village hall and the church of stone and brick with a big steeple. All date from after the mid-19th century. Blackwater is right on the point where the Hampshire, Berkshire and Surrey boundaries meet.

Hawley Common to the south and west is a large area of the original heathland vegetation, with a lake towards the southern end. Good walking.

HAYLING (O)

Hayling Island! Hayling Island!
What did I expect to see?
Beetling cliff and chalky highland,
And the salt spray splashing me?

John Betjeman continues 'but this was quite the wrong picture'. However he admired the reality, 'the ripple and suck of a smooth tide flooding over silvery mud and the salt, sand-coated vegetation of the marshes. A stately Georgian crescent, worthy of Brighton itself, but unfinished, two large stucco Georgian houses near it, and some Italian-style villas behind, show that Hayling Island has been loved for its sands for more than a century'.

Betjeman summarises Hayling neatly: until the 1820s this flat island was agricultural, with a few tiny settlements, but after the building of the first bridge to the island in 1824, the sandy southern shore (the only extensive sandy beaches in Hampshire) led to seaside development. The first attempts in the 1820s were not very successful, despite a book published in 1826 to extol its advantages including the views of Spithead 'bedecked with wooden walls, all bristling with the mighty engines of terrestrial thunder': meaning the Navy.

The medieval settlements and their churches are sensibly inland. St Peters church, north Hayling, has the remains of the village around it, with several thatched cottages, one with clapboard walls, more usually found here for barn walls. The church has a belfry and spire covered with cedar shingles. The rest of the building is late 12th or 13th century with simple lancet windows throughout. Three late medieval wooden benches survive and above the chancel arch good woodwork. The east wall leans amazingly and rests on a large buttress.

The whole of the northern part of the island is still rural, with thatched cottages dotted about, as well as more recent buildings. The harbours either side suddenly come into view, and everywhere is flat. The Hayling Billy Leisure Route, a footpath along the disused railway line up the western side of the island is particularly good for seeing birds from, and Black Point in the south-east corner a good viewpoint for Chichester harbour wildfowl, waders and gulls.

St Mary's church is towards the south, rebuilt inland after the original church was washed away in the early medieval period, when the sea removed the southern part of Hayling, and more land was inundated to become parts of Langstone and Chichester harbours.

Elegant spire, on a short but large tower and the wooden porch basically medieval. Close by a really large ancient yew, split into several different trunks, and hollow. The church is mid 13th century: the chancel is Early English in style, with typical lancet windows; but the nave, built a little later, is Decorated, the subsequent style. Here the style is very individual, perhaps influenced by France as the church was built by the priory which belonged to Jumièges. The arches flanking the tower have capitals of leaves which are a combination of Early English stiff leaf, very formal, with the freer style of Decorated. The east windows of the aisles are complex and very pretty. The pillars in the nave were originally Purbeck Marble, but they crumbled away and were replaced by granite in the 19th century. Very unusually the pillars continue above the capitals, then blending into the arch. Unusual and attractive clerestory windows. The font, contemporary with the church, has carved faces.

★ ★ *An interesting church: a rare chance to see the start of a new style.*

The southern part of the island is more built up, with a variety of housing including, particularly at the eastern end, many flat-roofed houses of the 1930s, which is when Hayling really started to take off as a resort. There are beach huts and amusement arcades and lots of pebble-dash close to the four miles of sandy beach, but somehow even this is still on a human scale, and the great variety of houses stops it being monotonous. The 1820s attempt at a resort is towards the western end of the front: Norfolk Crescent of yellow brick and the Royal Hotel. Norfolk Crescent has lots of curving railings, and the hotel

balconies. Both are attractive, and surrounded by modern buildings. There was a race course in front in the 19th century.

The road west runs through overgrown sand dunes to the ferry for Portsmouth (foot passengers only) which runs across the narrow mouth of the harbour. Sinah Common between the sea and road is good for birds. A pub stands on the point, and there are wide views of the Isle of Wight, Portsmouth opposite, Langstone Harbour and Portsdown Hill. A part of one of the Mulberry harbours constructed for D day can be seen just inside the harbour. On the road just before the point a pill box of similar date, and boats oddly supported on pillars on the shore line.

★ ★ *Church. St Mary's is a very interesting church, and the island offers good sandy beaches and good walking.*

HEADBOURNE WORTHY (E) A small village on a short tributary of the Itchen. Although close to Winchester it remains rural, with a few thatched cottages, some Georgian brick and modern houses all screened with big hedges and trees. The church of St Swithun is one of the small number of late Saxon churches in Hampshire, and its churchyard is totally enclosed by a small stream. Characteristic Saxon work includes flint walls with pilaster strips (vertical lines of stone) and long-and-short work on the corners. The

Long and short work on a corner of Headbourne Worthy church

chancel was extended and the short tower added in the 13th century. The odd extra bit at the western end is difficult to date. Inside, a re-set Saxon doorway leads into this western extension and on what was the outer wall of the original church is the Headborne Worthy Rood, a stone carving of Christ on the cross with the hand of God pointing down to him and figures representing St John and the Virgin either side. Sadly all the detail has been chiselled off, perhaps in the 16th century when representations of the crucifixion in churches were banned. The carving dates from about 1,000 A.D. and is similar to those at Romsey and Breamore. Outside Hampshire sculpture of this date is very rare.

In the chancel a brass to John Kent, a Winchester scholar who died in 1434. Around the chancel many simple tile-like memorials to rectors ranging in date from 1640 to 1947. High open screen of 1880s. The superb reading desk copies the stalls of Winchester cathedral of c. 1300, but was carved by the late 19th century vicar, as was the attractive font cover.

★ ★ *For the early date of the church and the remains of the rood.*

HEADLEY (F) (East Hants) starts at the bottom of the hill with the older village, but spreads for a mile and a half up to Headley Down, which is mostly modern. Development is still patchy, leaving good woody views on the descent.

Until 1870 Headley was only a hamlet, but by 1908 the VCH found 'a whole row of shops' and although much of the area was then heathland 'many roads are already marked out and many villas already built'.

The old village was around the church, with a few cottages to the north, the big Georgian rectory to the south. The church of All Saints has a late medieval tower, but the rest is 1859, re-using some long 16th century timbers in the roof. At the back of the church are big 18th century paintings of Moses & Aaron, from the side of a reredos. To the left of the altar is a fine panel of stained glass dating from the 13th century.

Headley Mill to the west of the village is both picturesque and still working. Downstream is a ford, and above the mill a large (four acre) pond to preserve enough water to work the wheel. All the machinery is still used and the millers are happy for people to look in and see it. Most of the buildings are 18th century, with the brick bridge dated 1796.

HEADLEY (B) (North Hants) On the boundary with Berkshire, well-wooded. Most of the village is recent, with the occasional older small-holder's cottage. The small brick church of St Peter in trees by the main road is of 1868.

HEATH END (B) Part of a large modern settlement right on the border with Berkshire, and difficult to distinguish from Tadley, Baughurst and Pamber Heath which adjoin. Wooded suburbia, with areas of birch, pine and oak. Only a little earlier settlement along the main roads.

HECKFIELD (C) A backwater, missed by all the roads, and with pretty, mostly brick cottages and houses. Fanny Milton (1780-1863) who became Fanny Trollope and the mother of Anthony Trollope the novelist, was born at Heckfield rectory and lived here until she was 21. She started writing when she was 50, producing *The Domestic Manners of the Americans* in 1831 after living there for a bit, and enraged the Americans by her revelations.

The church of St Michael has an unusual tower, the lower parts of which are roughly shaped Sarsen stone, not commonly used for building because it is so hard. The upper parts are puddingstone (with lots of pebbles in) with brick on the buttresses, corners and crenellation. The tower and the north aisle are early 16th century; the memorial to John Cresswell who died in 1518 states that he was 'lord of this towne at the tyme of byldyng of this steple and the new yle'. 15th century Purbeck Marble font, and lots of memorials including three early 17th century ones with small kneeling figures.

★ ★ *Church for odd building materials and unusual date.*

HEDGE END (J) The enclosure of Botley Common in 1863, led to the establishment of Hedge End village, but the few scattered Victorian villas, a pub and the church are now lost in a sea of modern development. There is little left of the strawberry growing and horticulture which thrived here for the century after enclosure. Bricks were made here too. The name presumably comes from its having been beyond the end of the hedges or enclosed ground. The church of St John the Evangelist is in the south-western part, stone with a spire but all of 1874. There are rather more Victorian villas in this part.

Cottages at Herriard dated 1824

HERRIARD (E) All through the hamlet is parkland, a reminder of the demolished big house. Opposite the church are several faintly classical brick cottages dated 1827 and 1828. The church of St Mary is mostly 1876, but the Norman entrance doorway and big chancel arch are partly original. 13th century chancel with lancets. A little medieval glass in a a square window in the chancel, but much more 1950s glass. Pretty 17th century screen now around the organ.

HIGHCLERE (A/B) Best known for its large mansion, set in a huge park. The village is to the west, with the occasional thatched cottage, but most of the houses are obscured by the many trees and hedges. The church of St Michael is on the edge of the park, near the village, and is a replacement of 1870. Low and dark inside, with (unusually) a rose window at the east end, and an elaborate reredos with stone surrounds and paintings. Up by the altar a big monument to Robert Sawyer who died in 1692, theatrical curtains and so on, typical of the date. By the entrance is a memorial to Richard Kingsmill, also large, but Elizabethan. Sawyer and Kingsmill both owned Highclere, and their portraits can be seen in the castle. Plain wall tablet by the door to the 6th Earl of Carnarvon who died in 1987. Peculiar monument in the south aisle with a black urn and two books, part of the memorial to Thomas Milles (d.1740).

Highclere Castle is a mansion (the largest in the county) not a castle at all. In medieval times there was a bishop's palace here on the site of the present house.

The current entrance passes over the new main road on a high bridge, as if it were passing over a moat. The park is massive and beautiful. Even Cobbett (who hated the owners) admired it 'according

to my fancy, the prettiest park that I have ever seen. A great variety of hill and dell. A good deal of water' (1821). Good trees, with lots of large cedars on the way in, grown from seed brought back from the Lebanon in the 18th century. Many other varieties too, some of them carefully grouped by Capability Brown who landscaped the park in the 1770s. The closely planted avenue is of lime. Sidown Hill to the south is covered with trees, and on the top is Heaven's Gate, an eyecatcher or folly of three arches, now reduced to its brick core. Beacon Hill, further round, is bare downland.

The house, despite its great size, looks like an architectural model, partly because it is set in a vast lawn, and partly because it is so regular. It was rebuilt in 1840 to designs by Sir Charles Barry, the architect who designed the new Houses of Parliament in 1835. Barry used an Elizabethan style, but imposed classical regularity on it. It is this symmetry and the windows (wrongly proportioned for Elizabethan) which stop Highclere looking like a 16th century house.

The vast interior is not by Barry, but a less well-known architect Thomas Allom, who was employed from 1860 by the son of the earl who built the house. The entrance is through a small Gothic vaulted room, with rich marble columnettes and paved floor. The huge library is fitted in imitation early 18th

Richard Kingsmill's monument, Highclere church

A temple in the grounds of Highclere Castle

century style, similar to that of the 18th century house demolished to make way for this one. A desk and chair belonging to Napoleon are in this room. The Music Room is decorated with 18th century ceiling, embroideries etc preserved from the old house, and displays a selection of material about the family. The Drawing Room is of 1900, in rococo style, with many family portraits including Richard Kingsmill who owned Highclere in the 16th century.

Upstairs many bedrooms are open to visitors. The main staircase is impressive with good woodwork, but the central hall does not succeed as a Gothic ensemble. Parts are good, but the greenhouse roof is incongruous, and the design weak. The dining room is in Jacobethan style (a Victorian combination of Jacobean and Elizabethan) with many fine portraits including Charles I and Robert Sawyer who owned Highclere in the 17th century. In the basement is a display of ancient Egyptian material, a tiny part of the discoveries made by the 5th Earl of Carnarvon early this century. He and Howard Carter found the tomb of Tutenkahmun in 1922, the pinnacle of their work. Most of the 5th Earl's collection was sold after his death, but these artefacts were rediscovered in 1987 sealed in a cupboard between the Drawing Room and the Smoking Room. Part of the servants' quarters are on display.

The flower gardens are a little way from the house, and include a white border, the 'secret' garden, and a glasshouse with many exotics. Jackdaw's Castle is a Greek temple built in 1743 with columns from Berkeley House, Piccadilly, a typical park ornament.

★ ★ ★ ★ *A perfect park, the house less beautiful but worth seeing.*

HIGH CROSS (K) Wide chalk valleys, still with many hedges, a calm landscape. Several tile hung cottages besides the flint and brick ones. The small church of St Peter is 1862 with an oddly octagonal tower, all neat flint, with some Norman inside moved here from the old church at Froxfield Green.

HIGHFIELD see SOUTHAMPTON NORTH

HILL HEAD (N) Now a large area of housing, stretching back from houses on the shore until it joins up with Stubbington, but until 1900 it was simply 'a few cottages and fishermen's sheds at Titchfield Haven' (VCH). This western end, the mouth of the river Meon, is still wild because **Titchfield Haven** is a nature reserve. The estuary has been protected from the sea since 1612 when the Earl of Southampton, who owned Titchfield and the estuary, built the wall and sluice gates to improve the grazing, and also constructed a canal parallel with the river from Titchfield to the sea. This was very early for canal building, which didn't take place on a large scale until the 18th century. Remains of the canal's course and some masonry can be seen off the road north to Titchfield, close to the first severe bend in the road (see also **TITCHFIELD**)

The Nature Reserve covers more than 300 acres of reedbed, freshwater marsh and fen, right up the river Meon to Titchfield and is particularly good for over-wintering wildfowl, gulls and waders. Regular tours around part of the reserve are offered (fee:lists) and start from the information centre just north of the little harbour. A footpath runs along outside the southern part of the reserve and gives good views of it, and another path continues north to Titchfield (see canal above).

The tiny harbour and sluices have been much altered since the 17th century, but the gates still prevent the rising tide from entering the marshes. The harbour houses a few yachts.

Extensive views from all along the shore to the Isle of Wight, with the open water of Spithead to the left, and Solent right with Southampton Water behind. Fawley Power Station and the oil refinery are clearly seen on the other side of Southampton Water.

Hill Head seems far more rural than its neighbour Lee-on-Solent, with winding roads which descend to the shore and much more scrub and trees. The houses on the front are less formally arranged, and some are right down on the shore. Only a few shops in the middle.

1,000 acres of farmland to the west of Hillhead are managed as a nature reserve called Brownwich and Chilling. Many footpaths have been created, some leading from the car parks inland at Thatcher's Copse (off the road from Titchfield Haven to Titchfield) and Hook Lane (further west) to the shore. Parts of the woodlands are now being coppiced again, and trees and hedges replanted. In the middle of the reserve is Brownwich Pond, good for wildfowl and waterlilies.

★ ★ ★ *Area for walking.*

HILLIER GARDEN & ARBORETUM (H) (near Ampfield, east of Romsey) A vast garden established by the Hillier family of nursery fame, given to the County Council and now open to the public (fee:lists). The formal name arboretum is slightly off-putting, but much of the area is laid out as gardens, and the tree plantings are interesting. All the plants are labelled, and the gardens are good at all times of the year. Bulbs and smaller plants are used as well as the shrubs and trees that Hillier's are famous for, all laid out in walks, a bog garden, pond and so on. The undulating ground gives good vistas, and several areas have mature oaks. The Brantrey Woodland to the south is only open in late spring for its azaleas.

Now covering 160 acres, this must be the best garden in Hampshire, well worth repeated visits at different seasons. Spring is magical, and the autumn colouring spectacular.

★ ★ ★ ★ *For the gardens, probably the best in the county.*

HINTON ADMIRAL (L) Park-like, because of the trees of the big house, away behind the church. Tiny village, with good brick houses. The church of St Michael is all brick, pretty 18th century classical tower, rest c. 1875 and Gothic with an especially good stone reredos. Short avenue of big trees up to the church.

HINTON AMPNER (J) Simply a hamlet, running up the hill to the big house, with several estate cottages. The church of All Saints is close to the house, and almost seems part of the park. Pretty wooden bellcote of 1879. The church was restored then, but on the north and south walls single pilaster strips (vertical narrow bands) show that this part of the building is late Saxon. Inside, towards the west end, is a simple round-headed doorway of the same date, with a door inscribed 'Nicholas Lacy gave this door February 1643', made in the first year of the Civil War. The building is plain inside, with lots of good memorials, some brought from the demolished church at Laverstoke. Katherine Stekely who died in 1679 has perhaps the best: a bust sheltering in a curtained niche. The inscriptions are worth reading.

Opposite is a spirited 1935 monument, and up by the altar a fine black slab for Ralph Dutton who died in 1985 (see the house). Two monuments to children, one a baby of ten days who died in 1601, with an effigy, and another closer to the altar. Lots of brasses with inscriptions. Jacobean pulpit, elaborately carved. Stunning 1970 stained glass in the east windows.

The house (fee:lists) is close to the church, looking handsome and authentically Georgian, but in fact built in 1937 and reconstructed after a fire in 1960. There had been a manor house here from Tudor times, and a small Georgian house was swamped in the 1860s by being enclosed in a much larger Victorian Tudor house. When Ralph Dutton inherited in

The drawing room, Hinton Ampner

1936 he reduced and rebuilt his grandfather's house creating what must be the best neo-Georgian house in the country, furnished with a connoisseur's collection of fittings, paintings and furniture. The Drawing Room is the finest room, with window shutters from the Adelphi, London (built by the Adam brothers) and doorcases and fireplaces from another late 18th century house. Wonderful furniture all through the house, much of it Regency and handsome carpets.

Ralph Dutton started planting the trees in the park even before he inherited, and the view from the terrace in front of the house is down a valley of classic English parkland, with hardly a cottage visible. The gardens are a mixture of formality and more wild parts, and the gardens seem much larger than they really are because of the close plantings. Views from many parts. Ralph Dutton's book *A Hampshire Manor* (1968) describes the rebuildings of the house and the making of the garden, as well as the history of Hinton Ampner.

★ ★ ★ ★ *House.*

H.M.S. MERCURY (J) (4 miles east of Droxford). Not a ship but a naval base isolated amongst the downs east of the Meon Valley. The road runs right through the middle. Here all the Navy's communications specialists are trained.

HOLYBOURNE (F) Alton has expanded to meet this village, but the middle is still villagy, with a good variety of houses and cottages. The novelist Mrs Gaskell (*North and South* etc) bought a large house in Holybourne in 1865, and died there the same year. Right by the church is a large pond fed by springs – the holy bourne of the name. Originally it bubbled up right next to the church entrance. Springs were holy places in pre-Christian times, and this is an interesting association of Christian Church and pagan site.

Norman tower, with a 19th century spire on top. Inside, the big aisle makes it lop-sided. Good corbels with heads, 14th century, hold up the roof of the nave.

★ *Church.*

Holybourne pond and church

HOOK (N) (South Hampshire near Hill Head) A remarkably unspoilt rural hamlet, and an odd one as it was the adjunct to a large house which burnt down in 1905 leaving only the cottages. The Nook (now a shop) was the wheelwright's workshop with an 18th century house attached, and the row of cottages with elaborate glazing are estate cottages of 1846. These are around the tiny triangular green, and just off it is the blacksmith's house and Old Smithy.

The Hook Valley, the shore and much of the area inland is part of a large nature reserve. The shore has many specialised sea-side plants, and inland towards Warsash are woodlands.

HOOK (C) (North Hampshire) Little here from before the Second World War. The White Hart is the exception, a fine 18th century inn, with unusually the bay window (supported on columns) weather boarded. Brick church of 1937. A few Victorian cottages. Woods to the south, now bisected by M3.

HORDLE (M) has the odd thatched cottage and earlier brick house to remind one this was once part of the New Forest, but it is mostly modern development, admittedly with many trees. The church of All Saints is in the rather separate southern part, brick and stone of 1872, with pretty contemporary fittings including the pulpit, reredos with good tesserae and the organ case. Good new embroidery of the village school.

HORNDEAN (K) started as a hamlet on the junction of the roads from London to Portsmouth and Emsworth/Havant, but the motorway now acts as a by-pass. There are a few Victorian flint or Georgian brick houses and cottages, but the dominating building is Gale's Brewery, mostly dating from 1869 with an assertive brick tower right on the main road. The street eastwards is rural, and up the hill towards Blendworth is parkland. Horndean was the terminus of the tramway from Portsmouth, and from 1903 when the service started many cafes were set up to supply teas to those who came out from the city for the woodland walks which abounded in the area.

HORSEBRIDGE (H/D) A hamlet right down on the River Test, which amazingly had a railway station (line now closed). The Test is wide, shallow and beautiful here, crossed by a bridge which is

certainly wide enough for a horse. The bridge had its slope increased greatly to put the road at the right angle to cross over the railway. Horsebridge Mill is large, red brick and early 19th century. Just to the south along the Test footpath is Horsebridge station, beautifully preserved even down to a parcels office (private: not open but visible from the footpath).

HOUGHTON (D/H) A single street running parallel with the River Test, rather spread out. At the southern end Houghton Mill, Georgian and classical, the side away from the road having a pediment. The river is large here. The main street has some thatch, with plain brick or brick and timber framing, along with many Edwardian cottages, presumably estate cottages. The church is up a side street, surrounded by large houses and their garden walls. The church of All Saints has a 19th century timber spire and shingled tower, and although the church is basically medieval much of the detail is 19th century.

Houghton Lodge to the north of the village, off the Stockbridge Road was built in the late 18th century as a big fishing lodge. The house is deliberately picturesque in style, with odd roofs, tall chimneys and decorative windows. The gardens are open to the public (fee:lists). Major features include the acre walled garden, enclosed by cob walls, the sweeping lawns which descend to the river, and a proper shrubbery with large trees. At the far end of the shrubbery is a flint grotto. A hydroponicum, growing plants in water, has recently been constructed.

★ ★ ★ *Gardens, picturesque.*

ABOVE *Horsebridge Mill*
BELOW *Houghton Lodge*
BOTTOM *Flint folly at Houghton Lodge*

ABOVE   *St Catherine's Hill*
LEFT   *St Cross Church, Winchester*
BELOW   *Winchester Cathedral*

TOP LEFT   *Exbury Gardens*
LEFT   *Mottisfont*
BELOW LEFT   *Waggoners Wells*
TOP RIGHT   *Jenkyn Place, Bentley*
ABOVE   *Breamore Countryside Museum*
BELOW   *The River Test*

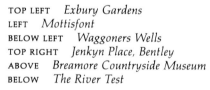

ABOVE *Keyhaven marshes.*   BELOW *Westgate, Southampton*

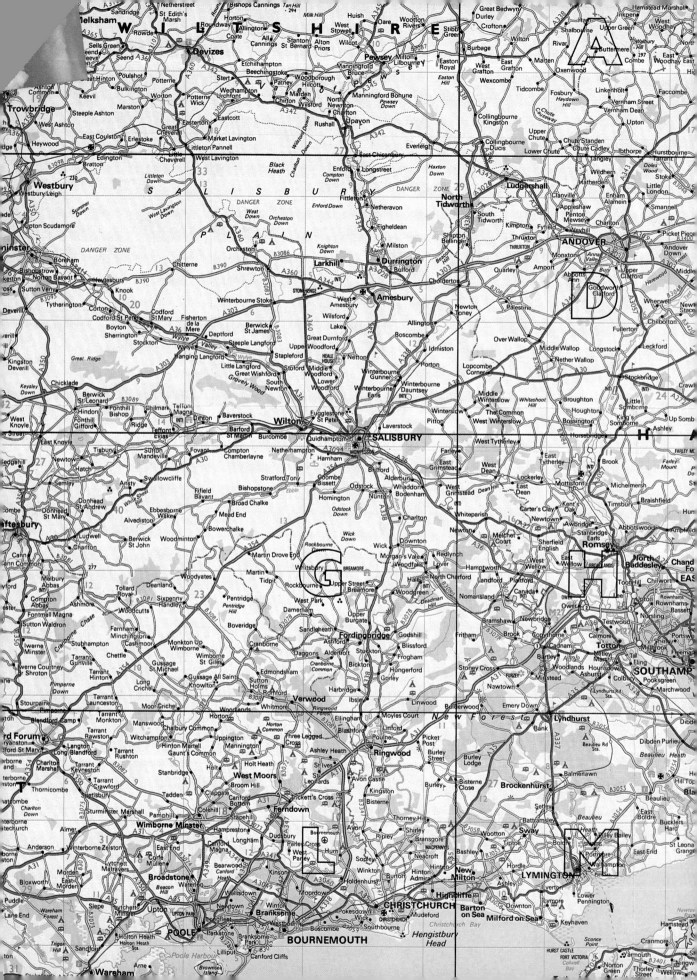

LEFT   *Highclere Castle*
ABOVE   *The windmill, Bursledon*
BELOW   *Palace House, Beaulieu*

ABOVE   HMS Victory
TOP RIGHT   *Portsmouth Point*
BELOW   *Southampton Docks*
RIGHT   *Buckler's Hard, Beaulieu River*

ABOVE *Deer in the New Forest.* BELOW *Early morning, New Forest*

HOUND (J/N) A vast but empty parish until Netley developed. The land is not good agriculturally, and only supported a small hamlet. The area around the church is still quite empty and rural. The church of St Mary survives as a simple medieval building because a new church at Netley was built in the 1880s. St Mary's church Hound is just a nave and chancel, basically 13th century with characteristic simple lancet windows, even in the east. The simplicity of the church is the ideal setting for the superb modern stained glass of the chancel, all by Patrick Reyntiens (see Odiham). The east windows are of 1959, a stunning composition of bright colours combined with painted lines. The side windows have slightly different colouring and are more abstract.

★ ★ *Church, tiny but with some of the best modern glass in the county.*

HUNTON (E) (just north of Stoke Charity) A hamlet in the valley of the River Dever, with a few timber framed cottages, some thatched, and the big house. The tiny church of St James is beside by the river, Georgian brick and earlier flint, very simple inside. The road east runs beside the river, and is picturesque.

HURSLEY (H) A village full of good brick buildings ranging from the 17th to the 19th century, a few timber framed, others with a little tile hanging. Some of the new houses are of good design too.

The village is well known for two different reasons. Since 1958 Hursley Park House has belonged to IBM, who have increased the buildings there considerably, housing their development laboratories. Vickers used the house in the Second World War for aircraft development, including the Spitfire. However, the most famous person associated with the village is John Keble (1792-1866) who was vicar here from 1836-66. He was one of the leaders of the church reform movement of the 1830s and 40s which transformed and revitalised the Church of England. The reforms led to more ritual at services, more services being held, resident 'professional' clergy, and great changes in the design of church buildings. Guided by the architect Pugin, the movement decided that some types of architecture were more Christian than others: classical churches were wrong. 'Correct' Gothic architecture was supposed to emphasise the Church's antiquity

and continuity. Many churches were 'restored' or completely rebuilt to fit in with these ideas, and Hursley, designed for Keble, is a good (and early) example of what the Oxford movement thought a church should be. Most of the church was classical Georgian brick: this had to go, but the west tower was preserved from the earlier church and the rest was designed to match. The neat building was finished in 1848. Inside the church is wide and light, with a high narrow roof, timber and elaborate. The complete set of stained glass commissioned for the church just after it was built survives. Really elaborate pulpit, font and cover, all contemporary with the building. Brass memorial to Keble on the chancel floor. He paid for the building of the church with the proceeds from his book of hymns *The Christian Year*, first published in 1827 and so successful that it went through 95 editions in his lifetime. A second collection, *Lyra Innocentium*, was published in 1846, specifically to help pay for the building. Keble had been professor of poetry at Oxford 1831-41, and his major memorial is Keble College Oxford.

Keble is buried outside the south-west corner of the church, beside the path to the vicarage, under a granite slab with a foliated cross. Nearby is a huge mausoleum of 1797. The (ex) vicarage is Victorian flint and brick, faintly classical.

Inside the church, under the tower, is a classical memorial to the Cromwell family. Richard Cromwell, Oliver's son, married the daughter of the owner of Merdon Manor, the forerunner of Hursley Park House. He was made Lord Protector after his father's death in 1658, but withdrew to exile in France for 20 years from 1660. Subsequently he lived partly at Hursley, and was buried there in 1712. The Cromwell family left Hursley in 1718, and the development of what had been only a manor house into a large mansion began.

The minor road running west from the north end of the village passes very close to Merdon Castle, an Iron Age earthwork adapted by the Bishop of Winchester as a castle in 1138, during the Anarchy of Stephen's reign.

To the south-east of Hursley is another mansion, set in a park. **Cranbury Park** is a huge crimson brick house, built in the 1790s and designed by George Dance. A footpath leads through the park, which is wooded all around a vast grassy area in the middle dotted with trees. A distant view of the house is possible, and the

The follies at Cranbury Park

footpath makes a good walk. The access from the east is strange: from the car park at Otterbourne Hill, west of the road, the footpath is taken over the Chandlers Ford bypass (a very busy road) by a high bridge. Past a pretty Swiss cottage lodge, and through the wood, the main house comes into view, and the footpath passes close to a little stone tower (with a house attached) and some ruinous arches. These were built in the 1760s as ornaments to the park, to look romantic from the house. They were built from the ruins of Netley Abbey, and include genuine medieval masonry.

★ ★ *Village and church*

HURSTBOURNE PRIORS (D) Along the Bourne valley and spreading along the crossroads, brick and flint houses and cottages, a few still thatched. To the east the woods of Hurstbourne Park, the big house. Right by the church a cricket ground with thatched pavilion. This is a famous area for fishing, chronicled in the fishing classic *Where Bright Waters Meet* (1924) by Harry Plunket Greene (1865-1936) the singer and fisherman.

An avenue leads down the short drive to St Andrew's church, with its entertaining mock Norman brick tower of 1870, styled to fit with the real Norman doorway. The arch to the north chapel is handsome Norman, probably originally the chancel arch. In the arch is the Oxenbridge tomb of 1574, large and impressive with two effigies and much decoration. The children are in a frieze below, those who died before their parents carrying skulls.

The north chapel behind is Elizabethan, simple and un-churchy. Early 13th century chancel.

★ ★ *Church for Norman, neo-Norman and monument.*

Hurst Castle from the air

HURSTBOURNE TARRANT (A/D) A

really pretty village, and a favourite place
of William Cobbett, who stopped here
often when writing *Rural Rides*. He
usually referred to it by its old name of
Uphusband. Anna Lea Merritt's *A Hamlet
in Old Hampshire* (1902) describes life in
the village in the late 19th century. She
died in 1930 and there is a memorial
plaque in the church. Jane Austen often
visited the village when staying at
Ibthorpe.

The main road descends steeply into the
village, which lies along the wide valley,
with the smooth chalk hills rising each side.
Lots of thatched cottages line the stream,
which only runs intermittently. Bigger
Georgian brick houses, a fine one to the
west of the church with impressive brick
gatepiers dated 1685. This is Rectory Farm,
and next to it are big thatched barns, some
weatherboarded. In the large yard a little
timber-framed granary on steddle stones.
The Rectory the other side of the church is
smaller scale, but has a pretty brick and
flint stable yard. Opposite is the Victorian
brick and flint school.

The church of St Peter has domestic
clerestory windows added in the 17th
century, a weatherboarded tower and a

late Norman doorway with lots of
patterning. Inside it is all medieval, and
although restored (and the chancel
altered) in 1890 the size and shape are the
same as when Jane Austen came to
services. Big timbers at the west end to
hold up the 15th century tower, 13th
century round pillars, and lots of 15th
century plain bench ends. Doubtless the
14th century wallpaintings were covered
with whitewash in Jane Austen's time
They show the quick (live) and the dead
(skeletons), and the Wheel of the seven
deadly sins, less well preserved and with a
text painted over part of it. The big
George III Royal Coat of Arms would
have been new when Jane Austen was
here, and in the chancel are memorials to
the then rector, Peter Debarry and his
four daughters who she refers to in letters
as 'the endless Debaries' and whose visits
she avoided returning, with excuses such
as: 'It is not an uncommon circumstance in
this parish to have the road from Ibthorp
to the parsonage much dirtier and more
impracticable for walking than the road
from the parsonage to Ibthorp'.

Rookery Farm, where Cobbett often
stayed, is just to the south-west of the
cross-roads in the middle, on the Andover

road, easy to spot because rooks still nest
there.

Ibthorpe is up the valley from
Hurstbourne Tarrant and seems
remarkably unchanged. Thatched cottages
of brick and flint with some timber
framing, all very neat, with the higher
land on either side still wildish. There are
a couple of larger Georgian houses – the
one higher up the valley is Ibthorpe
House where Jane Austen stayed.

★ ★ ★ ★ *Village with Ibthorpe, for itself
and Jane Austen, William Cobbett
associations.*

HURST CASTLE (M) (east of Milford-
on-Sea) Hurst spit is a long thin gravel
ridge which protrudes half way across the
Solent to the Isle of Wight. The channel
between the two is only ¾ mile wide, but
has two deep water channels and a tidal
race fierce enough to bring ships to a
standstill. The marshes which have
formed behind the spit are an important
nature reserve especially for birds, and the
head of the spit has been used since the
16th century as the site of a fort to guard
the Solent from hostile ships.

The fort can be reached either by
walking the mile and a half along the spit,

or by the ferry from Keyhaven. The whole area is flat, so that sea and marsh unite.

The middle of Hurst Castle is one of Henry VIII's small forts like the one at Calshot. Hurst was more complex, having a twelve sided tower in the centre surrounded by a single storey outer part and a moat. The moat has gone, but the rest survives.

The entrance is in one of the big wings added to the original fort in 1861-75, over a drawbridge which has a narrow gauge railway running across it. The railway was installed in the 1880s to make transporting the heavy ammunition for the huge guns easier.

To the left of the entrance is the 16th century castle (built 1541-4), now half submerged in the 19th century work. The original gateway is still used. The central tower was greatly altered inside in 1803, when the fort was repaired and brought up-to-date. The brick vaulting and the central brick pier with staircase date from this time. Guns would have been housed on the roof, much altered, which gives panoramic views of the Solent and the Isle of Wight, with the redbrick Fort Albert (1850s) clear on the Isle of Wight and the Needles to the right.

Two of the original bastions can be seen: the third (seaward) was filled with concrete to make it stronger in the 1850s. All three originally contained at least two tiers of guns.

The fort was adapted 1803 and again in 1850-6, but the later alterations were immediately outdated by improvements in explosive shells, and the big wings were added either side of the Henrician fort in 1861-75 to house huge new guns. There were housings for 30 big guns, each with a massive iron shield outside set in the granite masonry, all to protect them from ships firing back.

On the back wall are two lighthouses: the metal one dating from 1911, a re-placement for the 1865 brick one. There has been a lighthouse on Hurst since 1786, but the large independent one to the north dates from 1865. The building at the base of the large one was for generating acetylene for the light. The small houses on the spit were for the lighthouse keepers. From the late 18th century there was an inn here, and several other cottages, making up a small perma-nent community, as well as soldiers garri-soned in the fort, which went on in use until the end of the Second World War.

★ ★ ★ *Hurst Castle, for the odd landscape and the castle itself.*

HYDE (G) (1½ miles south-east of Fordingbridge) Quite a dense village, just into the Forest, hilly and woody. On the common between Hyde and Frogham is the cricket pitch. Off the common, away from the village, is the church of Holy Ascension, 1855, grey and red brick with complex window tracery. Blissford and Stockton to the north are similarly hilly and woody hamlets.

HYTHE (M) Enormously expanded since 1945. The old part is down by Southampton Water, but apart from the pier and the recent promenade, the town ignores the sea. The High Street runs parallel to the shore, blocking it.

Ferries run from Southampton to Hythe about every half hour during the day, tying up at the 700 yard pier of 1879 which has a small electric railway communicating with the land. Tiny carriages. The middle of the town has nice 18th and first half of the 19th century buildings, mostly rather plain. Prospect Place on the north and St John's Street to the south are as good as the High Street. All buildings are small scale: the pedestrianised High Street is so narrow that it is difficult to imagine how traffic managed. At the southern end of the High Street is a modern development, with The Promenade behind, which gives extensive views over Southampton Water

The railway on Hythe Pier

with the town, its industries and docks northwards, and more rural bits southwards. Hythe itself has a shipyard and other industries fronting the shore. It was the maintenance base for Southamptons flying boats into the 1950s when services ceased.

The church of St John is a big brick building with stone dressings of 1874.

IBSLEY (G/L) In the Avon valley. Lots of thatch and timber framing. The small brick church of St Martin is much later – 1832. One good monument of 1627 to Sir John Constable. He and his wife kneel with a large fruiting vine between them, from which biblically spring busts of their five children. Slender stone bridge (Georgian) over the river to Harbridge.

Moyle's Court ¾ mile to the south is a big mid 17th century brick house, now a school. Dame Alice Lisle lived here (see Ellingham). Good brick garden walls. Very wooded area. Gravel workings, some now lakes between Moyle's Court and Ibsley.

IDSWORTH (K) (1½ miles south of Chalton). The village and even the big house have moved or disappeared, leaving the little church of St Hubert standing alone in the fields. Happily it was completely neglected in the 19th century and so escaped heavy-handed restoration.

What remains of the settlement is in a wide valley, fringed by woods on the east with the county boundary on top. The buildings to the south of the church are the remains of the manor house and its walled gardens. A new house, Idsworth House, was built to the west in 1852 to be away from the railway which runs along the bottom of the valley, regularly shattering the rural silence. The 1852 house can be seen from the road to Horndean, large, brick, neo-Jacobean.

The church is set back from the road, and the field in front of it was probably the site of the deserted village of Idsworth. At the bottom of the grassy path are duckboards to cross what is now an intermittent stream. Inside the little porch the door is stiff and the handle obstinate, but persevere because the interior is worth seeing. Basically this is a small Norman church of nave and chancel, all simple and typical of many built at that time. Few survive, as they have been extended and rebuilt. On the north side is a little Norman window and further along a door. The other side wall was rebuilt in the 16th century.

Idsworth

The interior and fittings seem untouched, but in fact they were sensitively restored in 1914. The west gallery is mostly of that date, and on one of the beams underneath is an inscription recording the restoration. The rest of the woodwork dates from the 17th or 18th centuries. The box pews and simple benches are largely original, as is the pulpit with its pretty scrolled supports for the shelf.

On the plastered frame in the middle of the ceiling (it supports the bell-turret) is a Royal coat of arms with an inscription recording 'this chapel restored' 1795 and 1824. The east window and two of the north windows are very simple Gothic in wood and presumably date from one of these restorations. The chancel tie-beams had classical trim added in Georgian times, but the charming homespun plaster ceiling with its medallions dates from 1914, an amazingly convincing reproduction.

In the chancel are 14th century wall-paintings which survived because of 19th century neglect. Around the east window are two large figures of St Peter and St Paul (the original dedication of the church) with angels above. On the north wall two tiers of scenes probably represent the life of St Hubert as he cured a madman who thought he was a wolf and there is a wolf-like animal with a man's face. The lower tier depicts scenes from the life of St John the Baptist, with Salome dancing with swords in front (and looking as if she is about to break in half) and the head of St John being presented to Herod. These scenes are very lively, a contrast to the serene saints around the east window.

★ ★ ★ *Church for its fittings, wall-painting and setting.*

ITCHEN ABBAS (E) seems to consist of large modern houses, with lots of trees. A few old cottages with timber framing. The church of St John the Baptist is down by the river Itchen, and is in an individual neo-Norman style of the 1860s, incorporating original Norman work from the old church in the outer arch of the porch and the chancel arch. In the south-east corner of the churchyard, close to an ancient yew, is the grave of John Hughes who died in 1825, the last person to be hanged in England for horse stealing. W.H. Hudson, the naturalist, lived nearby for three months in 1900, when he was writing part of *Hampshire Days* (1903), a chapter of which describes the Itchen, its flowers and wildlife.

John Hughes gravestone at Itchen Abbas: the last man hanged for horse stealing

ITCHEN BRIDGE see **CROSSHOUSE, SOUTHAMPTON CENTRAL.**

ITCHEN NAVIGATION (H/J) Even before the 18th century when canals were built transport by water was important. Some rivers were improved, with locks and even partially new courses, to make them suitable for barges. The Itchen is one of these navigations, built in the late 17th century from Winchester to Woodmill, Swathling from whence the barges used the wide estuary of the Itchen to reach Southampton. The Navigation also supplied water for water-meadows all along its route. The usual cargo in the 19th century was coal to Winchester, where Blackbridge Wharf, the terminus of the navigation, still survives. The navigation was never busy, and the construction of a railway along the same route in 1840 removed most of the traffic. The last barges ceased operating in 1869. Much of the 10½ mile route is a footpath and can still be traced, perhaps most impressively at Shawford. See also Swaythling, Otterbourne, Winchester.

ITCHEN STOKE (E/J) A small village, with lots of thatch and timber framing, flint and brick. Rather too much traffic. Opposite the church the school house, an all flint cottage, unusually with huge flints making the arches over the windows.

The stone church of St Mary sits high above the road, looking tall and un-English. It was rebuilt in 1866 to the design of the vicar's brother, in miniature imitation of the exquisite 13th century La Sainte Chapelle, attached to the Royal palace in Paris. Inside a porch runs the width of the building, with low stone benches. These and the coloured marble columns and dense decoration of the walls give an odd effect in such a confined space. The main church is more effective, tall and thin like French churches. Only the apse really gives anything of the effect of Sainte Chapelle, with vivid blue and red glass like the original. The lower parts of the walls have a dense small scale flower pattern carved in the stone, the roof has complex painting and the floor good patterned tiles. The west wall, with simplified rose window above is extremely decorative. Behind the altar is golden glass, and the floor is a maze represented by tiles. On the pulpit and the bench ends are complex cast-iron decorations, originally gilded. The font is flamboyant black marble from California, with white and honey coloured stone as

ABOVE *The Itchen Navigation near Shawford*
BELOW *Itchen Stoke church*

well. Remnants of enamelled inserts.

Two good brasses of women on the west wall, one kneeling, of about 1500, the other Joan Batmanson who died in 1518.

In the churchyard sheets of wild daffodils. A path down to the river, nearly opposite the church, leads along the river to Ovington, ½ mile away.

★ ★ ★ *Church.*

ITCHEN VALLEY COUNTRY PARK

(north of the M27, east of junction 5, south of Eastleigh) 400 acres of meadows and woodland, with way-marked paths. Adventure playground for children, and displays about the natural history in the visitor centre (free:lists), a new building constructed like an old barn from oak felled by the 1987 storm. Guided walks and other events.

★ ★ ★ *A bit noisy because of the motorway.*

KEYHAVEN (M) A hamlet on the mainland, with the marshes caused by Hurst spit in front. Low-lying, and consisting of a few Georgian cottages and some more recent ones. The Gun Inn has a cannon on its signboard, referring to the armaments of Hurst Castle out on the spit, but it could have been a punt gun since the wild-fowl hunting in the marshes was always popular. Next door is Hawker's Cottage, built by Colonel Peter Hawker (1786-1853) one of the most famous 19th century sportsmen. His published diary makes shocking reading today – killing 16 coot with one shot, or in eight weeks of the winter of 1829, 574 wildfowl including swans, geese, ducks etc and 29 waders.

There are many boats here, and the extensive marshes support a large population of birds including wild fowl and breeding colonies of black-headed gulls and little terns. Ferries run to Hurst Castle regularly in the summer, and boats to the Isle of Wight are also available in season. See also **HURST CASTLE**

KILMESTON (J) One of the few villages on the sparsely populated chalk downs west of the Meon Valley. Spread out, the southern part with park-like fields and a large plain Georgian brick house. The cottages are varied, brick and flint, stuccoed, tile hung and even a few thatched timber-framed ones. Many 19th century estate cottages, and a couple of big farmsteads. The church of St Andrew is towards the north end of the village, very plain and of 1876. Opposite the church Kilmeston Manor, redbrick of the early 18th century, extended and heightened late the same century. From the road just below the church is a fine view of Hinton Ampner house.

KIMPTON (D) A small straggling village, but rural, and picturesque close to the church, with a green (the pump surviving in one corner) a little stream and a long curving blank cob wall, the back of thatched farm buildings. Beyond the church are open meadows. The path to the church leads past the brick and flint chequered wall of the central farmhouse which has a Georgianised front on a much earlier jettied house.

The church of St Peter and St Paul has a tower dated 1837 in panelled brick and flint, a style more commonly found in cottages and houses in the area around. The rest of the church is medieval, although the brick outer wall of the aisle is a rebuild of 1702. Inside the arches of the aisle simply die away into the supports: no pillars. The chancel is 13th century, with some simple lancet windows and the small tomb chest with brasses of Robert Thornburgh (died 1522) and his two wives, one with two children and the other a crowd. English inscription. Behind the altar a very rural wall monument of 1658 with pick, shovel, hour glass and skull and cross-bones. 1812 Royal coat of arms.

★ ★ *Church and setting.*

Kimpton church

The Navy and the Sea

Hampshire's long coastline, with the enclosed harbours of Langstone and Portsmouth, sheltered estuaries and so on, has been used by Navys since Roman times, with Porchester Castle built as a naval base in the third century AD. From late medieval times Portsmouth was the main base of the emerging English Navy.

Portsmouth and Gosport in particular have been dominated by the Navy since the Royal Dockyard was established in the 17th century, with both towns expanding rapidly as the Navy grew. The history of the Navy is superbly displayed in the Royal Naval Museum, Portsmouth, and at Eastney (Portsmouth) the Royal Marine Museum traces the history of these naval soldiers.

Gosport was the supply depot for the Navy, with victualling yards, powder stores and so on, and the Naval Hospital at Halsar, a huge classical 18th century building. Gosport became the base for submarines, and has the Royal Navy Submarine museum, with several submarines on display.

Although the Dockyard is closed, Portsmouth remains a major naval base, so there is always shipping passing in and out of the harbour. The Dockyard is one of the most interesting places in the county to visit, with three historic ships, two museums, and the

Horatio Nelson

surprising number of the old Dockyard buildings to survive wartime bombing.

The *Mary Rose* is the earliest ship, Tudor and famously recovered recently from the bed of the Solent. A fine museum displays her contents and explains the history of the ship. *HMS Victory* was Nelson's flagship at Trafalgar (1805), the great naval battle which he won, but died at. His cabins are still furnished as they were in his time.

The third ship, *HMS Warrior*, of the mid 19th century, has been completely refitted, down to all the plates for each mess and is the most atmospheric of the ships.

The Navy have never had a monopoly of the Hampshire coast: Southampton has always been a commercial port, and even Portsmouth has dealt with a little cargo. Today the distinction between Portsmouth as naval and Southampton as commercial is still true in broad terms, with the huge new container port at Southampton, but Portsmouth now has large numbers of ferries. Southampton Maritime Museum has superb displays on the history of Southampton Docks etc.

The sheltered anchorages, harbours and estuaries, along with an easy supply of oak from the coastal forests led to Hampshire becoming a ship-building county. Bucklers Hard, near Beaulieu, is the best place to see displays of the peak of the industry in the 18th century, and boat building and ship fitting still survives at places like Bursledon and Woolston, Southampton.

Royal Naval Submarine Museum, Gosport

The most romantic part of the history of the coast (at least with hindsight) is the smuggling, which was certainly carried on almost as a normal business, at many of the smaller coastal places, particularly the lawless New Forest. Langstone still feels like a smuggler's haunt, and indeed was one. Many places inland have reputed smuggler's storage places and secluded paths called Smugglers Walk or some such whereby the booty was taken inland for sale

The smaller coastal places like Langstone, Lymington, Emsworth and so on were ports in medieval times, but now they, with the Hamble estuary (the largest and most important of them all) are mostly yachting centres. Some attempts were made to involve Hampshire's coast in the new 18th century fashion for sea-bathing. Southampton was for a while a spa, and Regency seaside terraces were built at Alverstoke and Hayling. Southsea developed as a resort in the later 19th century, but it was not until this century that Hayling and the extreme west of the county around Milford on Sea became popular holiday areas.

★ ★ ★ Portsmouth: Mary Rose *and Museum; Royal Navy Museum;* HMS Victory; HMS Warrior. *Other places: Maritime Museum, Southampton; Buckler's Hard, near Beaulieu.*

★ ★ ★ *Royal Navy Submarine Museum, Gosport; Royal Marines Museum, Portsmouth; see also Museum of Dockyard Apprentices, Portsmouth; The Dockyard, Portsmouth; Old and New Docks, and Town Quay, Southampton.*

HMS Warrior, *Portsmouth*

Portsmouth Harbour

The Army & Fortifications

Hampshire is always thought of as a Naval county, but in fact the Army has been just as important, with many forts and barracks, and several important soldiers associated with the county. Portsmouth's great naval base had to be defended, and from the 18th century both Portsmouth and Gosport were garrison towns. Winchester had large barracks from the late 18th century, and Aldershot became one of the main Army bases from the middle of the 19th century when a large area of infertile heathland was taken over for training.

Aldershot is still full of soldiers, and has several military museums, most of them regimental. Winchester no longer houses regiments, but has almost as many regimental museums. Portsmouth has lost many of the barracks, but one survives as Portsmouth Museum, and the city has the fine D-Day Museum. At Middle Wallop the Museum of Army Flying superbly displays this aspect of the modern Army.

The surviving fortifications start much earlier, and altogether must form one of the best series in the country. Portchester Castle's outer walls are Roman, and inside is a medieval castle. The walls and gates of Southampton and Winchester, with the defences along the Point in Portsmouth, are also impressive survivors. The next oldest forts are part of the chain built around the coast by Henry VIII to defend anchorages. Calshot, Hurst and Southsea Castles were all built in the 1530s and 1540s, to counter the threat of invasion by France and Spain. All continued in sporadic use, and so have been altered, but Calshot still gives a good impression of what these small forts were originally like.

These earlier forts are (with the exception of

ABOVE *Calshot Castle*. BELOW *Fort Brockhurst*

Portchester) small, but the Palmerstonian forts (see entry) of the 1850s and 1860s were both big individually and built in large numbers. Fifteen forts, with other gun batteries and redoubts, were built in a chain around Gosport and Portsmouth, five of them along the top of Ports Down, a commanding and impressive position overlooking Portsmouth Harbour. A few have been demolished, but three are open to the public, including one of those built as an artificial island in Spithead. Fort Nelson, on Ports Down, also has quantities of guns of all dates displayed.

Several famous Army people have Hampshire connections. Florence Nightingale (1820-1910) lived during the winters at Embley Park, East Wellow, until 1853 when she finally managed to escape into nursing, greatly against her family's wishes. She hated the 'petty grinding tyranny' of unmarried women's family life.

Nursing then had a very low reputation. The Crimean war and her successes there liberated her, but destroyed her health. Her work for sanitary and nursing reform (especially for the Army) continued for the rest of her long life. She worked unceasingly, showing for example, that most hospital patients died from diseases of poor sanitation or bad hygiene, not the injury or disease which had put them into hospital. She was a maddening woman, devoted to hard work and utterly inconsiderate of others' feelings, although

Portchester Castle: the Roman Wall with its bastions

ABOVE *Aldershot Military Museum*
RIGHT *The first Duke of Wellington*

she could be kind. She was also amusing and aware of her failings. On a letter objecting to one of her actions in the 1890s (when she was old and famous) she wrote 'Shall I royally disregard it – or shall I give them a BUSTER'. Although she did not entirely approve of the design, the great Army hospital at Netley was one of the results of her work. The most famous soldier associated with the county was also long-lived and plain spoken. (He was the first to write 'Publish and be damned'. The First Duke of Wellington (1769-1852) was given a country estate by Parliament after his great victory at Waterloo (1815). He chose Stratfield Saye for its fine agricultural land. Wellington was the third son of an aristocratic family. His mother thought her 'ugly boy Arthur' was 'fit food for powder', so he was put into the Army, becoming the most successful general of his time. While he lived in Hampshire he was a politician and advisor to the Royal family.

He is buried at St Paul's, and there are many memorials including a huge equestrian statue at Aldershot and another just outside the park at Stratfield Saye.

Military Museums
★ ★ ★ ★ *D-Day Museum, Portsmouth; Museum of Army Flying, Middle Wallop.*
★ ★ ★ *Aldershot Military Museum; Airborne Forces Museum, Aldershot; Royal Corps of Transport Museum, Aldershot; Royal Green Jackets Museum, Winchester; See also: Army Physical Training Corps Museum, Aldershot; Light Infantry Museum, Winchester; Ghurka Museum, Winchester. Royal Army Dental Corps Museum, Aldershot; Royal Hampshire Regimental Museum, Winchester; Royal Hussars Museum, Winchester; Queen Alexandra's Royal Army Nursing Corps Museum, Aldershot; Second World War Aircraft Preservation Society, Lasham.*

Castles and fortifications
★ ★ ★ *Fort Brockhurst, Gosport; Portchester Castle.*
★ ★ ★ *Calshot Castle; Fort Nelson; Hurst Castle; Southsea Castle; Spitbank Fort. See also: Portsmouth Point and Defences; Southampton Town Walls; Winchester gates and walls; Stratfield Saye for the Duke of Wellington; The Wellows for Florence Nightingale; Royal Victoria Country Park, Netley.*

BELOW *D-Day embroidery, D-Day Museum*

KINGSCLERE (B) A small town just off the chalk. Until the later 19th century this was the largest parish in Hampshire – more than 17,000 acres, a reflection of the infertility of the land and thereby the sparseness of villages. The town grew up at the meeting point of several important roads, and had fairs and markets in medieval times. By 1800 the population was only 2,000, and it now seems more like a large village than a market town.

The best street is Swan Street leading south from the church, with many 18th century brick buildings, mostly grey with red detailing. The Swan Hotel is particularly good, as is the building next door. Scattered around the town are a few buildings entirely of grey brick, an unusual choice.

North Street has Georgian buildings (a few with weather boarding) and some attractive 1860s brick cottages, and George Street westwards has older buildings too. The informal square around the church has a variety of buildings, Georgian onwards, and an elaborate lamp commemorating Victoria's Jubilee of 1897.

The church of St Mary is prominent, plain and Norman in style but externally mostly dating from 1848. In the south transept a big memorial of 1670 with two good effigies. 1848 patterned glass in the chancel. The high windows give the effect of a Norman church inside.
★ *Church.*

KINGSCLERE WOODLANDS (B) As the name suggests this was once all woodland, and the arable fields are still surrounded by big hedgerows and copses. The settlement is so scattered that the different parts have different names. **Plastow Green** is the oldest part, with some thatched cottages, but the church of St Paul (1845 with a later spire) is to the east at **Ashford Hill**, standing alone.

KINGSLEY (F) A sandy area, with a large wooded common to the south-east. Lots of footpaths through the common, and car parks on the edge. Good walking. The old church is by the cross-roads to the west of the village. St Nicholas has older parts in the dark brown heathstone, and the rest red brick of 1778. The new church of All Saints is well sited in a knoll in the middle of the village, with a large pond below and the Common stretching off. The church dates from 1876 and is of the pale local malmstone. The village is quite large, with some older cottages, and

originated as a clearing in the forest. On the ridge road north to Wheatley are hop kilns, wide views eastwards.

Stubbs Farm to the north-west of the village is open to the public (fee:lists) in summer and offers a woodland walk, lakes and farming display.

KING'S SOMBORNE (D/H) A large village close to the Test valley with many thatched cottages, especially along the road to Little Somborne, where there is a cruck cottage and a weatherboarded thatched barn as well. The stream runs alongside the road. The name probably comes from the village having belonged to the King at Domesday, and certainly soon afterwards a large hunting park was established to the west of the village: part of its enclosing bank survives along by the river Test and can be seen from the footpath to Houghton.

The church of St Peter and St Paul is on the main road and mostly dates from a heavy restoration of 1886 Inside, the right hand pier closest to the chancel is original, early 13th century with graffitti close to that date scratched on it. In the chancel the 13th century stone effigy of a priest, and under a mat two early 14th century brasses with almost identical male figures.
★★ *For village.*

KING'S WORTHY (E) Runs north from the river Itchen, with handsome Georgian houses and some thatched cottages spread right through it even on the side roads. By the church is a tiny triangular green with a few cottages, one thatched. The church of St Mary is mostly of 1864, with an unusual octagonal vestry by the entrance, with a mock-medieval stone chimney pot. The tower is medieval. Unusual Royal coat of arms of 1774, a square turned on its point, with 'ribbons' added on for the churchwarden's names.

Abbots Worthy is a picturesque hamlet to the east, with many thatched cottages. The lane leads down to the river Itchen and joins up with footpaths leading along either side of the river east to Easton or south to Winchester. Lovely river landscape. Worthy Park, to the east again, is a classical yellow brick house of 1829.

KNIGHT'S ENHAM (D) A hamlet now on the edge of Andover's expansion, but still agricultural. A big Georgian ex Rectory, a farm and the church virtually make up the settlement, but the church of

St Michael and All Angels is medieval and must have been the centre for a wider area. 18th century table tombs crowd the graveyard in front. Thin shingled tower and more substantial timber framed porch. Now only a nave, and chancel, with between them an unusual wooden framed arch still retaining the rood beam. Big painted panels, two with the Creed and Lord's Prayer, and one wall covered with memorials and two big funeral hatchments. Crowded but charming.

Around the back outside, reset over the vestry window is a strange Roman looking stone head, perhaps Norman.
★★ *Church for its small-scale charm.*

KNIGHTWOOD OAK (M) (at the south end of Bolderwood Ornamental Drive (see entry)) is one of the oldest trees in the New Forest, probably dating from around 1600. It was pollarded and so has several trunks. 400 years seems to be the maximum life of an oak on the poor soils of the Forest, and the Knightwood Oak is clearly reaching the end of its life. Close by the Queen planted a new oak in 1979, the 900th anniversary of the establishment of the forest. A notice close by points out a beech and oak which are so close together that the branches actually unite, uncommon with two different species. Large old pollard beeches all around, and the marked path leads to an animal pen used by Verderers when they round up ponies or cattle.
★★★ *For old forest.*

LANGRISH (K) was part of East Meon until 1894. The church of St John is on the main road, a flint and stone building of 1870 prettily set amongst trees under the hill. The village is on a side road, with several malmstone cottages and a little thatch. Handsome countryside, with a tall wooded ridge running parallel to the village, set back a little.

LANGSTONE (O) A former hamlet on the shore opposite Hayling Island, beside the present bridge. Earlier it was the base for the small ferries to the island and the haunt of smugglers. From the main road a causeway footpath leads along the shoreline. Just inland, set at an oblique angle to the road, is a row of brick cottages, built in 1860 for coastguards, and a little along the shore is their look-out tower (now part of a house) in similar style. The pub by the main road is Georgian, and the shore here gives the best view of the rest of the hamlet,

Langstone

dominated by the black tower of a windmill. Odd to have a windmill right on the shore. Neville Shute the novelist lived here from 1934-40, when he was at Portsmouth Airport.

All the shore gives wide flat marine views, with Hayling Island to the south, Warblington distinctive with a thin tower eastwards, Langstone Harbour with Sussex shore beyond, and usually lots of boats. From the western side of the main road Portsmouth Harbour is seen with the bigger buildings of the town on the skyline.

The causeway leads to the bottom of the one inland street of old Langstone, which has many simple Georgian cottages, one long row still thatched. The door sills here and along the front are raised to keep out the spring tides, which creep up the street. The Towers is a very fancy mid-Victorian house, with even a dome. The private chapel of the Towers is now St Nicholas church.

A footpath leads on past another simple Georgian pub, behind the tide mill and windmill and past a small nature reserve teeming with birds especially wildfowl. The footpath leads on to Warblington (see entry), and is very rural, although large new roads roar nearby.

★ ★ ★ *For the hamlet and its views, a superb place to watch the tide creep up.*

LASHAM (E/F) Lots of thatched cottages, many of them plain brick, and a big pond close to the church.

A little brick building to the east of the church, with big doors either end and windows looking like a garage next to Pepper Box cottage and right on the road, is a traction engine shed. On the road up to the airfield is a granary on steddle stones. The church of St Mary dates from 1866, flint with a shingled tower and spire.

To the north of the village is an airfield which started in the Second World War, and continues in use with gliders as well as conventional aircraft. In the north-east corner are the aeroplanes (and one helicopter) of the Second World War Aircraft Preservation Society, seen clearly from the road but open for closer inspection (fee:lists) . To the south, off the road from Bentworth are the remains of a station on the Alton-Basingstoke Light Railway, built cheaply in 1910 and closed in 1938. All the stations were built of corrugated iron like this one which is now a coal yard.

LAVERSTOKE (E) A complicated village in the Test valley, which has taken over the adjacent hamlet of Freefolk. Laverstoke mill in the centre was where Henri Portal, a French refugee, started making the newly invented watermarked bank note paper in 1724. Portals had (and have) a monopoly in this specialised type of paper. Part of the Georgian redbrick house remains, surrounded by later brick and flint buildings. Every time William Cobbett (a passionate opponent of paper

money) rode by one of the paper mills in the area he exploded 'I hope the time will come when a monument will be erected where that mill stands, .. inscribed *the curse of England.*'.

To the north-east of the mills is Laverstoke House, built for the Portals in the 1790s, yellow brick and elegant. The house and park are visible from the road.

The village is mostly along the side road to the south, starting with small older cottages, but progressing to a variety of Victorian and later estate cottages along one side of the road.

St Mary Laverstoke is just to the west of the village, north of the main road. It sits well on the hillside, but is not particularly interesting. All of 1896. Small Victorian school below it, and on the main road below a long thatched and half-timbered range of cottages amazingly built so late as 1939.

Freefolk is just over the river from Laverstoke, with the churches only a good stone's throw apart. There are a few flint and brick cottages around the church, and more along the main river and road. The church of St Nicholas is tiny, basically probably Norman but with few features to give the date. It looks uninteresting outside, but the roundel with '1703' over the door records a 'beautification' of that date. Inside the cornice, probably the six gilt wooden candlesticks (with wooden candles) and the rustic classical reredos survive from the 1703 work. The reredos is partly on

LEE (H) (south of Romsey) Not really a village, but a scatter of 19th century estate cottages (from the Broadlands estate) and a few thatched earlier ones spread about the wide flat valley of the River Test. An unusual landscape, the hedges all full of big trees and seeming remote from Southampton which starts only a couple of miles south. Lord Palmerston had a small chapel built here in 1862, in red and yellow brick, now converted to an art gallery. The road north to Romsey has what seems to be a large ditch beside part of it: the remains of part of the Andover Canal which ran from Redbridge to Andover (see entry). Close to the turnoff for the church the dry canal curves away from the road towards the railway.

LEFT *The testament board in Freefolk church, Laverstoke*
BELOW *Lee on Solent church*

the south wall, a huge thing with naive portraits of Moses and Aaron, and marbled surround. The side panels are still in their original position, with rather elderly and tired looking baby angels holding up the texts.

The other wall is dominated by the vast and complex memorial to Sir Richard Pawlett, who died in 1614. His two wives kneel in recesses below, his effigy and his helm and spur above, the original ironwork still around. The 15th century wooden screen was moved to the back of the church to form the front of the family pew. A rare survivor in Hampshire, still with some of its original paint. Above are two funeral hatchments and, in similar style, the Royal Coat of Arms for William III.

★ ★ *St Nicholas church Freefolk, for its fittings.*

LECKFORD (D) A mixture of thatched cottages, timber framing, prim Victorian brick with flint panels and rather more severe rendered houses. Compact village. The church of St Nicholas is not impressive externally, although it is all medieval apart from the bell tower of 1934. The woodwork inside is interesting: unusual Jacobean pulpit with arches under the sounding board; classical screen of 1926; and in the chancel big Italian stalls of about 1600, brought here in 1923. The chancel arch is off centre, giving a lop-sided feel. 12th century table-type font.

★ *Church.*

LEE ON SOLENT (N) Founded in the 1880s as a health resort; until then it was only a few farms. It soon had a railway and pier, but both these have gone. Edwardian and Victorian villas line the straight road along the top of the short cliff, interspersed with modern houses and some smallish blocks of modern flats. Wonderful marine views, with the Isle of Wight straight ahead, Spithead left and Solent right. There are a few shops on this Marine Parade, but most of them are in the road parallel inland. The church of St Faith is to the north of the town centre in Osborne Road, and is a surprise: an impressive building of the 1930s. Outside redbrick with the windows oddly arranged – large ones in the upper storey and tiny ones below. Inside it seems huge, white with smooth parabolic arches across the church right down its length, and tiny arches on each side making minute 'aisles'. The east end has tiny lancet windows flanking a stone altar, an unusual arrangement. Plain fittings, white and low with wooden tops.

Between Lee and Hill Head is *HMS Daedelus*, the search and rescue helicopter station. One of the helicopters is on display at the entrance. The big slipway used to be used to launch seaplanes, and until recently hovercraft were tested here. The airfield was established in 1910.

Lee probably never formed an architectural whole even before some of the villas were demolished for flats, but the views are splendid, and the church is one of the best modern ones in the county and so.

LEIGH PARK (O/K) (north of Havant) A huge area of new housing built from the 1950s by Portsmouth Corporation as overspill from Portsmouth and to replace the many bombed houses.

Sir George Staunton Country Park on the Petersfield Road out of Havant, has been made from the remains of the gardens and grounds of the original Leigh Park, the estate bought in 1946 by Portsmouth. Leigh Park Farm trail (fee: lists) is the southern part of the original gardens, where Staunton's house was. It was demolished in 1863, but the library, an addition of 1832 in the Gothic style survives. The building looks like a folly: octagonal with mock gothic windows. Inside originally was a large library of Chinese books: it now houses a display on Sir George Staunton, his life in China and his house and garden here.

All through both parts of the gardens

Sir George Staunton's library, Leigh Park

are fine trees, many labelled, survivors from the 19th century gardens. Greenhouses, a walled garden (with crinkle-crankle or wavy wall), a vinery and fishponds cluster in this southern area, while to the east is the farm, with many different animals including some bold fallow deer, foxes, old varieties of pigs and cattle, and a display including several horse-drawn vehicles. The farm buildings themselves are attractive, early 19th century brick with arched windows.

Leigh Park Gardens are the northern part (free entry). Good trees again. The path leads to the site of the later house, now simply a terrace overlooking the lake, as the house (built 1863) was demolished in 1959. The lake was created by Sir George Staunton, and in the 1830s the islands were all adorned with follies: one was a fort, with a battery of Purbeck stone, pierced for nine guns. To the left of the terrace, on the way down to the lake is the best surviving folly, the shell house. Built in 1828, and now surrounded by trees, the inside was lined with shells from Hayling Island set in patterns. Only the ghost of the patterns can still be seen . The outside is still decorated with pebbles, flints and so on. To the north, seen more easily from the main road, is The Beacon, outside the present park, looking more like a tiny classical temple, and built in 1830.

The Sir George Staunton Conservatory is close to the Middle Park Way entrance to the gardens. Inside (fee:lists) several different types of tropical rainforest vegetation are laid out in great profusion. Impressive plants and worth seeing. Beyond the gardens are 1,000 acres of the Country Park, with many paths through the woodlands.

★ ★ ★ ★ *All parts of the garden well worth visiting: the farm especially good for children.*

LEPE (M/N) Not a village: only a single row of slate-clad houses, and one house which seems to be right in the sea. Trees down to the shore. Lepe Foreshore Country Park has good parking (fee Easter-Sept.), and offers walks along the shore in either direction. Superb views of the Isle of Wight and all the Solent. The deep water channel is close in to shore here, so ships are constantly passing. Sandy beach. The concrete blocks lining part of the beach are the remains of a hard where sections of the Mulberry Harbours for the 'D' day invasion of France were made. Larger blocks further up the beach are also remains of the harbours. In 1805 this was still 'the common place of embarkation' for the Isle of Wight, despite the lack of any harbour.

★ ★ ★ ★ *Landscape.*

Fossils over a window at Linkenholt

LINKENHOLT (A) Up on the chalk downs of North Hampshire, a dispersed village. The church of St Peter is a replacement of 1871, but the Norman font, decorated with zig-zags etc survives from an earlier church. Small 1871 school next to the church in matching style. Both Church and school have one window arch ornamented with a row of fossil sea urchins (from the chalk), and were designed by William White the architect of Lyndhurst church.

★ *Church and school.*

LINWOOD (G) A hamlet right in the New Forest with small hills; forest to one side and open lawn or heath the others.

LIPHOOK (F/K) Close to the borders with Surrey and Sussex, and more like them than Hampshire. It was only a small settlement on the road from Portsmouth to London until the 20th century. This original hamlet survives at the northern end of the present town, where all the roads join. The Royal Anchor is a big coaching inn whose central block with the deep roof dates from the 17th century. There are a few other Victorian or older cottages here, and along the Portsmouth Road. Flora Thompson (1877-1947) lived here from 1916-28 because her husband worked at the post office. She wrote a good deal here, including parts of *Lark Rise to Candleford* (see also Bramshott). Outside the new post office just to the south of the main cross-roads, is a bronze bust of her. **Bohunt Manor** at the south end of the main street opens its gardens to the public (fee:lists). The lake is the central feature, with many types of duck and other birds. Woodland walk, and small formal gardens. Good spring bulbs.

★ ★ ★ ★ *Gardens, partly for the wildfowl.*

LISS (K) Right on the border with Sussex, and still villagey and scattered despite growth encouraged by the main-line railway. **West Liss** is small, but has the parish church of St Peter, built in 1891 but with the tower added in 1930. The south porch is 1930 too, with a small sculpture by Eric Gill above the door. In the outskirts are several buildings of the local malmstone, rather darker in colour here,

Little Somborne

almost ochre. **East Liss** is large and modern, as is most of **Liss Forest**. The western end of Liss Forest is rural, sandy, with deep roads, lots of trees and several ponds. See also **BURGATES**.

LITCHFIELD (B) Now a cul-de-sac, but until recently on the main route north. The noise of the road is still heard, but otherwise the village is recovering. Very rural, with a large farmyard right on the street. Well treed graveyard, full of snowdrops. The small flint church of St James is mostly Norman, with some original small windows. The sequence of construction is difficult to work out, but the south aisle has been demolished and the arches filled in. Fine corbels with heads in the chancel and an unusual 17th century wooden screen between nave and chancel. Either side of the main road to the north is a group of prominent Bronze Age barrows called Seven Barrows. Only five can be seen easily although there are actually ten. Seven is a magical number often inaccurately used in names.

★ *Church.*

LITTLE ANN see ABBOTTS ANN

LITTLE SOMBORNE (D) A few cottages, the big house and a small church, set in parkland depleted by the storm of 1990. Marconi, the inventor of radio once lived in the big house.

The church of All Saints is tiny and simple, basically Saxon and Norman. The west end externally has a pilaster strip (vertical stone line) and the west corners have long and short work, both Saxon features. The eastern end is of about 1170. The footings of the tiny chancel are outlined in stone, and around the corner are indications of the footings of a tiny hermit's cell which once opened into the church.

Inside the blocked doorway leading to the cell can be seen, and in the east end is the blocked chancel arch. The western end has an open bell frame dating from 1590, with a contemporary bell – it is unusual to be able to see this so clearly. Up in the north wall is a Saxon window with double splay, that is the glass is in the middle of the wall with splays angled to both the inside and outside. 17th century timber roof.

★ ★ *Church for the Saxon work.*

Up Somborne is now larger than Little Somborne, but has no church. On the road through is Rookely House, early 19th century imitation Gothic, and up the

one side road is a cruck cottage.

LITTLETON (D) Now almost on the outskirts of Winchester, with many larger modern houses. The old village is at the north end, with a few timber-framed or thatched cottages. Church Lane is rural, with a cottage behind the church with an unusual chimney breast of brick and flint chequered. The church of St Catherine is small and mostly 1885.

At the south end of the village is Flower Down with several Bronze Age barrows preserved, including a large disc barrow, (ie a barrow consisting of a small mound in the middle surrounded at a distance by a circular ditch and bank). A large sarsen stone has been reset close to the road.

LOCKERLEY (H) A big green and a few thatched cottages in the south with another triangular green to the north, totally separate. Otherwise scattered like other settlements in this clayey area. Big church of St. John Evangelist north of the railway line. Stone, with an impressive spire, all dating from 1889.

LOCK'S HEATH (N) The heath was enclosed in 1866, and strawberry growing quickly followed, becoming a major industry after the railway station opened at Park Gate in 1888. 1930s ribbon development on the major roads, but in the last ten years many large housing estates have been built, and industrial estates too, totally changing the area. A big new shopping centre has been inserted, happily surrounded by big strips of open land still containing many oaks.

The church of 1895 is a plain stone building in the east of the settlement. To the south, close to Titchfield Common, is the Sir Joseph Paxton pub, interestingly named not after the designer of the Crystal Palace but after a variety of strawberry. There was a jam factory here to process some of the fruit.

LONGDOWN (M) (south-east of Ashurst) Small, but with two attractions. **Longdown Dairy Farm** (fee:lists) is fascinating, and well laid out for the visitor, who sees every part of milk production from day old calves to the automated milking process. Lots of other interesting animals including pigs, goats, handsome varieties of chicken and variously coloured rabbits which don't mind being picked up. An interesting combination of a working, large-scale farm and lots of animals for children.

The New Forest Butterfly Farm (fee:lists) is just to the south of the dairy farm, and has a large tropical butterfly garden under glass with exotic butterflies (and tiny birds) and a smaller area with British butterflies and moths. Both exotics and natives can be seen as caterpillars, chrysalises and flying. An insectarium has tarantulas, scorpions and so on, and outside are aviaries, dragonfly ponds, short woodland walk, and an adventure playground.

★ ★ ★ *Longdown dairy farm, interesting for children and adults.*

★ ★ ★ *New Forest Butterfly Farm for those interested in butterflies.*

LONGPARISH (D) The village really is long, running beside the River Test for more than two miles, under several different hamlet names. Very rural and low-lying with thatched cottages of brick, flint or timber-framing, or a combination of the three. Thatched barns too, and cob walls.

The church of St Nicholas has a handsome chequered stone and flint tower (15th century) while the rest of the church is 13th century with heavy Victorian restoration. 18th century bird-bath type font. One of the stained glass windows is dedicated to the memory of a First World War airman, and shows an airfield of that date.

Colonel Peter Hawker, a famous 19th century sportsman lived at Longparish House, and his published diary of 1809-53 includes much detail about the area, especially the shooting and fishing. In the first week of September 1815 he bagged 90 partridges, 11 hares, 2 quails, 1 snipe and 1 rabbit. In 1818 he failed to keep count of the trout he caught out of the Test here, but reckoned they weighed about a ton: the previous owner took double that amount by dragging the river.

★ *Church*

LONGSTOCK (D) Spread out along the side of the river Test, just up the valley side. Pretty, with lots of thatch and some brick houses. The main street north of the church is all thatched cottages, picturesque but not self-conscious. St Mary's church is 1880, with an impressive chancel including big wooden angels in the roof by William White, the architect of Lyndhurst church. The road across the river has many bridges over different streams, and thatched fishing huts. Very picturesque. One of the courses of the

At Longstock

river between Longstock and Fullerton is actually the Stockbridge – Andover canal, maintained here for fishing. **Longstock Water Gardens,** off the road to Fullerton are occasionally open and well worth seeing, having been described as 'one of the loveliest water gardens in the country, possibly in Europe'.

★ *Church* ★ ★ ★ *Gardens, but rarely open.*

LONG SUTTON (F) Compact despite its name, with several brick or timber framed cottages especially close to the church. To the east are the large neo-Georgian buildings of the Lord Wandsworth Agricultural College, 1915 onwards with impressive gates. The church of All Saints is 13th century. Very pretty chalk niche at the east end of the aisle. The chancel is very un-Victorian, still with the original slit windows deeply set in the walls. The big wooden bell tower supports (15th century) are in the middle of the nave. The three bells of 1520 have badly spelt inscriptions: 'IBE LEVE IN GOD THE FATHER OUR FATHAR WICH ART IN HEVEN HAL MARI FUL OF GRAS [GRACE]'. Massive medieval chest in the aisle.

Well a hamlet to the east really does have a prominent well in the middle.

★ ★ *Church for the original east end etc.*

LORDS HILL see SOUTHAMPTON WEST

LORDSWOOD see LORDSHILL, SOUTHAMPTON WEST

LOWER BULLINGTON see **BULLINGTON**

LOWER FROYLE see **FROYLE**

LOWER TEST NATURE RESERVE see **SOUTHAMPTON WEST**

LOWER WIELD see **WIELD**

LYMINGTON (M) A proper market town, and also a small port. The settlement was a medieval new town, founded here in about 1200 because Lymington-Yarmouth was the shortest sea-crossing to the Isle of Wight. The ferries still run, now carrying cars as well as foot passengers.

Celia Fiennes in the 1690s found Lymington 'a seaport town, it has some few small ships and some little trade but the greatest trade is by their Salterns'. Lymington salt, made by evaporating sea water, had been produced from at least the 12th century, and had a high reputation. From the 18th century Lymington supplied most of southern England and exported salt as far as America. By 1800 4,000 tons a year was being produced, but the high cost of transporting coal was too great, and the industry was gone by the 1860s. The salterns, where the sea water was boiled, were down by the sea shore, away from the town and estuary. Wine was imported in medieval times and ships were built from New Forest oak; yacht building started in the 1830s.

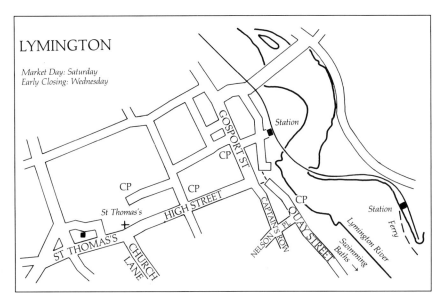

LYMINGTON

Market Day: Saturday
Early Closing: Wednesday

The main medieval street, High Street, runs up the hill from the quays. It is wide, to accommodate the market which still lines the road on Saturdays. The quay has a couple of good modern buildings amongst the older ones, and is open to the estuary with its muddle of boats, mostly sailing boats but occasionally fishermen's. On the opposite shore is the pier for the Isle of Wight ferry. Best to start at the quay, walking up Quay Hill, cobbled and pedestrians only. Small scale, 18th and 19th centuries with bow windows. Nautical shops mix with restaurants and jewellers. The High Street at the top leads on for more than half a mile, lined with mostly 18th century houses (many with shops underneath) varying from the dominant red brick to yellowy ones, some rendered and painted. A few iron balconies. Difficult to pick out individuals when all is so good, but no.73 in yellow brick up towards the church is very imposing, three and a half storeys high. A shoe shop no.41 on the other side has an ornate Victorian cast-iron shop front. Opposite the church is Monmouth House, red brick but earlier than most of the houses, dating from the late 17th century.

The church of St Thomas is a prominent landmark, with its cupola coming into view from about halfway up the hill of the High Street. The plain tower was built in 1670, but the cupola is 18th century. The Georgian interior is good. Large galleries of plain columns of c. 1800, and a pretty ceiling of 1910. Lots of monuments which look odd on unplastered stone walls. Huge entrance

hall with staircases either side (leading to the gallery) added in 1911, lined with big achievements of arms. Henry Lyte (1793-1847) was curate of this church, and wrote many famous hymns here, including 'Abide with me' and 'Praise my soul, the King of heaven'.

St Thomas Street continues beyond the church on a smaller scale, but still with many Georgian buildings. Church Street is also pretty and has two crinkle-crankle (curving in and out) garden walls – the further one was built by Dennis Wheatley, the novelist, who lived in Grove Place (behind the wall – demolished) from 1945-1969.

The happily named Captain's Row and Nelson Place lead southward, down river from the Quay, and are lined with smaller 18th and 19th century houses, all still domestic. Quay Street and Bath Road are also patchily good, with either boats or factories lining the estuary side of the roads. The swimming baths at the end of Bath Road were made from a saltern called King's Saltern.

To the south of the town a couple of lanes lead down into the marshes where the salterns were. As the shore gets closer the oaks get smaller and finally disappear. Miles of good walking in this strange marsh landscape, with concrete walls all over the place, the rectangular remains of the salterns and wide views of the Isle of Wight. Many footpaths, including the Solent Way which runs on the shoreline and a track to Keyhaven. A sailing club uses one of the big saltern pools which survived because it was converted to an oyster bed after the salt industry failed. There were pumping mills close by, and some of the surviving waterways were constructed for the barges which took the salt away.Hurst Castle is clear in the foreground.

ABOVE *Up from the quay at Lymington*
BELOW *Dennis Wheatley's crinkle-crankle wall Lymington*

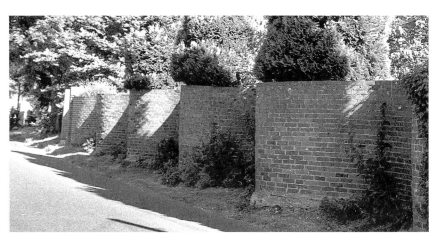

Down Pennington Lane is the old pub, the Chequers, whose name is a pun from the people who checked the salt-tax. Several large Edwardian houses are dotted about the higher parts.

To the north is **Buckland Rings** a simple double banked enclosure, probably Iron Age. It is not accessible, but impressive from the road with oak-covered banks and ditches.

★ ★ ★ ★ *Town, and walking area, especially the marshes.*

LYNDHURST (H/M) The name means wood of lime trees, a now uncommon species in the Forest. Lyndhurst is the 'capital' of the New Forest, the only town of any size within it. The administration of the Forest has always been based here, in the Queen's House (mudlingly the building is known as King's House when the reigning monarch is male). Lyndhurst was probably a royal manor in late Saxon times, and has certainly been one since the Conquest, when William made it the centre for the forest. A Royal manor house has existed on the same site since at least 1300, and parts of the present building in High Street next to the church, date from a 17th century reconstruction. Large handsome brick house, with the Verderers' Court attached at one end. Here this descendant of the medieval forest court still meets six times a year to deal with problems of animals and other rights in the Forest. The Court's real name is Court of Swainmote and Attachment. (Open only when the court is in session – list of dates outside).

Lyndhurst is full of hotels, restaurants and cafes, and the High Street is mostly Edwardian – Hudson in *Hampshire Days* (1903) complained that it was 'a vulgar suburb, a transcript of Chiswick or Plumstead in the New Forest where it is in a wrong atmosphere'. Time has softened our attitudes, and the mostly brick and tile buildings seem faintly picturesque today. The Crown Hotel opposite the church is a bit large, with tile-hanging and half timbering typical of its date (1896, despite the 1600 claimed on one part).

The New Forest Museum (fee: lists) opened in 1988 in a fine new brick building off Lyndhurst's main car park. First a multi-projector slide show, the changing forest, then displays about many aspects of the forest – trees, shipbuilding, famous people, and the fine New Forest embroidery, designed in 1979, the 900th anniversary of the forest. Shop with many books about the Forest,

Boulton's Bench, Lyndhurst

and a Tourist Information Office. A good introduction to the Forest, and a good place to find out more about it.

The church of St Michael is prominent, partly because it sits on a large mound. This is the third, or possibly fourth, church on the site, and was built from 1858-70 to designs by William White. John Betjeman, an early connoisseur of Victorian architecture, found it 'the most fanciful, fantastic Gothic style that I ever have seen, and I have seen a great deal'. White was a distinguished Gothic Revival architect and this is his most important building. Imposing externally, the building is even more impressive internally, the walls in exposed brick patterns of yellow, while and red. Complex pillars with thin purbeck marble shafts and brick above. Attractive naturalistic carving of flowers and leaves on the capitals. The roof is plainly boarded, but the supports are life sized angels with musical instruments. Huge reredos, wallpainting by Lord Leighton showing Wise and Foolish Virgins. Above fine stained glass by Burne-Jones, from the firm of William Morris. To the left of the altar, looking like part of the building, a handsome tomb of Caen stone and highly coloured marbles, to the Hargreaves who contributed greatly to the building of the church. Another window by Morris in the south window of the short south transept. At the west end a fine memorial by Flaxman moved from an earlier church, a woman mourning by a broken column, 1798. In beside the rather odd marble font, another fine memorial – Ann Frances Cockerell,

1882. The marble effigy lies on a shelf, with mosaic above and below. It was designed by her husband.

Outside in the graveyard, opposite the short south transept, is the Hargreave family vault, where the ashes of Mrs Reginald Hargreaves, the original for Lewis Caroll's *Alice in Wonderland*, are buried. A plaque marks the spot.

To the east of the town is an extensive 'lawn' or open grazing area where there are always ponies. Boulton's bench (named after a 17th century Wood Warden of the Forest) sits on a large natural knoll, surrounded by big yew trees. Good views of Lyndhurst. Large Edwardian houses line the main road: they are found all over the Forest, presumably because it became a fashionable place to live from around 1900, but there are more in and around Lyndhurst than anywhere else. Pike's Hill to the north is a happy mixture of older cottages and newer houses, mostly brick.

Swan Green to the west is picturesque, with a row of thatched cottages and a green now mown for cricket.

At Swan Green, near Lyndhurst

Holidays Hill Reptiliary, 2 miles west of Lyndhurst on the A35, (free: lists). Badly signposted, but worth finding. Set in the Forest beyond a caravan site are several large concrete enclosures with examples of all the reptiles and amphibians found in the New Forest, in natural settings. The adder, smooth snake, grass snake, sand and common lizards, slow worm, toad, frog and three types of newt are all here, although on dull days some of them may be concealed in the undergrowth. Well worth visiting.

★ ★ ★ *For anyone interested in natural history.*

★ ★ ★ *New Forest Museum*

★ ★ ★ *Town, Lawns and Church, although you may hate the Church.*

MAPLEDURWELL (E) Wriggly roads with lots of trees and hedges, and a pond at the road junction. The church of St Mary is up a damp cul-de-sac with lots of willows, and is mostly 19th century.

MARCHWOOD (H) One of the villages along the eastern side of the New Forest which has grown out of all recognition because of industrial development since 1945. From the Southampton side the two chimneys of Marchwood Power station (built 1952-5, stopped generating 1982) dominate, but in the village the vast incinerator is just as prominent. The village has grown recently, but still seems too small for the massive church of St John the Apostle, built in 1843 of yellow brick and stone. Large spire. Some painted decoration inside, and a good modern stained glass in the east window. The 1840s font is a copy of the 12th century one in Winchester Cathedral.

MARTIN (G) One of the pretty villages of the western chalk – until 1895 it was in Wiltshire. The mile long village street curves, with wide verges, a little winterbourne stream and a great variety of fine cottages in brick, flint and timber framing. Even a little greensand. A few Georgian brick houses. In the middle a tiny triangular green with trees, pump and low thatched cottages. A sunken lane (Sillen Lane) leads from the green a mile to the car park for Martin Down nature reserve (below).

At the north-west end a simple primitive Methodist chapel of 1829, and near the middle the church of All Saints. In front of the tower, standing alone, is the grave of William Lawes (1800-1886), the Isaac Balcombe of W.H. Hudson's *A Shepherd's Life* (1910). The Winterbourne Bishop of the book is the village of Martin, and Hudson describes the life of two generations of shepherds (including William Lawes) and gives much detail of village life.

A typical village church, with bits of many dates. Heavily buttressed, mostly greensand tower, with a pretty 18th century spire. Inside the 14th century dominates, with an unusual domestic-looking bay window in the north side. Some good monuments, mostly classical. Simple barrel roof. **East Martin** has a fine thatched farm, farmyard and cottages, the garden bordered by a thatched cob wall with flint lower parts. **Tidpit** a hamlet to the south also has good cottages and farms.

To the east of the village amongst ploughed-up downland, close to footpaths, are two Neolithic Long Barrows – Grams Barrow and Knap Barrow, both good examples. See also Martin Down.

★ ★ ★ *Village, classic long single village street; great variety of cottages and houses.*

MARTIN DOWN (G) is right on the borders of Hampshire, with Dorset to the west and Wiltshire to the north. It is now a huge nature reserve, 900 acres of downland and scrub, superb for walking because it's so rich in flowers and far from roads. The north end is close to a busy road, but the south is completely peaceful. **Bockerley Dyke** is the boundary all along the south-western side. This bank and ditch was constructed in the fourth century, presumably to keep the Saxons out of what is now Dorset, and is still the county boundary. At the north-western end of the reserve the Roman road runs through a gap in Bokerley Dyke. To the south-west the modern A354 is on the line of the Roman road, but to the north-east the modern road diverges and the Roman road can be seen as an earthwork running characteristically straight. Bokerley Dyke, by contrast, wriggles along the ridge. At its maximum it is 100 feet across, the ditch still up to 9 feet deep and the bank up to 8 feet high. Originally the ditch would have been 5 feet deeper, a formidable barrier.

At the south-eastern end of the reserve on top of Blagden Hill is Grims ditch, an earlier boundary probably dating from the Bronze Age, and here crossed by Bokerley Dyke. Just below the hill top, where the modern track passes through a modern gap in the dyke there are two Bronze Age barrows (one large and well-preserved), and between them and Bokerley Dyke is the smaller bank of Grims Ditch, here running in a straight line. There are more Bronze Age barrows to the south-east on the Hampshire side of the dyke.

The reserve has several different types of grassland, including the now rare flat downland, along with scrub and woods. All this makes a rich habitat, with lots of flowers including masses of cowslips, and later several varieties of orchids. Many birds nest in the scrub, including nightingales and whitethroats.

The best way to get to the reserve is

Martin

along Sillen Lane, which leads from the little triangular green in the middle of Martin village to the car park. The lane itself is charming with huge hedgerows.

★ ★ ★ ★ *For downland, flowers, walking and archaeology.*

MARTYR WORTHY (E) A small village right down by the river Itchen, with footpaths down along the river or across to Easton. Really only one lane leading down to the river. The church of St Swithun has a Norman entrance door, and another in the opposite wall, but the chancel is neo-Norman of 1865. Bell turret of same sort of date. The Itchen is wide here, and pretty.

Chilland to the east is mostly modern, but the lane down to the river leads on to footpaths, one crossing the river.

MARWELL (J) (Colden Common, off the B2177 Winchester-Bishop's Waltham road). A large zoological park (fee:lists) with nearly a thousand animals, where many rare species are successfully bred, and not at all like an old-fashioned zoo. The animals are seen in a lovely wooded setting with paddocks and enclosures, and the complete circuit of the 100 acre site is a long walk. A 'land train' offers lifts, and in the summer season a miniature train runs through the middle (fee).

Marwell is famous for its big cats, from Siberian Tigers to Lynxes, but there are many more species → ridiculously tall giraffes, rhinoceroses happily grazing, tapirs, many types of monkey and birds. To see an exotic like a Red Panda sitting in a Hampshire oak tree, or a herd of zebras grazing is superb. A farmyard with tame domestic birds and animals is attractive to children, and there is an adventure playground. In the middle of the park is Marwell Hall, built in 1816 – an early date for a realistic looking imitation Tudor House. Most of the turrets and decoration are on the garden side. Very appropriately Marwell was a hunting park belonging to the medieval bishops of Winchester. Heartily recommended zoological park and good for a full afternoon out. ★ ★ ★ ★

MATTINGLEY (C) Half the village is in a wood, and the rest around a marshy green. 17th and 18th century cottages abound, mostly timber framed. Farmyard by the church with lots of weatherboarded buildings. The church is unusual – all timber framed with brick nogging (or infilling). The aisles were

added in 1867 and the whole building restored then, but much is original dating from the 15th century. Inside it feels like a hall, with cottagey windows. The posts supporting the aisles were originally the outside wall, like those in the chancel. Plainish roof. Tiny tower, shingled.

A rare survivor: most churches built like this have had the walls replaced by all brick, like nearby Rotherwick. To the east, in Dipley, a picturesque redbrick mill, close to the road.

★ ★ *Church.*

MAYBUSH see **SOUTHAMPTON WEST**

MEDSTEAD (E) Many 1920s bungalows on the outskirts, with the occasional earlier building. Larger houses in the middle. The small church of St Andrew has a weather-boarded tower, and inside, a fat Norman pillar with an inscribed date of 1713 (must refer to a repair). Nice 19th century roof and porch. Castle Street may be named after the earthworks a little out of the village, or the unusually named Castle of Comfort pub. Good views from the roads around the village.

Alton Abbey 1½ miles north-east of the village was founded in 1895: most prominent from the road is the flint and brick gatehouse of 1903, but there is also a church, and other buildings. The abbey belongs to the Order of St Paul for the Welfare of Seamen.

MEONSTOKE (J) Another Meon Valley village where the church sits apart – this

time in the water-meadows in what seems to be a damp site. Good brick, flint and thatch cottages right by it. St Andrew's church has an odd timber two-tier top to the tower, added in 1900. Inside it is a real village church: 13th century and early English in style. Shallow Norman font made from a huge lump of Purbeck Marble.

The village is just up the hill, with a superb High Street running parallel to the main road. Lots of Georgian brick houses all along, and halfway a good brick and thatch barn. The village burnt down early in the 18th century and these are the replacements. A footpath from the south end of High Street leads on to Droxford.

★ ★ ★ *Village and good walking.*

MICHELDEVER (E) A large and pretty village, full of timber-framed cottages, dozens of them thatched. Brick too, and pebble-dash. There is still a forge. Opposite the church a neat 1870 school with clock tower. The church of St Mary looks odd from the outside because the

Micheldever

Meonstoke church

brickworks, the older part of the village in the north'. This is still true.

The church of St Mary is best known for its unusual wooden tower, only just attached to the church. Externally the weather-boarding has been renewed several times, but the timber frame inside is late medieval. The rest of the church is flint, with a big 12th century chancel. Much of the rest in 1847. One chancel window has remnants of 15th century effigy of a cross-legged knight. Behind this, on the wall, a most unusual small memorial tablet of 1538 with tiny figures on either side.

Opposite the church porch is a field called Agincourt. Here on 16th July 1415 the English army of Knights and archers camped on their way to France and the Battle of Agincourt.

★ ★ *Unusual church tower.*

MIDDLE WALLOP (D) virtually links Over and Nether Wallop, but is sparser than Nether Wallop. The river runs beside the road, and there are several thatched cottages. More settlement on the

crossroads. No church, but the village is well known because the Second World War airfield just to the north-east has been the centre for Army Flying since 1958 and has a large museum (fee:lists). Displays trace the history of Army flying from Victorian balloons and kites, through the Royal Flying Corps, the development of helicopters from the 1940s, and right up to the Falklands. Film Show: more than 10 planes and 8 helicopters displayed. Fine reconstructions and general displays, now being extended to include gliders. The planes and helicopters of the base can be seen from the museum, and every two years (even numbers) for a weekend in July there is an air show here open to the public.

★ ★ ★ ★ *Museum of Army Flying, fascinating for anyone interested in the Army or flying.*

MILFORD ON SEA (M) A substantial old village which developed as a seaside resort from the late 1880s. Many large late Victorian and Edwardian houses

ABOVE *Micheldever church*
RIGHT *1538 memorial in Michelmersh church*
BELOW *Michelmersh church*

middle is a brick octagon. Conventional and pretty, early 16th century tower. Inside the very unusual, classical style octagon nave fits well. It was designed in 1808 by the architect George Dance (see also East Stratton).

The chancel is 1880, but in it are three Regency memorials by Flaxman, the centre a seated woman, with either side sculpted panels, all of high quality.

Just north of the village is **Northbrook** with a few thatched cottages.

Micheldever Station more than two miles to the north grew up around the railway station, a simple classical building of neatly squared flint, with a verandah all round dating from 1840. It was originally the station for Andover. A pub and a few other buildings seem contemporary with the railway, and more have been built since.

★ ★ ★ *Church and village, church for its nave and the Flaxman memorials.*

MICHELMERSH (H) Narrow roads, some deep, with some older cottages close to the church. In 1908 VCH found 'the more modern and growing part of the village, with its shops and modern villas is in the south of the parish, near the

116

survive but on the outskirts are modern flats. More blocks are replacing the large houses on the sea front. The White House right on the shore is a notable landmark: wings enclose a courtyard open to the sea, and the main house has little towers.

R.E. Stevens in his book *The New Forest Beautiful* (1925) reproduces the contemporary attitude towards these seaside developments. Milford, 'a kind of super garden suburb by the sea', has 'dream-like bungalows amid the wind-tossed scrub oak of the cliff-top, which suggest romance in every line'. The development of Milford (and neighbouring Barton on Sea) has ousted the oak and replaced it by evergreens, but dwarfish oaks, all leaning away from the sea, still survive in the rural gap between them.

Superb views, with Hengistbury to the west, Isle of Wight ahead and eastwards, and Hurst Castle on its spit just along the shore. The low cliff dies out on the eastern side of the town, and the shingle spit of Hurst starts.

The centre has a small wildish park with a stream, and a few 18th and 19th century houses mixed in with the Edwardian, but the great surprise is All Saints church, just north of the shopping centre. A good example of a 13th century (Early English style) church, remarkably complete. The tower has a fine corbel table with heads on top, but a rather small replacement spire of 1827. To the right of the porch outside on the corner of the window is carved a man playing the bagpipes (15th century). Inside, apart from the three fat round pillars which survive from a Norman church, all is 13th century. Simple lancet windows.

The many pointed arches are complemented by the wooden roofs, which date from 1640, and are particularly elaborate over the crossing, with big bosses. Lots of classical style memorials around the church, ranging in date from the 18th to the 20th centuries. A small Victorian stained glass window on the north side of the chancel shows King Charles I, who was held prisoner in Hurst Castle in 1648, just before his trial and execution.

★ ★ ★ *Church, as a complete and good example of Early English style.*

MILLBROOK see **SOUTHAMPTON WEST**

ABOVE *Milford-on-Sea church, with* LEFT *Man playing pipes*

MINSTEAD (H) A large, spread-about forest village, whose pastures contrast with the surrounding forest. Some pretty thatched cottages. Good names – one part is London Minstead, another Seaman's Corner. In the centre a small green where the road leads up to the church of All Saints. From the gate the church looks just like a house: all gables and little extensions. The attractive brick tower (dated 1774) is the only slightly ecclesiastical bit. Rustic porch dated 1683 leads to the even stranger interior. It

RIGHT *Minstead church*

117

Conan Doyle's grave, Minstead

seems to have two naves at right angles to each other, because the south transept is so big, and the real nave is absolutely stuffed with galleries. The lower handsome one is 18th century, but this did not give enough seating so above is a plain one of 1818. The result is a combination of theatre set and church, small scale and charming. The three levels of congregation face a three-decker pulpit of the 17th century. Off the chancel are two private pews, completely separate rooms, one even with a fireplace. The only medieval remnants are the 13th century entrance door and chancel arch, and the Norman font, with crude carvings. The south transept or second nave was added in 1792, and has all its fittings down to rows of hat pegs at the back, which are also found at the back of the real nave.

Conan Doyle (1869-1930), the creator of Sherlock Holmes, is buried on the south side of the graveyard by an oak tree, marked by a large cross. He bought Bignell Wood in Minstead late in his life as a holiday home and the village (and indeed most of the Forest) is the background for part of his historical novel *The White Company* (1891). He was originally buried in the garden of his home in Sussex, but was moved here in the 1950s.

Furzey Gardens on the north-west outskirts of Minstead were designed and planted in 1922, covering 8 acres of undulating ground. The plantings are informal, and incorporate several large old oaks and other forest trees. Woodland predominates, and the garden is particularly well planted with azaleas, some of great size. Heathers too, and brooms. Good daffodils and other bulbs in spring, and all sorts of wild flowers. Water garden and pond and close to the pond a small building thatched with heather. Most trees and plants are labelled, and in one corner is a selection of pine miniature houses, one a tree house, to entertain the children. Close to the entrance is the original timber frame and brick cottage, open to the public. Tiny, with a big chimney stack up the centre, a large open fireplace and an awkward staircase: a rare opportunity to go into an ordinary 17th century cottage which has not been modernised. The barn-like building is a gallery selling local crafts.

★ ★ ★ *Furzey gardens, well worth seeing at all times of the year.*
★ ★ ★ *Church, because of the fittings, removed from most churches by the Victorians.*

MOCKBEGGAR see **GORLEY**

MONK SHERBORNE (B) Woody, slightly undulating landscape, with many oak trees. The church of All Saints is to the south of the village. Outside the Victorian tiled tower dominates, with a much earlier stone stair turret. The 14th century porch with its heavy oak timbers largely obscures the Norman doorway. Inside there is a big Norman chancel arch with odd heads in the supports. 1650ish pulpit, in an earlier style, and plain Elizabethan bench ends.

The west end seems all wood, with the bell frame and oddly the 19th century screen and Jacobean communion rails. The Norman font is a peculiar shape, with heads (one original) dripping from the lower part.

★ ★ *Church for the good mixture of dates.*

Monk Sherborne church chancel arch

MONKWOOD (E/F/J/K) Quite large but mostly recent, an agricultural settlement of between the wars like Beech, with rectangular field divisions, lots of glasshouses and poultry houses, and no real centre. To the west the road goes down a steep picturesque hill through woods.

Monxton

MONXTON (D) Crammed into the river valley, with lots of thatched cottages. A footpath leads up to the church from down by the river. St Mary's church is a replacement of 1854, with an individual bellcote with tiny spire. Interesting contemporary stained glass, patterns only. The Norman capitals to the chancel arch were re-used from the earlier church, and close to it a pretty brass with cut-out figures to Alice Swyre, 1599.

MORESTEAD (J) A hamlet seemingly composed of largish houses on a surprisingly fast road. The church (no dedication) is small and simple, basically medieval but details mostly 1873 'Norman'. The brick bit at the west end was built as a school in 1833. Lots of snowdrops in the graveyard.

MORTIMER WEST END (B) Hilly and wooded, only sparsely settled. Only really one street, with a plain brick church of 1856.

MOTTISFONT (H) Much visited for its famous rose garden and the remains of the priory. Worth walking through the village as well, since it is picturesque, especially up by the parish church where two thatched brick cottages sit gable end on to the path. Many larger houses, mostly brick and tile, with lots of trees.

St Andrew's is a real village church, of many periods. Short shingled spire.

ABOVE *Mottisfont, with* BELOW *The smoking urn by Rex Whistler*

Handsome Norman chancel arch. The big memorial by the altar has a row of small figures, and dates from 1584. The chancel has much 15th century stained glass, brightly coloured patterns or more delicate figure work. The lower part of the east window with big figures is largely restoration. Exposed in the nave is a 17th century clock mechanism, now working again.

A priory was established here in about 1200, sited close to the 'font' or spring which still wells up in the grounds producing 200 gallons a minute. The priory was not large, but built a church (now the house) with cloisters and other buildings on what is now the lawns in front of the house. In 1536 the priory was abolished and the land and buildings acquired by Lord Sandys, who exchanged two villages – Chelsea and Paddington – for them. He converted the buildings into a house, although most of his money was spent on his new house, The Vyne, in north Hampshire, and it was his son who completed the conversion. In the 1740s the house was cut down to one wing and modernised.

From the car park a bridge over a branch of the river Test leads into the superbly treed grounds. This south front of the house is the most complex, all being re-facing of the medieval church, with the truncated wings either end faced in stone, the rest red brick. Flanking the classical centre are corner turrets of the

1540s house with small windows. From this side it is difficult to believe that the building is basically a church, but round the short (river) side is a large medieval arch which led from a chapel into a transept. The north facade looks much more like a conversion, with medieval buttresses all along the wall, and at the east end bits of another large medieval arch emerge. The lower arched-top windows are 16th century, the upper larger ones 1740s. Only a small part of the house is open. The Cellarium, a 13th century undercroft, is well preserved with vaulted ceiling. The original ground surface is 2 feet below the present one, making the pillars look rather short. Inside the main house are 16th century doorways and a fireplace from Sandys house and little bits of the medieval church, but the ground floor is very austere. Upstairs is an extreme contrast: the corridors and staircase have walls painted to look like plaster in the early 19th century. The drawing room must be one of the most extravagant rooms of the 20th century. It was decorated by Rex Whistler in 1938/9 with *trompe l'oeil* painted plaster in peachy pink with blue velvet curtains trimmed with (fake) ermine. The overall effect is blowsy and vulgar, although the big paintings of 'trophies' in the panels are fine, the 'pelmets' convincing and the smoking urn in painted niche superlative. On one of the 'cornices' a forgotten paint-pot is

painted. Very fine 18th century overmantel mirror. The glass finger-plates and bell-pushes were engraved by Whistler's brother Laurence, and the original designs for the room are on display.

The grounds around the house are not extensive, but are charming with lots of specimen trees including mulberries and a giant plane, 100 ft high perhaps 250 years old, one of the earliest to be planted in England. The layout of the grounds dates from the 1930s, incorporating an earlier small summerhouse, a handsome classical stable block of 1836, and an ice house. A five minute walk upstream, along a tree-lined path, leads to the Fishermen's hut, a charming rustic building with intricate decoration made from twigs and small branches. In 1972 the National Trust planted its collection of historic roses in what had been the walled kitchen gardens. These are beautifully laid out, with many other plants, and show the vigour and beauty of the earlier varieties. They smell wonderful, and all are labelled not only with their names but also their date of introduction. Species roses too. Often crowded in June/early July, but well worth seeing.

★ ★ ★ ★ *When the roses are out, but disappointing to see so little of the house.*

NATELEY SCURES (C/F) (1 mile south-west of Hook).

Not a village now, just a church and farm in extreme contrast with busy dual carriageway close by. Tiny Norman church, all dating from about 1200. Outside it looks like an upturned rowing boat because there are no aisles, only an apse and nave. Bellcote added in 1865. Elaborate single door, one capital with a mermaid. Few and small windows. The gallery is supported on the beam put there for a gallery of 1591, as a little brass plate on it records. This must have been one of the earliest. Lots of memorials, including oddly on one wall four shaped like hearts, clubs, diamonds and spades. Brass of 1661 on west wall, with long inscription.

★ ★ *Rare survivor – most churches have been expanded from such small beginnings.*

NETHERTON see FACCOMBE

NETHER WALLOP (D)

A large, dense village, with wandering streets full of thatched cottages, all set across the river valley and up the hill. Good views: a village to walk around. To the south a big plain rendered house looks down the valley, with lots of walled gardens and outbuildings. Many pollarded willows along the river. Lots of thatch and timber framing, best overlooked from the church of St Andrew which is up on the hill. Good river view from east of churchyard too.

The church tower is dated 1704, and in front of it is a small pyramid with a flame on top, the memorial to Dr Francis Douce who died in 1760. The entrance is through a Norman doorway, with an old timber door. Much of the church is Norman, but difficult to explain in detail. Above the chancel arch are the remains of an 11th century wall painting with Winchester style angels, cut by the Norman chancel arch. All the eastern part is 1845. There are three other wall-paintings in the nave: a bell on the tower dating from about 1704 when it was rebuilt; two on the side walls of the early 15th century, simple and of few colours, one showing St George and the dragon. Under a mat in the nave a brass to a woman, 1437. Simple old wooden benches survive in the aisles.

★ ★ *Church for the Norman parts and the wall-paintings.*

NETLEY (J/N)

An unusual village. Inland is **Old Netley**, described in 1908 as 'a picturesque hamlet of timber framed cottages with trim old-fashioned gardens' but rapidly increasing in size. This part is still small, but mostly modern. The village of Netley proper lies beside Southampton Water. Until the 19th century the shore was only occupied by a Cistercian Abbey, but in 1856 the foundation stone for the huge buildings of the main British Army hospital was laid by Queen Victoria.

The village of Netley grew up outside the Hospital, and has hardly any buildings earlier than the mid 19th century. One of the handsomest is the classical railway station of 1867. Originally there were larger Victorian villas overlooking the sea, but now there are many low blocks of modern flats. Smaller Victorian terraced houses on the landward side, backed by modern development.

The wide Southampton Water gleams in any sunshine, and every type of shipping passes through on its way to Southampton. On the opposite shore is the New Forest, rather dominated by the oil terminal of Fawley. To the north the main road runs down through the miniature cliff to the shore, all tree lined, a fragment of romantic landscape which remains amongst the modern development.

The church of St Edward the Confessor is close to the abbey, but was not built until 1886, replacing the old church inland at Hound. The 1886 church is stone, with coloured marble used for some of the fittings.

Netley Abbey is to the north of the village (fee:lists). It was founded in 1239, originally by monks from Beaulieu. By 1300 they had built a substantial church and monastic buildings around a cloister.

The abbey was dissolved in 1536 and the buildings were converted into a house. The setting for the ruins is pleasing – sloping lawns and big trees.

The usual entrance is through the southern part of the cloister, much adapted in the 16th century with square-headed windows and brick alterations to the walls. The Cloister has lost its covered walk. The church end is impressive, a proper picturesque romantic ruin, which is how the site has been regarded since the mid 18th century, after it ceased to be used as a house.

Horace Walpole, who later built himself the first Gothic revival house, admired Netley Abbey extravagantly in the mid 18th century: 'The ruins are vast and retain fragments of beautiful fretted roof, pendant in the air, with all variety of Gothic patterns of windows, wrapped round and round with ivy ... on each side breaks in the view of the Southampton Sea, deep blue, glittering with silver and vessels ... In short, these are not the ruins of Netley, but of Paradise'.

The church was large, and the eastern end and south transept give some idea of its original splendours. The matching north transept was carted off to Cranbury Park (see Otterborne) in the mid 18th century to make an ornament for the park there. The big bases for the piers to support the tower crossing have areas protected from the elements. These have inscribed devices and one an inscription 'H DI GRA REX ANGL' for Henry III who became patron of the abbey in 1251.

The range off the south transept includes the chapter house where the monks met, and a narrow room, still with its rib vaulting, and a stone cupboard and piscina. Fragments of medieval tiles have been reset in part of the floor.

The infirmary at the south end of this block also has the rough part of its vault surviving, and a big stone fireplace. The main drain, with a stream running in the bottom, passes through this room to odd effect.

The small building detached from the rest is the Abbott's lodging, also 13th century and solid inside with most of the vaulted ceilings surviving.

Most of the area around the abbey has filled with housing. Opposite the abbey, on the shore, is a large late 19th century house called Netley Castle, with crenellations and a tower. This is all bogus castle, but concealed in the middle of it is a simple block built by Henry 8th in 1542 as a small fort, opposite Calshot Castle.

Netley Abbey

South of the village is **Royal Victoria Country Park**, created after Netley Hospital was demolished. Only the chapel survives from the hospital, built in 1856. It was 1,424 feet long, (then one of the longest buildings in the world), and ran along almost the full length of the open part of the park, parallel with the sea. It was the first and largest Army Hospital, treating so many soldiers during the First World War that a huge hutted annexe had to be built inland. The railway ran to the back of the hospital, where some rails remain, and there was also a long jetty into Southampton Water.

The chapel is now a museum (fee:lists) with good displays (including videos) on the history of the Solent coast and the hospital. The tower is accessible, and gives an even wider view of Southampton Water.

The Country Park has ¾ mile of shore, huge grassy areas, and inland more woodland and scrub, 200 acres in all. It is deservedly popular.

★ ★ ★ *Royal Victoria Country Park and the museum.* ★ ★ ★ *Netley Abbey, a romantic ruin.*

NETLEY MARSH (H) Mostly 20th century houses, with Totton's development spreading out to meet it. The large church of St Matthew was built in 1855, and must have served a scattered rural congregation as there is little evidence of pre-20th century houses. The church's design is strong and individual, and inside it has, unusually, two chancel arches one behind the other, needed to hold up the tower. **Woodlands** to the south has some earlier houses and cottages, and abuts the New Forest.

NEW ALRESFORD (E) 'New' because Old Alresford is the original village to the north: New Alresford was founded in 1199 by Bishop de Lucy of Winchester. At the same time the Bishop built a huge earthen dam to form Old Alresford Pond, not as was once thought as part of a canal to Winchester, but for a great fish pond and to supply water to mills. The pond was cleaned regularly: after it was emptied and the silt cleared out in 1253, the pond was restocked with 1072 roach, 603 bream, 229 perch and 115 pike.

The pond was originally 200 acres, but silting has reduced it to 30. Still very good for birds, especially over-wintering wildfowl. The dam which holds the water back is 20 ft high and 400 feet long, with the road on top. The best place to see it is from below. A footpath from the north-west end of Broad Street leads

ABOVE *Broad Street.* BELOW *West Street, New Alresford.* LEFT *The fulling mill*

down past a big brick mill, with the mill stream falling down steps. The dam towers to the east, and further along are watercress beds. Following the footpath along the river leads to War Memorial Gardens and then the fulling mill, a fine timber framed thatched building which straddles the stream. The footpath continues along the river to the bottom of The Dean. Fine river scenery all the way.

The original town forms a T, with one street wide to allow room for the market. Even when full of cars Broad Street is impressive. Most of the medieval houses were destroyed in fires of 1689 and 1736, but their replacements are handsome late 17th or 18th century buildings. At the north end is a tiny fire station, late 19th century, and opposite that is a fine late 17th century brick house still preserving its original mullioned and transomed windows. Some buildings are stuccoed, others tile-hung, many brick.

East and West Streets are narrower, but still with good buildings. National Westminster Bank, early 18th century in East Street, and the Bell and Swan Hotels (both coaching inns) in West Street are attractive. The Town Hall is a disappointment, yellow brick, plain and 19th century. Behind is the church of St John Baptist, mostly of 1898, large but not interesting. Showy tiles in the chancel, especially the east wall with gilt decoration. The tower is 14th century, with a brick top of the 17th century, and set externally quite high in the west wall, is a little Saxon crucifixion. Close to the tower are the gravestones of several French prisoners of war, taken captive during the wars with Napoleon.

Gravestones of Napoleonic prisoners-of-war at New Alresford

Station Road close by leads to the railway, part of the **Watercress Line** (see entry). A big warehouse in the yard dates from 1873, about ten years after the line opened.

Alresford was famous for its sheep fairs, originally held in Broad Street, but in the 19th century out on the Sutton Road to the east. Just out of the built-up area is Hurdle House, the brick and flint building where the hurdles were stored, now a dwelling.

On the west side of the town is a big house, Arlebury Park, with a double avenue of trees in front. Further out a fine brick toll house.

★ ★ ★ ★ *Town, best explored (including the riverside paths) on foot, perhaps along with Old Alresford.*

NEW FOREST BUTTERFLY FARM see **LONGDOWN**

NEW MILTON (M) Edwardian in the middle, mixed in with a lot of modern. Big pond just north of the town centre, and just south of the railway line a wonderful brick water tower of 1900 heavily

The water tower, New Milton

disguised as a castle. This new part of Milton only developed after the railway arrived in 1888. The church is to the south-west, in Old Milton. Tiny 17th century stone tower, the rest brick with the nave 1831. East end 19th and 20th century. All plain but handsome.

The **Sammy Miller Museum** (fee:lists) is to the west of the town centre, containing about 150 motor cycles ranging from some of the earliest pre First World War models up to the present, and storing the trials bikes used by Sammy Miller. Some of his trophies are displayed, and a reconstructed workshop of the 1920s. Road racers and speed record holders too. Must be the best motorcycle museum anywhere.

Right on the county boundary is the house called Chewton Glen, now a hotel but in the late 18th century the family home of the Marryats. Captain Marryat (1792-1848)who wrote *Children of the New Forest* was brought up here.

★ ★ ★ ★ *Sammy Miller Museum, for anyone interested in motorcycles or the history of transport.*

NEWNHAM (C/F). Large green in the middle, with a pond. 17th century timber framed houses scattered around the green, including one large one. The church of St. Nicholas was rebuilt in Norman style in 1847. The real Norman chancel arch, tower doorway and nave west doorway were re-used. Tower with small saxon-style top.

NEWTON VALENCE (F) A small village on the chalk, with a proper village pond. The church of St Mary is up what appears to be a private drive. It is basically Early English, including the tower (brick top of 1812) but has been heavily restored. Lots of good memorials. Huge ancient yew in the churchyard. The Manor House is close, the yellow brick part 18th century, the malmstone bit earlier. The parish has good field names including 'the Devil's Pleasure' and 'Dripping Pan Field'.

NEWTOWN (J) (South Hampshire) Like Soberton Heath, its neighbour, with a few older cottages outnumbered by recent buildings. Scattered oak woods. Large flint church of 1858 in amongst pine trees.

NEWTOWN (B) (North Hampshire) Right on the border with Berkshire. The timbered Swan Inn is the first Hampshire building one sees coming south. The area is too sparsely settled to seem like a

village, but in fact it was a medieval new town, founded by the Bishop of Winchester in 1218. The town flourished until the 17th century, but after that virtually disappeared. The church of St Mary and St John Baptist is a replacement of 1865, large and neat, with a spire. The area is well wooded.

NOMANSLAND (H) So called because it was not included in any of the New Forest keeper's areas, and so was under no-one's jurisdiction. High, with the green having a long view northwards. Most of the parish is in Wiltshire, but it is a typical New Forest mixture of brick houses.

NORLEYWOOD (M) (2 miles east of Lymington). A hamlet right on the southern edge of the New Forest, well treed. Narrow road, some cob and thatch cottages amongst the more modern houses.

NORTHAM see **SOUTHAMPTON NORTH**

NORTH BADDESLEY (H) Until the First World War North Baddesley was only a few farms along the ridge, with the little church and manor house on the highest point at its centre. In the last fifty years a large area has been developed to the south, away from the church.

North Baddesley church

The north part of the parish is still rural, and from the church the views are all wild and woody. The Knights Hospitallers, a medieval military religious order who looked after pilgrims, owned Baddesley, and from 1365 this was their headquarters for Hampshire. Their buildings were on the site of the 18th century brick manor-house opposite the church.

The church of St John is small and charming. Externally the tiny brick tower (dated 1674) hardly rises above the nave roof. The rest is a mixture of flint and stone, medieval. Inside there is no chancel arch, but a wooden screen dated 1602 which probably came from North Stoneham. A 15th century table-tomb in the chancel is dwarfed by a huge wall monument above, a classical extravaganza of 1620, much too big for the church.

The land of the Hospitallers was seized by the King at the Dissolution of 1536 and in 1553 it was bought by John Forster who had been steward of Romsey Abbey. A rhyme was still current in the 17th century:

'Mr Forster of Badsley, was a good man
Before the marriage of priests began.
For he was the first that married a nun,
From which he begat a very rude son.'

★ ★ *Wild landscape and church.*

NORTH STONEHAM (H/J)

Not really a village, but until the late 19th century a huge parish (more than 5,000 acres) served by a medieval church. The church is within the park of the big house, now demolished, but the dominant feature in the landscape is the motorway which cuts along this thin green gap between Southampton and Eastleigh. Half a mile north of the church is the aptly named hamlet of Middle, with a few old cottages, but all the little medieval settlements have been completely overtaken by the growth of Bassett and Swaythling to the south.

Just north of the church is Park Farm, the farmhouse converted from the stables of the big house of 1818. The name Park is a reminder that this was the medieval deer park of Hyde Abbey.

The church of St Nicholas is worth seeing, but is only open mid-morning to mid-afternoon weekends June-September. Unusually for Hampshire most of the church is ashlar, that is stone dressed to large regular blocks. Although there has been a church here since before the Norman Conquest most of the present structure dates from around 1600

North Stoneham church

although some of the windows are earlier medieval. The unusual big lead panels in the porch are war memorials by Eric Gill. Inside the church is open because there is no chancel arch, and chapels make the nave as wide as the chancel. In the tower opening is fine engraved glass of 1970, a big panel by Jean Mair. The side windows have reset fragments from a complete scheme of 1826, destroyed by bomb blast in the War.

The windows at the east end are medieval, the centre one in its original position, although elaborated internally during the restoration of 1826. The side windows are reset. They possibly came from St Mary's Southampton which was demolished in the 16th century. The church has interesting memorials: the most unusual is a black stone slab now under the carpet in front of the altar. It dates from 1491 and is a communal memorial to Sclavonian (Dalmatian or today Yugoslavian) oarsmen who propelled the Venetian galleys which came to Southampton to trade. It seems unlikely that they were buried here, so far from Southampton, and probably the stone was moved here from the demolished St Mary's Southampton. The biggest monument is to Thomas Fleming, Lord Chief Justice, who died in 1613, and his wife. Big reclining effigies, he in his official robes, and eight kneeling children below. Fleming signed Guy Fawkes' death warrant. The colourful and large marble memorial is to Admiral Lord Hawke, called the father of the British Navy, who died in 1781. The marble relief shows the battle of Quiberon Bay, where the Admiral was victorious over the French in

1759. As the inscription recalls 'whenever he sailed Victory attended him'. There are other good memorials of the first half of the 19th century, including one to John Fleming who died in 1844 with a fine portrait medallion by the local sculptor Lucas (see Chilworth).

★ ★ ★ *Church as an interesting rebuilding of 1600 and for its fine memorials.*

NORTH WALTHAM (E)

A big village, dense with wriggly roads. Lots of flint and brick, some thatched cottages and timber-framing. Big pond and a separate green, both picturesque. The church of St Michael is in a commanding position at the head of the green. Flint with a shingled spire, and mostly dating from 1865 with a little medieval inside. Brash Victorian school close by.

¾ mile south on the main road, the A30, is the Georgian Wheatsheaf Inn, where Jane Austen used to collect the family's post, delivered to the inn by stage coach. She walked over from her home at nearby Steventon.

NORTH WARNBOROUGH see ODIHAM

NORTHINGTON (E)

The estate village which went with The Grange. Rows of neat estate cottages off the road and running parallel with the valley. The church is slightly higher up, and very prominent. Hilarious wall, with terracotta pierced inserts and the top made from knapped flints, looking like an armadillo. The church of St John Evangelist was expensively rebuilt by the Barings of the Grange in the 1880s, but it is not

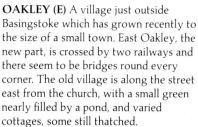

OAKLEY (E) A village just outside Basingstoke which has grown recently to the size of a small town. East Oakley, the new part, is crossed by two railways and there seem to be bridges round every corner. The old village is along the street east from the church, with a small green nearly filled by a pond, and varied cottages, some still thatched.

The church of St Leonard was re-built in 1869 incorporating some original 15th century detail including the west doorway. Good memorials including a brass of 1487 and alabaster figures of 1520 inside.

Malshanger to the north is a large late Georgian house with a thin tower of about 1500. The area around feels part of a large estate, with tree-lined lanes, woods, and neat Victorian estate cottages.

ODIHAM (F) A handsome small town, the High Street and the area around the church filled with houses and cottages ranging in date from the 16th to 19th centuries. The High Street is long and lined with good buildings. Some were refronted in the 18th century like the George Hotel, whose 16th century timber-framing is visible on the side. Almost opposite a small and charming 18th century shopfront. At the eastern end Marycourt with a huge shell-hood over the door, early 18th century. More timber framing on the streets to the church. The High Street curves round at the west end, and the Priory can be glimpsed through the trees. 16th century brick porch and oriel window, and a 15th century flint range. A good town to walk around, with something to admire at every turn.

particularly stylish. Outside knapped flints, both flushwork and chequer work, with a big tower modelled on those of Somerset. From the entrance porch a lane leads straight to the Grange.

Inside some good fittings including the chandeliers and candle holders, the pulpit with its own staircase, and in the tower the Baring family monument, with two large angels, one holding a big key, and a vault entrance in stone beneath. All 1848. Busts of Lord and Lady Ashburton of the Grange c. 1875.

★ *Church.*

NURSLING (H) A tiny village right on the River Test, now sadly dominated by the M27, whose roar can be heard even inside the church. Large pylons complete the modernisation. The core of the village is just a few nice cottages, a large house built in 1778 as the Rectory, and the church. There are a few other detached bits, including a housing estate and a large industrial area, all cut up by big modern roads and gravel pits. The church of St Boniface is mostly 14th century, with a big timber steeple. Jacobean pulpit, and in the south transept a fine monument of 1613, Sir Richard Mille and his wife: both effigies uncomfortably propped upon their elbows. She has a fashionable long slender torso. Classical contrast in the monument of 1751 to Thomas Knollys. Grove Place (now a school) a little to the north-east, is an Elizabethan brick house. To the south a cul-de-sac leads to Nursling Mill through a partly industrial, partly agricultural area. Manor Farm has lots of agricultural buildings and a big Georgian farmhouse. Nursling Mill is large, redbrick and dated 1728, slightly altered but still with two overhanging bays for loading. A footpath leads on to the river and then Testwood.

★ ★ *Church.*

OAKHANGER (F) Only a small village with several thatched cottages and the huge golf-ball like structures of RAF Oakhanger. The little brick church of St Mary Magdalene (1873) is in the centre. Several buildings are of local dark brown heathstone. Shortheath Common to the north is large and wooded, with many paths and a large pond. Several car parks give access.

High Street, Odiham,

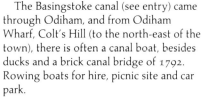

ABOVE *The Pest House, Odiham*
ABOVE LEFT *The Basingstoke canal at Coltbridge, Odiham.* LEFT *Odiham Castle*

Behind the church, to the south, are little brick almshouses of the 17th century, and in the south-west corner of the graveyard the pest house, built about 1625 to house those with diseases then thought to be infectious. From 1780-1950 it was an almshouse. Recently restored, and open generally at weekends.

North Warnborough to the north-west is a separate settlement but with houses and cottages like those in Odiham. Not so dense or so picturesquely arranged, but some thatch survives and a couple of jettied buildings. Georgian brick. The river and canal both pass through the village.

Odiham Castle is ½ mile to the west, best approached via the canal path as there is no reasonable road access. The castle was small, a halfway house for the King's journeys from Windsor to Winchester. Six sides of an octagonal keep survive, with holes where the windows were. It was built in 1207, and in 1215 King John set off from here for Runnymede to sign Magna Carta. The site is moated, but the canal cut through part of the earthworks in the 1790s.

★ ★ ★ ★ *Odiham town and* ★ ★ ★ *interesting church.*

OLD ALRESFORD (E) Disconcertingly, mostly more recent than New Alresford, which has a medieval church. The village is small, with some thatched cottages and a big triangular green. To the north, Southdowns, of brick and flint, originally The Industrial Home for Girls, built by the Hon Misses Arabella and Matilda Onslow of Upton House (one of the big houses in the village) in the mid 19th century. They also paid for the school and almshouses.

The Basingstoke canal (see entry) came through Odiham, and from Odiham Wharf, Colt's Hill (to the north-east of the town), there is often a canal boat, besides ducks and a brick canal bridge of 1792. Rowing boats for hire, picnic site and car park.

The church is to the south of the High Street, and in front under an open roof, are the stocks with one end a whipping post with iron clamps for the arms of the victim. All Saints is a large church, the flint parts 15th century (with 19th century windows), the tower brick (finished 1649) with lots of detailing including pilasters with pretty capitals. The porch, doorway and door are 15th century. Inside the nave is lop-sided because one side has more arches than the other. Impressive west galleries of 1632 either side of the tower, with stout pillars like supports in ships. The font is of chalk, 1634, with an inscription in difficult to read black letter

script, reading 'My help is from the Lord who made heaven and earth' (Psalms). At the west end a rare object – a hudd or graveyard shelter for the rector to stand in when taking funerals in bad weather. This one was used between 1859-91, a wooden frame covered with cloth. Nearby the parish chest, dated 1662. 1660 Royal coat of Arms (the date of Charles II Restoration) and very carved pulpit, 1634 with strapwork and flowers in vases. The church retains a remarkable number of 17th century fittings. The two east windows have splendid modern stained glass, that in the lady chapel a memorial to Neville Chamberlain's sister, all blue with a little green and gold. Both are by Patrick Reyntiens, who lived in Odiham (there is more of his glass at Hound). Three 15th century brasses behind the reading desk, and more in the lady chapel including two early 16th century women with their children.

Up the hill, alongside the church, are several large 18th century houses. Old Alresford Place, on the opposite side to the church, was built as the Rectory. Mary Sumner, the wife of the rector and mother of Heywood Sumner the artist and archaeologist, founded the Mother's Union here in 1876, as recorded on her memorial in the church.

Old Alresford House, behind the church, was built by Admiral Lord Rodney (1719-92) famous for defeating the French and Spanish fleets but a notorious gambler and womaniser. (Open in August only fee:lists). He built the house in the 1750s with part of his prize money, married and lived here happily with his wife until she died in childbed in 1757 (her memorial is in the church). He married again, but managed to become so short of money that from 1775-8 he lived in France to escape his creditors. When war broke out between France and England he had to borrow money from the French in order to return. He is buried in Old Alresford church, the rebuilding of which he helped to pay for, but his main memorial is in the crypt of St Paul's Cathedral.

His house is very plain and classical, built with red bricks from Bishop's Waltham. The forecourt has fine ironwork: the entrance doorway is of the 1760s, later than the house and more elaborate. The ceiling of the morning room has fine plaster, the eagle in the middle commemorating the name of Rodney's first ship. The dining room has 18th century French panelling, and the chapel wing has 1950s painted decoration. Rodney's bedroom upstairs looks out over the miniature park which he created, and along the terrace are small French cannon captured by him. All is small scale (for a big house) and enhanced inside by the vivid colours of recent redecoration.

The church of St Mary was rebuilt in the 18th century: the body of the church in 1753 and the tower in 1769, the dates being recorded on a stone on the tower. Stylish brick tower, with stone dressings: the church banded flint and stone. The church was slightly gothicised by Mary Sumner and her husband, to make the unacceptably classical building into a 'proper' church, but the interior still feels 18th century. Good naturalistic carving of plants including hops and grapes on the stone corbels of the 19th century alterations. Monument to Mary Sumner, plain with good lettering, and a huge flamboyant one to Mrs Jane Rodney,

Rodney's first wife, who died in 1757 aged 27. Big angel on the memorial to Esther North, 1828, wife of a rector here. Displayed in a case at the back, a clarinet played in the church band in the middle of the 19th century, and under the tower, in the entrance the Royal coat of Arms of Victoria, painted in 1837, the first year of her reign.

In the churchyard is a large mausoleum, built in 1839, the interior lined with marble and a handsome Italian marble relief of the Virgin and Child of about 1500. Opposite recently refurbished watercress beds, typical of the area.

★ ★ ★ *Church* ★ ★ *Old Alresford House.*

OLD BASING (E/B) Famous as the site of Basing House, scene of the most famous siege of the Civil War, and levelled to the ground afterwards.

Basing House (fee: lists) is best approached from the car park to the south-west. A path leads along the river, under railway arches to the 16th century brick Great Barn, with impressive timbering inside. This was the scene of fighting early in the seige, briefly taken by the Parliamentarians in 1643, but retaken immediately by the defenders. The rest of the farm and buildings date from after the Civil War, unsurprisingly as much of the village was destroyed during the long drawn out seige.

Inside the gateway to Basing House is what looks like a defensive moat but is actually the dry bed of the Basingstoke Canal which cut through the ruins in the 1790s. Beyond are the earthworks of the Norman castle, most prominently the motte, not on a high mound like most, but with an enclosing bank and ditch. In front of this are two outer baileys, less heavily defended. These early medieval defences enabled Basing to become a stronghold in the Civil War. In the 16th century William Paulet, who served Henry VIIIth, Edward VIth, Mary Tudor and Elizabeth Ist (he said (in Latin) "I am made of the pliable willow, not the stubborn oak") built a massive house here, partly inside the motte and partly on one of the baileys. The buildings were of brick, and rivalled Royal palaces in size. Today only the lowest parts of the Old House in the motte survive, and the brick walls can be traced showing for example the detached round towers at the entrance, the flint-lined cess pit and the cellars. A display has some of the finer architectural features of the building, including the head of a Roman emperor. The only

The barn at Old Basing

drawings of the house are difficult to interpret, and it was totally destroyed at the end of the seige, partly by fire and partly deliberately. The village used the ruin as a quarry for building materials, and many of the narrow red bricks of the village houses originate there. The garden

Part of the house ruins at Old Basing

wall, has two dovecotes, one thatched, and it is intended to reconstruct a Tudor Garden inside.

The village is picturesque, and the best cottages are between the House and the church. Neat brick and thatched cottage opposite the church. Behind the church a barn of the small bricks converted to a house, and opposite it a large house (Church Lane House) built as the workhouse in 1836, but again of small Tudor bricks. Good cottages continue along the road to the large railway arch, and even beyond. The park at this end contains Oliver's Battery, earthworks thrown up by the besiegers. The railway line passes right through Old Basing on a high embankment, very intrusive.

The church was damaged in the siege, and after the Restoration of Charles II in 1660 a national appeal was made for money to restore it. Basically, an early 16th century church although the brick walling is 17th century restoration. Little classical west doorway, which has been associated with the architect Inigo Jones because he was one of the prisoners taken after the seige. Surprisingly a statue in a niche survives above: one would have expected the Parliamentarians to remove it. Inside big and light, under the central tower the Norman side arches are the earliest surviving part.

The five monuments to the Paulets are on either side of the chancel, looking more like part of the building than tombs. The two on the left (north) are William Paulet's parents and grandparents, on the right (south) William Paulet who died in 1572 and probably his oldest son who died in 1576. The large north and south chapels were added at the same time as the tombs, and although the William Paulet and son tombs have classical details on the freize, they are otherwise identical to the earlier ones.

Unusually the south chapel has wooden tracery in the windows. In the north chapel a stylish memorial by Flaxman to the 6th Duke of Bolton who died in 1794, portrait bust in a circular recess. 1660 (year of the Restoration of the monarchy) Royal Coat of Arms, very naive with a chequered floor background. 1622 pulpit, highly decorated. In a west window impressive modern stained glass.

★ ★ ★ *Ruins and for church.*

OLD BURGHCLERE see BURGHCLERE

OLD MILTON see NEW MILTON

OLD WINCHESTER HILL (J) (east of
Corhampton). A large chalk downland Nature Reserve, partly short turf and partly scrub or woodland with the typical trees and bushes of chalk – yew and juniper. Rich in plants and butterflies, and large enough to give an idea of what vast areas of the chalk looked like before they were ploughed. William Campden described the hillfort on the highest point in 1637: 'there mounteth up an high *Hill*, environed in the top with a large rampier, and they call it Old Winchester: at which by report, there stood in old time a citie, but now neither top nor toe, as they say, remaineth of it'. Folk memory could hardly have stretched back to the Iron Age, when the hillfort with its simple single rampart was built, but the name remains.

There is good car-parking by the road, and many walks through the reserve, some strenuous, especially getting up to the hillfort. The views over the Meon Valley and further west to the New Forest and south to the Isle of Wight make the climbs worthwhile.

★ ★ ★ ★ *One of the best areas to see downland, but popular so best to avoid weekends and holidays.*

OTTERBOURNE (H/J) is still a village,
and surprisingly small and rural in comparison with its southern neighbour Chandler's Ford. The wooded hill and village street have some modern development but the street retains many 19th century and earlier buildings. Charlotte M. Yonge, the prolific Victorian novelist, was born here in 1823 the

Brambridge House

daughter of the squire of the village. She lived from 1858 until her death in 1901 in a house opposite the church. She wrote more than 160 books, mostly religious novels and is buried close to the memorial cross to John Keble (see Hursley) near the entrance to Otterbourne church. Keble was a friend and a great influence on Charlotte Yonge.

Otterbourne (and Ampfield) churches were designed by her father, with the help of a professional architect from Winchester, Owen Carter. Otterbourne was built in 1838, and is a real period piece. This was early in the Gothic Revival, before architects like Pugin had determined suitable styles for new churches. Charlotte Yonge, writing about it sixty years later, admitted that 'mistakes were made from ignorance and lack of authoritative precedent'. The church is broadly Early English in style, with a wierd bellcote copied from one in Wiltshire (now with its top missing). Grey brick was used, Caen stone imported for dressings, and old oak fittings were acquired. The apse was added in 1875.

A good picture of Otterbourne, Hursley and the surrounding hamlets through the 19th century is given in Charlotte Yonge's *John Keble's Parishes* (1898), which also describes all the churches in the area being built.

For Cranbury Park (to the west of Otterbourne) see **Hursley. Brambridge House** right down in the flat valley floor to the east of Otterbourne was rebuilt after a fire in 1872. A huge avenue of trees leads up to the house. Maria Smythe (better known as Mrs FitzHerbert) who

The Itchen at Otterbourne

became the Prince Regent's illegal wife in 1785 spent her childhood here. Narrow wriggly road across the valley. Footpaths run up and downstream from the bridge along the Itchen Navigation (see entry). Rural apart from the parallel railway.

★ *Church.*

OVERTON (E) In the 16th century Overton was regarded as a town, with a weekly market and several annual fairs. Even in 1912 the one remaining fair sold an average of 30,000 sheep. The town was founded in 1217 as a new town by the Bishop of Winchester. The grid plan is typical of medieval new towns, and the wide main street is reminiscent of Alresford. Overton declined, so that by the 1920s it was much the same size as it had been in the 1220s. The large paper mills to the north reversed the decline, being set up after the First World War to supply bank note paper to foreign countries. Now the old centre is enclosed by much modern development.

In the middle is a flinty Victorian school, now a library, not decisive enough for a focal point, and while there are pleasant individual houses in some quantity they do not build up to a picturesque whole except perhaps in the wide side street, where there are plain Georgian brick cottages and some thatch.

The church of St Mary looks well from the village, standing across the river valley in what was the original village. The stout tower dates from 1909, and much of the rest is Victorian externally with medieval features like the Norman arcades surviving inside.

Quidhampton is the name of the village settlement, to the north, now part of Overton. The big ponds on the Test were for the paper mills, and a much smaller and picturesque brick corn mill survives above them.

OVER WALLOP (D) Less dense than Nether Wallop, but with some thatched cottages, and some cob. In front of the church is a river meadow. The church of St Peter was virtually rebuilt in the 1860s, with a new chancel and tower with the rest of the church thoroughly restored by J.L. Pearson, a fine architect with a fondness for wrought iron, which he used here. Effective 1860s tile reredos with mock-medieval figures in the tiles.

Near Ovington

OVINGTON (E/F) Unselfconsciously pretty, running down the hill from the big house (with a Gothic cottage lodge dated 1839) to the river. The house is surrounded by an immensely long flint wall. Handsome brick, timber framed or flint cottages everywhere, many still thatched. In the middle a brick and flint farmyard, with a barn dated 1838. The church of St Peter was rebuilt in 1866, flint and stone with a fancy wooden top to the tower. Elaborate pulpit and reredos, with a reproduction table-type Purbeck Marble font.

A path leads from the north end of the village, by the pub, to Itchen Stoke, alongside the wide clear River Itchen. Very beautiful, with willows and other trees. To the east of the village, the handsome brick mill and millhouse, up a narrow and pretty road with a watersplash.

★ ★ ★ *Village and river walks.*

OWSLEBURY (J) The odd timber framed and thatched cottage, but predominantly modern buildings. The roads around are very picturesque, with many trees especially yews. The church of St Andrew has a complex plan, with the west tower dated 1676. Iron pillars supported the aisles, but they were handsomely panelled in wood in 1956. Big 1794 monument right up by the altar with a good bust. A serpent, a primitive wind instrument, used in the church band in 1840, is on display.

★ *Church, odd date.*

PAMBER (B) Several separate hamlets. **Pamber Heath** in the north, right on the

Pamber priory church

county boundary is a big modern settlement with a few older houses in the middle. **Pamber Forest** was a medieval forest, and still retains some areas of oak although there is a good deal of coniferous plantation. In the middle are **Pamber Green** and other rural hamlets, while at **Pamber End** in the south is the church of Pamber priory, now alone with an old farm and a big pond. The pond is the remainder of the extensive monastic fish ponds.

The Benedictine priory was founded about 1120 as a cell of Cerisy-la-Forêt in Normandy, and was dissolved in 1414 because by then Normandy was part of France, with whom England was at war.

Only the chancel of the church of 1150 survives. The wall of the nave looks like a boundary wall on the right leading up to the church. The crossing with its low tower is now the entrance. Although the chancel is only part of the original church, it is perfect, with long high simple lancet windows, and unusually a pair of circular ones.

The low arches either side at the west end were to side chapels, now gone. In one an oak effigy of a knight, early 14th century and over life size. In the entrance several 12th century grave slabs, one with a leafy cross and inscription. Otherwise the fittings are simple.

★ ★ ★ *Church, even though a fragment, as a complete architectural scheme.*

PALMERSTONIAN FORTS Portsmouth and Gosport were surrounded in the 1850s and 60s by a ring of the most advanced forts in the world, designed to prevent the French from being able to take England's most important naval base and anchorage. The line cutting off Gosport was the first to be built, in the 1850s, but rapid advances in long-range gunnery made them obsolete before they were completed. Explosive shells were replacing simple cannon balls, and the range of large guns was doubled during the 1850s.

The five forts of the Gosport line were originally intended to have linking earthworks. A further five on the Ports Down hill and one at Fareham were built 1860-68, but the three in the sea at Spithead took longer to complete because of difficulties in building on the shoals. Some sites had to be changed because they were on shifting sand, and the design of the sea forts was altered to include more iron after tests had shown that guns could easily destroy granite.

The Ports Down and Spithead forts were based on the latest military strategy, derived from the Crimean and American Civil Wars.

The forts never saw any fighting, although they were in military occupation until after the Second World War. Some have been demolished, and others are used by the Services, but three are open to the public. These were the last self-contained forts to be built in England, successors to the Iron Age hillforts and medieval castles, a concept now completely outdated by aerial warfare.

Fort Brockhurst ★ ★ ★ see Gosport; Fort Nelson ★ ★ ★ see entry; and Spitbank Fort ★ ★ ★ see Southsea, Portsmouth.

PARK GATE (J/N) Now bounded by the motorway, Park Gate grew up around an earlier form of transport: the railway station was one of the main gathering points for the strawberries grown in the area. Special trains ran all through the season, and in 1913 over 3,000 tons of strawberries were sent out from this station alone. The sending of strawberries by train stopped in 1966, but the redbrick station survives, with the adjacent station master's house now a restaurant. Fruit is still grown in the area, but modern housing and industry dominate.

PAULTONS (H) (at Ower just north of the motorway, 7 miles west of Southampton centre). Paultons (fee:lists)

was a large mansion, demolished in the early 1960s and taken over as a leisure park in 1980. The house has completely gone, but the ten acre lake has been restored. There are gardens, including a sort of Japanese rockery, and over 100 varieties of wild fowl, but the park is mostly visited for the children's adventure playground (very good) and other entertainments for the under 12s – pets, miniature railway, small theme displays, big dinosaur models in a swamp, etc. There are also a Romany Museum with a large collection of the brightly decorated vans etc; a Village Life museum with reconstructions of a smithy, wheelwright's shop etc and many objects, and a waterwheel of 1860 working sawing machinery. Small collection of animals including deer, llamas and the odd-looking large rodent, the capybara. Wildfowl on the lake, and many large aviaries with other species from colourful parrots to exotic starlings. A 2 mile woodland walk is offered.

★ ★ ★ ★ *For the under 12s.*

A gypsy wagon at Paultons

PENNINGTON (M) originally a village to the west of Lymington, but now difficult to distinguish from the town. **Lower Pennington** leads down into the marshes which line the shore. Good walking country (see also **LYMINGTON**). Pennington village is north of the main road, with the older houses on two roads which made a V shape, an unusual street pattern. A few thatched cottages, and more Victorian ones. The elaborate Victorian school and simpler church of St Mark (1859) are at the head of the V streets.

Lymington Vineyard is to the west of Pennington church and is open to the public (fee:lists). Besides the vines and wine-tasting, there is a slide show of the year in the vineyard and a herb garden.

PENTON MEWSEY (D) Dense centre, but still with a field in the middle. Rural despite the proximity of Andover. The church of Holy Trinity is small and pretty, mostly 1888 in Decorated style, with clear glass apart from some 15th century remnants. Intricate brick and flint Victorian old Rectory next door.

Penton Grafton is named separately but seems part of the same village. Pretty pond.

PETERSFIELD (K) A real market town, all on a human scale, albeit marred by the traffic which pours through because it is on the main road from London to Portsmouth. The town seems to have been founded in the 12th century, and still retains a good many Georgian buildings.

The centre of the town is the Square, with the parish church on one side. Until its demolition in 1898, the town hall stood between the church and square, blocking one from the other. One timber-framed house survives (unusually with flint infilling), but most of the buildings around the Square are Georgian or Victorian. On Wednesdays and Saturdays there is a market, but on other days it is dominated by the lead statue of William III dressed as a Roman in the middle. Latin inscriptions explain that this was sculpted in 1757, 'Sir William Jolliffe wishing to leave some memorial of the loving zeal which he himself had devoted to the cause of liberty and of liberty's Royal champion WILLIAM III provided in his will for this statue to be erected in the town'. It was transferred here from Sir William's garden in 1812 after the house

The Spain, Petersfield

was demolished, and was originally gilded.

Sheep Street has 16th century timber-framing and Georgian cottages and leads to The Spain, an informal green surrounded by handsome, mostly Georgian houses of red or grey brick or painted. The name is supposed to come from Spanish wool merchants who traded here.

The High Street is luckily not the main through road, but runs at right angles across it. A great variety of buildings from timber-framed to modern. At the back of 16 High Street, midway along the north side is Petersfield Physic Garden, recently established on the big back plot of one of the town houses. It has been laid out like a 17th century garden, physic because it supplied herbs for medicines. An orchard and topiary too, all the trees and plants being those known in the 17th century.

The Portsmouth Road southwards is called Dragon Street, with several Georgian buildings, the best being Dragon House in red and grey brick. Like so many apparently Georgian houses this is only a new front, with a much older timber-framed house behind. At no. 38 is the Teddy Bear Museum (free: lists) with displays of these beasts and other toys.

The London Road north is College Street. Close to the junction with High Street is the Red Lion, one of several large coaching inns needed on this important route. It seems to have been refronted in Regency times with shallow bow windows. At the north end of College Street is the original building of Churcher's College, 1729 of chequered red and grey brick. The college was

founded to educate boys to go into the East India Company, but changed in the 19th century to an ordinary school. The big Victorian stone buildings of the school are out on the London Road. Much of the rest of the middle of town has occasional Georgian buildings, and there are several late 19th century churches and chapels.

The church of St Peter on the Square is an interesting, basically Norman building. Unusually the aisles continue on either side of the tower. Inside it is clear that a central tower was originally intended, and the lower stages survive inside as a superb composition with the chancel arch.

William III at Petersfield

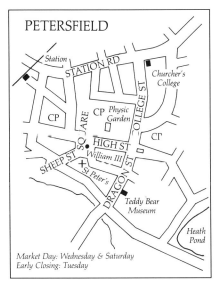

PETERSFIELD

Station

STATION RD

Churcher's College

CP

CP Physic Garden

COLLEGE ST

SQUARE

CP

CT

HIGH ST

SHEEP ST

William III

St Peter's

DRAGON ST

Teddy Bear Museum

Heath Pond

Market Day: Wednesday & Saturday
Early Closing: Tuesday

The arch itself is heavily moulded and zig-zagged, and above it is a triple arch, even more decorated, and above that a simple window.

The entrance doorway and the one opposite are Norman, but everything else externally is Victorian Neo-Norman. Many good monuments around the church especially those to the Joliffes. They are mostly at the west end, placed here after the restoration of 1873, and include one to John Sainsbury by Flaxman with two mourning figures. The roof was raised to give a clerestory at the restoration, and the chancel detail (including the impressive wall tiles) is all of that time too.

★ ★ ★ *Church for the Norman work.*

To the south-east of the town is Heath Pond, formed in 1867 from a swamp. Large, and with boats to hire. Some birches remain from the original heathland. On the north-east side are nine quite large Bronze Age barrows, some with ornamental clumps of pines on top. Good view of the chalk hills beyond.

★ ★ ★ *Town.* ★ ★ ★ *Church.*

PITT (H/J) A hamlet just to the west of Winchester, where there are more thatched roofs than tiled ones. The little flint and brick chapel was built in 1858 as a school room and chapel by the novelist Charlotte Yonge of Otterbourne. Pitt's isolation is about to be destroyed by development.

PLAITFORD (H) On the county boundary with Wiltshire and the New Forest boundary. The area is more agricultural than most of the Forest. The church of St Peter is small and charming, set away to the north of the village, on the side of a wide shallow valley. Basically 13th century and flint, but sympathetically altered in the mid 19th century. Inside everything is small scale, with a handsome gallery of about 1800 complete with its bench-like pews and a recent (1980) royal coat of arms. Lots of medieval floor tiles reset by the altar. Timber spirelet of 1850.

★ *Setting, scale.*

PORTCHESTER (N) Much visited for its fine Roman fort with medieval castle, the best in the county. The name now encompasses a huge suburban area, but on the promontory which runs out into Portsmouth Harbour much of the old village is preserved, and inside the castle is an interesting Norman church.

The village. A survey of 1405 shows that the settlement then extended from the Castle, all along Castle Street and around the cross-roads on the main route from Portsmouth to Fareham (now the A27). Although it had pretensions to being a town, Portchester was never really more than a large village until the 1930s. Since then thousands of houses have been built.

North of the A27, off the road going up the hill, is Portchester railway station, a small intricate flint building of 1848, a survivor from when the Portsmouth line was first built. Virtually nothing of the old village survives at the A27 end of Castle Street, but from the White Hart pub to the Castle there are lots of Georgian brick houses and cottages, and even one 16th century timber-framed thatched cottage. The road curves and widens to encompass a small green with an oak tree planted to mark the Jubilee of 1935.

The houses are a mixture of red and grey bricks or rendering with a little flint painted various colours. Many have the little lead firemarks which showed in the 18th and 19th century that they were insured with a particular company, whose own fire engine would come to put out a fire. Doors and windows are mostly simple. Perhaps the best individual house is St Vincent, built of chequered red and grey brick in the later 18th century by one of Nelson's Captains and named after the battle of Cape St Vincent. Good iron railings. Opposite is an oddly narrow house.

One lane from the green leads to the castle, the other to the shore (as a footpath) passing Portchester House with lots of Venetian windows (the centre part with high circular arch) which was used as the Officer's hospital for Napoleonic prisoners (see Castle). This lane is really rural, a surprising survival in Portchester, with arching hedges and even fields.

The Roman Fort. Portchester is the only Roman fort in northern Europe surviving in something like its original form. The outer walls enclose more than 8 acres, and were built in the 280s. It was probably originally a base for part of the Roman Fleet which was clearing the Channel of pirates. The enclosing walls have been repaired many times since the third century, and six of the original twenty bastions (little semi-circular towers) have been demolished. Parts of the original masonry show lines of red tiles used as bonding courses. The walls were originally 20 ft high and 10 ft wide,

but their width was halved by medieval robbers who quarried the inside face for building materials. The Roman land and water gates have gone: they were recessed just inside the fort, on the same site as the surviving medieval ones, but larger. There was a double ditch around the outside, including along the shore. When the fort was built the shore-line was further out.

A good deal is known about the date and use of the castle from the excavation of a large area on the south side of the interior, away from the later medieval castle buildings. It seems that both civilians and soldiers lived inside the fort from about 300, in timber rather than masonry buildings. Some Germanic or Saxon soldiers seem to have been present in the 4th century, along with women and children, presumably their families. Occupation continued through the 5th century after the Roman withdrawal in 410, and probably right through the 'Dark Ages' until about 700 when more substantial timber buildings were erected. Parts of the interior of the fort were used for agriculture. In 904 King Edward acquired the fort to re-use as one of his strong points in the defence of Wessex against the Danes. A large aisled (timber) hall was built about 1000, and a little later a masonry tower was built, possibly a bell-tower. All these buildings are only known from their traces in the soil.

The medieval castle. From around 1120 a castle was built in one corner of the Roman fort, and most of its buildings survive, albeit some of them as shells. Unusually this is a castle where we know about all the buildings, and all their different phases, because more than half the area inside has been excavated.

The gatehouse, with its bridge over the redug moat, has been gradually extended outwards so that the innermost part is Norman and the outermost 16th century, with two other phases in between. Proper castle-sized modern timber doors. The medieval enclosure seems small and cosy compared with the wide open space of the Roman fort, and the huge square keep is much more impressive than any of the Roman buildings would have been. The keep and the outer wall of the castle are Norman and are easily distinguished from the later buildings because they are ashlar (that is properly squared, flat-faced blocks of stone laid in regular courses) while the later medieval buildings are more random and include flint. The Roman wall survives here to its full thickness, making

ABOVE AND RIGHT *Portchester Castle: the disturbed ground in front of the graveyard marks the site of the excavations*
BELOW *Richard II's palace, Portchester Castle*

the outer wall of the Castle.

On the right as one enters are shells of buildings which were adapted about 1600, with square-headed windows and doors, and some brick. Next to the entrance is an odd juxtaposition – a doorway of about 1600 with the remnants of a Norman doorway above, decorated with Vs. The outer wall is Norman.

Assheton's Tower in the right hand (north-east) corner was part of the Constable's house, which also extended along the curtain wall, but only the basement survives there. The 14th century tower is an impressive shell, surreal inside with all the floors gone but windows and fireplaces still there.

The opposite corner has the palace built for Richard II between 1396-99. He abdicated in 1399, and died soon after so he never used the grand buildings here. Although they are inside the castle defences the large number of windows show that it was intended as a Royal palace, not part of a fortress. The main room, a large hall was on the first floor and the protruding stone-vaulted porch contained the staircase leading up to it. Norden, the King's Surveyor described this in 1609 as a 'verye fayre and spacious

Portchester church, in the Castle

hall, to which was an assent by a fayre stone stepps' but 'ruynous' because the lead had been removed from the roof. In the angle between the two ranges a passage leading from the hall to the private quarters in the smaller range can be seen at first floor level. Under the hall were service rooms – kitchen, storage etc 'darke and malincoly' according to Norden. A little gate in the corner of the west range led out to a latrine tower, now gone. Although these buildings are roofless, they are still impressive, and enough remains to understand them.

One of the small buildings in front of the keep was a chapel (with a large arch) and the original entrance was in same position as the modern stairs. The keep was built about 1120, and made higher around 1150, the earlier part having the buttresses. The large crack down the north face dates from 1247. Norden in 1609 thought that the keep 'annoyeth the rest of the howse THE castle by raflaxe of the chimneye smoake and therefore is thowght fitt to have it takinge lower by the halfe'. Luckily the keep was not reduced to half its height. Although the floors all date from the Napoleonic Wars or even more recently, the building is very atmospheric. An original spiral staircase adds to this, although the wooden ones are easier. Very good new display in the keep graphically explaining the long history of the castle. From the top of the keep the view is stupendous, truly panoramic and well worth the climb. The castle buildings below seem almost in plan, and Portsmouth Harbour mouth to the south, lined on one side with buildings and cranes. To the right (west)

one arm of the harbour runs up to Fareham, while the other continues to the head of the harbour, the castle marking the split. Acres of mud when the tide is out. Ports Down limits the view to the north with Portchester village in the foreground and suburbs stretching up the hill.

The Castle was used all through the earlier medieval period, losing importance from the fourteenth century as Portsmouth was founded and grew up at a more convenient point on Portsmouth Harbour. In 1415 Henry V and his army camped here on their way to Agincourt, and the castle was used in the Civil War. However its most crowded time was the 18th and early 19th century when prisoners-of-war were housed here. The peak was the Napoleonic wars when the Castle held as many as 5,000 prisoners, in the keep and in temporary wooden buildings out in the Roman fort. The basement of the keep was used as a theatre around 1800, and the prisoners even produced operas with proper orchestra and singers. The public were admitted, but after several prisoners escaped the theatre was stopped. The south-east corner of the castle was a detention place and has many inscriptions carved into the walls, and more are to be found in the keep and other places.

The Land Gate is basically Norman on the same site as the Roman gate although half the width, and re-using the Roman wall for its north side. The inner Norman arch still survives, but much of the building was altered in the 1390s.

The Water Gate has a very simple arch on its inner face, now known to be Saxon,

but its exact date is unclear. It can be matched at Titchfield church. The rest of the building is 14th century.

Postern gates. There were two Roman postern gates in the middle of the north and south walls. The southern one was blocked in medieval times, but the northern one survives, narrowed to a quarter of its width in the Norman period.

A walk right round the outside of the castle gives changing views of the sea and the buildings. On the north side, beyond the car park is a bank and ditch added to the defences in the 14th century, and closer to the sea is the sailing club, originally the Powder House where gunpowder was stored in the 18th and 19th centuries.

Church. In the opposite corner of the fort from the medieval castle is the Norman church of St Mary, built 1133-1150 as part of an Augustinian Priory. This moved over Portsdown Hill to Southwick in about 1150, possibly because the priory found it difficult to co-exist with the castle. The church became (and remains) the parish church. The other Priory buildings including a cloister, stretched from the church to the south wall of the Roman fort, where, high up in the wall, a row of latrine shoots survive, also seen clearly on the external face.

The west front of the church is an impressive Norman facade, the doorway arch particularly elaborate and with a window above with decorated pseudo windows either side. Inside the nave is very plain, barn-like because the windows are high, and with four high rounded crossing arches. All is Norman except the east end, which was rebuilt by Sir Thomas Cornwallis, Constable of the castle, about 1600. His memorial in the east wall has a portrait bust in armour, and is very classical. His east window is simplified Gothic. The Norman north transept has arcading and an arch to a chapel which has been demolished. The south transept has gone.

The font of about 1150 is of a more lush style than the church, with foliage scrolls and animals around the top and arcading below. On the north wall of the nave a big Royal Coat of Arms dated 1710 commemorating the restoration of the church with £400 granted by Queen Anne. The timber roofs from this restoration survive.

★ ★ ★ ★ *Portchester is well worth visiting to see the village and church, the fort and castle.*

Ports Down

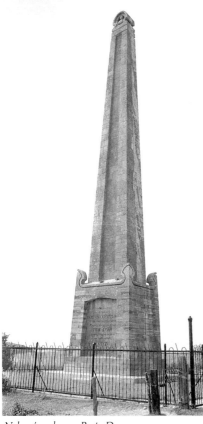

Nelson's column, Ports Down

PORTS DOWN HILL (N) An outlying chalk hill prominent behind the coastal plain between Bedhampton and Fareham, and providing the backdrop to views from Portsmouth. 'A narrow lofty eminence, running east and west for nearly seven miles. On the south, it commands a noble view of the British Channel, with its majestic feature the Isle of Wight, which is here seen through nearly its whole length. The dark blue tints of the New Forest mingle with the horizon in the west: on the north the eye commands the extensive vale of the Forest of Bere and on the east, the graceful spire of Chichester Cathedral appears rising above the level of the wolds of Sussex. To enliven and animate the whole, multitudes of ships and vessels, of every denomination and size, are seen'. (Britton and Bayley 1805)

A fair and horse-racing used to be held on the hill, and in the 1690s Celia Fiennes found it 'pleasant for Sports Hawking and Hunting' for the inhabitants of Portsmouth (then only Old Portsmouth), but now the most prominent features are the Palmerston forts, running from Fort Wallington in the west (see Fareham) to Fort Purbrook in the east. Fort Nelson is open to the public (see entry) and Fort Southwick still in use. Towards the west end close to Fort Nelson is Nelson's memorial, a column with a bust on it erected in 1807, two years after his death, and sited to look out over Portsmouth harbour. Car parks in many places along the top.

★ ★ ★ *The views, especially over Portsmouth Harbour, are superb, even at night with the lights of Portsmouth, Portchester, Fareham and so on.*

PORTSMOUTH (N) A small port which grew up during the 12th century as a replacement for Portchester, and remained small until the fifteenth century. From then onwards it developed as a naval and garrison town, expanding with the growth of the navy. In the 1540s John Leland wrote that the town 'standeth in a corner of an isle being the name ... this isle

Portsmouth from Gosport

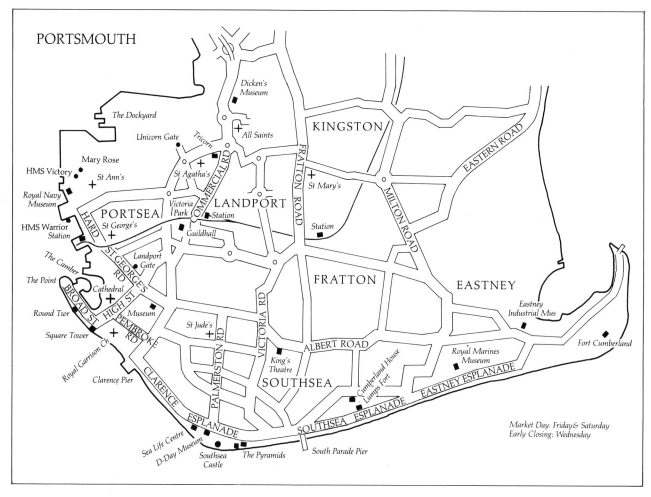

PORTSMOUTH

Dicken's Museum

KINGSTON

The Dockyard

Unicorn Gate · *Tricorn* · *All Saints* · EASTERN ROAD

Mary Rose

HMS Victory · *St Ann's* · *St Agatha's* · *St Mary's*

Royal Navy Museum · PORTSEA · *Victoria Park* · LANDPORT · *Station* · *Station* · MILTON ROAD

HMS Warrior Station · *St George's* · *Guildhall*

The Camber · *Landport Gate*

The Point · *Cathedral* · FRATTON · EASTNEY

Round Twr · *Museum* · *Eastney Industrial Mus*

Square Tower · *St Jude's* · ALBERT ROAD

Royal Garrison Ch · *King's Theatre* · *Cumberland House Lumps Fort* · *Royal Marines Museum* · *Fort Cumberland*

Clarence Pier · SOUTHSEA · EASTNEY ESPLANADE

Sea Life Centre · SOUTHSEA ESPLANADE

D-Day Museum · *Southsea Castle* · *The Pyramids* · *South Parade Pier*

*Market Day: Friday & Saturday
Early Closing: Wednesday*

---

berith good corn and grasse'. The town was only a small area right on the mouth of the Harbour, the Old Portsmouth of today. It took a long time for the town to grow out of the corner of the island, but by 1800 the population was 33,000 – by far the largest city in the county. By 1901 it was 187,000, almost as many as today – 190,000.

From the late 19th century Portsmouth was an important area for stay making, and then corsets, an industry which is now virtually extinct. Locally it was said that the only things made outside the dockyard were corsets and beer.

The naval name for Portsmouth is Pompey. The rest of the county used to regard it as a tough place, full of drunken sailors, but since the Dockyard closed and many new industries and cross-channel ferries arrived, this image has changed.

Portsmouth now has more museums than anywhere else in the county, with the greatest concentration in the Dockyard and along Southsea front. The historic ships are the most popular, offering the unique opportunity to see the 16th century *Mary Rose*, the 18th century *Victory*, and the 19th century *Warrior*.

Navy Days in the summer mean that current Naval ships are on view, and the fine Royal Navy and Royal Marines Museums are always open.

The geography of Portsmouth is difficult to grasp on the ground, partly because it is so flat, and partly because the various areas merge into one another. War time bombing and post war redevelopment have removed many of the older buildings, and the demolition of the defences of Portsmouth and Portsea in the later 19th century opened up the previously enclosed areas and blurred their boundaries.

Most of the churches of Portsmouth date from 1890s-1950s, with the greatest number 1900-1916. Many are brick and some are quite large. Only those which are prominent or of particular interest are mentioned individually in the text.

The city is liberally dotted with pubs, many of them tiled, some exuberantly Tudor, and were built from 1890s-1930s. The typical housing is grids of straight streets lined with terraced houses, having tiny or no front gardens. Almost all late Victorian or early 20th century.

Old Portsmouth
The Cathedral ★ ★ *Royal Garrison church* ★ ★ *The Point and the Defences* ★ ★ ★

The Dockyard
Mary Rose and Museum ★ ★ ★ *Royal Navy Museum* ★ ★ ★ *HMS Warrior* ★ ★ ★ *HMS Victory* ★ ★ ★ ★

Portsea
St George's church ★ ★

Southsea
Spitbank Fort ★ ★ ★ *Sea Life Centre* ★ ★ ★ *D-Day Museum* ★ ★ ★ *Southsea Castle* ★ ★ ★ *Natural History Museum, Cumberland House* ★ ★ ★

Eastney
Eastney Industrial Museum ★ ★ *Royal Marines Museum* ★ ★ ★

Landport
The Dickens Museum ★ ★

Kingston
St Mary's church ★ ★

Hilsea

North End

Old Portsmouth

This is the original town, founded in the 12th century, and until 1700 the only settlement of any size on the whole island. Until the bombing of the Second World War and redevelopment afterwards it was full of 17th and 18th century houses, but they now only survive in patches.

The Landport Gate of 1760 survives in its original position on St George's Road, now looking like part of the sports ground. The road side is the inner face, not so impressive. Until the 1870s the defences of Portsmouth, a moat and complicated ramparts, stretched right round the town, with this as the main entrance.

The High Street starts at the landward end with Portsmouth Grammar School, built in 1856 as barracks. Some Georgian houses survive. The cathedral was hemmed in by houses, but now sits in an open site. Behind the cathedral, particularly in Lombard Street and St Thomas Street, are picturesque groups of 17th and 18th century town houses.

Portsmouth Cathedral. Until 1927 Portsmouth was within the large Winchester diocese, but in that year Portsmouth Diocese was created, and St Thomas's church became the cathedral, • and was greatly enlarged. Externally is a difficult building to understand. The western parts are of the 1930s, with a short nave only now being completed. Side aisles enclosing the 17th century choir. The '30s parts are in smooth Norman style, and include arches cut through the tower, making a complicated plan.

The middle of the church was the nave of 1683-93, now the choir, classical with simple pillars. Only one of the wooden galleries survives, but the splendid pulpit is 1693. On one of the pillars an elaborate Royal Coat of Arms of William and Mary, 1694, wooden and carved by the

Portsmouth Cathedral

Dockyard's Master Carver. The southern aisle, added in the 1930s, is the Navy aisle, built with contributions from the Navy. In the floor is a beautifully lettered slate slab to the memory of those who died in the *Mary Rose* in 1545. The ship is being preserved in the dockyard. The captain of a later ship of the same name, Admiral Sir John Kempthorne, is commemorated by a monument.

The chancel is the most distinguished part of the church, the only surviving bit of the original, founded in 1180, and dedicated to St Thomas Becket, martyred only ten years earlier. The vaulting is plaster of 1843, and the chancel arch is the same date. The altar with its suspended canopy is of 1939, and in the south aisle is the memorial to the Duke of Buckingham, Charles I's favourite, who was murdered in Portsmouth in 1628. Big classical memorial with figures. To the north of the tower, on the east wall is a

fine pottery plaque of the Virgin and Child, made in Florence about 1500 by Andrea della Robbia.

On top of the plain 1690s tower is a pretty cupola of 1702 with a lantern over. This was really a lantern, a light to guide sailors into the harbour. Right on top is a gilded weathervane in the shape of a ship, dated 1710. (The one now on top is reproduction: the original is displayed inside).

★ ★ ★ *Church for the chancel and the 17th century parts. Good fittings.*

The Point is the narrow strip of land which makes one side of the mouth of Portsmouth harbour. It was technically outside the town of Old Portsmouth, and was a tough area, full of pubs. Many older buildings survive, including several of the pubs. As a viewpoint the far end is magnificent: the narrowness of the harbour mouth means that all the vessels passing through are close, and when a big

The mouth of Portsmouth Harbour with The Point (left)

Round the corner from the Point are many earlier houses with modern neo-Georgian filling the gaps made by bombing. On the shore, actually overhanging the water, is the timber clad Quebec House built in 1754 as a bathing house: sea water was taken into the baths at high tide and trapped there. The little square is still called Bath Square. The Portsmouth Sailing Club premises are an early 19th century sail loft, and to the south along the shore are deliberately picturesque late Victorian seaside houses, one with a fancy look-out tower.

The town and dockyard were defended from attack by sea from medieval times, and the best surviving parts of the defences are along the shore of Old Portsmouth. On the point is the Round Tower, now mostly 16th century

ABOVE *Looking into Portsmouth Harbour along The Point.* BELOW *Quebec House* RIGHT *The Camber*

ferry or naval ship goes past it seems as though the land is moving. The Isle of Wight ferries dock close by, but the channel ferries go on further up the harbour. Opposite on the far shore is Gosport, with the two big blocks of flats, and to the right is *Warrior* and *Victory*. Harbour installations are all around, and the small Gosport ferries dash across regularly. Grey naval vessels pass through, and submarines, which are based at Gosport.

Broad Street, the road to the point, has many 18th century houses on one side, and the harbour (The Camber) on the other, with fish for sale and many types of boats in the complex of inlets. In the middle of the warehouses etc on this eastern side is a pub, a surprising and popular position.

HMS Invincible *passing The Point, Portsmouth*

rebuilding, whose top offers the best view of the harbour mouth, and an extensive panorama of the Solent.

The defences were linked together as a walkway in the 1930s, so one can walk along the top of the wall (really a gun battery of the 1680s) to the Square Tower, built in 1494 but refaced in 1827. The building has had a series of uses – as a powder store, and from 1780 as a store for the Navy's meat. In 1823 a semaphore tower was built on top, to signal to ships in the Solent.

From the street the gilded bust of Charles I is prominent in the otherwise plain building, with a fulsome inscription recording the King landing here in 1623. From the street the Sally Port or gate through the wall can also be seen, with plaques recording a few of the many people who have passed through it to take boats to their ships anchored in the Solent. On the pavement is a bronze sculpture of two huge smooth links, placed here in 1980 to commemorate the links with Australia. Many of the emmigrants left England by the Sally Port.

Beyond the Square Tower, on the upper level, a wider part is the Saluting Platform. The walls stop just beyond, but the earthen defences start. Running right round the landward sides of Old Portsmouth were complicated zig-zag banks with moats in front, and this is the only surviving part of them because they were levelled in the 1870s. Although there were defences from the 14th century, this part dates from the elaboration of the later 17th century.

This walk along the defences offers history mixed with superb sea views. The Point and the defences ★ ★ ★.

The Royal Garrison church is tucked in just behind the defences, with Grand Parade in front. The church has had an eventful life, finally being bombed in 1941. This left the nave roofless, but it remains a very sturdy and tidy ruin. The building was originally a hospice for pilgrims, the present nave being a long hall divided up into bays where they slept. It was founded in the 13th century, and the surviving buildings are of that date, but heavily restored and with the west bay added in the 1860s. The chancel (fee:lists) is full of furnishings of the 1860s, with pretty tiles and choir stalls. Original stone vaulting, post war stained glass including several Second World War soldiers. Lots of photographs and documents relating to the building, and to the Governor's house which stood between the church and the defences. Catherine of Braganza and Charles II were married in the Governor's House in 1661. ★ ★ *Church.*

Grand Parade and Battery Row to the east have some Georgian and Regency houses surviving, and these with the rampart give the best idea of Portsmouth as described in Jane Austen's *Mansfield Park* (1814) where the Price family take their exercise on the ramparts with the rest of the inhabitants of the enclosed town.

Pembroke Road leading towards Southsea has big early Victorian houses.

The City Museum and Art Gallery (fee:lists) is just outside Old Portsmouth, housed in the Clarence Barracks of 1880 which were built on part of the area of the defences of Old Portsmouth. (The line of the defence can be followed quite clearly today by the playing fields parks and military buildings constructed on it). The Clarence Barracks look more like a straightened out French chateau, especially on the garden front where there are conically roofed turrets. Formal gardens this side, and on the entrance side a few modern sculptures. The museum displays a large collected of furniture and modern crafts, with little on the history or archaeology of the area. Temporary exhibitions too. ★ ★

The Dockyard

The Royal Dockyard, building, repairing and fitting out ships for the Royal Navy was half the reason why Portsmouth existed as a town. The other half was the sheltered anchorages for shipping available in the harbour and out in Spithead.

The original medieval harbour was the

Portsmouth Museum, originally Clarence Barracks

Camber, protected by Portsmouth Point, but in the 1490s the first dry dock in the world was constructed in open ground at the water's edge on the site of the present dockyard. Ships were built and repaired here, but it was not until the late 17th century that Portsmouth became one of the most important Royal Dockyards. During the 18th century the dockyard (and so the town) expanded enormously and during the 19th and earlier 20th century it was the major employer in the area, with 22,000 people employed at the end of the Second World War.

From 1700 the wooden buildings in the dockyard area were replaced by brick or iron ones, and despite bomb damage in the Second World War, many still survive.

The Dockyard was closed in 1984, although much of it is still part of the naval base and therefore closed to the public. The southern part houses the historic ships and museums, and also has some fine buildings.

The public entrance to the Dockyard is right by the Hard, through the brick wall built in 1708 to enclose the Docks. The rather domestic looking building just inside the gate (used by dockyard police) is the original porter's lodge of 1708. On the right are three boathouses arranged

around a pool, the back one brick of 1843 and the flanking buildings timber clad of the 1870s and 1880s. The Navy's architecture was happily very conservative – all these buildings are Georgian in proportions. The pond they surround is of 1665, used to store masts before use – they split unless stored wet.

One of the timber-clad boathouses houses the **Mary Rose Museum** (fee:lists). The ship *Mary Rose* sank in the Solent in 1545, in front of Henry VIII and the captain's wife. The ship was rediscovered under the mud of the Solent, excavated and the surviving half lifted in 1982. The museum is superbly laid out and displays the history of the ship, its significance in the development of ships and guns, and many of the objects found inside her. All the wooden artefacts on board were preserved, and some of the most interesting objects are wooden including a backgammon board, the barber-surgeon's chest with all its contents, and many simple bowls and platters. Reconstructions of parts of the decks and the barber-surgeon's cabin, along with a film give a good idea of the ship, the people who sailed her and their lives. The half of the ship which survived its 400 years in the sea bed is displayed in dry dock beyond the *Victory*. The *Mary*

ABOVE *The* Mary Rose *under conservation*
BELOW *Domestic objects from the* Mary Rose

Rose is undergoing treatment to dry out the timbers, which will take several years, but can be seen from viewing platforms.

HMS Warrior (fee:lists) is moored on the other side of the road. This huge ship was the Navy's first ironclad warship, built in 1860 and restored from the iron hull to its original condition at a cost of nearly £9 million. She is the largest of the preserved ships in Portsmouth Harbour, and despite all the fittings being reproduction, the most impressive. She was revolutionary because she was actually constructed of iron rather than simply sheathed with it, and was far larger than any contemporary warship, with larger guns and more of them. The ship was normally propelled by her sails, as she could only carry enough coal to use her engines sparingly.

As with *HMS Victory* the contrast between conditions for the crew of 300 and the officers is extreme. The crew lived on the main deck in just the same way as the **Victory's** crew, while the officer's quarters are opulent. The re-creation is superb, with even all the plates and tubs for every mess. Down below, the engines can be seen but it is the huge expanse of the upper and main decks which make the greatest impression.

★ ★ ★ ★ *HMS Warrior.*

The three huge brick buildings on the left hand side of the road on the way to *HMS Victory* were built as Naval storehouses in the 1760s-1780s. Simple but handsome, with classical detailing and good proportions, looking too sophisticated to be just storehouses. The extremely long brick block opposite the middle store, running for more than 1,000 feet, was the ropery, where rope was made for the Navy. In the 18th century Portsmouth Dockyard was one of the

largest industrial complexes in the whole country.

The storehouses now contain the **Royal Navy Museum**, recently redisplayed and giving a thorough history of the Navy and the men who served in it. One big area concentrates on Nelson and Trafalgar, and is ornamented with many ships' figureheads. This area helps one appreciate the *Victory* and the great battle against the French at Trafalgar, the turning point in the Napoleonic Wars. Other displays explain the rise of the Navy, attitudes towards it, development of the ships and so on, bringing the story right up to the Falklands.

★ ★ ★ ★ *Royal Navy Museum*

HMS Victory, the ship used by Nelson at the battle of Trafalgar (1805), is a remarkable survival. She was built in 1759 (2,500 oak trees were used) and survived the 19th century partly as a relic of the battle and partly as a guardship in the harbour. In 1920 the decision was made to restore the ship, and she was placed in the dry dock where she still remains. Parts

are fitted up to show what they looked like when the ship was in use: the extreme contrast between the Admiral and Captain's spacious mahogany fitted out cabins with their elegant furniture and the gun decks where the crew ate, slept and fought is a reminder of the effects of the class divisions of the period, reflected here as on land. The spot where Nelson fell mortally wounded, and the place on the orlop deck where he died are marked by plaques. The orlop deck is claustrophobically low.

★ ★ ★ ★ *Fascinating to walk around an 18th century ship.*

The *Victory* dry dock and the basin behind with more dry docks (one of which now contains *Mary Rose*) date from 1801, but parts beyond the open area are survivors from the 1690s. All the docks are lined with Portland stone, as are the sides of the basins.

A little of the complex of buildings beyond the area open to the public can be seen by walking up the road immediately to the right of the entrance gates. Through the new security gate can be seen the big redbrick Royal Naval Academy of 1730, and further along Admiralty House of 1780s in the then fashionable yellow brick. The Dockyard church of St Ann is beyond these, not visible. Those interested in Georgian church architecture may obtain a pass to visit St Ann's from the police at the gate. It was built in 1785 and has a fine plaster ceiling 'rose' and many naval memorials.

East along Circular Road, past several anchors and other naval memorials is the Unicorn Gate, one of the elaborate 18th century entrances to the dockyard, moved here in 1868. To the east is the **Museum of Dockyard Apprentices**, occasionally open to the public.

★ ★ ★ ★ *The Dockyard is interesting in itself, and the range of historic ships and museums makes it a must for visitors.*

Portsea

A separate town from Old Portsmouth, established about 1700 on the waste ground between the old town and the Dockyard. By 1800 the population was 22,000, triple that of Portsmouth, and Portsea had been enclosed by a rampart on the landward side from the 1770s. Until the Second World War Portsea was full of 18th century houses and cottages. Bombing destroyed most of them, and they have been replaced by dull modern buildings. Small pockets of Georgian survive.

HMS Warrior

Pubs on the Hard

The Hard is the road along the shore, once full of pubs and brothels catering to sailors. Trains come right down to the shore at Portsmouth Harbour, and ferries run to the Isle of Wight. The railway embankment cuts prominently across the road. Under the railway arches are a tatooist, cafe and **Old Portsmouth Toy and Doll Museum ★** (fee:lists). To the south along the shore a mixture of naval and conventional shops.

The best surviving building is **St George's church,** in St George's Square just back from the Hard. Built in 1754, it looks just like an American church of the 18th century, brick, with three tiers of domestic-looking windows and a complicated plan and rooflines. Inside there are big galleries and a classical arrangement of windows behind the altar. The church was restored after bomb damage. The rest of St George's Square is mostly modern. Isambard Kingdom Brunel, the famous engineer, was born in the Square in 1806, and Walter Besant the novelist in 1836. His novel *By Celia's Arbour* (1878) describes life in Portsea.

In Kent Street to the north of the church is another survivor – the Beneficial Boy's School of 1784 a classical barn. Close by in St George's Way a few Georgian houses survive.

★ ★ *St George's church.*

Portland Terrace, Southsea

Southsea

Sometimes considered a separate town from Portsmouth, but really it is not. The first building here was the Castle (see below), but it was not until 1790 that houses started to be built to the east of Old Portsmouth. The earliest faced the ramparts of the attractively tree-covered defences, and a little of one of these, King's Terrace, still survives.

The present extensive Common along the shore was preserved from development because it belonged to the Government and was used for military purposes. Thus the 19th century buildings had to be constructed a good way back from the sea front, as they still are. The growing suburb spread eastwards through the 19th century, with tall terraces facing the Common (some now replaced by modern blocks of flats) and a greater variety of houses inland. From the beginning Southsea had a large proportion of upper-middle class residents including retired Army and Navy officers, and until about 1860 it was more a high class residential area than a resort. A local architect Thomas Ellis Owen was responsible for much of the development before 1860, building classical styled terraces and villas in big plots along winding roads, with lots of trees.

The best area to see his work is at the north end of Palmerston Road. Here he built St Jude's church in 1851 to serve the new suburb. The church is of small flints, and more interesting as a focal point with its pretty spire than as a building. Just to the south is Portland Terrace, one of his finest buildings, classical and stuccoed,

dating from 1847. There are several other terraces in Southsea, and also his distinctive villas, quirky and varied in style. Infilling has taken away much of their leafy setting, but the roads still curve in the picturesque manner. The Vale to the west of Palmerston Road is the best preserved area.

After about 1860 Southsea developed as a seaside resort, with piers, hotels and a railway. H.G. Wells, who was employed in a Southsea draper's in the 1800s hated it, and soon escaped into teaching, using some of his experiences later in his novel *Kipps*. Conan Doyle came to Southsea as a doctor in 1882 and stayed for 8 years. The first Sherlock Holmes story *A Study in Scarlet* was written while he was there.

By about 1900 the whole of Southsea was developed, so that almost all the buildings are 19th century.

The seafront reflects Southsea's growth as a resort, which probably peaked in the 1930s, before foreign holidays were common. Starting at the western end, there is Clarence Pier, which was first built in 1816, but now dates from 1960 because it was bombed in the war. The buildings are characteristic 1950s seaside, now with rather a period flavour – space invaders etc and a big fun fair. Just to the south is the anchor from Nelson's *Victory*, the first of many naval memorials along the shore. The largest is the Naval Memorial to those lost at sea in the First World War.

From the seafront the three circular forts actually in the Solent are prominent, looking like neat circular islands. They were constructed on high points in the

Southsea seafront

seabed as part of the 1860s defences of Portsmouth (see entry: Palmerstonian Forts). The closest, **Spitbank Fort**, has been restored and is open to the public. Boats leave from Gosport Pontoon and Clarence pier (fee:lists) and the whole trip takes about two hours. The fort is simpler in plan and more compressed than the land forts. Guns have been replaced in some of the galleries, and there are passages everywhere.

★ ★ ★ *for an unusual fort.*

The Sea Life Centre (fee:lists) displays a great variety of live fish. The deep sea tank is impressive and another has flat fish. Small sharks.

★ ★ ★ *Interesting, perhaps especially for children.*

The D-Day Museum was opened on the 40th anniversary of the Allied Invasion of Europe in 1944 which forced the final defeat of Hitler. Portsmouth was the main port used by the invasion fleet. One part of the museum was constructed to house the 83 metre long Overlord embroidery, privately commissioned in 1968 as the equivalent of the Bayeux Tapestry, embroidered 900 years earlier to commemorate another cross-channel invasion. The Overlord tapestry is superb, modern in style graphically illustrating scenes from the invasion and the preparations for it. The rest of the museum is as good, using set pieces and sound to tell the whole story of the invasion.

★ ★ ★ ★ *Heartily recommended.*

Southsea Castle was built by Henry VIII in 1544 as part of a series of forts along the south coast (see also Hurst and Calshot Castles) and it was from here that he saw the *Mary Rose* sink in 1545. The castle was the only building in Southsea

until the 18th century, and was sited there to be close to the deep water channel so that guns could fire into any invading fleet. The present shape of the outer works is like that of the 1544 fort, but it has been modified many times. The entrance has the Royal Arms of Charles II, recording 1680s alterations. Inside, the central square keep of 1544 survives, but the staircases and gun platforms are of 1850, replacing earlier ones. Much of the brick around the castle dates from 1814 when the interior of the keep was adapted. The spooky tunnel (really a caponier, a protected way through which soldiers could move to get better positions to shoot attackers) is 1814 too. In the keep is a good display on the military history of the Portsmouth region. Planted oddly on one side of the Castle is a small lighthouse of the 1820s.

Good views from the gun platforms, especially seawards where the Castle's successors, the three Palmerston forts actually in the Solent, can be seen. The castle saw use in the First and Second World Wars, and only became a museum in 1960.

★ ★ ★ *Southsea Castle.*

Beyond are the distinctive buildings of The Pyramids, the modern equivalent of a pier, with indoor pools etc. South Parade Pier yet further east has had a chequered history. It was first built in 1879, destroyed by fire and rebuilt in 1908 in opulent Edwardian style. This pier was badly damaged by fire in the 1970s, but has recently been restored to something like the original. A walk to the end gives extensive views.

The Canoe Lake was once a wild pond surrounded by marsh, one of several on Southsea Common. The rest were

abolished when the Common was levelled in the 1880s, but this one survived in a much more formal style. Larger late Victorian houses surround it, and on the north side is **Cumberland House** (on Eastern Parade) which houses the city's Natural History Museum (fee:lists) with good displays on life in ponds and rivers (including live fish etc), geology and natural history of the area, ecology, the ice age etc. Graphic displays, good for children (and adults). In summer the butterfly house has live butterflies.

★ ★ ★ *The house is early Victorian, one of the earlier ones this end of Southsea.*

On the shore further east is Lumps Fort, an early 19th century gun battery adapted as part of the 1860s defences. The interior is Southsea Rose Garden, very pretty. The concrete remains of the ramparts date from the Second World War. Beneath them is **Southsea Model Village** (fee:lists) with miniature houses and so on, set in a garden. Beyond Lumps Fort is Eastney (see entry).

Inland there are several different shopping areas. Albert Road is particularly interesting because of the flamboyant Edwardian King's Theatre prominent on a corner plot. Lots of small shops.

Eastney

The south-eastern corner of the island, with mostly 20th century housing. The area runs to Langstone Harbour, where a wide spit makes the entrance narrow, and the tides race through the gap. A passenger ferry runs to Hayling and there are many small boats.

On the north side of the bay, which is muddy, are the remains of the entrance to the Portsmouth and Arundel Canal, which ran to the basin at Commercial Road shopping centre. It was the shortest and most unsuccessful of Hampshire's canals, opening in 1882 and closing five years later having leaked sea water into the town water supply. The redbrick lock to the sea survives, with a bridge over it, and a short length of the canal, preserved because they are used by a sailing club.

A path leads north along the shore, giving flat views across Langstone harbour with its mud and birds. There are a few older houses down on the shore.

On the seaward side of the entrance is Cumberland Fort, unusually dating from the 18th century. From the road it is mostly concealed by its own defences. Mostly earthen ramparts.

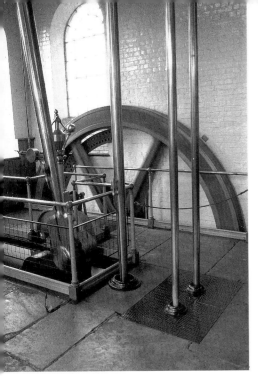

A beam engine in Eastney Industrial Museum

Eastney Industrial Museum (fee:lists) is centred around the 1887 Pumping Station with its two huge beam engines. The building and all the machinery are a monument to Victorian engineering, which solved the problem of sewage disposal on the awkwardly flat island. The engines are in steam regularly, and best seen then. Other displays on industrial archaeology, and in an adjacent building are three large gas engines of 1903, also used for pumping sewage. Fascinating for those interested in industrial archaeology. ★★*Museum.*

Portsmouth Arts Centre in Reginald Road Eastney, has changing exhibitions throughout the year. It is housed in a big Edwardian school, with one entrance inscribed in stone 'Manual Instruction'.

Westwards is Eastney Barracks, built in the 1860s for the Royal Marines. Big plain brick blocks, with a high water tower masquerading as a castle tower. The most elegant building is the stone officers mess, now **The Royal Marine Museum** (fee: list). Entrance to this is from the road along the seaside. One of the best military museums in the county, showing the development of the marines, originally soldiers on board ship, from their establishment in the 17th century up to the Falklands. Large area of displays with vehicles outside, and interesting to see the ornate interior of the building. ★★★ *Museum*

Landport

Named from the landward gate of the town defences. A small settlement grew up here from the 18th century, expanding rapidly after the ramparts were levelled in the 1880s. The Guildhall was built here in 1890, and Commercial Road developed as a shopping area. The Guildhall is in rich classical style, of white Portland Stone. It was gutted by bombing in the Second World War, and lost most of the small towers and its steeple, but remains impressive, with the grand flight of steps to the main front. The Square now has modern buildings on two sides. Big statue of Queen Victoria. A path leads through the north-west corner to Victoria Park, created when the defences of Portsmouth were obliterated in the 1880s. Lots of military and naval memorials, and a good aviary.

The late Victorian Roman Catholic cathedral of St John Evangelist is on the west side of Victoria Park, of brick and stone with pretty windows.

Beyond the south side of the Guildhall is a similarly classical building of stone, originally the Municipal College, which opened in 1908.

The street south from Guildhall Square (Guildhall Walk) contains the best mixture of Victorian building in the town. The White Swan pub is Victorian Tudor at its most exuberant, and the Theatre Royal next door is also good with a cast iron frontage, dating from 1900. The fine plasterwork inside has a riot of nautical emblems. The terracotta Prudential Buildings are of 1891, and on the other side are the domes and minarets of the Palace Cinema (1924).

Commercial Road to the north was badly damaged by bombing and rebuilt mostly in Portland Stone: it was pedestrianised in 1977 and has a large modern fountain with heraldic beasts set in the middle.

Off Charlotte Street is the Tricorn, a startling modern development of 1966, all concrete with prominent ramps. Very

Portsmouth Guildhall

ABOVE *Guildhall Walk, Portsmouth.* BELOW *All Saints, Landport*

unpopular, it has not proved successful for shops. Cascades, a more recent shopping mall, is next door, and in a totally different style – neo-Victorian. Close by, isolated by the modern roads, is the church of St Agatha, an 1890s brick barn externally but with Heywood Sumner's fine scraffitto and mosaic decoration inside.

Another church left in an exposed position by modern roads is All Saints towards the north end of Commercial Road. This was designed by Jacob Owen (the father of Thomas Owen the Southsea architect) in 1827, and is a fine example of pre-Victorian church. Outside it is neat and regular, nothing like a real medieval church, and inside it is all slim cast iron and plaster vaulting. The chancel was added in 1877 in proper stone, but fits well with the light-hearted original. The main body of the church has recently been divided and the back part turned into a hall with a ceiling at conventional level.

The area around is all modern flats and maisonettes, apart from one small area of early 19th century houses. This little bit of Old Commercial Road is preserved because Charles Dickens was born in one of the houses. Now a conservation area, and with through traffic removed, it is the one area to give the feeling of early 19th century Portsmouth. 393 Old Commercial Road, **Dickens' birthplace,** is open to the

145

public as a museum. His family lived here for only a few months after his birth in 1812. Dickens' father worked in Portsmouth Dockyard, and the house is now furnished as it might have been when the family lived there. Dickens returned several times to Portsmouth later in life, most notably to research the part of *Nicholas Nickleby* set in the town. He managed to discover the terrace of four houses, but was never sure which one he was born in. Interesting house both for the Dickens relics and as a lower middle class home of the early 19th century. Small, but well furnished.

★ ★ *More for anyone interested in Dickens.*

Kingston

St Mary's Kingston was the church for the whole of the island outside Old Portsmouth. Kingston was a little cross-roads settlement, with a small population until the 19th century, but then expansion was fast and the church was rebuilt in the 1880s on a scale to match. The outside is pebbly flint, large and high with an impressive tower that was for a long time the highest building in Portsmouth. Inside the nave is enormous, with only a tiny chancel. The hammer beam roof is interesting, and there are many other rich Victorian fittings.

★ ★ *Church, somehow rather alien and cold, but impressive.*

Hilsea

The north part of the island, and was only a roadside hamlet until the late 19th century. There had been small forts to defend the only bridge to Portsmouth island since the 17th century, but in the 1740s the whole of the north side of the island was fortified by the building of the Hilsea lines, an earthen rampart with moat in front. The lines were modernised in the 1860s when the Palmerston forts on the hill were built.

The motorway now roars along parallel with the lines, with earthworks on a larger scale than the defences or the little creek which makes Portsmouth an island.

The western part of the lines was modified in the 1930s when Hilsea lido was constructed. The moat was formalised into a boating lake, and some of the area planted as a park. The rampart remains at the back, with trees. The eastern parts are rather wild, and the steep rampart is mostly tree-covered. The central section is fully accessible, and the

brick-lined parts on the back of the corners can be seen.

There were barracks in Hilsea from 1780, but most of them have recently been demolished. Gatcombe House, a big Georgian house taken over by the barracks survives, and one large Victorian building. Opposite the barracks is Hilsea Farm, a simple 17th century timber-framed house, still with its barns and so on, now completely out of place surrounded by modern housing.

A farm in the eastern part of Hilsea was taken over as an airport in 1932, and adjacent Langstone Harbour was intended to become a marine airport for flying boats. In 1933 the Airspeed firm moved their air craft factory to the airport. Neville Chute was one of the partners in Airspeed. The airport closed in 1972, and the area is now virtually covered by factories and housing.

North End

The western shore of the central part of the island has the unromantic modern ferry terminals and Whale Island just off the shore. This is largely man-made, constructed from dredged material in the late 19th century. It belongs to the Navy and is not accessible, but a small car park by the bridge to the island gives wide views of the northern part of the harbour, with cranes everywhere, the grey naval ships and dockyard in the background and closer the more colourful car ferries and their terminal. Close to the turn from the big modern road to the ferries is a fine Victorian tudor pub, the Air Balloon, with extravagant figures and so on. Flathouse Quay to the south is the small commercial port for cargo ships.

At **Fratton** is the big St Mary's Hospital, mid 19th century onwards, and close to it the Victorian castellated stone Prison.

Copnor has a smallish park in the middle, but otherwise typical Portsmouth grids of straight roads are filled with terraced houses.

MAINLAND PORTSMOUTH

Cosham

In 1908 VCH described Cosham as dividing into two parts: East Cosham along the road to Havant 'chiefly residential houses surrounded by pleasant gardens' while the other was the commercial centre, still then rural enough to have a weekly cattle market. Some of the villas survive on the Havant road (a

few of them Regency), but the area has developed to cover virtually all the land, and even the reclaimed parts to the west now have commercial buildings.

Cosham station is in the south of the old High Street, and dates from 1847. The level crossing next door has contributed greatly to traffic problems since until 1930s all Portsmouth's traffic passed through Cosham. The High Street is mostly modern.

Cobbett thought when he saw this area in 1823 that 'it is impossible that there can be, anywhere, a better corn country than this .. from Bedhampton to Fareham are not less than eight square miles of cornfields, with scarcely a hedge or ditch of any consequence' Cobbett was sure that corn was cut earlier here than anywhere in the country, the harvest normally starting in July. The whole of his eight square miles of cornfield has disappeared under bricks and mortar.

To the south-east of the railway station is the huge Highbury estate, built in the 1930s, one of the first big areas of housing off Portsmouth island. The terraces and semi-detached houses have distinctive scrolls under the roofs. Cosham had no church, and the building of this large estate meant that one was needed badly. St Philip's was built on the edge of the estate in 1936, with all the costs being met by Lady Mary Harrison, in memory of her husband Sir Heath Harrison. The vicarage and church hall form a three-sided courtyard with the church.

The church was designed by Ninian Comper, one of the most important church architects of the 20th century. Outside the building is austere, faintly early 19th century in style, but as John Betjeman wrote 'you would never know from its outside how breathtaking is the interior'.

The inside is certainly a surprise – square and high with crisp plain vaults with simplified classical capitals on thin pillars, all painted white. Against this serene background the vividly coloured fittings make bright episodes. The altar canopy first takes the eye – gold and intense blues. The font cover is similar, and both have fine paintings – of angels on the canopy and a dove on the font cover. The west gallery holds the organ, the gallery plain white, the organ gilt and blue.

By contrast the communion rails all around the free-standing altar are plain dark wood, as is the pulpit. Comper

St Philip's church, Cosham

designed the silver, vestments, altar frontals – everything. The stained glass in the east window is incomplete, but the part which was done is effective.

Comper described the mixture of styles he used here as unity by inclusion, ie using features from all styles. Here he succeeded in producing a wonderful church in diverse styles which all come together superbly.

★ ★ ★ *Church, best 20th century church in the county (and probably beyond).*

Drayton

Part of the continuously built up area on the mainland, but only a farm until the late 19th century. The church of the Resurrection in Lampeter Avenue was built in 1930, reflecting the recent growth of the area. Ports Down is always in the background, with a row of houses along the top.

Farlington

Famous to bird-watchers for Farlington Marshes on the edge of Langstone harbour with its thousands of over-wintering wildfowl, waders, gulls and little tern colony. There are car parks off the A27, and a footpath leads right round the landward parts.

In 1891 Portsmouth Park race course was laid out at Farlington, with a railway station built specifically for the traffic. Horse-racing ceased in 1915, and the area was used as a dump for ammunition which was broken up there during the 1920s. The area has now been built over.

The church of St Andrew is on the old main road from the east. It was virtually rebuilt in the 1870s by the distinguished architect G E Street and is particularly effective inside.

Next door is the old Rectory, plain and early 19th century. This seems to be the only old building in Farlington – the rest is 20th century.

Paulsgrove

Virtually only a house on the A27 until after the Second World War when it rapidly developed as a vast housing estate. From 1928 for ten years the lower slopes towards Wymering were a horse racing course, with motor cycle racing as well. Racehorse Lane leading over the railway commemorates this short-lived enterprise: the whole area of the race course is now built over.

The centre is a small park with shops on one side and the church on the other. Ports Down rises steeply behind, one part cut away by a big chalk pit.

Port Solent

A marina and new housing to the east of Portchester, set inside the large earthworks of the motorway. There are shops around part of the marina, which has a lock to keep the water in this upper part of Portsmouth Harbour which would otherwise be mud at low tide.

Widley

Just over the top of Ports Down on the main coach route north. In 1908 it was a small secluded hamlet with only a few cottages, church and farmhouse. Now it is really a suburb of Portsmouth. The replacement church Christ Church, is close to the main road, Neo-Norman of 1874, and appears suddenly coming from Portsmouth, just over the crest of Ports Down.

Although the west is still farmland, on the east of the main road Widley joins up with Purbrook. To the south on the crest of Portsdown Hill is the George, the last

Fort Widley

coaching inn on the London-Portsmouth route. Modern roads have altered its habitat.

Fort Widley to the west is one of the 1860s Palmerston forts, with a magnificent view over Portsmouth and Langstone harbours.

Wymering

A small medieval village on the slope of Ports Down which has been swallowed up by the expansion of Portsmouth. Surprisingly the village centre survives, with the church, manor house and cottages.

The church of St Peter and St Paul was thoroughly restored in 1860, with a pretty bell turret. Behind the church is the Georgian rectory, and to the north-west is the large manor house (now a Youth Hostel) dating from the 17th century onwards, a proper accretion of wings and different dates. A few older cottages including a handsome flint one with verandah.

Further up the hill are the large buildings of the Queen Alexandra Hospital, founded in the early 1900s as a military hospital.

PORTSWOOD see SOUTHAMPTON NORTH

PRESTON CANDOVER (E) Larger than the other Candover villages, with a Victorian church (of St Mary) in the middle, and the remains of an earlier one a little southwards. Between the two are two large Georgian houses on either side of the road.

PRIORS DEAN (K) (west of Hawkley) In

1900 Hudson recorded a saying in villages around that you had to cut the nettles down in order to find Priors Dean church. When he saw it there was only the church, an ancient yew, a farm and a few cottages, and surprisingly that is all there is today. The hamlet is in good chalk countryside, still with many hedgerows and small woods.

The name came because the village belonged to Southwick Priory. The church is tiny, basically Norman but 'restored' in 1856. The churchyard is dominated by an ancient fissured yew, one of those which are thought to be a thousand years old. Inside the chancel arch and most of the fittings are 1856 apart from the bellframe and the monuments. Up in the chancel are a series from the Compton family of nearby Colemore. The earliest are the brasses on the floor, 1605. The four wall monuments are to Sir John Compton and his wife, 1653 with busts; two of their daughters opposite, both of whom died before their parents, one aged only 21 but having had four children; and finally the heir, a grandson of Sir John who died only four years after his grandfather. They form an interesting series of closely contemporary monuments, gradually becoming more classical, and are individually attractive. Fragments of another monument of similar date are reset around the nave.

A mile to the north is Goleigh Farm, an impressively large timber framed building.

The whole hamlet ★ ★ ★ for its lack of change, and for the church monuments.

PRIVETT (J/K) In 1900 Hudson found Privett church a 'jarring and discordant thing ... ' with a 'gorgeous yet vacant and

cold interior'. Hudson disapproved of new large churches in the countryside, but today we can appreciate fine Victorian churches for their own sake, not as imitation medieval. Holy Trinity, Privett was built in 1877, designed by Arthur Blomfield and paid for by the Nicholson family, distillers, who lived in a large house just to the north of the village, now demolished. They spent a great deal of money on the church, but Blomfield gave them good value producing a large and impressive church in the Early English style of the 13th century. The 160 ft spire is visible from miles around, somehow looking slimmer than it does from close to. Externally the body of the church is undressed flint and stone, a busy surface but organised within a regular framework, typically Victorian. Its position on the top of the hill is fine, with extensive views, but the church is surely far too large for the village at any date. The walls inside are not plastered, but lined with faced stone. The red stone around the lower part came from Dumfries, the almost white from Bath, the yellow from Ham Hill, Somerset, and the steps are from Yorkshire. The floors have Italian mosaic, and the best fittings (all of which are 1877) are the stone pulpit and font, and the colourful chancel.

The village is small and most Victorian, with a lot of flint in the buildings.

★ ★ Church, a rich example of its date, in a fine setting.

PURBROOK (N/O) A village over the hill from Portsmouth, which has grown largely since the Second World War. Still rural to the West. The church of St John is a replacement of 1843, and is next to the later Victorian school in the middle. Both are built of large flints. A few other earlier buildings survive, including a Georgian house and some cottages, but most of Purbrook is 20th century. Off Stokes Road (which leads east from the centre) is Old Van Diemens Road with a complicated cottage dated 1844 on the corner and then a row of single storey cottages named after Van Diemen, the Australian explorer who discovered Tasmania in 1642. To the south-east is Fort Purbrook (not open) one of the Palmerston forts.

QUARLEY (D) One of several pretty villages in the borderlands with Wiltshire. Rural, with thatched cottages and good brick houses scattered about over the small hills. The little church of St Michael

Quarley church

is on one of these hills, and its most notable feature is clear from the road: a Venetian window (with three openings, the centre one arched and larger than the others). This became a popular style during the 18th century, and this one is particularly interesting as it is so early, being dated 1723 on an inscription which also names William Benson and Henry Hoare as the designers: Benson designed Wilbury House, close by in Wiltshire, and Henry Hoare had Stourhead, Wilts, built in 1721, both classical houses.

The church is simply a nave and chancel: the bells are hung in a little shelter outside the north wall of the church. One is medieval, one dated 1686 and the last was recast in 1905.

The nave of the church is 11th century and a church was recorded here at Domesday. In the north wall are the outlines of original door and window. The big plain font is probably Norman. Vivid plain Victorian stained glass in the side windows, and inappropriate figured glass in the venetian window. The elaborate late 17th century twisted balusters in the pulpit and screen came from a staircase in the old Amport House.

To the south west of the village is Quarley Hill, an Iron Age hillfort with single bank and ditch, but also with outworks which seem to be Bronze Age field boundaries. A footpath leads close to the hillfort.

★ ★ *For church window and general interest.*

QUEEN ELIZABETH COUNTRY PARK (K) (4 miles south of Petersfield) A huge country park, which divides into two separate parts. **Butser Hill** is the second highest point on the Hampshire

chalk, 887 ft. A track leads to the car park right on top (fee). Panoramic views, the most extensive from any Hampshire hill, with the Isle of Wight clear to the south, the sea at Solent and Spithead in front, and the flat islands of Portsmouth and Hayling. Inland the views are as good, and the downland of the hill and the areas around is worth exploring on foot. Hang gliders and model aeroplanes use the top of the hill.

The rest of the country park is on the eastern side of the A3, and is beech forest planted in the 1930s. Dozens of footpaths lead through the steep wooded slopes, and access for cars is possible to some areas (fee). Forestry demonstrations are given regularly. Small exhibition in the Park Centre. Regular guided walks and other events. See also Butser Ancient Farm.

★ ★ ★ *One of the best areas of Hampshire for walking, both on the high downland and in the forest.*

QUIDHAMPTON see OVERTON

RAMSDELL (B) Rural, lots of trees, but with a rather more dense village centre than many of these northern villages. The little Christ Church is a striking building of 1867, brick, flint and stone with a tiny spire. Currently there are fields of daffodils being grown here.

The interestingly named **Charter Alley** adjoins the north-east, and **Ewhurst** to the south-west has a footpath through woods and around a long lake which offers a good walk.

REDBRIDGE see SOUTHAMPTON WEST

RHINEFIELD ORNAMENTAL DRIVE
(M) (south-west of Lyndhurst). A contrast to Bolderwood opposite, as this New Forest road is lined with large old conifers of several different types, planted informally from the middle of the 19th century. Rhododendrons and azaleas too. Rhinefield Lodge was, as the name implies, a keeper's lodge but a large Elizabethan style mansion was built there in 1890, and it is now a hotel. Lots of car parks all through the ornamental drive.

To the south, at the Ober Water river, there are two nature trails laid out along the stream and through the heathland and woods.

★ ★ ★ ★ *For walking in the ornamental drive, or at Ober Water.*

RINGWOOD (L) A border town, sitting right on the River Avon which divides Hampshire from Dorset. On the western edge of the New Forest and the crossing of several roads, and an obvious site for a town. There was already a mill and church here at Domesday, and the town has grown steadily since, with a notable market, still held on Wednesday mornings. Ringwood seems strangely cut about by recent roads: the so-called bypass actually cuts through the town, and other new roads destroy the old street pattern.

The big new car parks on the north of the town lead oddly into the delivery areas or backs of most of the recent large shops. Preserved amongst this recent development is **Ringwood Meeting House** (now a museum), built in 1727 and containing all its original fittings. Plain and unchurchy outside, and inside filled with plain pews and galleries. In the centre of the pews is a rare table pew, with a table in the middle used as a solemn seat for testifying and for the fathers of the church to gather round on sacrament days. Upstairs in the galleries are displays of photographs and objects relating to the history of Ringwood (fee:lists) ★ ★ *As a very complete and early non-conformist chapel.*

The High Street has many small Georgian brick houses, mostly now with their lower parts converted to shops, mixed with Victorian and later development. The Crown Hotel at the western end has decorative tile hanging. Further along towards the market place is the classical Corn Exchange of 1866, now a shopping centre. The market place forms a wide triangle, with in the middle the elaborate Jubilee lamp of 1887. Lots

of small Georgian houses around the market place, brick or stuccoed. All of Ringwood has many alleys off the streets, some with small cottages, others still with stables or other outbuildings. By the entrance to the church a much larger mid 18th century house with a pillared porch and Venetian window, sadly painted but faced with mathematical tiles (wall-hung tiles which look like bricks). Just behind is another big Georgian house.

The church of St Peter and St Paul was rebuilt in the 1850s, and is thus rather uniform. Large and plainish, with a handsome chancel. Much 1850s stained glass, which suits the church well. Survivals from the earlier church include many 18th century memorials and funeral hatchments, and the handsome brass chandelier of 1729 under the tower. In the chancel brightly coloured carpets made by a vicar about 1905.

The town mill and several other buildings behind the church were demolished in 1936 to make way for the first Ringwood bypass, now widened. West Street leads from the corner of the market to the river.

Monmouth house, on the right is so

ABOVE *Ringwood market place.* BELOW *Bridge over the Avon at Ringwood*

ABOVE *Monmouth House, Ringwood*
RIGHT *Rockbourne Roman villa*

named because the Duke of Monmouth was held in a house on this site after his attempt to become king failed in 1685. Next door late medieval timber framing and thatch, and opposite Bridge House Hotel, Georgian brick. Two bridges lead over the Avon, very rural with the Jubilee Gardens despite the closeness of the main road. The Fish Inn, thatched 18th century is picturesque.

Christchurch Road leads south from High Street, and at the junction is Greyfriars (Ringwood Community Association) the finest Georgian house in the town, redbrick and three storeys. Smaller Georgian houses and thatched cottages continue for a surprisingly long way along Christchurch Road, and the turning into Coxstone Lane is crowded with thatched cottages. The lane leads down to Bickerely Common, a riverside meadow.

The Manor House, stuccoed Georgian and dated 1737, is just up Southampton Road, which then crosses the present bypass and becomes the old main road with houses ranging from Georgian to the present.

The New Forest Owl Sanctuary (fee:lists) is at Crow to the south-east of Ringwood. Here many types of British and foreign owls can be seen and barn owls are bred for release in the wild. Regular talks and demonstrations of owls and birds of prey.

A town well worth walking around. The chapel ★ ★ ★, *and the New Forest Owl Sanctuary* ★ ★ ★

ROCKBOURNE (G) To the south of the village is the monumental entrance to West Park, a large house demolished in 1945. In the grounds, visible from the road south of the village is the Eyre Coote Monument, a pillar over 100 ft

high with a complex top, commemorating Lt General Sir Eyre Coote who lived in West Park. He was victorious in India from the mid 18th century and died there in 1783.

The village street is pretty, plain brick or brick and timber-framed houses, either facing the street or gable end on. Lots of thatch, a winding road with trees and many small bridges over the river. The church is towards the north end, up what appears to be a private drive. The footpath leads up to the church by a large topiary bird. Looking down north from the churchyard one sees Manor Farm, with many old farm buildings, parts of medieval houses and a chapel (medieval bits are of stone).

The church of St Andrew has a tiny oak shingled spire of 1630, but it is basically an early Norman church, later extended and adapted. Having only one aisle makes it seem lop-sided. Good roofs. Heavily restored, and the porch added in 1893. The chancel has many memorials of the Coote family of West Park, including the most famous, Sir Eyre Coote, whose memorial and portrait are by the organ. According to a contemporary eulogy he was 'Polite, obliging, affable and free/ From distant pride and dull formality'. There is another memorial to him in Westminster Abbey. Two standards are still preserved in the church. Fine 1520ish triptych displayed in nave, and the west window has intricate German stained glass of 1893.

Just off the road to the south of the village is Rockbourne Roman villa (fee:lists), excavated from the 1950s. The footings of the walls of the courtyard house are laid out, and two mosaics and a hypocaust can be seen. Good displays in the new museum explain the development of the site from a simple Iron Age hut

through a small villa up to the large and complex fourth century house. The displays also explain the life of the people who lived there through the finds excavated.

To the north-west of the village is Duck's Nest (or Duke's Rest) Neolithic Long Barrow, set in trees just off a footpath in the downs.

★ ★ *Church,* ★ ★ ★ *Village, cottages etc.*
★ ★ *Villa, small but good displays.*

ROMSEY (H) A proper market town, which has expanded on the outskirts, but remains small scale in the middle. The main attraction is the abbey, a vast Norman church which sits just behind the market place. The town grew at the junction of the roads to Salisbury, Winchester and Stockbridge at a suitable bridging point on the River Test.

The middle of the town is a small triangular market place, with a rather dull statue to that lively man, Lord Palmerston (1784-1865) who lived at Broadlands. Several good brick buildings of the 18th and early 19th centuries. One corner has the Town Hall, brick and stone 1866. The big flint United Reform church has a gateway over the street, leading to the south side of the abbey. The church, gateway and so on are of 1888, all in a busy late medieval style. Oddly a river laps one side of the building. Lovely backwaters, beyond the church in Newton Lane with a variety of enviable houses, especially Temple Buildings in Abbey Meads dated 1820, white stucco with Gothic glazing.

South of Market Place is Barclays Bank, originally the Corn Exchange, classical for its date (1864) painted in pretty pastel colours. All the roads around the centre have good Georgian and early 19th century houses mostly small, especially

building in England (David Lloyd). The abbey was founded in 907 by Edward the Elder. The first abbess was his daughter Elfreda, who became a saint. None of the early buildings survive above ground: a small part of the footings of an apse from an early church can be seen exposed under the tower crossing. The surviving church was started about 1120 and finished around 1230, and is a remarkably complete Norman church, with only the Lady Chapel at the east end missing. A rich Benedictine nunnery, with Royal connections in the early medieval period – Maud who married Henry I in 1100 was educated here.

Externally the building is big and strong, with big round-headed windows, zig-zag decoration, and corbel tables with heads and animals. Low tower, castle-like, with wooden bell tower 1625 on top. The south doorway ('The 'Abbesses') by the tower is more elaborate, pretty with twisted columns etc. Next to it is the Romsey Rood, Christ on the cross, with the Hand of God descending from clouds above. Dating from about 1000 A.D., this must come from the earlier building, reset here.

Internally the walls are cut into three

ABOVE *Broadlands*
LEFT *Romsey side street*
BELOW *Romsey Abbey, the south doorway*

Bell Street leading into Middlebridge Street, The Hundred, Latimer Street and all that area. Palmerston Street has 17th century timber-framed survivors. Off Church Street and Cherville Street in the north was a large brewery, now converted to flats but with some of the Victorian buildings (including the distinctive tower) preserved. A good town to walk around, accumulatively fine. At the end of The Hundred the Police Station mid-Victorian, picturesque flint and brick. Bits of river everywhere.

King John's House, Church Court off Church Street, opposite the Abbey is both a museum and an interesting pair of buildings (fee: lists). The original building is the further one, of about 1230 (after the reign of King John). It has a first floor hall, small and domestic, with some original, if mutilated, door and window surrounds

surviving. Originally it had a central hearth: the fireplace is 16th century. In medieval times it was entered via a door in the western gable, which had a little building in front of it, now gone. Medieval graffitti on the walls and some red lines painted to imitate stonework. Downstairs a display on Romsey Abbey, Broadlands and its owners etc. the entrance is through the Tudor cottage, a timber framed building. This houses displays on the history and geology of Romsey and area.

Romsey centre seems compressed, and the **Abbey** is no exception. It does not stand apart, but in with the town. All the other abbey buildings have gone, but the church was saved by being bought by the town in 1544 after the dissolution of the monasteries for £100, and has been described as the second finest Norman

levels, each with different treatment. The nave starts by the tower with huge circular columns, changes to multiple smaller columns, and finally for the western three bays has pointed rather than round arches, and different columns and capitals. Probably this is not a different phase of building, but shows that the nave was being built as the style changed from Norman to Early English.

Good monuments at the west end, behind the font of 1912, including an elegant wall tablet to Viscountess Palmerston (1769) with Viscount Palmerston (1802) by Flaxman on the left. This is copied on the right. The reclining figure of a man is an 1858 memorial to Sir William Petty, a founder of the Royal Society who died in 1687. The small effigy is a girl who died in 1843, aged 3.

The bright curtain inside the abbesses doorway dates from 1961. The south transept has many memorials including the grave of Earl Mountbatten (1979). Above is a highly coloured wall memorial of 1658 with life-like busts, and children below, to earlier owners of Broadlands. Verses and 'An Anagram upon theire names JOHN and GRISSELL SAINTE BARBE ... BE IN SHARES IN BLEST GLORIE' An odd thing to put on a tombstone, particularly as it is not a perfect anagram. Close by a fine 14th century canopy, to which has been added the effigy of a lady some hundred years earlier.

The tower and the eastern parts of the church are the earliest, including some finely carved capitals with figures. In the chapel of St Anne, on the altar, is the late Anglo-Saxon Rood, or Christ on the cross. Rather blurred now, the background of gold showing up the surviving carving. Figures float around Christ. It is set in some remains of the 15th century wooden screen.

The floor of St George's chapel beyond has medieval tiles, some complex. In the north transept a rare survival: a painted wooden reredos of about 1525. Rows of saints above, an abbess (presumably of Romsey) bottom left.

The abbey has been 'restored' several times, mostly during the 19th century. Palmerston was reluctant to contribute in 1844 because the proposed alterations – opening up the west end of the church by removing the gallery and partitions – would not help with the major problems – 'from its size it is difficult to warm, and to fill with the voice'.

The only remaining part of the Andover to Redbridge canal (see entry),

Romsey Abbey, the Nave

constructed in 1794, is to be found in Romsey. The canal went out of use in 1859 having never been a great success. It runs north from Romsey station : it was the railway which finished off the canal. The canal walk has many trees and shrubs, and runs for about two miles.

The War Memorial gardens have the river running by, and a Second World War Japanese gun presented by Mountbatten. The bridge from the town to the gardens gives a good view, including a salmon leap alongside one of the weirs.

★ ★ ★ ★ *Abbey church*, ★ ★ ★ *Town.*

ROPLEY (E) A big and attractive village, dense in the middle, but with thatched cottages and Georgian houses over a wider area too. Lots of hedges and trees everywhere. One of the large houses to the west is Ropley House where John Duthy, the early 19th century author of *Sketches of Hampshire* lived. The church of St Peter is snugly in the middle of the village, and is mostly 1896. The brick and flint coffee and Reading Room close by was built in 1883. To the west of the church is a pond and more thatched cottages.

There are several large hamlets around. **Ropley Dean** is on the main road and has lots of Edwardian buildings and a station on the Watercress Line. **Gilbert Street** to the north-east is very rural and spread out. At Swelling Hill (the east end) the road cuts through little chalk cliffs.

The Hampshire Hunt has kennelled its hounds here since 1846, and still does. The kennels are to the east of the village.

To the north west of the village,

Ropley station

beyond Ropley Dean is Ropley Station, part of the Watercress Line (see entry). Locomotives are stored here, and the steam trains stop at the station, which is well furnished and particularly memorable for the topiary, a tradition at this station.

ROTHERFIELD PARK see EAST TISTED

ROTHERWICK (C) A big village, with a green and pond to the north, hedges and wide verges. Good brick or timber framed cottages, some quite large especially on the road from the church. The village hall, built in 1933, looks more like a collection of cottages. The church is almost all brick with a very plain 17th century tower. The nave was originally timber framed with brick infilling like nearby Mattingley, but in the 16th century it was made all brick. The cut off timbers coming down from the roof can be seen inside. One original window to the right of the door, with the others copies. The flint chancel is mostly 1870s, as is the small north aisle. The front of the nave has very plain 16th century oak benches: it is rare to see so many surviving. In the north chapel a huge monument with the inscription on a triangle to Frederick Tylney who died in 1725. A plain monument of 1583 up by the altar.

★ ★ *Church.*

ROWLANDS CASTLE (K) Right on the Sussex border, the old part of the village on one side of a long green, with the other side being mostly a wall bordering a

large house and then Stanstead Forest (in Sussex). The name comes from the small medieval castle largely obliterated by the railway. Roland was a legendary giant. There are two other small earthwork castles in the parish as well! Only a hamlet until the early 19th century, which accounts for the few Georgian and many more Victorian houses on the green, mixed brick and flint. The railway line from London to Portsmouth was constructed in 1859, with a station at Rowlands Castle. The original classical style station, well painted, survives at the east end of the village, and the big double viaduct closes the east end of the green and has decorative flint panels. At the other end is the flint Congregational church of 1881, and up the lane beside it a

remarkable, lavish Parish Hall of 1914. The church of St John is away to the south-west, mid Victorian and flint. Bricks were made in the parish in large quantities in the 19th century.

Finchdean, a compact hamlet to the north, has several Georgian houses, and was from the middle of the 19th century a centre for the production of agricultural machinery, with a brass and iron foundry. One chimney still survives. Steep hills either side, and the railway runs very close.

★ ★ *Both Rowlands Castle and Finchdean villages.*

ROWNER see GOSPORT

ROWNHAMS (H) Technically not part of Southampton, but it now joins up with the city and the M27 seems a more logical boundary. Until twenty years ago it was a leafy Victorian village, but new housing estates have transformed it. Many trees and hedges survive, along with some fields. The church of St John was built in 1856, fairly typical of its date, and with an evergreened graveyard. The treasure of the church is the painted glass, roundels reset in Victorian settings. Many are brown and yellow, a few in all colours. Mostly biblical stories. The roundels date from the 16th century.

★ ★ *Church for the glass*

RUFUS STONE (H) (1½ miles north-west of Minstead, north of A31). One of the earliest areas in the New Forest to be popular with tourists, perhaps because it is so close to Southampton. In the 1890s it was described as 'a pandemonium of trippers', with a cocoa-nut shy stand close

The Rufus Stone

by. Still very busy in summer, and best seen in the winter. Good oak wood around the stone, with beech further away on the car-park side.

The story is well-known, although the only facts supported from contemporary sources are that the unpopular William II, one of the conqueror's sons (generally known as William Rufus) went hunting the New Forest in August 1100 and was killed by an arrow shot from the bow of Walter Tirrel. Whether accident or murder remains uncertain, and elaborations such as Rufus's body being taken to Winchester on a charcoal-burner's cart are later additions. Rufus certainly ended up buried in Winchester, where is tomb can be seen. Tirrel's arrow was supposed to have glanced off a tree, but he fled the country immediately, and given Rufus's unpopularity murder was possible. It is far from clear exactly where in the forest this happened: this is the traditional spot, and from 1742, the supposed site of the oak from which the arrow deflected was marked by a triangular stone. As the present memorial states the stone was 'much mutilated' and in 1841 its remains were encased in 'this more durable memorial' – a triangular cast iron pillar.

★ ★ *Historic interest, and good forest.*

SANDLEHEATH (G)
Almost a suburb of Fordingbridge, with mostly brick houses scattered along the main road, and occasional evidence of market gardening. The small church of St Aldhelm is brick too, of 1907.

SARISBURY (J/N)
In 1912 there were only 'two or three inns, a church, a schoolhouse, and a few cottages standing round a stretch of village green, alongside of which runs the Southampton road' (VCH). The green survives although it is now mostly cricket pitch. The motorway makes the road less busy, but the area has almost filled with modern housing. On a corner of the green is the church of St Paul, built in 1836 of brick with simple lancet windows. The stone chancel, was added later. The nave is very wide, and feels wider still because of the shallow transepts. Complexly carved Victorian stone pulpit.

To the south, on the road to Warsash, is **Holly Hill Woodland Park**, a large area of hilly woodlands, with lakes and from the lower parts, views of the Hamble. Once the grounds of a big house, now open free as a park. To the south, linking up with the park, is Wendleholme, more woodlands and saltmarsh, part of a large nature reserve along the shore.

★ ★ ★ ★ *Area for walking.*

SELBORNE (F)
World famous because of Gilbert White the author of *The Natural History and Antiquities of Selborne* (1788). He was born in the village in 1720, and died there in 1793. Although he was never vicar here, as his grandfather had been, he was curate for many years of either Selborne or nearby Farringdon. His book describing the natural history of the area is a classic, popular ever since written, and there have been more than 200 editions.

The landscape has always been extolled: Cobbett visited in 1823 and claimed that 'nothing could surpass in beauty these dells and hillocks and hangars'. This is still true. The attractive village has of course changed since White's time, but the landscape is perfect and happily much is now preserved by the National Trust.

Several houses in the village (including White's house, The Wakes) are built partly of Malmstone, the rather soft white stone from the greensand. Plestor House by the green has the hard brown stone, usually used for paths, in chips along the lines of mortar. White wrote that this embellishment had 'occasioned strangers to ask us pleasantly, "whether we fastened our walls together with tenpenny nails".' Off the green is the Old Vicarage, where White was born, and beyond the green are more thatched cottages. Good walking around the miles of footpaths, especially in the woods. The classic route is up the zig-zag which White constructed in 1753, a quick 200 ft up to the top of the wooded hangar which forms the backdrop to the village. At the top a sarsen, brought here by White and called the Wishing Stone. Perfect views from the top over the village and into the small scale wooded landscape beyond.

The Wakes, Gilbert White's home from 1730 until his death in 1793 is open as a museum (fee-lists). White planted a row of limes in front of the butcher's slaughter house opposite to conceal it, and two of the limes and the slaughter house are still there. The house has been added to since his time, but the study and great Parlour (which White added to the house in 1777) are still as they were in his time. Good displays on his writings, the geology and natural history of the area and Selborne Priory. The garden has been partly restored to what it was in his time: the orchard with naturalised plants and bulbs is especially good, but the best feature is simply the position – the lawns run into park-like pasture and the beeches of the hangar rise 300 feet behind. Perfection. A brick path leads to a reconstruction of the thatched wooden hut White called his alcove, from which he made many of his observations.

Upstairs are displays on Francis Oates (1840-75) an explorer of Africa, who brought back both natural history specimens and artefacts. He was an uncle of Captain Lawrence Oates (1880-1912) who died on Scott's ill-fated Antarctic expedition, who is the subject of another display.

The church of St Mary is behind a small green. By the path was a massive yew tree which in White's time measured 23 feet round. Cobbett found it 8 inches

The Wakes, Selborne

View of Selborne from the hangar

bigger in the 1820s. It fell in the storm of January 1990 has been heavily trimmed and replanted. Next to it is a granite pillar inscribed to the memory of a trumpeter who led the agricultural riot of 1830, when an attempt was made to burn down the poorhouse. The wooden door with its fine ironwork dates from the 13th century. The nave remains much as White would have known it, but the chancel was virtually rebuilt by his great nephew, the architect William White in 1856.

The fine Flemish painting behind the altar dates from 1520, and was given by White's brother Benjamin in memory of Gilbert White in 1793. 15th century bench ends made up into a reader's desk, with three small whole benches of the same date. The Gilbert White whose grave slab is by the altar was the author's grandfather.

In the south wall of the nave a stained glass window in memory of White, dating from 1920 the 200th anniversary of his birth. It shows St Francis with many of the birds White wrote about. Under the

altar close by many medieval tiles. A rare survivor – a wooden ladder dating from 1709, is hung on the wall. The painted Royal Coat of Arms cost £4.4.10d in 1785.

Gilbert White's grave is to the north-east of the vestry/organ chamber, marked by a simple stone with GW and his dates.

The wooded valley above the church makes a fine walk. At the south end of the village, in Limes End Yard, is a workshop where Romany living vans are restored and sometimes made. Attached is a good **Romany Folklore Museum,** showing all aspects of gypsy life and history. Lots of photographs, clothes, five or more living vans, and so on. Well worth seeing (fee: lists).

The road from Selborne to Blackmoor gives good views over the flatter countryside to the east, with the large golf-ball like buildings of RAF Oakhanger – they enclose radar – sitting oddly in the rural landscape. A mile and a half along the road are the Selborne brickworks, one

of the few still operating in the county. To the south-east are extensive orchards.

★ ★ ★ ★ *White associations, landscape, walking, village.*

★ ★ ★ *Romany Museum, not huge but authentic.* ★ ★ ★ *The Wakes.*

SHALDEN (F) A small, rural village with a big farmyard in the middle, including an impressive flint and brick barn. Many flint walls, and cottages of mixed flint and brick, or timber-framed. The small flinty church with a tiny bell turret is of 1865, and its graveyard gives good wide chalkland views.

SHAWFORD (J) Not really a village, but a well-treed, large hamlet which grew up because of the railway station on the line from London to Southampton, opened in 1840. The hamlet was then part of Compton, with only a few houses, a mill and an inn. Most of the houses are late 19th century, and the larger ones were presumably built for early rail commuters to Winchester. No church, only a Mission Hall by the station, with a few shops. Down in the river valley is Shawford House, a stone mansion of 1685.

The hamlet is on the side of the Itchen valley, which is wide here and beautiful. What seems to be the western stream of the river is in fact the Itchen Navigation (see entry). Footpaths run up and downstream along the Navigation, through the water meadows which are surprisingly wooded. Just downstream are the remains of one of the locks, with brick walls lining the banks. It ceased being used in the middle of the 19th century because the railways were cheaper and more efficient. Here the railway runs parallel with the Navigation, so that periodically the deep rural quiet is shattered by trains.

Just north of the railway station is a car park which gives access to the Navigation, and to Compton Down which is chalk downland now with quite a lot of scrub and trees.

Good walking country. Right on the top, close to the main road, is a large wooden cross, a memorial to the many soldiers who marched by in the First World War.

SHEET (K) (1 mile north-east of Petersfield). Now joins up with Petersfield, but really a separate village. From the small triangular green (filled by a magnificent horse chestnut) the narrow village street runs down, bordered by a trickle of water and with many attractive Victorian cottages. Some timber framing around the Green. Stone church, rebuilt in 1869.

SHEDFIELD (j) The mostly Victorian village is neatly sited between the two main roads which skirt the vast triangular green. Although it had a small church from 1829 the settlement was tiny into later Victorian times, and did not become a parish until 1894. The older houses and cottages are around the cross-roads at the Winchester road, but the Victorian school, church and more of the village are down the side road, all spread out and well treed.

The church of St John is unexpectedly large and interesting: pretty imitation Decorated style externally of stone, and inside the Hampshire speciality – brick lined. All this dates from 1880. Complex stone and brick pillars with leafy capitals and serrated edges to the arches. Well carved stone corbels above, alternating heads and foliage. Most of the bricks are red or crimson, but the patterning also uses grey, yellow, black and blue. Characteristic late Victorian fittings include the stone pulpit and reredos, and the wooden font cover and screen, the later being so late as 1927. Bright stained glass on one side. Worth seeing. In the churchyard survives the simple brick tower of the old church, 1829.

North-west along the road to Shirrell Heath is a big brick house (New Place) of very strong character, designed by Lutyens in 1906.

The Common is large and rough, with grassy areas, scrub and trees. The whole of Waltham Chase, Swanmore, Shirrell Heath and beyond looked like this into the 19th century – one large heath. Good views across the common.

★ ★ *St Mary's church, good later Victorian church, brick interior particularly interesting.*

SHERBORNE ST JOHN (B) The older cottages are all rather small and of brick. The church of St Andrew is interesting. Externally the brick parts dominate. The tower is 1837, with oddly chamfered corners, but the pretty porch is so early as 1533. Domestic-looking, with inscriptions over both doors, spelling the donor's name a different way on each. The inner has kneeling figures of the donors, and an injunction to pray for their souls. Lots of graffitti on the soft stone.

Inside the church is large and has many

interesting fittings. The Brocas chapel in the north-east was built about 1420 to house monuments for the family. The largest of about 1530 is in the arch to the chancel – Ralph Peall and his wife, who was the Brocas heiress. Their effigies both hold hearts. Several brasses, the earliest of 1350 on the wall with half figures, the others of around 1500 on the floor. Medieval tiles too. A mixture of glass in the window, including early 16th century Dutch of fine quality.

In the chancel the bust of Richard Atkins (died 1653) sits effectively against a black background. The pulpit is an elaborated example dated 1634 'MAD BY HENRI SLY'. The 17th century reading desk has three sides, like those used in libraries, and the panelling behind the altar and altar rails are the same date.

★ ★ ★ *Church for the porch and the fittings.*

SHERFIELD ENGLISH (H) The name is further complicated by having a hamlet called The Frenches just to the east. Wide busy road, with lots of trees and the houses spread out. Lavish brick and stone church of St Leonard, a replacement of 1902. Short octagonal tower with flying buttresses. The building would be more at home in London. Inside is more classical, with odd pillars. Side windows and 'screens' have simple Art Nouveau stained glass; the upper panels in the pulpit figures of Temperance, Justice and Charity, 16th century Dutch.

★ *For unusual date.*

SHERFIELD ON LODDEN (B/C) The main village is around a huge and varied green, so big that different parts are scrub covered, wooded or open. Some timber-framed cottages, and near the middle a school and schoolhouse of 1737. Big ponds and marshy areas. Many older house sites in the area are moated, and the best is a mile south, behind the Victorian St Leonard's church. Sherfield Court, a handsome Georgian house is beside the church, the replacement for the old house which stood inside the moat, which is still filled with water.

Longbridge Mill, to the north is picturesque with big sluices.

SHIPTON BELLINGER (D) On the border with Wiltshire, and with the main part of the village off the main road. A stream runs alongside the village street, which is mostly Edwardian brick houses, although with a few earlier cottages, occasionally still thatched. The church of St Peter has attractive irregular flint and stone chequering, but is basically of 1879. Small shingled tower.

SHIRLEY see SOUTHAMPTON WEST

SHIRRELL HEATH (J) Proper market gardening country where the fields carry all sorts of crops and there are yet more inside the greenhouses. Most of the houses are along the single 'main' road, with older small-holders' cottages now mixed with more modern housing.

SILCHESTER (B) A large Roman town called Calleva Atrebatum with Iron Age antecedents, which was deserted in the 5th century. Silchester is one of the few Roman towns which did not continue to develop. Almost all the others, like Winchester, are buried beneath modern towns, while Silchester is farmland.

LEFT *The Roman amphitheatre, Silchester*
ABOVE *Angels on the screen in Silchester church*

The defences of the town are still clear and enclose 80 acres. None of the buildings inside survive above ground level, though 19th century excavations revealed a partial plan – only the solid masonry building. Houses, shops and temples were found, as well as the market place (forum) and the main administrative building (basilica). A large complex of bath buildings was also found, and what has been interpreted as the earliest Christian church in the country.

The village church of Silchester is just inside the Roman town wall, and is in the area of the Roman town which had pagan temples, a coincidence perhaps, but a strange one.

The town walls are best seen on the east and south. Outside the wall by the church is a duck pond adapted from one of the two Roman ditches which ran along in front of the wall. The wall is made of layers of flint with narrow layers of limestone, and dates from around 260-280 A.D. To the south and round the corner the wall survives to a greater height and the lower parts of two gates can be seen, one for pedestrians, the other one of the main entrances to the town. It is possible to walk all round the defences, although the south is the best preserved part, and a footpath runs across the middle of the town (see below for Calleva Museum).

The walls have been admired as a romantic ruin since the 18th century. In 1833 a traveller was very struck by the site. 'The whole stands upon a high lonely part of the country with only a rude low church and a single farm-house in the neighbourhood, but commanding a most lovely and almost boundless view over woody plains and blue skyey ridges on all sides of it'. (Lord Jeffrey). Romantic travellers could not have found a more suitable spot for lingering over the contrast between the placid picturesque present and the ancient classical bustle.

To the north of the church, outside the town walls, is the Roman amphitheatre, constructed at about the same time as the start of the Roman town in the 50s or 60s A.D. and adapted with a stone wall on the inner face in the third century. The lower part of the wall survives, and the steep earthen bank which had seats for spectators. Amphitheatres were used for gladiatorial combats, wild beast shows and public executions. Close by, and an odd juxtaposition, is a thatched timber-framed cottage.

In front of the north side of the wall the ditch can be seen, still damp in places. Beyond the north-west corner of the town the modern road cuts through an outer earthwork which was part of the defences of Silchester's Iron Age predecessor, which started in the mid first century BC and was replaced by the Roman town.

The church of St Mary is a typical and interesting village church, which disappoints only because one expects a church whose graveyard is bounded by a Roman town wall to be more exotic. Materials robbed from the Roman town were used for the church (eg at the west end where Roman tiles can be seen making the corners of the 12th century building), but it has no other relationship with the Roman.

Basically the church is 12th and 13th century, with lancets in the side walls of the chancel, surrounded by the original simple wall-paintings. In the south aisle a 14th century tomb recess, with the effigy of a woman. The sober 18th century pulpit has a domed tester dated 1639, but the best woodwork is the screen, early 16th century with a frieze of angels, wings spread, managing to run and kneel simultaneously.

Next door to the church is the manor house, brick and timber-framed. There are few houses around the church, and the main modern settlement is to the west, and here, in the north-east corner of the village is **Calleva Museum** (free;lists) housing a very good small display about the Roman town. Much of the material from the excavations is on display at Reading Museum (Berkshire). Silchester Common makes a big green in the centre of the village, with some 18th century brick houses and modern.

★ ★ ★ *Silchester Roman town walls and amphitheatre.* ★ ★ *St Mary's church.*

SMANNELL (D) Really only a hamlet, but with the church of Christ Church, designed by William White in 1857, very like his church at Hatherden nearby. Flint

Cottage at Smannell dated 1873

and brick outside, with a peculiar bellcote, lined with brick inside and patterned. Painted decoration as well in the apse. Absurdly low pillars to the aisle. Simple roof of steel and wood. Worth seeing.

Little London to the north lives up to its name by being mostly modern, but the rural setting and few thatched cottages contradict it.

★ *Church for William White interest.*

SOBERTON (J) Even without the separate settlement at Soberton Heath to the south, the village straggles for two miles along the hillside parallel with the river Meon. Cottages, brick and some timber framing, and farms are mixed with Edwardian houses and modern infill along the single road. Some cottages, like those in the middle bit where three trees fill a little triangle, have been extended or amalgamated to form large houses. The northern part has a rectangular green with the pub, a vast battlemented flint house (Soberton Towers) of the 1890s, and the church of St Peter and St Paul.

The detailed building sequence is difficult to untangle, but basically it is 12th and 13th century, with a very unusual triple arch to the tower. The pretty south transept is late 13th century and early English in style, with a long window on either side of a window-like niche. Wallpaintings of about 1300 survive around these windows, showing

Soberton church tower

willowy female saints, and elsewhere on the walls are much cruder rosettes and lines imitating courses of stone. Purbeck Marble tomb of 1521.

The chancel is a mixture of medieval styles, all fitting happily together. In the north aisle, tucked in a corner, a very classy monument to Thomas Lewis (1747) by Scheemakers. Bust with two cherubs.

Outside there are wide views across the valley. Most of the handsome tower was rebuilt in the 16th century, chequered knapped flint and stone with stone screens in the bell-openings.

★ ★ *Good village church and position.*

SOBERTON HEATH (I) has a few heath cottages, along with modern infill. The only remnants of the heath which once covered the acid gravels are the furze bushes in the hedges.

SOPLEY (L) Right on the edge of the Avon valley, with such a small bridge in the middle that the roads have had to be made one-way. Lots of 18th century cottages and the odd house, all brick, a few thatched. Still has a farmyard right in the middle, and a forge. The big house, now Moorlands Bible College, to the south, has large brick lodges of 1875. Just below the church, down a little cliff, is the large brick mill.

The church of St Michael stands on what seems to be an artificial mound: this is not uncommon in Hampshire. The church is wholly medieval, but thoroughly restored in the 19th century. All brown heathstone outside and creamy stone inside. In the porch an elegantly painted board with the names of the churchwardens, 1714. On the organ a large embroidery of the village, 1984, very good. 13th century Purbeck marble effigies of a man and a woman on either side of the entrance.

★ ★ *Good village church.*

SOUTHAMPTON COMMON see **SOUTHAMPTON NORTH**

SOUTH BADDESLEY (M) (1½ miles east of Lymington). A hamlet in the remote southern part of the New Forest, more agricultural than foresty. A school and a few houses, with the church of St Mary of 1858. Small and rendered, in style more like the 1830s. Tiny tower.

SOUTH STONEHAM see **SWATHLING, SOUTHAMPTON NORTH**

SOUTHAMPTON (H/J) Today Southampton is a big bustling city (the largest in the county) of more than 200,000 inhabitants, most of them living in the suburbs or villages swallowed up by its expansion. Despite bomb damage in the Second World War and much modern development it is an interesting city to visit, with a large and attractive shopping centre, and a surprising number of historic buildings, many of them open to the public. Parts of the Docks are being converted to marinas or housing. The medieval town walls survive, and a walk around them takes in many of the older buildings. There are five very good museums (four of them free) and a medieval house restored to its original appearance. The city is green, and full of parks, while just to the north is Southampton Common, a huge area of wild woodland and grass.

★ ★ ★ ★ *p.160* The Town Walls
★ ★ ★ ★ *p.164* Tudor House Museum
★ ★ ★ ★ *p.162* God's House Tower
★ ★ ★ ★ *p.167* Wool House (Maritime Museum)
★ ★ ★ *p.160* Bargate
★ ★ ★ *p.163* Medieval Merchants House
★ ★ ★ *p.164* St. Michael's Church
★ ★ ★ *p.165* Southampton Hall of Aviation
★ ★ ★ ★ *p.169* Southampton Art Gallery

Ocean Village and Town Quay are the best places to see the Docks.

The description below is divided into: History of the Town; The Town Walls and Castle; The Town Centre; East of Town Centre; The Docks; and Outer Southampton.

History

The medieval walled town is not on the same site as its Roman and Saxon predecessors. Roman Southampton (Clausentium) was across the Itchen at Bitterne, and Saxon Southampton (Hamwic), was to the north-east of the medieval town, running north from St Mary's church. There is little to be seen of either, but excavated material from both of them, and from the medieval period, can be seen in God's House Tower, the archaeological museum. Southampton started to grow on its present site from around 1,000 AD, and Canute was proclaimed King here in 1014 suggesting that the settlement was of some size by then.

The city is now so large and flourishing, and has so many buildings surviving from its prosperous medieval days, that one assumes that growth has

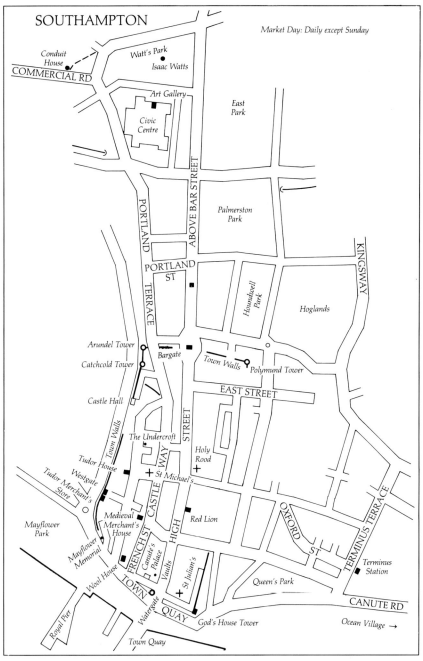

SOUTHAMPTON

Market Day: Daily except Sunday

Conduit House
COMMERCIAL RD
Watt's Park
Isaac Watts
Art Gallery
Civic Centre
East Park
ABOVE BAR STREET
PORTLAND TERRACE
PORTLAND ST
Palmerston Park
KINGSWAY
Houndwell Park
Hoglands
Arundel Tower
Bargate
Catchcold Tower
Town Walls
Polymund Tower
Castle Hall
Town Walls
EAST STREET
The Undercroft
CASTLE WAY
Holy Rood
Tudor House
Westgate
Tudor Merchant's Store
Mayflower Park
Medieval Merchant's House
FRENCH ST
HIGH STREET
St Michael's
Red Lion
OXFORD ST
TERMINUS TERRACE
Mayflower Memorial
Wool House
Canute's Palace
Vaults
St Julian's
Queen's Park
Terminus Station
CANUTE RD
Royal Pier
TOWN QUAY
Watergate
God's House Tower
Ocean Village →
Town Quay

water and sea-bathing in the same place. Jane Austen lived in the town in the early 19th century, and in the 1820s when William Daniel visited Southampton during his epic *Voyage round Great Britain* he thought it could just still be considered a commercial town, 'but it partakes more of the character of a watering-place, and a constant residence for genteel families who prefer the still waters of retirement to the noisy current of fashionable existence'.

The coming of the railway and the construction of the docks from the 1840s destroyed the town's tranquillity, and the spa faded away while the city grew commercially. The population increased from about 13,000 in 1821 to almost 48,000 in the town centre and the docks (St Mary Street etc) areas alone in 1871. Suburbs like Shirley and Freemantle to the west and Portwood to the north grew up from the 1830s, and still the city continues to expand.

The Town Walls and Castle

Medieval Southampton was defended by a stone wall with towers and gates, and a surprising amount survives. The defences began with an earthen bank and ditch on the north and east, constructed from 1200-1250. The Royal Castle filled part of the western shore-line and had stone defences, but the rest of the shore was left only partially defended because easy access was needed to move goods from ships to stores. This lack of defences allowed the pirate raid of 1338 (called the French Raid) to land at the western quays and sack the town, looting everything they could find, including the King's wine, and burning many houses. After this the stone walls were built right round the town, although not completed until about fifty years later. The walls, towers and gatehouses were maintained and altered until the mid 18th century, and despite the demolitions after that date, a great deal remains.

The best place to start a walk around the walls is **Polymond Tower**, the north-east corner of the medieval town. Now a shell, it was built in the 14th century, and was originally three stories high. An impressive length of wall, (originally with two ditches outside it) runs towards Bargate on the west, surrounded by modern buildings. A footpath leads through some of these to **Bargate**, one of the finest town gates in the county, now isolated on its own roundabout with 1930s buildings circling

been steady. This is not true. Southampton had a large trade from the Norman Conquest, first with Normandy and then Bordeaux for wine, and although the French Raid of 1338 affected both town and its trade badly for at least a generation, both recovered well. In the 15th century there was so much trade with Italy that there was a large Italian community living in the town, one of whom even became Mayor. With the rise of London as a port and the decline in Italian trade Southampton's fortunes declined. When Celia Fiennes visited in

the 1690s she found it a 'very clean neat town' but 'now the trade has failed and the town almost forsooke and neglected' with even the guns from the castle removed 'tho' by most its thought the best scittuated [SITUATED] port for ships to ride and take their provisions in' – a virtue much appreciated by the many smugglers it attracted.

From the 1740s the town revived, not as a port but as a spa and sea-bathing resort. Both had become fashionable, and Southampton was lucky in being able to offer Chalybeate (iron-bearing) spring round. Until the 1930s this was the main entrance to the town, as it had been since the core of the gate was built in about 1200. The surviving part of the Norman gate is to be seen in under the main arch, a round-headed gateway. The inner, southern side of the gate is flat, dating from the 14th century but with most of the window detailing etc dating from a restoration of the 1860s. The Roman in the niche is George III, placed here in 1809. The outer, northern, side is much more complex and impressive, with 14th century semi-circular towers and the outer arch and tower added in about 1400. The statues flanking the entrance are 18th century lead lions. Southampton's trams used to run through the Bargate, and had to be especially low to do so. **The Guildhall** in the upper part of the gate, is now a museum, displaying local history and folklore. A 13th century fireplace and a doorway survive inside. Set in the pavement just outside Bargate is a memorial to Southampton's role in the Second World War.

Flanking Bargate Street, the wall continues to the west, with a 1980s suspension bridge filling the gap made in the 1960s for a new road. Arundel Tower (also known as Windwhistle Tower) marks the corner, and beyond the wall turns south. Until this century the cliff (lined by the wall) marked the shoreline, difficult to comprehend today when a vast area has been reclaimed (see The Docks). Just to the north, outside the walled town was the chalybeate spring which the 18th century visitors to the spa drank, thinking it medicinal. Now there is an odd circular modern building. **Catchcold Tower** is an early 15th century addition, well preserved and with three gunports. Beyond the tower the wall curves out to meet the defences of the Castle, which already existed when the walls were built. The steps down to the road, called Forty Steps, were built in the early 19th century.

The Castle was probably built soon after the Norman Conquest and the plain piece of wall between Catchcold Tower and the buttressed part dates from about 1270, when the Castle was extended. Above, on top of the cliff, is a row of 19th century houses called Forest View, their view now obstructed by the buildings on the reclaimed land. The buttressed wall is the earliest part, dating from the 12th century. Behind the wall are the only two buildings surviving from the Castle. First is **Castle Vault**, built about 1193 for

Catchcold Tower, Southampton

storage of the goods unloaded at Castle Quay, which is under the present road. A small round-headed door and tiny window mark the vault, and then there is a larger door flanked by buttresses. This is Castle Watergate. Beyond, and easy to see from the stairs and walkways, is **Castle Hall**, built in the earlier 12th century with a hall on the upper floor and another storage vault on the ground floor. Originally the floor between the two was timber (the big holes for the joists are clear) but later it was vaulted in stone and this has been partly reconstructed. The remains of a stone spiral staircase between the two floors can be seen in one corner. The last Castle building, seen from the walkway, is a well-built narrow masonry enclosure, actually a garderobe or lavatory built in 1252, and carefully constructed so as to be flushed by the tides.

The high motte or mound with a stone-built keep of the Norman Castle was just into the present town. Nothing remains of the buildings but the motte is still detectable between Castle Way and Upper Bugle Street, emphasised by the fourteen storey block of flats (called Castle House) built on it in 1963. The footings of the eastern Castle Gate can be seen in Castle Lane (with some handsome Georgian brick houses close by), and the much more substantial remains of the north wall of the bailey (or outer enclosure) can be seen in the car park just to the north, off Castle Way. This big wall does not look right for a defensive wall because the lower parts are open arches, but in fact these arches are only footings

for the upper wall, and were originally concealed in an earthen bank. The wall dates from around 1250. The rest of the castle area has been built over repeatedly. Jane Austen and her family rented a house in this area in 1807-9. Their garden ran back to the walls and the house may have been where the pub (Castle Tavern) on top of the walls now is. Little survives of the buildings she knew: most of the area is modern housing.

Returning to the town walls, after a gap with 1980s flats (the area was cleared of slums and rebuilt by 1903: these are replacements) comes the most unusual part of the defences. In the 12th century large stone houses were built here, close to West Quay which was one of the main landing places for goods arriving by sea. There was no wall or bank here until after the French raid of 1338, but then the seaward walls of the houses were incorporated into the defences, with their windows and doors blocked up. These can still be seen in the inner part of the wall (see also *Tudor House*). A second stone wall was built in front on arches to support a wall walk, and gaps were left between parts of the two walls so that things could be dropped on attackers. The gun ports (holes in the wall for guns to be propped in) are the earliest in England. In one of the arches is the Blue Anchor postern, a small gate leading into a very narrow lane. The Baths, part of Southampton's spa attractions, were built here in the later 18th century on the shoreline: coincidentially the 1962 swimming pool is close to their site. Further along the walls part was

The Royal Standard pub replacing part of the town walls

demolished and the Royal Standard pub built in about 1810. Next door is the **West Gate**, small and plain, dating from the middle of the 14th century. This is the gate by which Henry V and his army left England in 1415 on their way to France and the Battle of Agincourt. The passengers for the *Mayflower* also left through here in 1620. Inside the gate a couple of Georgian brick houses survive, and on the other side, against the wall, the **Tudor Merchant's Store**. This is a mid-15th century timber-framed building originally built in St Michael's Square as part of the Fish Market and moved here and re-erected in 1634.

The final surviving stretch of wall at the south-west corner has arches like those near Blue Anchor Postern, but only the southern two are original. The others are reconstructions of 1900. The view from the top of the walls here is extensive, with many buildings on the reclaimed ground in the foreground, the container docks beyond, and Southampton Water with the chimneys of Marchwood Power Station clear on the other side.

The wall survives only as a stub for a little way along the southern side of the town, behind the Mayflower memorial, but can be picked up again at the bottom of High Street where part of the **Town Watergate** survives, despite having been sold for £70 in 1803 for demolition to improve the access to the quays. (See **The Town Quay** for all the other buildings in this area).

Winkle Street runs parallel with Town Quay, and on the north side is *St Julian's church* built about 1190 as the church for God's Hospital. Much restored externally, internally it still has a Norman chancel arch and Norman capitals. Behind the church is a courtyard with the almshouses of the Hospital, rebuilt in 1861. Very rural, a surprise here.

God's House Gate and Tower mark the south-east corner of the walls. From about 1300 there was a gate here with a small tower projecting from the wall. This survives, with the arch having many ribs across its little vault. Attached to it is a much larger building: God's House Tower, built about 1400 to protect the sluice which allowed the tide to fill the town ditch and then trapped it. The water flowed in under the building, and also worked a mill. Since it was converted in 1960 to be the town's archaeological museum, most of the interior can be seen. Very good displays on Roman Southampton (Bitterne), Saxon Hamwic and life in the medieval town (free:lists).★ ★ ★ ★

The town walls continue for some way north, but are less interesting on this east side. The East Gate was completely demolished in the 18th century. Lower Canal Walk marks the line of the walls, named after the extension of the canal from Redbridge, a failure because the tunnel was badly engineered. Further north, over Briton Street Back of the Walls marks the line, and at the north end of that street is the Old Bond Store of the

1840s, a heavy but attractive brick building with an overhanging roof and barred windows, looking rather out of place amongst the modern buildings. It is an unusual survivor as most of the earlier warehouses were either bombed in the Second World War or demolished more recently.

Medieval Houses and Vaults

Southampton was prosperous from early in the medieval period, and although there was no building stone available locally, the inhabitants could afford to import it from the Isle of Wight, France and Dorset. Substantial remains of two of the earliest houses survive, and so do many of the stone vaults constructed beneath them. These large cellar-like rooms were built for secure storage, shops and workshops and range in date from the 13th to the 16th century. None are open to the public except that under the Medieval Merchant's House, but many can be peered into, and some (usually The Undercroft and Quilter's Vault) are opened up on the regular guided walks around the town.

Tudor House (Bugle Street) (p.oo) and Medieval Merchant's House (French Street) (p.oo) are open to the public, and the Red Lion (High Street) and The Duke of Wellington (Bugle Street) (p.oo) can also be seen as they are public houses. Ruins of medieval stone houses can be seen at the back of Tudor House (or from the Esplanade) (p.oo) and in Porter's Lane (p.oo). Close by are vaults which can be peered into. Others are in Simnel Lane (p.oo) and French Street (p.oo). If there are excavations taking place in the old town when you are there more vaults will probably be exposed. the Wool House (p.oo) is a superb medieval commercial building.

The Duke of Wellington pub

Town Centre

Above Bar Street is the main shopping street, devastated by bombing in the Second World War and rebuilt in a mostly dull style in the early 1950s. All is of fine white Portland Stone, but in the lower part of the street most of the buildings are only two stories and so are unimpressive, particularly as the street is so wide. Now pedestrianised. Just below the junction with Civic Centre Road is one of the few buildings to survive the bombing – the late Victorian Prudential House, elaborate terracotta, smooth and used like stone. The terracotta was made by Blanchards of Bishops Waltham. In the park opposite is a poor statue of Lord Palmerston with intricate plantings of shrubs and heathers. There is a vast expanse of parks on this east side, mostly with large trees.

Good views of Bargate (see p.oo) down the street. On the right half way down is Portland Street, where one side of the street survived the bombing. Plain stuccoed terraces, with iron balconies and railings, built 1830. At right angles is the slightly later Portland Terrace, larger in scale but otherwise similar.

High Street (or Below Bar as it is sometimes called) runs south from the Bargate. Until the bombing this street was admired by many visitors. John Leland in the 1540s thought the street 'that goith from the barre-gate to water is one of the fairest streates that ys yn any town of al England, and it is welle buildid for timbre building'. There is more brick in the modern buildings here, and more 19th century survivals including several flamboyant early 20th century stone banks (and one plain classical one of 1928). Further down on the left are two coaching inns, first The Star (1840) with its big coach arch, handsome iron balcony and Royal Coat of Arms. Below is The Dolphin, Georgian red brick with huge bow windows to the first and second storeys (with another Royal Coat of Arms). This is the one building associated with Jane Austen's stay in Southampton to survive. She danced at balls here while living in Southampton 1806-9. The plain early 19th century extension to the hotel is yellow brick, typical of its date.

Holy Rood Church has been preserved as a bombed ruin as a memorial to those in the Merchant Navy who died in the Second World War. The 14th century tower survived, although the spire went, and the nave is now a garden. At the other end is the roofless chancel. A large anchor lies in the nave, and under the

tower is a stone memorial to the crew of the *Titanic* (who mostly came from Southampton) moved here from the common.

Opposite Holy Rood is the elaborate stone bank of 1867, the best of the city's middle Victorian commercial buildings to survive the bombing. Below and opposite is Holy Rood Chambers with busy terracotta matched by the Post Office opposite. The left hand block of the Post Office (1894) has the most complex decoration in pale orange terracotta made by Blanchards of Bishops Waltham. Above the Post Office the Red Lion looks imitation timber framed, which the facade is, but inside it is genuine 15th century with the original hall and gallery and a Tudor fireplace.

The lower part of the High Street has many office blocks, and a large wholesale fruit market but is only sparsely built up and incoherent architecturally. The street leads down to Town Quay (see entry). At the bottom, on the right are three stone vaults, all later medieval. Around the corner in Porter's Lane is Canute's Palace, a roofless ruin, originally with large

rooms for storage on the ground floor and a hall on the far part of the upper floor. Some original Norman window surrounds survive. It is a century later than Canute.

The short **French Street** which leads up from the Town Quay is also little built up at this end. The roofless stone building is the Weigh House, mid 13th century with a vault underneath and possibly used to house the weigh beam. It was converted to a school in the 1930s but bombed in 1940. Above on the opposite side is a big warehouse of about 1900 now used as a store. At the head of the street is **Medieval Merchants House**, recently restored and open to the public (fee:lists). Timber framed at the front and stone elsewhere, it now stands alone amongst modern flats but originally would have been surrounded by similar buildings, some timber framed, some stone. Dating from around 1290 (and damaged in the French Raid of 1338), it is one of the earliest merchants houses to survive in England. The lowest storey is the vault where merchandise was stored, and above, the first room is the shop where it was sold, now reconstructed as it would have been in medieval times. Along the passage is the hall, the main living room, open through two storeys and with a fireplace. Behind is a smaller parlour or office, and upstairs two bedrooms. All the rooms are furnished with reproduction medieval furniture hangings and pottery, giving a good idea of the life of the people who lived there. The kitchen would have been a separate little building out in the yard.★ ★ ★

Bugle Street runs parallel with High Street and the west walls, and was an important street in the medieval town. It starts by the town quay with the Woolhouse (now the Maritime Museum see **Town Quay** entry) and retains several redbrick Georgian houses. Many low blocks of modern flats. The Duke of Wellington pub (on the corner) is a fine late medieval timber-framed house, altered inside in the 17th century. Opposite St Josephs, the plain yellow brick later 19th century Roman Catholic church is another good group of Georgian and earlier houses. The street opens up to St Michael's Square, with **Tudor House** (a museum) on the left. This was built about 1500 and although the very impressive frontage to Bugle Street was heavily restored in 1900, it gives a good impression of what a large timber-framed Tudor town house looked like. Big windows on the first floor, and open timber-framed porch. Inside the impressive two-storey hall of an earlier house, probably of about 1450, was preserved and re-used as part of the Tudor House. The stone fireplace in the first room is original, as is much of the upstairs with Tudor ceilings. South of the hall an 18th century addition sticks out into the garden. Downstairs there are good displays on cooking and sewing.

The Tudor garden was replanted in 1982, and is a charming display of features which would have been found in a 16th century garden, created with only those plants and shrubs known at the time. In the lower part of the garden an arch, which is all that remains of St Denys Priory (see Northam), leads on to a wall walk with the large bronze canon given to the town by Henry VIII. Below the shell of a large Norman house is preserved, its western wall incorporated into the town walls in the 14th century (see **Town Walls**). Norman round-headed doorways and windows can be seen: like the surviving Castle buildings the lower floor was used for storage and the upper part living accommodation. The reconstructed Norman chimney was brought here from a demolished house in the town. Within the filled-in arches are holes for guns, thought to be some of the earliest gunports in the county, 14th century.

St Michael's square once housed Southampton's Fish Market, and is

Tudor House

dominated by the church. **St Michael's Church** is the only medieval church left in the old town. Big and plain externally with a slender 165ft spire rebuilt in 1887 to make it higher and so a better landmark for shipping. Inside the church is odd because it is so wide. In the middle is the Norman tower, whose arches frame the altar. This is the earliest part of the church, and has gradually become enclosed by additions. In 1829 the aisles were reconstructed to allow galleries (since removed) to be inserted, and the plastered arches are all of that date, with only a little Gothic detail. This is typical of the 1820s, known to the Victorians as Carpenter's Gothic because it was often wood where it should have been stone. The contrast between the thin, light 1820s work and the central Norman tower is very effective. The eastern end is medieval, but most of the windows are 1820s.

The church has some fine fittings: at the west end is the tomb of Sir Richard Lyster, chief justice of England, who died in 1567 and lived in Tudor House opposite the church. The tomb has been re-erected and some bits are missing. Next to it is a handsome carved wooden cupboard, with an inscription inlaid along the top recording that 'John Lyngeom of this towne alderman erected this presse and gave certaine books'. He died in 1646. There are two fine 15th century brass lecterns, one from the bombed church of Holy Rood. Both have eagles and are supported by lions. The one with a little winged demon between the eagle's feet is the earlier, and one of the best in the

country. The Tournai (Belgium) marble font is one of four in Hampshire: large with roundels of grotesque beasts gnashing their teeth. It dates from about 1170.

The main east window has post-war glass with the five former parish churches of Southampton represented on the lower part.

★ ★ *Church, for the building and its fittings.*

On the opposite side of the Square, beside Tudor House a tiny lane leads down to the town walls, and although the modern flats on one side detract, the other side and the walls still give the feeling of a medieval lane. On up the street there are more modern flats, but at the corner of Simnel Street, beneath a 1902 redbrick council house, is one of the finest medieval vaults, very like a room, with windows, a groined vault and a fireplace. Called **The Undercroft**, it dates from the early 14th century and was perhaps a shop as well as a store. To the north lies the Castle area (see **Town Walls** entry).

East of Town Centre

The Oxford Street area to the east of the town centre is different from the rest of the town being urban and industrial, tightly packed together and dominated by the Old Docks, whose cranes are always visible. Platform Road and Canute Road mark the original shoreline, but since the 1840s the docks have moved the sea up to 1½ miles southwards. Queen's Park at the western end is small by Southampton's standards, but has some fine trees. Dock gates and shipping offices line the south of the road, but at the north east corner of the park are some of the plain handsome terraced houses built in this area from the 1830s with characteristic semicircular bow windows at first floor level. There are more in Oxford Street and Bernard Street. Oxford Street also has a splendid tiled pub (The London Hotel), a huge Salvation Army block of 1908 and some unusual shops.

Terminus Terrace is named from the Terminus Station. The first railway into Southampton opened in 1840 with its station here, and although the main station was moved to its present site in the mid 19th century, the original station building survives here. It was designed in 1839 by the distinguished architect Sir William Tite, stuccoed and classical in style, and is one of the earliest railway stations to survive. Now a casino, and not looking at all railwayish. Behind it part of the railway canopy survives, covering a car park. Some way behind the station is a large redbrick building (now a store) with faintly Gothic windows. This was a railway shed, part of the station.

Canute Road commemorates the Viking who was proclaimed King of England in Southampton in 1014. The legend of his sitting on the shore and commanding the rising tide to stop rising is supposed to have happened here. Canute was soaked: he was not trying to prove he could control nature but to demonstrate to over-flattering courtiers that he could not. The corner of Canute Road and Terminus Terrace is filled with South Western House (1872), built as a hotel. Big, brick and stone in French Renaissance style, with a florid entrance in Canute Road. The car park with good iron entrance pillars, is where the track was. Further along Canute Road is the Canute Hotel of about 1840 with a notice stating 'NEAR THIS SPOT AD 1028 CANUTE REPROVED HIS COURTIERS'. The entrance to Ocean village (see Docks entry) is opposite.

Up Royal Crescent Road close by is **Southampton Hall of Aviation**. The large new hangar is needed to house a huge flying boat of the 1940s, one of those which used Southampton Water as its base from the late 1930s. Lots of information, well displayed, about the important local aeroplane and flying boat industry, and eight other aeroplanes on display, plus a helicopter and a hang glider. Well worth seeing. (fee:lists). ★ ★ ★.

The St Mary Street and Six Dials area was the centre of the 8th century port of Hamwic, the forerunner of Southampton, then the largest town in England and one of the most important ports in Saxon Europe. Founded about 700 AD, it lasted for about 150 years. The shore of the Itchen was used for the ships, and the population is estimated at several thousand. It gave its name to the county, Hamtunscire. There are no remains to be seen unless an archaeological excavation is taking place, but there is a good display in God's House Tower, the archaeological museum.

St Mary's church at the south end of St Mary's Street marks the site of a major Saxon church, but it was rebuilt several times and the present large stone building dates from 1880, with the impressive tower and fat spire (part of the original 1880 design by the well known architect G.E. Street) not being added until 1914. The church was damaged in Second World War bombing, and the body of the church was heightened in the subsequent restoration. North of the church is part of the college, a long brick building, which was the Workhouse, rebuilt in 1867.

Between St Mary's church and the town walls, a visitor of 1635 found 'many pleasant gardens, orchards, cherry grounds, and walks, and a fine bowling ground, where many gentlemen, with the gentile merchants of this town, take their recreation'. Part of these gardens survive as Hoglands Park, but most of the area has been built upon. A suburb developed from the 18th century, and by 1850 nearly 2/3 of the town's population lived in the St Mary's area, 21,000 people. All the area to the shoreline was filled up with small-scale housing for the dock and railway workers.

St Mary's Street preserves the line of one of the Saxon roads, and is now a cheerfully scruffy small-scale shopping street with many second-hand shops. Halfway up is the covered market. All the early Victorian housing to the east has been demolished and replaced in the 1960s by blocks of flats, with only the short stubs of adjoining streets left with their 19th century buildings. Six Dials at the north end has become rather posher, with antique shops.

Crosshouse is the newish name for the area just round the corner of the Itchen from the Old Docks. The area used to be called Chapel, and from the 13th century there was a tide mill here. The Saxon port of Hamwic used this shore for its boats,

Queen's Park

and shipbuilding started by at least the 17th century. From medieval times until 1875 a large annual fair was held here, on open ground close to the town centre. The new car park in Crosshouse Road is on part of what was the enclosed mill pond, filled by the tides, and the little Cross House (a stone shelter for those waiting for the ferry) stood on the cross ere the causeways of the two ponds met. The little conical roofed stone structure is the one permanent feature in this area, built in medieval times. Until the 19th century and the expansion of the docks there were only two mills, a small wharf and the cross house in this isolated area. Ferries across the Itchen ran from here, and in 1836 the floating bridge was built, powered by steam. The floating bridge continued to function until 1977 when the huge Itchen bridge opened.

The car park in Crosshouse Lane gives panoramic views of the Itchen, its industries and ships. Upstream both sides are lined with wharves and factories, large and small, with shipbuilding and cranes. Northam gas works marks the curve of the river, and the only natural things to be seen are trees way upriver and Pear Tree Green opposite. On the far side of the river, just upstream from the bridge was the famous Spitfire factory (see **Woolston**).

The bridge itself is difficult to scale until a double decker bus goes over it, then one realises its immense height: in the centre it is 80 ft high, which looks too large until one of the large cargo ships goes under it.

Below the bridge the two sides of the river are contrasting. This side is big new neo-Georgian houses, part of the Ocean village development on the Docks, whereas the other side is shipbuilding with large premises. A great variety of

Looking upriver from the Itchen Bridge

shipping can be seen from the Crosshouse Road car park, ranging from frail rowing skiffs to huge sand or gravel ships.

Cars are not allowed to stop on the **Itchen Bridge**, so it is well worth walking for the panoramic views its height affords. The walk to the middle is shorter from the Woolston end. Downstream has shipbuilding on the left and the new houses of Ocean village replacing the docks on the right. Over Southampton water, filling the middle is Hythe, with Fawley Oil Refinery visible downstream. Over Ocean village and the old Docks is more of Southampton Water. Looking upstream is the curve of the river and all the wharves lining it. St Mary's church spire is clear on the left bank and beyond, the slim tower of the Civic Centre. Much of Southampton to the north is visible. On the right bank is Itchen and Pear Tree Green, still green. The railway runs along the top of the river cliff, dividing the housing on top from the industry below.

The Docks

Southampton has always been a port since it has an ideal position at the head of Southampton Water with sheltered anchorages. The 'double' tide phenomenon is another natural advantage: the Isle of Wight splits the rising tide, giving a double surge and thus a long period of high tide.

In the medieval period there were quays and jetties under the western town wall (now dry land) and to the south of the walls at Town Quay, which still survives although much altered. Medieval ships were small, and so only needed shallow water, but after the port started to revive in the early 19th century facilities were needed for larger vessels.

The Harbour Commission was set up in 1803, taking over from the Corporation, and they extended Town Quay, and demolished the medieval Watergate to improve access from the town. In 1833 Royal Pier was opened, stretching out into the deep water from Town Quay so that steamships could land passengers. Soon afterwards, in the mudlands to the east, construction of the first dock began. Finished in 1843, this is now Ocean Village (see below). Right from the start Southampton's docks were linked to the railway system, which meant that goods or passengers for London could be unloaded or disembark at Southampton and go on by train rather than taking ships round to London, a major factor in the 19th century growth of the port.

Southampton specialised in passenger traffic, so the history of its Docks mirrors the development of sea passenger trade all through the 19th and 20th centuries; a period of enormous expansion and finally decline. When the Docks opened in the 1840s regular scheduled services were just starting, made possible by steam propulsion and made profitable by carrying mails, but sea travel was uncomfortable and only undertaken as a necessity until the late 19th century when much larger and more comfortable vessels were built. Finally, Kipling could write 'Yes, weekly from Southampton/Great steamers, white and gold/Go rolling down to Rio'. And so they did, rolling regularly to far-flung ports. Southampton has been the country's main trooping port since the middle of the 19th century: more than 8 million Allied troops embarked from Southampton during the First World War, and many of the ships carrying troops to Normandy for the invasion of 1944 left

from the Western Docks.

These Old or Western Docks were extended by the construction of two more docks in 1890 and 1911, pushing out southwards for over a mile into Southampton Water. These larger docks were used by the huge luxury passenger liners which regularly crossed the Atlantic, including in 1912 the ill-fated *Titanic* on its maiden voyage. In the 1920s and 30s Southampton was the largest passenger port in the country, with regular world-wide services. This prosperity continued into the 1950s, with cruise ships as well as passenger liners, but the growth of air travel has virtually destroyed it. Ironically Southampton was the main base for the fore-runners of todays land-based aircraft, the flying boats. They used Southampton Water for passenger services from the 1930s until services ceased in the 1950s.

From 1927-34 the New or Eastern Docks were built on the other side of the town centre, reclaiming 400 acres of land and creating 1½ miles of deep-water berths. The King George V dry dock at the east end of the New Docks opened in 1933.

The most modern part of the port is the Container Terminal, to the east of the Eastern Docks; also on reclaimed ground. The first berths opened in 1968, and it continues to expand while the Western Dock shrinks and parts of it become marinas. The only ferries still using the port are local ones to Hythe and the Isle of Wight, and cruise ships are only rarely seen. The Esso oil terminal at Fawley handles huge quantities of crude oil, but it does not seem part of the Docks. Fruit, a trade which began in the 1890s, is still imported, as are cars, grain and wine (which was a medieval import here).

The commercial docks are not accessible to visitors, but Ocean village is, and the Town Quay gives good views over the Old Docks. The New Docks are easily seen from a distance, and the King George V dry dock is visible from a footpath. Shamrock Quay gives an idea of the private quays along the Itchen, which can also be seen from Woolston or Itchen, or the other side of the river.

Town Quay is the road which runs along the south of the town, originally the water-line, now extended by Royal Pier and the quay called Town Quay. In front of Cuckoo Lane and the remains of the town walls are two memorials: the larger of 1913 to the *Mayflower* which set off from Southampton in 1620, but had to call at Dartmouth and Plymouth on the way; and the smaller to a stewardess who sacrificed herself to save passengers in 1899. Further along is the former Yacht Club, an attractive building of 1846, Italian in style with columns below and nice window detailing. In complete solid contrast opposite is the 14th century **Wool House**, now the Maritime Museum. The front to the road was rebuilt in the 18th century, but the rest of the building is original, including the

ABOVE *The Wool House*
RIGHT *Royal Pier, Southampton*

complex wooden roof inside. French prisoners of war were kept here in the late 18th century. The displays on maritime Southampton are superb, with a large model of the docks, lots of ship models and good displays explaining it all. Also power boats, with a real one of 1933, all shiny metal. ★ ★ ★ ★ (free: lists).

Opposite is the florid Royal Pier, a proper seaside building of 1930 added to the pier which opened in 1833, but rebuilt in the 1890s. The 1833 pier was for the steam boats to France, the Isle of Wight and the Channel Islands, the main business of the port then. The 1890s buildings at the seaward end were burnt recently. Mayflower Park next door is

one of the less attractive parks of the town, but does give good views over Southampton Water with Marchwood and the Army supply ships opposite. From the western end of the park the long low buildings on the shoreline of the New Docks are very close, as are the moored ships. The higher buildings are the Solent Flour Mills, built in the 1930s to process imported grain. Southampton Boat show is held in Mayflower Park each year.

The big brick warehouse on the road called Town Quay (dated 1866) has been converted to offices and flats. Close to it is the Sun Inn, of one storey, the only one of the temporary buildings put up after war-time bombing to survive. It is built

Ocean Dock, Southampton, in 1959. The United States *is passing (l to r) the* Oxfordshire, Mauretania *and* Hameric.

SS Sheildhall *at Ocean Village*

grain: these are for the exports. Coasters and smaller ships used Town Quay until recently, while the main eastern docks opposite were used by big liners.

Ferries run from Town Quay regularly to Hythe on the other side of Southampton Water and the Isle of Wight ferries (ships and hydrofoils) run from between the Quay and Royal Pier. Their floating pontoon is part of a Mulberry Harbour, the artificial harbours made in Southampton for the Normandy invasion of 1944.

Ocean Village is now new blocks of flats and houses with a big shopping centre constructed around a dock, but it was until the early 1980s part of the Old Docks. This was Southampton's first enclosed dock, built in the mudlands from the 1830s and opened in 1843 with railway lines running right down to the dockside from nearby Terminus Station. Steamships carrying mail and passengers to the West Indies, Egypt, Australia and South America were the major users. All but one of the Victorian warehouses which lined the dock were destroyed by bombing in the Second World War.

Most of the troops and equipment for the Crimean War of 1854-6 left England via this dock, and it continued in commercial use until recently, being damaged by bombing in the Second World War and converted in 1968-72 for roll-on roll-off ferries to the Continent.

Today the dock is a marina for yachts, and historic ships are often moored here and open to the public. A Calshot Spit lighthouse boat is displayed outside the main shopping building, and regular trips by boat are offered. The SS *Sheildhall*, the last working cargo steamship, built in 1955, is open to the public (in stream on Bank Holiday weekends). In the

Southampton Docks

background are the working docks with impressive cranes. Parts of the area have still to be developed, and it is possible that the Maritime Museum will move here from Town Quay.

The Western or New Docks were created by filling in the large bay to the west of the old town of Southampton, moving the shoreline up to 2/3 of a mile south from its original position and reclaiming 400 acres of land. A mile and a half of deep water berths was created, big flour mills built to process imported grain and the inland area filled with industry. The docks were completed in 1934. Since they are still in use they are not open to the public, but can be seen from Mayflower Park, or Freemantle. A closer view is possible from a foot bridge over the railway at the western end, off Millbrook Road West. The bridge leads nowhere, but its slight elevation is enough to see the container docks with the huge cranes straddling railway lines, and just over the bridge is the George V dry dock, opened by the King in 1933. It was then the largest dry dock in the world and contains 260,000 tons of water, but can be emptied in four hours. The gate weighs 4,600 tons. Marchwood Power Station, across Southampton Water, seems very close. The new container port runs westward almost to Redbridge, and it is here that most of the port's business is now carried on. 300,000 containers were handled in 1983.

on the stubs of the walls of the bombed building. The domed brick and stone building to the left of Town Quay was built in 1923 as the new Harbour Board Office. The Quay now has modern shops and flats built on it, but there has been a commercial quay here since medieval times. The medieval quay was much shorter, and partly under the present road. It was extended several times during the 19th century, and is worth walking along to the end for the views over the Eastern or Old Docks. The Flying Boat terminal was on the eastern side of the basin enclosed by the Town Quay from the late 1940s until services ceased in the late 50s. The big buildings behind are grain silos: Southampton both imports and exports

At Ocean Village

Outer Southampton

The outskirts of Southampton are divided into three groups: the east, which are those over the Itchen; the north, and the west. The dividing line between the last two is not well defined.

Generally the history of most of the suburbs is similar: the land around Southampton was not rich enough to support good farming and frequent villages, so the only medieval settlements were Millbrook, Redbridge, Itchen and Woolston, all on the shore, and North and South Stoneham inland. In the Georgian period many country houses with large grounds were built in the countryside around the town. Portswood for example had two. Gradually since the 1840s with the expansion of the Docks these large houses have been demolished to make way for the city's expansion. Generally the further from the city centre, the later the development, but this is not uniformly true.

Rownhams, Chilworth, North Stoneham and North Baddesley are not within Southampton despite being so close and feeling as though they are part of the city. They have their own separate gazetteer entries.

Southampton North: The Civic Centre, Parks and Commercial Road; The Common; Bannisters Park; Bassett; Bevois Valley; Highfield; Northam; Portswood; St Denys and Swaythling.

Southampton West: Aldermoor; Freemantle; Lordshill; Lower Test Nature Reserve; Maybush; Millbrook; Redbridge; Shirley and Wimpson.

Southampton East: Botany Bay; Bitterne; Itchen; Pear Tree Green; Sholing; Thornhill; Townhill Park; Weston and Woolston.

Southampton North: The Civic Centre Parks, Commercial Road and Bedford Place. Southampton was alone amongst English towns in expanding during the slump of the 1930s: the New or Eastern Docks were constructed, and the vast Civic Centre built. Sitting to the north of the old town with a large park beyond, the Civic Centre's slim white 158 ft high tower is visible from a large area. The building houses the Civic offices, Police, and to the north the **Art Gallery** (free:lists). This has several handsome exhibition halls, a superb collection of paintings and shows a series of temporary exhibitions every year. Highly recommended ★ ★ ★ ★

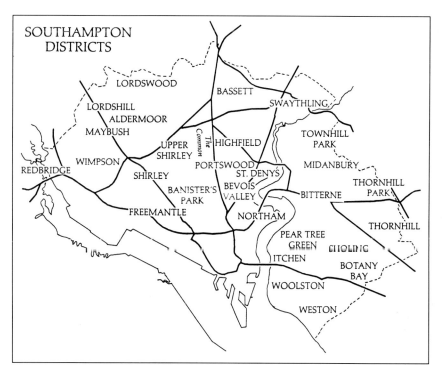

SOUTHAMPTON DISTRICTS

Behind the Civic Centre and then running south down to the old town are parks, which were originally the open arable fields of medieval Southampton, surprisingly preserved from development and turned into public parks in the 1840s. The Corporation bought out the grazing rights and made the parks as compensation for developing the Oxford Street area down by the Docks which had also been common land. Watts (or West) Park north of the Civic Centre was originally Marlands, really Magdalens from the Leper Hospital which stood here in medieval times. A statue of Isaac Watts (1674-1748) the prominent non-conformist stands in the middle of the park. It was by a local sculptor (see **Chilworth**). Watts was born in Southampton and is best remembered today for his hymns which include 'God Our Help in Ages Past' which is chimed by the Civic Centre clock close by. The Cenotaph beside Above Bar Street was designed by Lutyens, and opposite is the memorial to the engineer officers of the *Titanic*. The parks were planted as an arboretum in the 1850s, and still contain many specimen trees.

Commercial Road leads across the back of the Civic Centre towards the Railway station. It starts at normal domestic scale, with terraced houses mostly converted for commercial use, but soon the buildings get much larger. On the south is Mayflower Theatre, recently restored but dating from 1928. Beyond

are huge office and residential blocks of the 1980s. On the other side of the road, just before the church and beside Water Lane is what looks like a stone shed. It is in fact the 14th century Conduit House, which collected the water from a spring uphill near the Polygon. This was then piped down to the old town. Beyond is St Peter's church, designed by the Winchester architect Owen Carter in 1845 in Norman style with the tower imitating the one at Sompting which has been thought to be Saxon. The church is being converted to offices. Southampton central railway station is within the large office blocks opposite, having been rebuilt in the 1960s.

Bedford Place – Carlton Crescent area. In the 1820s Southampton expanded to the north, happily leaving the open fields of the town to become parks. An attempt to develop this area had already been made in the 1760s, with a polygon of houses built around a central mount, but only a little was built. The name still remains. The Carlton Place/Rockstone Place area is well worth walking around to see the large numbers of surviving Regency buildings.

Cumberland Place, facing Watts Park, has some stuccoed Regency houses surviving, with pillared porches and pretty iron balconies. Behind is Grosvenor Square, not completed in the Regency but with three large plain houses

169

of that period set around what should have been a garden, but is now a carpark. Yellow brick or stucco houses of the 1820s and 30s survive amongst more recent buildings in Bedford Place, and Henstead Road leading off to the west is rather more complete. The most impressive area is between Bedford Place and London Road. Carlton Crescent, characteristically laid out as a picturesque curve, is all big rather plain stucco houses with simple classical detailing, most of them joined by short walls so that the whole street frontage is built up. A few have pillared porches or iron balconies, but the overall effect is very restrained. All the houses are subtly different.

Carlton Place is in the same style, but smaller scale and Rockstone Place to the north has groups of three houses lining one side of the road, probably of the 1830s. On the corner with The Avenue is the Ordnance Survey Director General's House of about 1840, yellow brick but with fan-like decoration in stucco over the windows exactly like that found in 1820s stucco houses in the area. The Ordnance Survey moved to Southampton in 1841, after a fire drove them from the Tower of London. The Ordnance Survey is now at Maybush on the outskirts of Southampton. Many of the buildings were bombed, and the middle of the site is filled by the new Courts of Justice, a low block of yellow brick with an interesting modern Royal Coat of Arms in metal at the entrance. Below this a three-sided square of 1830s or 40s buildings survive.

There are more early Victorian villas, mostly yellow brick but a few stucco in this lower part of the Avenue, called Asylum Green after the Military Asylum (or orphanage) which preceeded the Ordnance Survey. Cranbury Place on the east has more yellow brick houses, fairly large, blending into later Victorian terraces eastwards.

The Common. Southampton's medieval arable fields have been preserved as parks around the town centre, and the town's communal grazing is also preserved, as the Common. The area is first referred to in documents in 1228, but it has belonged to the town for longer, perhaps even from Saxon times. The low banks which line the north and west sides are part of the ancient boundaries.

Nearly 400 acres still survive as a wild area of trees and grass, happily too informal to be called a park. Until the 19th century this was a good way outside

Southampton Common

the town, and the large number of trees made it a good spot for highwaymen. The last one was caught in 1775. The whole area is now peaceful, used only for recreation, but in earlier times it was much busier. At Cutthorn Mound, still surviving on the north edge, in the east corner of Burgess Road and The Avenue, the Court Leet was held once a year. Originally in Saxon times, this was a law court, but gradually it came to deal mostly with supervising the common fields and grazing. In 1670 the court moved to the more comfortable Guildhall.

Besides grazing and cutting hay, the area contained brick makers kilns from the 16th century to the early 20th. The town gallows were in the north of the common until 1785, when the last execution took place here. The Cowherds pub, in the middle of the common beside the Avenue is named from the cowherd who looked after everyone's cows. From the later 18th century he supplemented his income by using his house as an inn, popular because it was an attractive short walk from the town. From the middle of the 19th century many more trees were planted because grazing had ceased and the Common was becoming a park. Horse racing was held here in the 1820s and 30s, with a short-lived revival later in the century. Much more important was the supply of water to the town. The springs on the Common had been used by the town from at least the 16th century, but in 1803 a reservoir was built to improve the supply. This has gone, but the Paddling Pool behind the Cowherds and the Boating Lake to the north are both

reservoirs of the 1830s. The Cemetery Lake in the south-west corner was formed by gravel being taken out in the 1870s, and the Ornamental Lake was dug deliberately in 1888.

The common has probably been used by armies for exercises and as a camp since it was first formed, but it was used much more intensively as a permanent camp in the First World War, and again in the Second, when nearly the whole area was used, with a large prisoner-of-war camp as well.

There is much to explore on the Common, and the history and surprisingly varied wildlife of the area is well explained in The Hawthorns, (Southampton Urban Wildlife Centre) (free:lists) which is in the south part of the common, in the corner between Cemetery Road and the Avenue. Particularly good for children, with some live animals.

In 1846 the south-west corner of the Common was taken over as a cemetery, and laid out with all sorts of evergreens. It is a classic Victorian graveyard, now scenic, with its large evergreens and slightly decayed Gothic feeling.

Banister's Park is a very mixed area just south of The Common. Banister's Court was a farm which was rebuilt as a mansion in the 1790s, and demolished in 1927 to make way for development. Archer's Lodge, (bombed in 1940), also of the 1790s, was named after the Royal Society of Southampton Archers, founded in 1789. They met in this area. Some larger Victorian houses survive, but some have been replaced by blocks of flats. The Dell,

Southampton Football Club Ground, is in the south of the area, and the Hampshire County Cricket Club ground in the north.

Bassett is a huge area of north Southampton which has filled with houses since the First World War. The central area is hilly, with many trees, and Bassett Avenue (the continuation north of The Avenue) is well-wooded too. Bassett's church is on Bassett Avenue amongst the trees. St Michael and All Angels is late Victorian brick and stone, a daughter church to North Stoneham which is also used by Bassett.

Off Bassett Green Road, which runs through the north of the area is the tiny Bassett Green, with one big thatched brick cottage and another now with a tiled roof. This is the original settlement, and by the entrance is a small brick building constructed in 1812 as the school, but converted to a church in 1949. St Christophers is very small, but has stained glass and other fittings like a larger church.

The eastern end of Bassett Green Road has many houses designed by the Southampton architect Collins (see Highfield). Some are in three-sided closes off the roads, a very effective arrangement. Ethelburt Avenue, leading from Bassett Green Road to Stoneham Lane is the most characteristic part, still with an unmade wide gravel road, and with houses and terraces in a variety of styles, all handsome. They were built from the late 1920s to the 1950s.

Bevois Valley runs north from Northam along the Itchen and inland to the bottom of the Avenue. The name comes from legendary giant Bevis. A huge mound was interpreted in the 18th century as his castle, and incorporated into the grounds of a house which was named Bevis Mount. The grounds filled the area between the Avenue and Bevois Valley Road, which was then the edge of the river. In the 1760s this was 'a kind of wilderness thro' which are various winding gravel-walks, which are extremely romantic and agreeable and adorned with statues'. The house was demolished in 1940, but long before that the grounds had been covered in houses. The area is full of later 19th century terraced houses, but the main road in the valley itself is lined with unglamorous but very useful shops, many technical. There are a few larger Victorian houses on the main roads, and in the southeast corner of Bevois Valley, right by the railway line, is

Bassett Green

The Old Farmhouse pub, a real farmhouse dated 1611 which was swallowed up by Southampton's expansion but survived. It looks so completely out of place, that it is difficult to believe that it really is an old brick farmhouse. **Bevois Town** off the Avenue is a dense area of small late Victorian terraced houses.

Highfield. A small village developed here from the 1840s, gaining its own church in 1847. Development was slow until this century, but the area filled with mostly quite large houses between the wars. Some of these have now been replaced by blocks of flats, but the**Uplands Estate**, in the south-west close to the common, is the best place to see the work of the Southampton architect Herbert Collins (1885-1975). He designed hundreds of houses on the outskirts of Southampton from the 1920s to the 1950s, all of high quality, and in traditional materials, and all well laid out, taking every advantage he could from the sites.

The streets with little traffic are the best – Orchards Way and Uplands Way. The whole estate is voluntarily maintained so that all the houses are painted the same colour. Informal green areas were left between the houses. Opposite where Orchards Way meets Highfield Lane, is Glebe Court, also by Collins, but much denser development. Collins lived in Brookvale Road, where there are larger and more varied houses, first at no. 59 and then no. 38. (See also Bassett, Thornhill and Swathling.

Christ Church is just to the south-east of the Uplands estate, picturesquely set in

trees. All stone, it dates from 1847 onwards, with a good spire. Beyond the church a short sharp hill, up and down, leads to **The University**.

The University, which now has more than 7,000 students is really a post-war development. In 1850 Henry Hartley of Southampton left a large legacy to set up an institution for scientific, literary and classical studies, but this was not established until 1862 as his relatives contested the will. Hartley University College was established in the town, but moved to Highfield in 1919, becoming the University of Southampton (with less than 1,000 students) in 1952.

In the middle, off University Road, are the original redbrick buildings dating from before the Second World War, but to the east and west are many 1960s onwards buildings in modern styles, some large. The University has also spread into many of the Edwardian semi-detached houses in the area. The Nuffield Theatre of 1961 is one of the most striking, and is in the north-west corner of the campus. Close by is the Turner Sims Concert Hall. The John Hansard Gallery (between the two) shows a series of exhibitions throughout the year and is open to the public (free:lists).

Well designed gardens (perhaps small parks) run through the western side of the campus, ornamented with modern sculpture.

Northam. Until Northam Bridge was built in 1796, and the new road towards Portsmouth constructed, there was no settlement at Northam, although shipbuilding started on the riverside at least as early as the 17th century. The new road encouraged development so that building soon started and Northam was described in the 1820s as 'a small hamlet principally occupied by a few seafaring men, and the labourers at the wharf and yard for shipbuilding, which occupy its river front' (Duthy).

In 1820 Southampton's gasometers were erected here because it was a safe distance away from most of the inhabitants of Southampton who assumed they would blow up. Two are still there, the one with the external frame dating from 1902, the other from 1935.

Shipbuilding at Northam expanded from the 1820s, and from the 1840s there was also marine engineering. A big wharf was established for coal brought in by sea and others for timber, along with other industrial premises. The greatest growth was in the middle of the 19th century, when the river frontage filled with wharves and inland many small houses were built. Except along the main road, most of these terraces have been replaced by low modern blocks of flats. Along the shore all is still industrial, but one part of this is now accessible for the public. At *Shamrock Quay* the redbrick 19th century warehouses which line the shore have been turned into offices and workshops, and yachts are still built and repaired. It is not a large area, but an interesting contrast to Ocean Village and other docklands developments because the original buildings have been preserved and there are still many marine businesses.

Northam bridge was rebuilt in 1889, but tolls had to be paid until 1929 when the Corporation took the bridge over and made it free. The present bridge dates from 1954.

Portswood. This was never a real village. Portswood House was built in 1776 in the south (where Lawn Road is now), a large country mansion described in 1805 as 'a handsome building, situated on an eminence, commanding a fine view. Southampton Water, when the tide is up, forms a wide lake in front of the mansion'. This view was spoilt when the railway was built. Another country house, Portswood Lodge, was built in the north in 1800, but both have since been demolished. By the middle of the 19th century smaller houses had been built along much of Portswood Road. At the northern end on the east side of the road,

between Kent Road and the Red Lion pub, is an incongruous survivor, a little square Georgian Gothic lodge of 1775, with arches, windows and decorative crenellation. This was a lodge to Portswood House.

Off Portswood Road the area filled with houses from the later 19th century onwards. The long shopping street has great variety, including a large cinema of the 1930s, The Broadway, now used for bingo.

St Denys. Until the middle of the 19th century there were no houses east of Portswood Road, except the farm whose buildings incorporated the remains of the Priory of St Dennis, which had been founded in 1127 down by the river. Only one arch of the building survives, now reconstructed in the garden of Tudor House. After the middle of the 19th century the area filled with housing, and in 1868 a vast brick church was built, and a little later a big brick school next door. The church is early English in style, designed by Sir George Gilbert Scott.

Swaythling divides into three parts – along the main road down into Portswood, where there is an ordinary small shopping area; South Stoneham with the old church to the south-east, and to the north-east a fine piece of suburban development by the Southampton architect Collins.

There is one survivor from rural Swaythling. Tucked up among suburban development in Channel's Farm Road just over the railway in the north-west (off the Bassett Road) is Channel's Farm House, a proper thatched cottage. The Collins development is along Mansbridge Road, mostly three-sided courts of houses with large greens. They were built quite cheaply for a housing association from 1925 onwards, and include handsome neo-Georgian shops on the corner at the roundabout, with a characteristic Collins touch – a grassy bank in front. The whole development is very successful.

Along Burgess Road, otherwise lined with 1930s houses, is another Collins building – Swaythling Methodist Hall, built in 1932 as a combination preaching hall and cinema, with a big copper dome. It was converted to a church in 1960.

Mansbridge was the lowest bridge on the Itchen until Northam Bridge was built in 1796. The old bridge (a plain early 19th century stone structure) is now by-passed. The Itchen Navigation (see entry) used

the course of the river here, and so barges had to go under this bridge. A path leads downstream on the eastern side of the river through surprisingly rural countryside to Woodmill, which marks the end of the Navigation. The pools upstream of Woodmill were famous for their salmon, and were visited by Queen Victoria in 1847. She was later supplied with salmon from here. Woodmill marks the change in the Itchen from fresh to salt water, and there is a redbrick mill of 1820. This was the site of 'the curious works erected by Mr Walter Taylor, for the manufacture of *Blocks, Pumps*, etc for the service of the English Navy' made by the 'aid of ingenious machinery'. They were 'much cheaper, more certain in their operation, and more durable, than those formerly in use'. (Bayley and Britton 1805).

South Stoneham church is in the middle of southern Swaythling, the area where many of Southampton University's halls of residence have been built. The church of St Mary sits apart, looking very rural. Originally the parish included Eastleigh, Bitterne, West End and Portswood, which is why the church is quite large. The tower (stone like the rest) is of about 1500, late for tower building. The body of the church is basically 12th and 13th century, but was thoroughly restored, the south transept added and many windows put in, in the 1850s. The very fine chancel arch is late 12th century, with superb detailing. Most unusually it is made from chalk, a sensible stone to use

The Clerk Memorial in South Stoneham church

inside as it carves easily, but unsuitable externally as it washes away. 12th century Purbeck marble table-type font, with more decoration than usual.

The church has some very fine monuments: the earliest of 1540 in the chancel, an arched recess with table tomb, looking like part of the building. Opposite, Edmund Clerke, who died in 1632, kneels praying facing his wife, with their twelve children below. The inscription plays with the fact that Clerke was clerke of his Majesties privy seal, as was his father, grandfather and great-grandfather. Beside the altar a monument to Mary Jones who died in 1828, by a carver in Florence. The best monument is that to Edmund Dumner (died 1724) who employed the famous architect Hawksmoor to design South Stoneham House (see below): the monument may also have been designed by Hawksmoor. Big, and very impressive, with a central medallion of Dumner, theatrical curtains, and then a large architectural surround. Other good monuments around the church.

★ ★ *Church*

Southampton West:

Aldermoor used to consist of one large house (built about 1800) set in a hilly area whose very name suggests the area was not good for farming. Recently housing estates have filled the area, and the big house has been demolished, but many trees and open areas survive, most surprisingly a valley in the middle which is still partly farmed.

Freemantle was part of Millbrook until 1852, and then had only a large Georgian house. From that date it was developed with small detached or semidetached houses for the great increase in Southampton's population, with lots of Victorian corner pubs. Most of these survive, with occasional small blocks of modern flats. Until recently the area was very scruffy, and was often hidden under the euphemism of Lower Shirley. Today it is more prosperous. Christ Church fills the angle between two of the main roads, an impressive building with a big spire by William White who was also the architect of Lyndhurst church. Wide views of the docks from outside the church, which dates from 1865. Stone, unlike Lyndhurst, with elaborate windows. Inside there is a lot of brick.

In the middle of the 19th century there was a promenade for pedestrians along the shore, just over the railway line. Although the shore-line has moved away because of reclamation the path is still preserved.

★ *Church*

Lords Hill is mostly very recent development. Lordswood House was built about 1800 in what was then an area of poor farming quite distant from Southampton. It was demolished this century. Many trees and open areas survive, and the new developments have wide roads. A new shopping centre in the middle is not distinguished. *Lordswood* still survives as a large wood with many popular footpaths.

Lower Test Nature Reserve covers 270 acres of the marshy Test valley above Redbridge. The lowest parts are saltmarsh and although the tide penetrates a good way up the valley in the river, streams and ditches, the marsh gradually changes to fresh water. Public access is restricted to the northern part, and by car the easiest way to it is from the west, using the car park north of Totton. On foot there are several entrances from the east, including the Test Way. One foot path crosses the valley from the car park, and gives a good view of the low wet landscape. Good plants and birds, especially waders. The reserve belongs to the Hampshire and Isle of Wight Naturalists Trust, and there are display boards at the entrances to the footpaths explaining the natural history. The Mill house on the Testwood side of the estuary is handsome redbrick, and there always seem to be huge fish in the river here. Towards the car park is a faintly Gothic tower, a 19th century water tower which used to serve Testwood House, demolished in 1935. On the south-western side is a public hide, sited to look over an area used by many birds. The reserve is good for waterfowl and waders in winter, and many different types in summer.

★ ★ ★ ★ *For the walks in this odd landscape, a complete contrast to adjacent Southampton.*

Maybush has mostly post-war housing filling the area: 1930s semi-detached on the main road and more recent estates behind. The largest buildings are the headquarters of the Ordnance Survey, which opened in 1966. (Museum open by appointment, free;lists. Worth seeing). Just to the north, and also used by the O.S. is Crabwood House built in the 1840s when Maybush was open countryside.

Millbrook (H) was originally a village straggling along the main road from Southampton to Redbridge, along the shore of Southampton Water. Reclamation for docks and industry has moved the shoreline ¾ mile out to the deep water channel, and the new roads have destroyed virtually all the older buildings. Millbrook was a medieval village, whose parish included Shirley and Freemantle. The church of Holy Trinity was rebuilt on a new site in the 1870s, and is a prominent landmark with its huge stone spire, right by the main road. To the east, amongst the interwar housing, is a survivor from the old village, a large yellow brick house of the earlier 19th century. Thousands of 1930s houses in central Millbrook.

The north-western part was developed as a housing estate after the Second World War, along with Wimpson, Maybush and Redbridge.

Redbridge started as a small medieval settlement at the lowest bridging point on Southampton Water. The first part of the name means reed not the colour: the bridges are grey. From the 1790s it was the terminus of the Andover Canal (see entry), and by 1805 Redbridge was 'a populous hamlet' with 'a busy appearance and a considerable trade in coals, timber corn etc' (Bayley and Britton). A few Georgian brick buildings survive from this village underneath either side of the modern flyover. Beside the Anchor Inn is one of the canal warehouses, now converted to flats and the damp dip east of Redbridge railway station is part of the canal. The canal was not very successful. Canal barges were not seaworthy enough to reach Southampton along the shore. Attempts to extend the canal into the middle of Southampton along the shore-line foundered because the tunnel required was badly designed and built. In 1847 the route of the canal into Southampton was taken over by a railway company, who built their line along it. In 1865 another railway along the line of the canal north to Romsey was opened: here the severe curves of the route caused several derailments and the line was rebuilt. The railway companies reclaimed land on the shore, south of the track, for wharves and sawmills, so that today Redbridge is cut off from the estuary.

Both railway lines are still in use, but it is the bridges and flyovers which dominate the old centre. Two old road bridges are deserted just upstream: both are stone, with the larger eastern one dating from the 17th century, and the other inscribed hugely 'BUILT BY THE COUNTY' 1793. These were replaced in the 1930s by a concrete bridge, made very high so that the road could cross the railway to Romsey without a level crossing. Between 1865-1930s the level crossing caused enormous traffic jams since all the traffic to the New Forest passed through Redbridge. In the 1960s another bridge was added, widening the road. The railway crosses the estuary on a viaduct. The container port stretches to Redbridge now.

Most of Redbridge is post-war, with large housing estates to the north, including one large tower block. The church of All Saints is in this part, dating from 1965 and with a striking stained glass which dominates the small building. The area south of the main road which bisects the area is industrial. To the north-west, stretching across and up the marshy Test valley is the Lower Test Nature reserve (see entry).

St James church, Shirley

ABOVE *Decoration under a window in Shirley High Street*
RIGHT *Early Victorian house, Shirley*

Shirley was never a village. Originally it was part of the medieval parish of Millbrook, but in 1836 it became a separate parish and developed rapidly as a suburb of Southampton. The early Victorian centre was around St James church to the north-west of the present main shopping street. The church was built in 1836, of the yellow brick typical of that date in Southampton. The style is typical too, not serious Gothic revival like later Victorian churches but inaccurate and pretty. Handsome tower, and inside long plain galleries supported by iron columns. The chancel was added in 1881 in a surprisingly light-hearted style. Next to the church a strangely sunken park, once a brick pit. A few early Victorian houses survive around the church, all of yellow brick, but most of Shirley consists of later Victorian or early 20th century redbrick houses, mostly semi-detached although styled like terraces.

There is another early nucleus in Regent's Park Road, with several early Victorian villas stuccoed or yellow brick. The distinctive grey and red brick blocks here, one with a clock tower are Thorner's Charity which moved here from near the Civic Centre in the 1930s.

The main road through Shirley is a long and lively shopping street, mostly small scale but of great variety. At the north end it opens up to a modern shopping area. Several late 19th or early 20th century chapels or churches, the most spectacular of which is halfway along the main road. Of varied red bricks it is St Boniface Roman Catholic church of 1927, Byzantine in style. Further in towards Southampton, on the opposite side of the road is a handsome early Victorian house of yellow brick with 'Gothick' windows

and curvy barge boards, a survivor from Shirley's earliest days.

Upper Shirley is mostly later Victorian whereas **Shirley Warren** is more mixed and includes post-war houses. **Old Shirley** was on the road junction to the north, only a hamlet of which one thatched building (now a pub) survives incongruously amongst the modern developments.

Wimpson was described in 1911 as a little hamlet consisting of two farms, a 'group of cottages, the school and the Methodist chapel'. Post Second World War development has filled the whole area, with a circular road looping through Wimpson, Redbridge and Maybush. A couple of big tower blocks, but mostly smaller scale, with large open spaces. The only earlier building surviving is a pub in Wimpson Lane.

Southampton East

Botany Bay is one of the small settlements around Weston Common which have grown enormously this century. Wild areas of common still survive, particularly just north of Mayfield Park where there are ponds and a small study centre. Close by the railway is carried on a brick viaduct. A few rather mean 19th century cottages survive around a triangular green.

Bitterne covers a huge area on the eastern side of the River Itchen. On the peninsula created by the curves of the river was the Roman settlement of Clausentum, known from the late 16th century when the antiquary Camden recorded that 'a right honest gentleman there dwelling showed unto me the rubbish, old broken walls, and trenches of an ancient castle'. Occupation started about 70 AD, and continued into the late 4th century, with earthen defences on the landward side cutting off the peninsula. The settlement was not large and is best described as a small town, the earliest predecessor of Southampton, albeit on a different site. God's House Tower Museum has a good display about Clausentum.

A medieval manor house was built on the peninsula in Norman times, and part of it still survives. The building was badly damaged by bombing during the Second World War, but was converted into flats by the architect Herbert Collins. A small park beside the manor is inside the Roman settlement.

Until the first Northam Bridge was built in 1796 this area was only accessible by boat from Southampton, and was little developed. The bridge was part of a general improvement of the road from Southampton to Portsmouth, and was privately built, a turnpike road and bridge for which tolls had to be paid. Bitterne village grew at the top of the hill alongside this new road, slowly at first but faster from the middle of the 19th century, with the shore line being reclaimed for wharves and industrial buildings, and even the site of Clausentum covered with houses.

The shopping street of Bitterne has been by-passed, and the road pedestrianised. The buildings are small scale, and only the grey stone church of Holy Saviour is prominent, up near the top of the hill with a spire. It dates from 1852 and 1882 reflecting the date of most of Bitterne.

Bitterne Park upriver, developed from 1883 when Cobden Bridge was built across the Itchen. Northam Bridge, then the only other bridge, charged tolls, whereas Cobden Bridge was always free. Upstream from the bridge (which was rebuilt in 1926-8) is a park reclaimed from the river bank, and downstream are a few recent Docklands type houses. The Triangle, the shopping area just over the bridge, is mostly Edwardian and centres on a substantial combination clock tower

and drinking fountain of 1889, moved here from the middle of Southampton in 1935 because it was obstructing road improvements in the area of the Civic Centre.

Bitterne Park was not completely developed until the 1930s, and the church of The Ascension was not built until 1924-6, replacing a temporary building on the same site just to the south-east of The Triangle. The entrance is under the tower, with a fine mosaic on the wall inside dating from 1963. Stairs lead up to the church, which is very large, with plain stone piers. All the windows except the western one have square tops, unusual in churches of any period. The main screen is modern classical in style of 1959, very effective. Fine altar as well, a combination of Gothic and classical. The stained glass in the aisle and east windows dates from the 1920s and 30s, and are some of the finest of that period, combining bright colours with detailed monochrome scenes.

The church is ★ ★ as a good quality between the wars building.

Itchen. The inhabitants were described by John Bullar in 1819 as being 'quite peculiar in their manners. Any settlers in their district, who are not actual natives of the village, they describe as foreigners' The men were employed in fishing and their wives in selling the fish. The village was described at much the same date as consisting simply of one steep street up from the hard where the ferries beached. this has gone: when the floating bridge was established at Woolston (just down the river) in 1836 the ferries ceased and Itchen developed inland. From the 17th century smuggling supplemented fishing, and boatbuilding started.

The one steep street led up to Pear Tree Green, and there are a few 19th century terraced cottages surviving here. The other old part of Itchen, along the shore, developed into shipyards, many of which are now used for other industries.

Itchen inland has no real centre, but is a large area of later 19th century onwards development, joining up with Woolston to the south and Sholing in the east.

Pear Tree Green still survives as a large green in the middle of Southampton suburban development. The ancient pear tree was replaced in 1850 and again in 1951. The 1951 tree is at the north corner on the road to Bitterne, railed in and with a plaque. It doesn't seem very large

considering its age. Opposite, concealed by suburban development, is Pear Tree House, its Gothic facades of 1800 concealing a much earlier building.

Jesus Chapel in the middle of the green was the first church to be built on this side of the river, and was built in 1620 to save the people of Itchen crossing the river every Sunday. The original building is concealed by additions of various 19th century dates. Inside are several good 1830s and 40s memorials.

The whole area (except the green) is now filled by housing. The green gives good views of the Itchen, its industry and the high new bridge.

Until the late 18th century a procession was formed on St Peter's day, when an image of that saint was carried about the village to ensure good luck with fishing. This survival of a Catholic custom was explained by the isolation of the area.

Sholing is mostly 1930s with a few 19th century brick cottages, some of them single storey. The church of St Mary (1866) and the Victorian school are close together at the southern end of the parish.

Thornhill and Thornhill Park are names easy to muddle with Townhill Park, which is a more recent area of housing to the north of Thornhill. As in so many areas now which are part of Southampton, a country house (in this case a rather late one of about 1827) was demolished this century to make way for housing. The eastern part of Thornhill is the oldest, dating from the 1920s, with some small houses along the main road by the Southampton architect Collins (see Highfield). 1930s development filled the main road, and since the Second World War large estates have been built filling virtually the whole area, but leaving good quantities of trees and open spaces.

Townhill Park is very easy to muddle with Thornhill and Thornhill Park just to the south. The name comes from a big house of about 1800 with a well treed park now a college, and the area is densely developed with 1960s houses and low blocks of flats, and 1980s housing. Towards the north is a new shopping centre.

Weston. Most of Weston is very recent. The Victoria County History described it in 1908 as a 'small village' of 'a few thatched cottages and some newer-looking houses nearer the coast'.

The newer-looking houses have multiplied to form a large settlement with blocks of flats along the shore. Weston Lane has the shops and the stone church of Holy Trinity with a prominent spire, all of 1865. More elaborately decorated inside. All the parish overlooks Southampton Water.

To the north of the church is **Mayfield Park**, the remains of the grounds of a large house of the same name (now demolished) adapted as a public park. Towards the centre is a plain and large stone obelisk of 1810, and in the north one of the early Victorian lodges survives, a pretty building.

Weston Common is difficult to distinguish from Sholing now, with lots of 1930s housing, but it was originally open ground and a little remnant of that common survives through the middle.

Woolston is on the shores of the Itchen, opposite Crosshouse, and was always one of the places where ferries across the river from Southampton landed. The steam floating bridge of 1836 ran only to Woolston, making it the only important landing place from then onwards. The floating bridge has gone, replaced by a huge bridge of 1977, but the sloping hard which it used is still at the bottom of Woolston's main street.

Woolston has been a ship-building centre since the 1870s, when iron ships were produced, and gradually changed to supplying the Royal Navy. Naval ships are still made in the big buildings on the shore, but the most famous Woolston industry no longer exists. Upstream from the new bridge was the Supermarine factory which started making seaplanes and flying boats in 1914. Between the wars it was the most important aircraft factory in the area, and it was here that the Spitfire designed by R.J. Mitchell was produced for the Second World War. Great parts of the works were destroyed by bombing in 1940, and nothing now remains. There is a memorial to R.J. Mitchell under the new bridge, close to the site of the works.

Flying boat services ran erratically from Woolston from 1919, with regular services, mostly to the Channel Islands from 1923 into the 1930s.

By the 1860s Woolston had grown into a large village, mostly along the main road from the hard to Bursledon, and from the later 19th century onwards it spread over a much wider area. In and around Obelisk Road are many mid 19th century villas and cottages. The shops now extend along a cross-street as well as the main road. Just up from the hard is a very early cinema, the Woolston Picture House of 1912, now splendidly painted. Where the bridge meets the ground is a typical railway station of the 1860s, and further along, just beyond the roundabout is the Roman Catholic church of St Patrick of 1938. There is no medieval church in Woolston: the parish church is half a mile south of the main road and was built in the 1860s-80s to the designs of William White whose best building is Lyndhurst church. This one is simpler, although with a complicated plan and lined inside with different coloured bricks.

★ *Church*

SOUTH TIDWORTH (D) One of the ring of Army camps around Salisbury Plain. North Tidworth, difficult to distinguish from South, is in Wiltshire with the county boundary running along the east-west road at the main cross-roads. Just to the west of the crossroads are the surviving cottages of the original hamlet, one with unusually elaborate flintwork. In 1903 the Army came to Tidworth, and many large Edwardian buildings date from this first phase, alongside recent buildings. The row of shops to the east of the crossroads is basically Edwardian, and to the west are two churches of 1912, one Roman Catholic. Lots of sports fields and many trees.

To the south is Tidworth House, mostly Victorian, in a large and woody park. The church of St Mary on the main road close to the house is a distinguished Victorian building. Externally it looks rather solid steep roofed and with a crazy little spire, but inside it is rich, with plenty of carving and pillars of exotic stone.

★ ★ *St Mary's church, for its interior.*

SOUTH WARNBOROUGH (F) Most of the village is off the main road, with neat brick or timber-framed cottages, but a big Georgian house and the church are on the main road. The church of St Andrew has a Norman doorway, and the rest is basically medieval apart from the aisle which was added in 1870. Unusually the rood loft survives, with a reproduction screen underneath. At the west end is the heavy timber bell frame. In the chancel are many memorials to the White family, a surprising collection of early monuments. The earliest is the plainest, a tomb chest on the left hand side of the altar, of the late 15th century. A brass of 1512 behind it, and most prominently on the left hand wall a table tomb or possibly a re-used pre-Reformation Easter Sepulchre (used to house an effigy of Christ for Easter celebrations) with figures in the back and in inscription in English to Thomas and Agnes White who died in 1566 and 1570. Fourteen sons and six daughters are represented, those who died before their parents shown holding skulls. The inscription ends 'God save the Queen' ie Elizabeth. Another Elizabethan tablet above to one of their daughters, and another to a son. More 16th century Whites opposite. An Elizabethan bracket to the right of the altar and 16th century glass in the eastern window of the aisle.

★ ★ *Church, especially for the monuments.*

SOUTHWICK (N/J) Just over Portsdown from the Portsmouth/ Portchester conurbation, but a different world. A superbly preserved large village with an interesting church. The best part of the village is on the T-junction close to the church, with plain Georgian brick houses and cottages, and a few Victorian houses (and the school) of knapped flint, all in a fanciful style. Almost all the houses have dark red front doors showing

Southwick: timber framing and, on the right, timber cladding

The tomb of John Whyte in Southwick church

that they belong to the local estate which is still remarkably intact. Many thatched cottages survive, scattered all over the village, some of them 16th or 17th century timber-framed. In the road leading west from the church a rare example of a thatched and weatherboarded cottage. Both the other roads from the church have good buildings, the one to the north rather sparsely, the southern one more dense and attractive. The village pump survives, and behind the Golden Lion pub is its late 19th century brewhouse. All the machinery inside, including a steam engine, is preserved.

The Augustinian priors of Portchester moved to Southwick in about 1150, and although little remains of the large priory which grew here, the big house (an early 19th century mansion) is on the same site. This was taken over by the Navy during the Second World War, and was used as Eisenhower's headquarters in 1944, when he was Supreme Allied Commander. The house still belongs to the Navy, and is called HMS *Dryad*, the school of navigation. It is difficult to see from the village, but can be seen (with its surrounding modern buildings) from the road to Portchester over Ports Down. A modern 'suburb' for the personnel makes almost a separate part of the village.

The church name (St James-Without-the-Priory-Gate) is another reminder of the priory, for this is the village church, outside the Priory. Although there has been a church here since at least Norman times, most of the present building is a reconstruction of 1566, a most unusual date. John Whyte was granted Southwick Priory in 1538 at the dissolution of the monasteries, and it was he who rebuilt the parish church having demolished most of the Priory. He re-used some windows. The lower part of the tower is attractive chequering of knapped flint and stone, the upper part plain, nearly all flint and of 1566. The entrance is low and panelled, a preparation for the good fittings inside.

The 1566 windows are very plain, with square tops, and the arches to the north aisle are large and flat. Preserved in the arch between the north aisle and chapel is an elegant Purbeck Marble double capital with foliage which must have come from the Priory. The Norman font is Purbeck Marble too. Between the north chapel and chancel is the tomb of John Whyte the builder of the church. He possibly re-used a slightly earlier tomb chest from the Priory, which has brasses to him, his wife and children, and is medieval in style. Good lettering around the slab, in English. The large surround is by contrast classical and fills the arch.

Only the two big 18th century family pews remain, nicely fitted out with fabric. They make one regret the loss of the others. The pulpit is part of one of the pews but has its own window. The simple wooden gallery is supported on big twisted columns, repeated on a much smaller scale in the communion rails. Blocking most of the east window is an unusual painted wooden reredos of the 18th century with a classical painting of cherubs and doves in a pilastered surround. This is an unusual survival as it is not the sort of church fitting approved of by the Victorians. The stout brass candlesticks on the altar are late 17th century. On the outside of the east walls is an inscription recording the rebuilding of 1566.

★ ★ ★ *For the church, an attractive building of unusual date with interesting pre-Victorian fittings. A good village too, worth walking around.*

SOUTH WONSTON (E) An odd modern settlement high on the chalk downs, started about 1900 by a farmer who sold off plots for building, despite the lack of water. The area was so poor for farming that it was known as Starvedown.

Along the ridge are lots of 1930s bungalows, with more modern estates beyond. Farmland all around, and the village is more like a suburb than a rural settlement. The small church of St Margaret is of corrugated iron. The most distinctive building is the water tower, an inverted cone on stilts by the main road. **Worthy Down** to the south is an Army Camp.

SOWLEY POND (D) (2½ miles south of East Boldre) A medieval fish pond, extended about 1600 to form the water supply for a big tilt hammer of an ironworks, partly supplied by local ironstone, collected on the coast. This closed in 1822. Picturesque, with trees all around it.

SPARSHOLT (D/H) 420ft up on the chalk, high for a village settlement, but placed here because a deposit of the more fertile clay-with-flints covers the chalk. On the road in from the east is Lainston House, handsome redbrick of 1700, with a wide avenue of trees. The whole area is well-wooded, and the village itself is full of hedges and trees. The houses are sparse except right in the middle. Mostly brick cottages, some still thatched. A few are weather boarded. The church of St Stephen is largely 1880s, but the entrance doorway is classical of 1631, with a wooden door of the same date.

To the south-east is the hamlet of **Deane**, with a variety of cottages, and to the north-west Hampshire Agricultural College.

Sparsholt church doorway dated 1631

Literary Hampshire

Hampshire can claim Jane Austen as entirely its own. She was born at Steventon in the north of the county and lived there for the first twenty five years of her life. The next five years the family were in Bath, the only long period she spent out of the county, as in 1806 they moved to Southampton. Finally they settled at Chawton, close to Steventon. When Jane became ill in 1817 she was taken to Winchester for better medical attention, died and was buried there. She wrote very little while they were in Bath, so Hampshire can claim to be not only her home, but the place where she wrote all her six classic novels.

Her father was rector of Steventon, and the family was quite prosperous. Jane had six brothers, and one sister to whom she was very close. The whole family was scholarly, clever and bookish, all great novel readers. Jane wrote fiction from her early teens, some of which survives, and started writing what was to become (after mature revision) *Sense and Sensibility* when she was twenty. The early versions of *Northanger Abbey* and *Pride and Prejudice* were also written at Steventon before she was twenty six.

Through her family she was involved in the wider world in ways that do not show in her fiction. Two of her brothers joined the Navy and became Admirals; an aunt was threatened with transportation and imprisoned for 9 months on a false charge of stealing; and a cousin (later a sister-in-law) was widowed when her husband was guillotined in the French Revolution.

Jane's life was quiet with home and family (a wide circle) of central importance. She made visits (as her heroines do) for quite long periods, and there were short-lived romances. Cassandra and she helped keep

Charles Dickens birthplace, Portsmouth

house with their mother, and many letters survive describing Jane's everyday life. (See particularly Chawton and Steventon, but also Ashe, Deane, Hurstborne Tarrant, Portsmouth and Southampton.)

Many other novelists are associated with Hampshire. Charles Dickens was born in Portsmouth in 1812, and used the town in *Nicholas Nickleby*.

Charles Kingsley (1819-1875) is best known today for his novels especially *The Water Babies* (1863), but in his lifetime he was well known as a social and sanitary reformer, supporter of the Chartists, and as a poet. He was curate and then rector of Eversley in north Hampshire for 30 years, dying and being buried there. He wrote 8 novels, mostly concerned with social problems. *Alton Lock* (1850) has a Chartist hero, and shows the sufferings of the overcrowded towns, and *Yeast* (1851) shows the rural problems. Kingsley was a controversial man, ahead of his time, and well-loved by his rural parishoners.

Elizabeth Gaskell died at Holyborne in 1865. In her novel *North and South* (1855) the rural softer south is represented by the eastern edge of the New Forest. Although it claims less of the novel than the north, the Forest is used as an image of a better life.

Charlotte M. Yonge was a prolific and popular Victorian novelist, producing 160 novels and some non-fiction. She lived all her life at Otterborne.

The first Sherlock Holmes story *A Study in Scarlet*

Jane Austen.

Charles Dickens

(1887) was written while Conan Doyle was a Doctor in Portsmouth, so the county can be said to be the famous detective's birthplace. Conan Doyle also stayed at Emery Down in the New Forest in 1890 while writing *The White Company* set partly in the New Forest of the 14th century. Late in life he bought a cottage at Minstead in the forest as a holiday home, and he is buried in the churchyard there.

R. D. Blackmore, best known for *Lorna Doone* also wrote a good melodramatic novel set in the New Forest – *Cradock Nowell* (1873.

The most enduringly popular New Forest story is still *Children of the New Forest* (1847) by Captain Marryat. His family came from New Milton, close to the setting of the novel. He wrote sixteen novels for adults and six more for children, none still as popular as his New Forest classic.

Sir Compton Mackenzie described the odd settlement at Beech in several of his early novels, having lived there for part of the time in the 1890s.

Neville Shute is usually associated with Australia, but he lived at Emsworth and several of his novels have Hampshire settings, some including the growing aviation industry in which he worked. *No Highway* (1948) is largely set in the Air Research Station at Farnborough, and *Requiem for a Wren* (1955) describes part of the New Forest during the Second World War.

The author of *The Compleat Angler*, Izaac Walton (1593-1683), spent much of his later life in Winchester and Droxford. Two distinguished literary naturalists are associated with the county. Selborne is synonymous with Gilbert White (1720-93), who spent virtually his whole life there, distilling his local knowledge into *The Natural History of Selborne*. W.H. Hudson (1841-1922) was less firmly rooted, but his *Hampshire Days* and *A Shepherd's Life* (set in Martin) are also classics.

The county has a double claim on William Cobbett, the reformer. He farmed at Botley from 1805-12, putting into practice the advanced farming methods he preached, and his two favourite spots in the world were Hurstborne Tarrant and Weston, Southampton.

The Reverend William Gilpin, rector of Boldre in the New Forest 1770-1804, is perhaps not strictly speaking a literary worthy. He did publish five books of his tours in various parts of Great Britain, but these were aimed at defining the picturesque – those parts of the landscape worthy of being painted, of being part of a picture. He had a great effect on the way people looked at the landscape, the cult of the picturesque (and travelling to see it) being reflected in Jane Austen's novels for example. He was much more than locally important.

Keats is the best known poet associated with the county. he wrote 'The Eve of St Agnes' at Bedhampton, a poem very popular in Victorian times, and 'Ode to Autumn' while he was staying in Winchester in 1819:

Season of mists and mellow fruitfulness
Close bosom-friend to the maturing sun;
Conspiring with him how to load and bless
With fruit the vines that round the thatch-eaves run.

Bentworth produced George Wither (1588-1667), a prolific writer in prose and poetry. His first published work *Abuses Stript and Whipt* (1613) was highly critical of the government (and amusing) and he was imprisoned. He fought for Parliament in the Civil War, and was a fine poet, although Dryden was scornful: 'He forgot his notions as they fell,/And if they rhymed and rattled all was well.' From *Fair Virtue* (1622):

Her true beauty leaves behind
Apprehensions in my mind
Of more sweetness than all art
Or inventions can impart.
Thoughts too deep to be expressed,
And too strong to be suppressed.

Edward Thomas (1878-1917) is now best remembered for his poetry, although he wrote much prose. He lived for the last ten years of his life at Steep, and the dramatic landscape of the area figures in several of his poems.

Shakespeare may have stayed at Titchfield Abbey and might have written some of the sonnets there, but lack of contemporary information sadly makes this uncertain.

Three houses associated with writers are open to the public – Charles Dickens Birthplace, Portsmouth; The Wakes, Selborne where Gilbert White lived; and Jane Austen's house at Chawton.

Memorial to Edward Thomas near Steep

ST CATHERINE'S HILL see
WINCHESTER

ST CROSS see **WINCHESTER**

ST DENYS see **SOUTHAMPTON
NORTH**

ST LEONARD'S GRANGE (M) (1 Mile
south of Buckler's Hard) Granges were
outlying farms belonging to large
land-owners, usually used for storage of
grain or other crops. This one belonged
to Beaulieu Abbey, and the remains of the
medieval barn indicate the huge scale of
the abbey's farming. Only the gable walls
survive, 60 feet high. The barn was 216
feet long, and a more recent good-sized
barn shelters inside the ruins. Further
away from the road are the remains of the
13th century chapel and a handsome brick
and stone house of about 1700. From the
road west there are suddenly views of the
Solent, surprisingly close. The grange is
not open, but worth seeing from the road.

ST MARY BOURNE (D) Much denser
than most of the valley villages,
especially in the middle around the church
with lots of thatched cottages, brick flint
or painted. Almshouses of 1862 in flint
and brick. The river is small and wanders
through flat meadows either side of the
village. To the north-west is **Stoke**, a
separate hamlet with the river and some
thatch. Up the side road is a thatched
18th century octagonal brick building,
once a lodge to the big house. **Binley**
away to the north is a very rural hamlet,
some thatched cottages and a house with
unusual brick or flint lozenges on the side
wall.

The church of St Peter has an
Elizabethan tower, but the rest of the
church is mostly late 12th century and
puzzling inside because the square pillars
although seemingly all much the same
date, do not line up. Handsome 14th
century tomb recess in south aisle.

The church has the largest of the
Tournai marble fonts (all dating from
around 1170). Attractive carvings on the
side, and a base of 1927 made from the
same Belgian marble. Unusual 17th
century reading desk, with four positions
for books, more like one intended for a
library. One of the chains remains, used to
attach books to it for security.

STEEP (K) An odd village, with several
'Arts and Crafts' houses and cottages
dating from 1900 onwards, presumably

St Leonard's Grange

built by people attracted to Bedales, the
progressive co-educational school which
moved to Steep in 1900. Edward Thomas
(1878-1917) the poet and writer, was one
of these, and the three houses he and his
family lived in during the ten years before
his death are a cross-section of Steep's
geography and buildings. Much of his
poetry is based on the area around Steep,
and his wife's book *World without End*
(1931) describes their life there and many
of the people.

The dominating feature of Steep is the
wooded escarpment, the steep hill which
marks the edge of the chalk, falling away
in a steep slope to the greensand below.
One of the houses the Thomases rented is
on the top of this hill, along Cockshott
Lane which runs west along the hill, off
the road from High Cross. The Bee House
was new when they moved there, built on
Arts and Crafts principles of local
materials. The views are magnificent: 'We

A hangar near Steep

lived in clouds, on a cliff's edge' (Edward
Thomas). The lane leads along the top of
the hangar and after half a mile a footpath
leads downhill past a sarsen stone with an
inscribed slate dedicating the hillside to
the memory of Edward Thomas.

The footpath leads down to Berryfield
Cottage, another of the Thomas homes of
brick and malmstone tucked in the
winding lanes. Their last home was no.2
Yew Tree Cottages, right in the middle of
the village close to the crossroads with
the Petersfield Road. Between the
crossroads and the church is Bedales
school, with only one of the buildings
really visible from the road. This big
rendered building dates from soon after
the school arrived here in 1900.

The church of All Saints is rendered
outside, and dominated by the Surrey-like
tower and spire of 1875. Inside the 15th
century wooden door it is atmospheric
and medieval, with Norman rounded

arches and fat pillars. Unusual early 13th century font, large with arched decoration. Lots of modern fittings, the organ case and screen of 1953 being particularly effective. In the south wall are two long thin windows engraved by Laurence Whistler of 1978 in memory of Edward Thomas. The kneelers are notable, all the designs being based on the birds, plants, animals of the area.

★ ★ ★ ★ *Walking area along the steep escarpment with woods, or on the intricate lower greensand, with all ways views up to the wooded hanger.* ★ ★ *Church, good modern fittings.*

STEVENTON (E) Famous throughout the world as the birthplace of Jane Austen in 1775 and her home for the first twenty-five years of her life. Here the first versions of *Pride and Prejudice, Sense and Sensibility,* and *Northanger Abbey* were written, along with many juvenile works. Nothing was published until ten years after she and her family left Steventon.

Jane's father was rector of Steventon, and the family of six sons and two daughters lived in the rectory which was to the right of the drive going up to the church. The site is marked by a few large trees, and a pump enclosed by a fence. The building was demolished in the 1820s, and replaced by a new rectory which can be seen on the little hill opposite the site of the old one.

The village cannot be much bigger than when Jane was here – the population was 153 in 1801 and only 195 in 1981. A few old cottages survive at the cross-roads, along with Victorian estate cottages.

Steventon church

The church is up a ¾ mile drive – the Austens usually walked to services through the trees, descendants of which still line the drive. Opposite the church in their time was the Elizabethan manor house, now replaced by modern red brick buildings. Despite these the church of St Nicholas still seems remote. The entrance front is elegant with symmetrically arranged windows – unusual for medieval buildings. The details are 13th century. Small tower with Victorian spire. Inside the building is basically 13th century too, with tiny lancets in the chancel. The 17th century screen around the vestry at the west end was originally the manor house pew, and at the other end of the church. The rest of the fittings date from after Jane Austen's time, but up in the chancel are memorials to her brother James who became rector after her father, and his two wives, one of whom was also called Jane Austen. The chancel ceiling is early 19th century, and entertaining.

Part of an Anglo-Saxon cross in the church, dating from the late 9th century. It has interlace decoration including two inter-twined dragons. ★ ★ ★ ★ *church and area for Jane Austen associations.*

STOCKTON see **HYDE**

STOCKBRIDGE (D) Too big for a village, but surely not now a town. Its single wide street bridges the Test Valley, and looks large until one realises that it is only one plot deep. Five or six bridges cross branches of the Test, all of them virtually flat and imperceptible on the road: a local saying is that even the ducks have to duck to get under them.

In the middle, is the town hall, plain and of yellowy brick with a clock aloft. It was given in 1810 as a bribe in one of the many corrupt elections here: Stockbridge was a notorious rotten borough until the Reform Act of 1832.

The early 19th century Grosvenor Hotel, also yellow brick and with a huge bay sticking out into the street supported on columns, may also have been built from the proceeds of the elections, although racing and fishing profits probably contributed. The whole of the main street has handsome buildings in great variety and is worth walking through, right to the west end where thatched cottages overlook the river one with a Welsh inscription meaning 'Seasoned Hay, Tasty Pastures, Good Beer, Comfortable Beds'. It was used by Welsh sheep drovers. On the roundabout,

The river Test at Stockbridge

at the eastern end, the White Hart, early 19th century, with the front supported on iron columns. At the junction of Romsey road and Stockbridge is the old church with its cemetery, deserted in the 19th century when a new church was built in the middle. Only the 13th century chancel survives, small and somehow room-like. Interesting, with a nice communion table dated 1704, and a medieval door. The recent restoration has revealed ER monograms painted on the plaster, one dated 1588.

St Peter's church, with the spire, was built in the 1860s (spire 1880s) on a new site. Fine carving on the capitals inside, especially the chancel arch and north arcade. 12th century table-top type font.

Stockbridge is one of the centres for trout fishing on the Test: the Houghton Club which has its headquarters here is the oldest fishing club in the country, and the most exclusive. Stockbridge Races were held from 1753-1898 in June on Danebury Hill. They were very fashionable: the Prince of Wales' horses won two races in 1896.

Marsh Court a mile south of the town on the east bank of the river is a huge white house built from chalk and designed by Lutyens in 1901. It sits high and is glimpsed from the roads on both sides of the river.

See also Stockbridge Down, Danebury and Houghton Lodge.

★ ★ ★ *Small town.*

STOCKBRIDGE DOWN (D) (just east of Stockbridge off the A272 Winchester Road). More than 200 acres of grassland, not really downland because the grasses and abundant flowers are taller and coarser than those of true downland. On the clay which caps part of the area is low woodland and scrub, with a great variety of trees and bushes. On the north side of the reserve is the big rampart bank of Woolbury Ring, a simple Iron Age hillfort with only one bank and ditch. All the reserve gives wide views, and because it is undulating these views keep changing. Two car parks on the main road give easy access.

★ ★ ★ ★ *Walking, good grassland and scrub.*

STOKE CHARITY (E) Centred around a little cross-roads just up from the river, with a variety of houses and cottages, all some distance from the church which sits alone in the fields. Humps and bumps either side of the footpath to the church suggest that there once were houses here, and the village has grown away from the church.

The Norman church of St Mary and St Michael looks like a usual village church externally, with a shingled tower and spire, the rest flint.

The interior is a surprise, small but atmospheric and crammed with medieval and 17th century memorials. The lords of the manor were prosperous and living in the manor house from later medieval times until into the later 17th century, but then the manor house was demolished, and the parish was poor enough even in Victorian times for the church to be left unrestored, preserving a remarkable series of 15th-17th century tombs still in their original positions and a higgeldy-piggedly arrangement of floor levels which survive in no other Hampshire church.

Two of the 1480s tombs have brasses: in the nave Thomas Wayte who died in 1482, and between the chancel and chapel Thomas Hampton (1483) with an almost identical figure on the brass. Half Thomas Hampton's wife survives, and it seems likely that he had the chapel restored as well, since the windows, roof timbers, and

surviving bits of stained glass are of the same date as his tomb, as is the old glass in the upper parts of the east window, easily distinguished from the Victorian by its discoloration. Medieval floor tiles.

The outside wall of the chapel has the tomb, with a pretty arch, of John Waller, who died in 1526. Westwards is Thomas Phelipps (1626), much simpler and more classical. Set in the north-east corner of the chapel is a rare (but not beautiful) complete piece of church sculpture of about 1500 showing Christ appearing when St Gregory (Pope around 600) celebrated mass.

It is not known who is buried in the rather damp later medieval Purbeck Marble tomb under the first arch of the nave, but at the west end of the aisle are three 17th century memorials, the western one rather altered (and with a fragmentary piece of sculpture which does not belong to it on top) and the two smaller side ones to women.

★ ★ ★ *Church for the monuments.*

STONEHAM see NORTH or SOUTH STONEHAM

STRATFIELD SAYE (C) The house given by a grateful nation to the Duke of Wellington after the Battle of Waterloo. (fee: lists), and chosen by the Duke for the good agricultural land around. There are seven drives into the park, mostly with lodges which suggest a larger and grander house. Newly planted avenues stretch right across the main drives. The house has a surprising amount of Napoleonic material, bought by the Duke in Paris after Waterloo, and much French furniture. Long fronts to the house, stucco but painted brick colour. Most of it was

built in the 1630s, the Duke adding the outer wings, the porch and the conservatory. He originally intended to have the house pulled down, and build a much more impressive one, even having designs made for Waterloo Palace, but the money was not available.

The interior of the house was remodelled in the 18th century, with little from the 1630s house remaining. The hall has a gallery supported on wooden pillars, painted to look like marble, and is hung with tricolour banners presented by Napoleon to districts of France, and later presented to the Duke after Waterloo. Three Roman mosaics from nearby Silchester are re-laid in the floor, and all around are relics of the first Duke, and surprisingly also of Napoleon.

The library was fitted in about 1740, and has much regalia presented to the Duke after Waterloo on display, two locks of hair – one George Washington's, the other from the Duke's favourite horse, Copenhagen. Many of the books are from Napoleon's library. The Music room has more Copenhagen material, and horsey pictures. Under the staircase is one of the

Those desirous of seeing the Interior of the House, are requested to ring at the door of entrance and to express their desire. It is wished that the practice of stopping on the paved walk to look in at the windows should be discontinued.

The first Duke of Wellington's notice at Stratfield Saye. BELOW *Stratfield Saye*

radiators installed by the first Duke: he was well ahead of his time, and also fitted many lavatories. The stairs are part of the 1630s house. The sitting room has many family portraits. Next door is a room decorated with prints stuck directly to the walls, a fashionable style around 1800, but here dating from the first Duke's time and including prints of Napoleon and the Duke.

The Gallery was decorated with prints about 1795, but the Duke added the gilding between them, and the carpet was especially woven for the room in 1952. The gold and black, along with the French furniture and busts acquired in Paris after Waterloo, make the room exotic. The next two rooms have wallpaper of 1838. Many family portraits, and in the Drawing room the fine collection of paintings originally belonging to the King of Spain, which the Duke took from the French after the Battle of Vittoria in 1813. The dining room has fine Regency furniture, and the corridor marble busts of the Duke and some of his contemporaries, rather intimidating in this narrow space. Beyond a slate billiard table of 1837. Fine porcelain on display.

In the forecourt an unfinished bronze sculpture of St George and the dragon, dating from the 1820s. In one of the 1630s stable blocks flanking the drive is a wonderful display on the life of the first Duke, illustrated with many of his possessions, clothes (even underclothes), weapons and so on. One of the best displays I have ever seen, culminating in the massive (18 ton) ornate funeral car made for his funeral in 1852.

The grounds are extensive and interesting. In front of the house wide lawns, and the river with two islands. The Pleasure Grounds to the north have many specimen trees, including a group of the huge Wellingtonias which were

The Duke of Wellington's funeral carriage

The rustic summer house at Stratfield Saye

introduced from America at the time of the first Duke's death and named after him. At the northern end a charming slightly Chinese, summerhouse of rustic twig work, built to commemorate a visit of Queen Victoria in 1846, and incorporating the Queen's and the Duke's arms inside. The rose and shrub gardens are lovely. In a paddock closer to the house is the grave of Copenhagen, the horse the Duke rode through the later part of the Peninsular wars and at Waterloo. Close by an ice-house, used from the 18th century to store ice from ponds for use in the summer.

The **village** is to the west, with pairs of good Victorian brick estate cottages well spaced with big gardens. Half timbered victorian school, and a tiny infant school. A few more houses around the church, which is down another drive just to the south of the main house drive. The church of St Mary is a surprise – very plain classical of 1755, with a dome. It was built by Lord Rivers on a new site closer to the big house. Unusually for a church it has an open porch. Inside it is cruciform, and was restored in 1965, the 150th anniversary of Waterloo. Good pews, painted a striking blue-green. The organ is in the restored north gallery, which is where the first Duke sat for services. Lots of memorials. In the south transept Sir William Pitt and his wife, reclining effigies of 1640. Next to it, two mourning figures by Flaxman, the memorial to Lord Rivers who built the church and who died in 1803. Memorials to the 2nd-7th Dukes of Wellington (the first is buried at St Pauls). Up by the altar John Howsman 'who heere continued a paynful (ie painstaking) preacher by the space of 41 yeares' and

died in 1626. Lord Richard Wellesley's (died 1914) Memorial is by Eric Gill, very finely lettered. The alabaster font is 1901, copied from a Wren original.

To the east of the park, beside the east lodges, the Wellington Memorial, erected in 1863 after his death. Big pillar and base, with a 7 ft statue of the Duke on top.

★ ★ ★ ★ *House, museum and grounds.*

STRATFIELD TURGIS (B) Not really a village, but a collection of three hamlets. Stratfield Turgis had the small church, now adapted for secular use, but otherwise only consists of a square Georgian brick house enclosed by a moat, and a vast farmyard at the end of a cul de sac. **Turgis Green** is a little bigger, with a large stuccoed house, a fine timber framed cottage and a handsome early 19th century pub on the main road, but **Spanish Green** is again tiny.

STROUD (K) A small village on the main road from Petersfield, mostly Victorian or later.

STUBBINGTON (N) Usually linked with adjacent Crofton. In 1912 they consisted of 'a few dozen cottages and farms scattered over a tract of flat country, and only round the green in Crofton is there anything in the nature of a village'. The twentieth century has altered this: seas of development fill the area, and only around the old church at Crofton (in the north) is there any evidence of an earlier village. In the middle, by the green, is Holy Rood Church built from the 1870s in brick and stone. Much adapted inside for parish work after a fire of 1968 badly damaged the interior. By the entrance is an old thatched cottage, and the church of Holy Rood is a real village church, an accumulation of many periods and styles. It originally served a huge, if sparsely populated, area as a chapel to Titchfield. The west wall is brick of the 18th century, the east wall has huge brick buttresses and other walls lean alarmingly. Inside it is charming, simple and homely. Heavy roof, late medieval. Chancel arch with no pillars, and nice 'Gothick' panelling in the chancel with testament boards. Most of the church is later medieval, but the very plain south aisle is early 19th century. In the south aisle a big memorial to Thomas Missing who died in 1733, with a portrait bust.

★ ★ *As a proper village church.*

Museums, animals, birds...

Hampshire has more than 60 museums, which are very varied in size, aims and content. The many military and naval museums are listed under the sections on the Navy and the Army, but there are still a large number of more general ones.

The town museums, with their displays on the history, archaeology, natural history and so on of their areas are all worth seeing, and add greatly to visiting the area. Southampton is especially well served, with several museums illustrating the long history of the city. The Winchester City Museum and the Winchester Heritage Centre both provide a good introduction to that city and its many historic buildings.

Many of the local museums have good modern displays, but Alton, Fareham, and Havant must be singled out as being particularly well done. The New Forest Museum at Lyndhurst gives a good idea of both the history and natural history of the Forest.

The history of the countryside is well displayed in Hampshire, with reconstructions of several types of rural workshops and cottage rooms at Breamore Countryside Museum, alongside much farming equipment. The Hampshire Farm Museum is superb, a real

ABOVE *Owl at Paulton's Park.* BELOW *God's House Tower, Southampton's Archaeological Museum*

farmhouse and farmyard with all the proper buildings and animals. When only a few people are about, it feels like walking back in time. The Romany Museum at Selborne is very interesting, and there are displays on the same subject at Paulton's Park and Finkley Down.

The county is also rich in places to see animals, ranging from the little Reptiliary near Lyndhurst with all the native reptiles to Marwell Zoological Park with exotic animals in great variety. Birds are especially well represented, with Bird World superb for exotics, and The Hawk Conservancy just as good for hawks, owls and so on, with the added attraction of seeing them flown. Paulton's Park, Bohunt Manor and The New Forest Owl Sanctuary also have lots of birds.

Finkley Down Farm Park and Sir George Staunton Ornamental Farm must be the best places for small children to see domestic animals and farm, but the Hampshire Farm Museum also has some, all of old-fashioned types. Prehistoric domesticated animals can be seen at Butser Ancient Farm. There is one Butterfly Farm in the county, and the Sea Life Centre for fish. The Longdown Dairy Farm is a working dairy farm which can be seen in great detail, and it also has smaller animals for children.

Museums

★ ★ ★: *Breamore Countryside and Carriage Museum; Hampshire Farm Museum, Upper Hamble Country Park; Tudor House, Southampton; God's House Tower, Southampton; Maritime Museum, Southampton; Jane Austen's House, Chawton.*
★ ★: *The Allen Gallery and the Curtis museum, both Alton; Andover Museum; Fareham Museum; The New Forest Museum, Lyndhurst; Cumberland House, Portsmouth; The Romany Museum, Selborne; The Wakes, Selborne; Westgate Winchester; City Museum, Winchester; Winchester Heritage Centre; Bargate, Southampton.*

See also: *Willis Museum, Basingstoke; Bishop's Waltham Museum; Emsworth Museum; Eastleigh Museum; Sherings Fordingbridge Museum; Gosport Museum; King John's House, Romsey; Dickens Birthplace, Portsmouth; City Museum Portsmouth; The Museum, Royal Victoria Country Park, Netley; Havant Museum.*

For other types of museums see the following sections: Industrial Archaeology; Archaeology; The Navy and the Sea; The Army and Fortifications.

Animals, Birds, Fishes

★ ★ ★: *Bird World, near Farnham; The Hawk Conservancy, Weyhill; Finkley Down Farm Park, Andover; Longdown Butterfly Farm, New Forest; Longdown Dairy Farm, New Forest; Marwell Zoological Park, Upham; Sir George Staunton Ornamental Farm, Leigh Park.*
★ ★: *New Forest Owl Sanctuary, Ringwood; Sea Life Centre, Portsmouth.*

See also: *Butser Ancient Farm for sheep etc; Bohunt Manor, Liphook and Paulton's Park for wildfowl; Hampshire Farm Museum, Upper Hamble Country Park for old-fashioned farm animals; Hawthorns, Southampton Urban Wildlife Centre; Holiday Hills Reptiliary, Lyndhurst.*

ABOVE *Hampshire Farm Museum, Upper Hamble Country Park*
BELOW *A farm labourer's cottage reconstructed at Breamore Countryside Museum*

The Jubilee Hall, Sutton Scotney

SUTTON SCOTNEY (E) Once on the main road north from Winchester and an east-west road forming an important cross-roads, but now bypassed. There is no church, but the pebbledashed Victoria Hall with its clock tower (erected in 1897) sits in the middle looking a little bit churchy. Off the main road there are thatched cottages and Georgian houses, the side streets surprisingly picturesque. To the north, over the river, is an area called **Egypt** consisting of a few Edwardian and later houses and cottages.

SWANMORE (J) was part of Droxford until 1894, but the original hamlet has outgrown its parent. The cross roads centre has the Victorian school and the church of St Barnabas, mostly neo-Norman of 1846 (a briefly fashionable style), with a spire and so on added later.

SWANWICK (J/N) Has a few older houses scattered about, but is mostly modern. The railway station caused the expansion of fruit strawberry growing here from the 1880s, now rather swamped by modern housing estates.

Lower Swanwick is down by the bridge and river Hamble, with huge boat-builders' yards. Mostly modern, but a few older houses and a long row of low cottages near the car park on the shore. A footpath leads downstream through another boatyard. The banks of the estuary are low, mostly lined with small oaks and there are lots of small inlets. Half a mile along the footpath, around the curve of the river, the view opens up right down the Hamble to its mouth with Southampton Water and Fawley power station chimney can be seen in the distance.

Sway tower

SWAY (M) North boundary of the built-up southern fringes of the New Forest. Some 18th and 19th century houses, but much modern. Church of St Luke in the south of the village, 1839 and brick with a tiny stone spirelet. Later additions. Memorial in chancel to the builder of Sway tower, Andrew Peterson.

Sway tower 1½ miles south of the village, is a landmark from many miles around. Built from concrete, then a very new material, from 1879-85, it was simply a folly. Andrew Peterson constructed several other buildings immediately around it of the same material, some with smaller towers. He was buried under the tower in 1906.

SWATHLING see **SOUTHAMPTON NORTH**

SYDMONTON (B) A hamlet just under the chalk scarp, surprisingly with a church. A footpath leads up past the big house (16th-18th century) and the church of 1853 with a few medieval bits from the earlier church.

Ladle Hill is an Iron Age hillfort on a corner of the chalk scarp south of Sydmonton. It is the best example in the country of a hillfort abandoned unfinished. The whole of the fort is enclosed by a small ditch, presumably a marking out ditch, but the proper deep ditch is not complete, and is also interrupted by causeways. These suggest that the ditch was dug in separate lengths by separate gangs of diggers. There are several Bronze Age round barrows nearby, the one just to the north being a disc barrow (ie one with an outer bank some way from its small central mound). Good views from the fort, and indeed all along the top of this scarp.

See also Watership Down and Beacon Hill for the chalk scarp.

TADLEY (B) One of the villages on the Berkshire boundary which have grown enormously. A few older cottages survive, and Tadley Common is full of gorse and birch. In the northern part is the new church of St Paul, completed in 1965 with a distinctive triangular bell tower. Inside the windows are horizontal, with especial emphasis on the eastern part with stained glass. The parabolic arches make it look like a modern upturned boat. Modern pottery font. An effective and interesting building.

The old parish church is away in the south, completely different and still rural. St Peter's has a brick tower firmly dated by an inscription in Hampshire dialect 'Christfur Clifard Bricklayar 1685'. Same sort of date porch, and more inside – a big west gallery and pulpit dated 1650. These with the benches and wooden supports dominate the interior.

★ ★ *For both Tadley churches, interesting buildings with interesting fittings.*

TANGLEY (D) A well wooded hilly parish, many of the roads lined with trees. Handsome park to the south-west. No real centre to the village. The church of St Peter is surrounded by trees too, and is largely of 1875 by William White (see Lyndhurst). He used lines of tiles in the walls like the Roman masonry at Porchester Castle. The steeple is later Victorian. Inside the tiny apse is on Norman foundations and the little chancel arch is partly original too. The unusual lead font with its thistles, roses and so on dates from the early 17th century, probably the reign of James 1, king of England and Scotland.

★ *Church*

TESTWOOD see **TOTTON**

THORNEY HILL see **BRANSGORE**

THORNHILL see **SOUTHAMPTON EAST**

THRUXTON (D) A big village, with many thatched cottages, a stream beside the street and a green, but known to most people only for its motor racing circuit. The Second World War airfield to the west of the village was taken over in 1959 to be used for motor racing, although it continues as an aerodrome.

The village is worth walking for its cottages: the village hall is of two stories, having been built in 1817 as a Methodist chapel. The church of St Peter and St Paul has a squat classical ashlar tower of 1801, an unusual date, built because its predecessor collapsed. Externally at the east end is an odd priest's door with elaborated surround, inserted in 1869, cutting a tomb inside the church.

Most of the rest of the church is 1869, built of very large flints, but the 1839 north transept is in the local panelled brick and flint style. The chancel is dominated by early memorials including three tombs with arches, one of 1520 with rather re-carved effigies and a big brass to Sir John Lisle 1407.

In the nave an unusually late oak figure of a woman in Elizabethan costume, a memorial effigy. All around is bright stained glass of 1857, and huge boards with texts along the bottom of the roof. More in scrolls on the walls.

★ ★ *Church, particularly for memorials.*

TICHBORNE (J/E) A few cottages disposed on each side of a lane that winds above the river, with two or three farm houses and a small parsonage. High up, above this, on the acclivity of a green knoll, stands the church'. So John Duthy described the village in the 1830s, and so it remains today.

It is famous for the Tichborne Dole, and the Tichborne Claimant. The dole, a bequest originally left for the poor by Lady Mabella Tichborne in the 13th century, is still given annually: a gallon of flour to adults, and half a gallon to children, for all the inhabitants of Tichborne and Cheriton. The Tichborne Claimant caused one of the longest trials of Victorian England: a long-lost heir appeared from Australia to claim the estate. He lost the court case and ended up with fourteen years penal servitude, but several people in Tichborne believed he was the real heir. The case caused international publicity, and is supposed to have cost the Tichborne estate 92,000.

The village is charming – handsome farms on the outskirts and in the middle brick cottages and houses, some timber framed and thatched, including a fine jettied brick house of about 1600 the Old Post Office: Church cottage on the lane to the church is dated 1729 largely in brick on this side. The best view is from the church, with the big house just visible in the trees down over the river, and the rest of the village spread out in between. Beside the church is the school, now a house, built in 1843 of brick and flint.

The church of St Andrew has a plain brick tower of 1703, but inside much is medieval. The chancel is 11th century, probably dating from just after the Norman conquest but still with little double-splayed windows on each side. Fragments of medieval stained glass in the east window. The rest of the church is basically 13th century. Superb Jacobean box pews, with lots of shallow decoration in the front ones, less in the middle, and the back one in the south aisle as plain as a cattle stall. Jacobean communion rails too, and a splendid George II Royal coat of arms at the back, painted on canvas. Big simple Norman font with 17th century wooden cover.

The north chapel, cut off from the rest of the church by painted iron railings, is the Tichborne chapel, with good family monuments. The railings are probably Elizabethan, with small skulls and crossbones on the large finials. Big funeral hatchments above. Huge monument to Sir Benjamin Tichborne who died in 1621, with his wife Amphillis, and on the side of the chest very high quality representations of their children, shown as adults. Touching monument to Richard Tichborne who died in 1619 'after he had lived one yeare six monthes and too daies'.

★ ★ ★ *One of the most charming small churches of Hampshire, and an unspoilt village.*

TIDPIT DOWN (G) is off the Cranborne/Tidpit road, and suffers from comparison with its much larger neighbour Martin Down. There are fewer flowers at Tidpit, but good views as it is high on the chalk. Many earthworks including the Bronze Age ditch and bank boundary of Grim's Ditch which wriggles on the north boundary.

TIDWORTH see **SOUTH TIDWORTH**

TIMSBURY (H) A small village right down in the Test valley, rural but largely modern. Big manor house, and small church of St Andrew. Basically medieval, and unrestored, although the chancel arch is Victorian. Full screen at the back, with 1788 Royal coat of arms, and a cupboard inscribed 'BOOKES GIVEN BY TIMOTHY GOODACKER MINISTER OF THIS P 1713'. The books are still in the cupboard. 16th century benches, and a rustic screen of the 15th century, the sort of simple piece which rarely survived Victorian restorations. The pulpit is 17th century with the Protestant inscription 'WO IS UNTO ME IF I PREACH NOT YE .. GOSPEL'. Bright 1967 glass in the east window, and 15th century fragments in the side windows.

★ ★ *For an unrestored small village church.*

TIPTOE (M) Wonderfully named. One of the usual forest edge villages, recently greatly enlarged. The church of St Andrews sits on a triangular island in the lanes, looking rather like an elaborate Edwardian village hall.

TITCHFIELD (N) Although village sized, Titchfield is a well preserved 18th century small town. In medieval times it was the centre of the second largest parish in Hampshire, more than 16,000 acres including Swanwick, Warsash, Locks Heath, Crofton, Lee-on-the-Solent and Hill Head. Much of the area was heathland, until the later 19th century when strawberries were cultivated. Earlier industries were much more diverse: tanning, brick-making, parchment dressing, and cloth weaving. There was a market here before Domesday, probably on the site of the Square, and the establishment of the Abbey in the 13th century encouraged growth. Surprisingly Titchfield was also a port, with the small medieval ships able to get right up the Meon at high tide to the town. The Earl of Southampton dammed the mouth of the Meon in 1611 and had a canal built up to the village, one of the earliest in the country.

From the later 19th century the village was regarded by others around as rather rough and tough, and from the 1880s the 'Bonfire Boys' annual celebration on 5th November was part of this image. The combined carnival and bonfire used to include burning a tar barrel in the Square, and whilst that no longer happens, the day is still lively and the evening bonfire huge. Originally the effigy burnt on the fire was not Guy Fawkes but the first Earl of Southampton.

The village was by-passed as early as 1928, and the direct road from Fareham in the east down the hill from Catisfield only

dates from 1811 when the
Titchfield-Cosham Turnpike Trust was set
up. They built a new bridge (still
surviving) over the Meon. Before that
traffic from the east had to come into
Titchfield from the south and up through
the Square. The entrance from the east is
dramatic, as one house was demolished in
1811 to let the Turnpike in, and it is like a
missing tooth – a gap just wide enough
for the road whose surroundings change
immediately from rural to urban.

The Square is the centre, lined with
small-scale houses, cottages and shops,
mostly Georgian fronted but many older
behind. All the roofs are covered with
little red tiles, accumulatively adding to
the picturesqueness, while the houses are
brick, or painted. This was where the
market was held, and the little timber
market hall is now reconstructed in the
Weald and Downland Open Air Museum,
near Chichester, Sussex.

The Bugle is a coaching inn which had a
new front added about 1820, with three
storey bays (the top ones false) and a
semi circular porch. Behind the Square
many outbuildings survive – stables,
workshops and so on, and alleyways lead
past them. It is rare today to see so many
old subsidiary buildings surviving. The
Queen's Head in High Street is another
unspoilt inn.

South Street has older cottages, several
of them timber-framed with jettied
(over-sailing) upper stories. West Street
also has Georgian and earlier cottages and
houses running up the hill. At the corner
of High Street and East Street, along an
alleyway, is Old Lodge, very different
from the rest of Titchfield – larger and
17th century brick made into patterns.
East Street is totally lined with Georgian
and earlier cottages and houses. Mill
Street was cut by the bypass in 1928, but
over the main road is Abbey Mill, large

ABOVE *Titchfield Square*
RIGHT *Titchfield church*
BELOW RIGHT *The tithe barn, Titchfield Abbey*
BELOW *The Earl of Southampton's
tomb, Titchfield*

and redbrick, rebuilt in 1834. Between this
mill and the church were the tanneries
which only closed in the 1950s. There is
still industry here.

To the north-west of the town is St
Margarets, a brick Tudor tower and
house.

The most famous aspect of the church
of St Peter is the often-pictured view up
Church Street with Georgian cottages
framing the church tower. The simple arch
entrance is Saxon, originally part of a
porch, but its exact date is uncertain
because it is so plain. It could be as early
as 700 AD. The upper parts are later, the
join marked by rows of red tiles like

Roman work. The lozenge patterned iron gates into the church were made at the nearby Funtley ironworks. The inner entrance is a Norman doorway with lots of decoration. The left aisle is 15th century with high thin pillars, the right Victorian. The chancel and chapel are basically medieval, the chapel belonging to the abbey and taken over at the dissolution by the Earls of Southampton.

On the back wall is an unusual wall-painting, repainted in a folksy style in 1951. The stone font carved with figures is 1951 too. Fine carved beasts on the 14th century capitals between chancel and chapel.

The chapel is dominated by the Southampton monument, erected in 1594 in memory of the 1st and 2nd Earls of Southampton. It is a magnificent piece, alabaster, marble and painted with three finely detailed effigies. On top is the first Countess of Southampton, with her husband and son either side on the middle tier. On the lowest part are four small kneeling effigies of their children. The boy is the third Earl of Southampton, Shakespeare's patron. Shakespeare dedicated his first published poetry to him, and possibly also the sonnets. The sonnets extolling marriage are thought to have been written to Southampton: 'Look in thy glass and tell the face thou viewest/Now is the time that face should form another'. He did marry and 'form others', and the small memorial on the wall of the chapel is to one of them, Lady Mary who died in 1615 (a year before

Shakespeare) aged 4 years 4 months. Fine effigy. A good display in the chapel explains the history of the church and area.

A path beside the church leads down to the canal with a footpath to the mouth of the river at Hill Head, just over two miles south. A good rural walk (see Titchfield Haven in Hill Head entry).

Titchfield Common to the west was described in 1905 as 'until comparatively recent times a stretch of waste heather land, being now cut up into small allotments generally consisting of a few acres of strawberry fields round a cottage'. A jam factory here processed the fruit for the Army and Navy Stores. There are still smallholdings, but also modern housing.

Titchfield Abbey (fee:lists) is half a mile north of the village, now surrounded by glasshouses and farms, not a romantic setting for the ruins. The abbey was founded here in 1232, and most of its buildings were late 13th century. At the dissolution of the monasteries in 1537 one of the administrators of the surrender of the monasteries obtained Titchfield, and rapidly converted it into a house. John Leland, the antiquary, saw it finished only a few years later in 1542 'a right stately house embatelid and having a goodely gate and a conducte (CONDUIT or fountain) in the middle of the court'. Wriothesley (pronounced Risley) who built the house became first Earl of Southampton, rising high in the service of both Henry VIII and his son Edward VI,

but falling from power in the 1540s. The second earl entertained Queen Elizabeth here, but the third Earl is the most famous, because he was Shakespeare's patron (see Titchfield Church). Possibly some of the sonnets were written here, and it is just possible that some of the plays had their first performances in this house, perhaps in the courtyard. The house continued to be inhabited until 1781, when it was largely demolished.

Only the 'goodely gatehouse' survives from the large house described by Leland, and that is roofless. It pretends to be defensive with turrets, mock arrow-slits on the ground floor and castellation on the top. The large windows in the middle show this fierceness is all a sham. The wooden doors are original. Inside much Tudor brickwork, although stone was used outside. The west end is brick too, with a stepped gable.

A little of the courtyard remains, with the cloister (converted to a courtyard when the house was built) laid out in the turf. The patches of medieval tiles were saved from the monastery and re-used in the house. Some have parts of inscriptions. A little of the 13th century entrance to the monastic chapter house survives.

All this area, where the monastic buildings are marked in the turf, was also part of the house, which extended beyond the present boundary.

★ ★ ★ ★ *Titchfield village, the church (and Southampton monument) and walks around the area. The abbey* ★ ★ ★ *interesting but ruinous, fascinating because of the association with Shakespeare.*

TOTTON (H) Once a small village, on the lowest bridging point of Southampton Water, and described in 1852 as 'picturesque, abounding with river and inland scenery and studded with agreeable residences'. Development soon changed that. By 1912 there were 'saw and flour mills, chemical manure works, brewery, and tar distilling and creosote works'. Eling is the original medieval settlement and has the church for the area but Totton is much bigger with industry and huge areas of housing. The centre is dominated by traffic which pours through from the bridge, and is mostly recent, and somehow rather suburban despite some huge shops. One reminder of the earlier High Street is the Georgian Crossed Keys pub close to the roundabout. Totton

Titchfield Abbey, the gatehouse

extends westwards with huge new housing estates, while *Testwood* to the north has both modern and 1930s housing. On the main road there are also 19th century villas. The church of St Winifred is on the main road, and was built in 1937 of brick.

Rumbridge Street and High Street to the south of the main road (and north of the bypass) together form a much quieter shopping street, with many small shops. Industry creeps in at the eastern end. South of the bypass are late 19th and earlier 20th century housing and a large industrial area leading down to the creek at Eling. See also **LOWER TEST NATURE RESERVE**.

TUFTON (E) A farming hamlet only a mile south of Whitchurch, with a few thatched cottages, big farm buildings, and a small church (St Mary). Norman nave, with simple chancel arch, but the 13th century chancel is very grand for such a small church, with arcading around the side windows. The big wall-painting is of St Christopher, 15th century. The church was modernised in the 18th or early 19th century – the big domestic windows, the handsome entrance door and the pair of wooden doors at the back with odd heads perhaps all date from the same time. George IV Royal coat of arms.

Testbourne to the west is also in the Test valley, and has a large Georgian farmhouse. The name, Paper Mill Farm, is a reminder of industry here.

★ ★ *Church for chancel etc.*

TUNWORTH (E) A hamlet with a long row of handsome brick cottages, and some good timber-framed ones. The path to the church is enclosed by a cob wall on one side and a close beech avenue on the other. The church of All Saints is mostly rebuilding of 1854, but inside are older fittings including an unusual 17th century wooden alms box.

TURGIS GREEN see **STRATFIELD TURGIS**

TWYFORD (J) A large village, with many good brick houses and cottages, but divided by the main road. Twyford House, towards the Winchester end of the village, is large and handsome early Georgian brick, and behind, facing the churchyard, is Mildmay House (once the rectory) of about 1700.

The church of St Mary is a surprise: a large striped brick and flint building of 1876 with a prominent spire. The architect was Waterhouse, best known for designing the Natural History Museum, London. Inside he re-used the Norman pillars, and a plain Purbeck Marble font of the same date survives. The chancel is darker than the rest of the church, with lots of wood. Simple Art Nouveau glass on the side windows.

In the churchyard is one of the ancient yews for which Hampshire is famous. When John Bullar saw this one in 1819 he admired the 'wide-spreading head ... so moulded and disciplined as to be brought very nearly to resemble the top of a considerable green hillock, elevated on a stump'. It still looks healthy, despite being trimmed.

★ *Church, more for those interested in Victorian architecture.*

Twyford Waterworks (¾ mile up the road to Morestead). Built in 1900 with later additions, but now redundant, although preserved. Besides the pumping station with its Triple Expansion steam engine there are limekilns, used to produce lime for softening the water. Limited openings (fee:list).

UPHAM (J) The main village, **Upper Upham**, is high at 300 ft. Lots of brick and flint garden walls, and many 18th and 19th century brick cottages and houses. Not consciously picturesque even at the classic duck pond, but certainly handsome.

The church (dedication not known) has a very short chequered brick tower of the 18th century, while the rest is 1881, but unusual inside because one aisle is much higher than the other, giving a very un-Victorian irregularity. Two big yew trees guard the gate.

Lower Upham is partly on the main road, and rather more dispersed, but has many smaller brick cottages and the occasional larger house. Brick and flint walls here too. Until the early 19th century the village was the centre of a large brush-making industry.

UP NATELY (F) One end of the Greywell tunnel for the Basingstoke canal is in this parish, and the overgrown most westerly surviving part of the canal. Towards the tunnel the canal is in woodland which has many footpaths. The northern part of the parish, between the motorway and the A30, is also picturesque, with a mill and the river.

The church of St Stephen was largely rebuilt in 1844, and the Norman doorway from the original church sits oddly in the 1844 flint and brick banding. Inside the chancel arch is Norman too, and the 15th century timber roof survived the rebuilding. Tiny chancel, and the communion rail of about 1700 is partly there, and partly as a rail in the gallery of the tiny tower. A Victorian collecting box is labelled 'Remember the Poor'.

★ *Church.*

UPPER BULLINGTON see **BULLINGTON**

UPPER CLATFORD (D) Dense in the middle, with lots of thatched cottages. The church of All Saints is by the river, close to the big brick bridge. Externally the good tower of 1578 (an unusual date for church building) and the 18th century brick porch are most obvious, but the most unusual feature is inside. Instead of a proper single chancel arch, two arches which once formed part of an arcade (dividing nave and aisle) were rebuilt as

the chancel arch. The effect is most peculiar, and probably dates from a re-arrangement of the 17th century. 17th century pulpit, and font (odd cover) dated 1629.

A little further east from the church is a charming tiny cast iron bridge, dated 1843 and made at Taskers, the Waterloo Iron Works, just up the road at Anna Valley. Lots of trout in the river.

★ ★ *For oddness of the church.*

UPPER FROYLE see **FROYLE**

UPPER HAMBLE COUNTRY PARK (J) (just north of junction 8 on the M27). The upper parts of the Hamble estuary have long been admired as picturesque scenery, and now a large area of the wood and shore form the Upper Hamble Country Park, more than 200 acres of woodlands with miles of footpaths which continue into the farmland around. A charge is made for cars entering the park, and there are many car parks.

Hampshire Farm Museum (fee:lists) is at Manor Farm to the north of the country park, and can also be reached on foot from Church Lane, Botley. The museum is entered through a big early 19th century brick barn, where good films on the blacksmith, wheelwright etc are shown. The farmyard then opens up, with animals and buildings combining to give a complete impression of a traditional Hampshire mixed farm in about 1900. The smells and sounds complete the authenticity – hens clucking around, dungheaps smelling and in the farmhouse the scullery smells of soap. The farm has an extensive array of buildings for the animals and for storing crops. The big thatched barn partly dates from the 15th century. All the buildings except the

Hampshire Farm Museum, Upper Hamble Country Park

steddle barn between the two big ones are original to the farm. The steddle barn of the late 18th century was originally built at Longstock. Farm machinery and carts lie around naturally in the farmyard, along with sheep and cows.

All the animals are of older breeds, like the saddle back pigs, and shorthorn cows. The farmhouse ranges in date from the 15th century onwards, and is furnished as it would have been in the early part of this century. Good garden too and a traditional pond with ducks.

Outside the farmyard are two more buildings brought from elsewhere: a wheelwright's shop from Nether Wallop and the forge from Hedge End. Both are occasionally used by craftsmen. At the end of the road are the remains of the old church of Botley, with just the medieval chancel remaining, now with many monuments.

In summer there are craft demonstrations on many Sunday afternoons, but perhaps the farm is best seen on a quiet weekday when there are few other people about. Then it does seem as though one has walked back in time.

★ ★ ★ ★ *For Upper Hamble Country Park and Hampshire Farm Museum, the park for the scenery and walking, the museum for the recreation of a 1900s farm.*

UPPER WIELD see **WIELD**

UP SOMBORNE see **LITTLE SOMBORNE**

UPTON GREY (F) An attractive village, with a pond by the crossroads surrounded by old brick and timber framed cottages, and a little barn on steddle stones. To the south are old cottages too, with parkland opposite.

ABOVE *Taskers' iron bridge at Upper Clatford.* RIGHT *Upton Grey*

The Vyne

The novelist Henry Fielding, was here in 1728, and disliked the village, writing:

'On the House-side a Garden may be seen / Which Docks and Nettles keep forever green. / Weeds on the Ground, instead of Flowers, we see, / And Snails alone adorn the barren Tree.'

He must have been one of the few not to admire the village, which continues up the hill from the pond to the church. The house above the church is Upton Grey House, which was drastically altered and enlarged in 1907, and whose gardens were designed by Gertrude Jekyll. The gardens are being restored and are occasionally open to the public.

The church of St Mary is an interesting and oddly arranged mixture. The plain brick tower is dated 1690. Internally the church seems to go in two directions because a large north aisle was added in 1715 – anyone sitting in it would have no chance of seeing the altar because the chancel is round the corner, a long tunnel away. The old nave gained new windows in 1715, and very simple pillars etc.

The 13th century chancel is so long because the first part is the crossing with the tower above. At the east end a big memorial with a portrait bust to Lady Dorothy Eyre who died in 1650 'in her youth a maide of honour to Q. Anne in her riper yeares' twice a wife. (the Queen Anne was James 1's wife). Other good memorials around the church. Fittings of note include a plain but faintly Art Nouveau pulpit and a 15th century font. The roof in the nave is dated 1608 on one of the main beams. On Royal Oak Day (29 May) large branches of oak are placed over the church porch and the lych gate, and smaller ones on each house, to bring luck for the following year.

★ ★ ★ *Church and village.*

VERNHAM DEAN (A) Lots of thatched cottages.

Vernham Street and **Littledown** (hamlets to the north) have more with farmsteads. The little church of St Mary is between Dean and Street, and has a highly decorated Norman west door. The rest is 1851. Close by a plain Jacobean brick manor house.

★ ★ *Cottages and good rural landscape.*

THE VYNE (B) One of the most interesting large houses in Hampshire, both historically, and for the building and its furniture. It was built in the reign of Henry VIII, adapted and given the first classical portico to be built in England in 1655, and had the superb staircase added in the 1760s.

The 16th century house was larger, with another block away from the entrance front and closer to the lake. What survives is quite large, however, all rosy red brick with diaper pattern in dark bricks. The windows are not original: a few round-headed windows in the basement of the entrance side are all that remain of the 16th century ones. The stone surrounds are of 1655, but they would have had windows like those in the stable block to the right, with upright and horizontal stone bars (mullions and transoms). The sash windows now in the house are 18th century.

The lake front is similar, but has in the middle the portico: pillars holding up a classical pediment. The columns are brick, rendered, and the portico wood. John Webb, pupil of Inigo Jones the first English Classical architect, designed this and some of the fittings in the house in about 1655.

The present entrance is through the Stone Gallery, which fills one wing of the house. Originally a dormitory for visitor's servants it was adapted as a greenhouse in the 18th century. Over the fireplace a terracotta bust of a Roman emperor in a big roundel part of the 1520s house. These were then very fashionable and are found at Hampton Court (one from Basing nearby is on display in the museum there). The three following rooms are still hung with the faded red damask bought for the house in 1760, probably in Italy, and have rococo plaster ceilings of the same date. Here, and throughout the house, are fine paintings and furniture, and splendid ceramics.

The Large Drawing Room and the Dining Room have fireplaces of the 1650s, and the latter has simple Elizabethan panelling. The Chapel Parlour has much better panelling, fine linenfold of the 1520s, with an 18th century plaster ceiling.

The Ante-Chapel was decorated in the 1750s, and is light-hearted, unconvincing Gothick. In the gallery above the chapel are the remains of the painted canvases used for the ceiling of the chapel in the 1750s, theatrical pretend vaulting. The chapel itself dates from the 1520s, and is considered the most perfect private chapel in England. Small, with big wooden stalls extensively carved, the decoration showing Renaissance influence. The poppy heads have putti, jugglers and women, and there are classical motifs in the cornice and elsewhere. Set in the floor are a large number of early 16th century tiles, tin glazed and with painted bright colours. They were found in the grounds and set here in the 19th century, but were probably part of the original building. Original too is the stained glass, which shows in the lower parts portraits of Henry VIII, Catherine of Aragon and

Chaloner Chute's memorial at the Vyne

Garden pavilion at the Vyne

Queen Margaret of Scotland. The middle has religious scenes, the top the arms of the Royal persons.

The tomb chamber was built to house the tomb of Chaloner Chute, Speaker of the House of Commons and the man who had the portico built on the house in the 1650s. He died in 1659, a hundred years before his great grandson designed the tomb and chamber. His effigy is superb showing him as a young man in the Speaker's robes, reclining on a straw mat.

The staircase is the most magnificent part of the house, designed by the owner John Chute, who also designed the tomb chamber and Ante-Chapel. Theatrical and classical, it is carefully designed to make the best use of the narrow space available, decorated extensively with classical detailing which was rather old-fashioned by the 1760s, when it was built.

The Print Room was decorated in 1815, in the then fashionable style of pasting cut-out prints directly onto the wall.

Upstairs the Library has 1840s bookcases, but a classical fireplace with palm fronds of the the 1650s, brought here from elsewhere in the house. The tapestries in the next two rooms were put here in the 1840s, ruthlessly cut to fit. They were probably bought for the house in the 1720s. The last room is the Oak Gallery, with some very fine panelling, part of the 1520s house. The panelling is linenfold, delicately carved with heraldic devices top and bottom, a few fanciful but mostly the arms and badges of contemporaries. Above the east door is the Arms of England. The classical fireplace is 1650s.

Nothing remains of the Tudor gardens, but a domed brick garden pavilion of the 1650s is classical in the same style as the Portico. This was imitated, probably in

the 18th century, for the lodges, at about the time the lake was created from the small stream. The smallish wild garden and the formal beds around the house are charming.

★ ★ ★ ★ *House.*

WALHAMPTON (M) A small

settlement on the opposite side of the river from Lymington. The Isle of Wight ferries run from here. On a small hill overlooking the river is the Neale Obelisk, a memorial to Admiral Sir Harry Burrard Neale, dating from 1840.

Walhampton House is to the north, now a school, large and neo-Georgian of 1912. Closer to the road is a late Victorian model farm, with Suffolk type decorative plasterwork, now a restaurant.

The memorial to Sir Harry Burrard Neale at Walhampton

WALLINGTON see FAREHAM

WALLOPS see MIDDLE WALLOP, NETHER WALLOP and OVER WALLOP

WALTHAM CHASE (J) As the name chase implies this was a hunting ground in medieval times. It belonged to the Bishop's palace at Bishop's Waltham, and until 1870 an area measuring 2 miles across was open and unenclosed, running down to the Meon Valley where it joined up with the medieval Forest of Bere. Bishops ceased hunting in the 17th century, and early in the 18th century Waltham Chase was home to a gang who blackened their faces, and were known as the Waltham Blacks. They were no more than organised poachers, but their nick-name still survives locally as byword for wickedness.

The area developed from the enclosure of 1870, and some small redbrick late Victorian villas survive from this time, but much of the village is recent.

WARBLINGTON (O) (west of Emsworth) Two distinct parts. The northern bit, inside the Havant bypass, now joins up with the suburbs of Havant and is largely modern. The road east from Havant centre has several older buildings including, just out of the town, Denvilles House, Regency yellow brick with a typical verandah. Warblington Lodge, near the junction with the bypass is the same date, and there are a few other older buildings between them. Most of the area is recent suburban development.

The other part of Warblington is to the south of the bypass, and is still rural.

Visible from the lane to the church, and from the churchyard, is the remnant of Warblington Castle, one side of a brick and stone gatehouse, all that remains of a large moated house built in about 1520. It looks like an odd tower, and was perhaps retained as a seamark, although it was also used as a dovecote. By the church a big weather-boarded barn and a farm. The church of St Thomas Becket is much larger than one would expect: it was originally also the parish church for Emsworth. In the middle is a Saxon tower (Victorian top), with simple round-headed openings visible outside. Medieval timbered porch on south. Inside the lower part of the tower was rebuilt in about 1200, with Purbeck marble pillars and leaf carving above. The nave and chancel are much the same date, the nave with

One of the watchmen's huts in Warblington graveyard

clustered pillars. Good memorials all round, with two medieval ones: a man in the north aisle, an effigy with a small representation of his soul being taken up to heaven in the back; and a lady of the 14th century in the south chapel, fine recess and effigy. Up by the altar a brass to Raffe Smalpage, 1588, showing him kneeling. Medieval floor tiles under the altar.

In the north-east and south-west corners of the original graveyard are little brick and flint watchmen's huts, built about 1800 to shelter the watchmen needed to prevent bodies being robbed from the graves of this isolated graveyard. Lots of good gravestones, some with ships. Footpaths and lanes lead to and along the harbour edge.

★ ★ *Church and landscape.*

WARNFORD (J) Meon Valley, and partly off the main road, with lots of larger houses in flint or brick, occasionally with tile hanging. All dates, ranging from a big thatched brick cottage on the north side to Hanover cottages of 1981 in the middle. Farmyard almost central, and the whole village threaded with watercress beds. To the south a vast Georgian rectory, and on the east of the main road, the church (park in entrance with wrought iron gates).

The church of Our Lady is in Warnford Park, which until 1956 also contained a large house (site to the north of church). Now the park, with its ornamental trees and river Meon running through, is left to Jacob and black sheep. The heavy square tower of the church is Norman, looking a little bit like a water-tower. Unusual circular bell-openings. Inside the porch, and opposite on the outside of the south wall, are two inscriptions in Latin, translated thus in the 1720s by Bishop Gibson:

ABOVE *Warnford church.* BELOW *One of the dedicatory inscriptions on Warnford church*

'Good folks in your devotions ev'ry day, / For Adam Port, who thus repair'd me, pray'

'All you that come here / Bestow a kind prayer / On the Church builders, / Both youngers and elders. / What pious Wilfred rais'd, / Good Adam increas'd'.

Adam de Porte held Warnford 1171-1213, and these very rare examples of medieval dedicatory inscriptions seem to mean that he restored, or added to, a church dating from the time of St Wilfrid, who converted the Meon valley to Christianity in the 7th century. This is impossible: the tower of the church dates from about 1175, and the nave from about 1210, so probably both were built by 'good Adam'. Perhaps a tiny bit of one of the walls survives from an earlier structure, and Adam was happy to give his church an ancient history associated with the famous saint.

Inside the nave is barn-like, because it is simple and has no chancel arch. Good 1634 chancel screen and woodwork under tower. Fine 14th century east window, and monuments to the Neale family who

lived in the park. On the left an architectural wall monument 1601, right more flamboyant (1621) with three effigies and a row of children, some carrying skulls to show they died before their parents.

Behind the church is 'King John's House', really the 13th century house of the St John family. The far end is a large hall, with pillars surviving to a great height. These supported the roof. Smaller rooms at the west end were for storage and perhaps cooking. Big flint walls. It was adapted as a ruin to decorate the park in the 18th century.

Warnford is famous for its snowdrops – the park and churchyard are full of them, and there are special openings in February when they are in flower.

★ ★ ★ *Church: setting, and snowdrops.*

WARSASH (N) On the estuary of the river Hamble and described in 1912 as a small village 'its inhabitants chiefly employed in the crab and lobster trade' (VCH). In the centre a peculiar water tower of 1906 with a tiled 'helmet'. Other Victorian buildings here, some small-scale Georgian terraces on the roads down to the shore and big thatched barns and a Georgian farmhouse on the road to the north. All else is modern. Virtually at the head of the estuary is the College of Maritime Studies, mostly new and looking like a small university.

Down by the shore the buildings are neither picturesquely or regularly arranged. There are car parks to view the shipping (mostly yachts) which continually goes up and down the river. Hundreds of boats are moored up the Hamble river, and on the opposite shore are the Hamble boatworks. The small

ABOVE *The Harbour Master's House, Warsash*
LEFT *The ferry shelter, Warsash*
BELOW *Warsash clock tower*

black and white striped 'castle' is the Harbour Master's. Several long jetties. Fawley can be seen across Southampton Water. Woody walk down river, marshes upriver with more woods beyond, all part of a large nature reserve. Upriver also is the little ferry to Hamble (the village across the river) which runs all day.

The church of St Mary is inland, and was built in 1871, soon after the parish was divided from Titchfield, halfway between the big house at Hook (who paid for it) and village of Warsash. More

attractive inside, with angels on the wooden roof of the nave, a wooden vault in the chancel and elaborately carved stone capitals in the chancel too. Odd pulpit, Victorian with panels like memorial brasses. The stained glass in the east window looks Victorian but is 1950. Hung up in the south aisle is a model of HMS *Hotspur*, the largest ship ever built at Warsash. It took three years to build the vessel, which was completed in 1810. The modern model was given to the church in 1975.

★ ★ ★ ★ *Walking along the shore.*

WATERCRESS LINE (E-F) Hampshire's only steam railway, running from Alton to Alresford, with stations in between at Ropley and Four Marks. The line opened in 1865 and originally extended to Winchester. It closed in 1973, but opened four years later as a preserved railway, running steam engines.

The ten mile trip passes through superb countryside, and all the stations are fully furnished, with signs, barrows, signal boxes and so on. At Alton the station is to the side of the British Rail one, and at Ropley the selection of steam locomotives is stored. Alresford gave the line its nick-name: watercress was sent by train to London from the extensive beds around the town.

The round trip takes an hour and a half, with good rural views all the way. Each of the stations is worth visiting too, especially Ropley with the steam engines and fine topiary. From Medstead veteran

buses run trips to Selborne and Chawton in the summer, and there is an exhibition about the buses.

★ ★ ★ ★ *For anyone interested in railways.*

WATERLOOVILLE (J/K) A coaching inn called 'The Heroes of Waterloo' was built in the Forest of Bere on the Portsmouth/London road at about the time of the battle (1815) and a settlement grew up around it and took its name. By 1850 there were 195 inhabitants, and the village gained its full name, possibly to avoid postal mistakes as there was another village near Liverpool called Waterloo. From 1903-35 the village was linked to Portsmouth by a tramway, bringing day trippers from the city for country walks. Harper described it in 1923 as an 'entirely modern neighbourhood ... wearing not so much the appearance of an English village to that of some mushroom township in the hurried clearings in an American forest'. Now a sizeable town with quite a lot of industry. The main street is no longer the main road to London: the town is by-passed and the M27 is the main route.

Few old buildings survive in the pedestrianised main road, but there are some on the side streets. The church of St George in Hambledon Road just to the north-west was totally rebuilt in 1970, with a plain concrete tower. Good modern fittings. Opposite is one of the few Victorian buildings surviving – Swiss Cottage, flint ornamented with small chips of flint in the mortar, and a really odd conical roof supported by a verandah.

Just along London Road, north of the main shopping part, a few Victorian villas survive, one flint, mostly rendered, a couple with verandahs. To the east is the Roman Catholic church with a convent attached, ranging in date from the 1880s onwards, some of it Byzantine in style, all brick arches. A little further north up London Road is a little bit of oak forest, a remnant of the Forest of Bere.

Victorian villa, Waterlooville

Churches

Medieval churches

One historic building in every village is visitable, and contains much of its story. The church may be interesting as a building, for its monuments and fittings, or it may have fine setting, but always it reflects the past and present of the settlement. Churches form the centrepiece of exploring a village.

Hampshire is a good county for churches, having examples of almost every possible date, some of them as fine as anything in the country. Winchester Cathedral stands head and shoulders above all the others, not just in size (it is the largest medieval cathedral in Europe) but in the quality both of the building and its fittings. Like so many churches it cannot be classified to one date: parts are Norman but much is later. Many other smaller churches are like this too, showing growth from Saxon times onwards.

It is impossible to describe all these smaller churches, with their many periods of buildings, but a fictional history applies to them all generally, although none exactly. A small Norman (or even late Saxon) church of simple plan with just a narrow nave and chancel (like the surviving tiny church at Ashley) had aisles added about 1200, with fat pillars and big pointed arches. Perhaps the chancel arch was enlarged to match. A flint tower was added soon afterwards, and the chancel was rebuilt on a larger scale in the 13th century, with simple lancet windows. This chancel probably had its east window enlarged in the 15th century. From the 15th century tombs and brasses were placed in the church as memorials and a wooden screen to divide the chancel from the nave. In the 16th century wooden benches were provided for the congregation.

In the 17th century a wooden pulpit was provided and the number of memorials about increased from the 17th century, and also the memorials grew larger. During the 17th and 18th centuries rebuilding only took place if something went badly wrong with the old building – a tower would only be built if the old tower fell down.

ABOVE *North transept of Winchester Cathedral.* LEFT *Stoke Charity.* BELOW *Inside Stoke Charity church*

From the 1840s the revival of the church led to increased building activity, even to the extent of demolishing the whole church and rebuilding it a more 'correct' medieval style. Many churches were 'restored' less thoroughly – perhaps the narrow old chancel arch would be demolished and a wider one inserted, and new pews provided. Few churches escaped the 19th century unscathed, and those few are now prized for their authentic atmosphere and fittings. The 20th century has been more careful in its repairs, trying to preserve rather than rebuild.

The lists below include the medieval churches, with other lists for Saxon and Norman, 1540-1800, and 19th century churches. They include the ones I think are most interesting and worth travelling to see, but there are many other churches listed in the Gazetteer which have good features or fittings, but are smaller or seemed less interesting to me. Many of these are worth visiting if you are in the area.

★ ★ ★ ★ *Winchester Cathedral; Eversley, for its association with Charles Kingsley; Steventon for its association with Jane Austen.*
★ ★ ★ *Beaulieu; Bramley; East Wellow (for Florence Nightingale association); Empshott; Farley Chamberlayne; Hambledon; Hartley Wespall; Idsworth; Milford-on-Sea; Minstead; North Stoneham (Southampton North); Odiham; Old Basing; St. Michael, Southampton; Sherborne St John; Stoke Charity; Tichborne; Titchfield; Upton Grey.*

Good positions: Beaulieu; Eversley; Farley Chamberlayne; Idsworth; Steventon. Good fittings/lack of Victorian restoration: Bramley; Minstead; Sherborne St John; Stoke Charity; Tichborne; Upton Grey. Mostly of one date: Empshott; Milford-on-Sea.

ABOVE *South Chapel, St Cross, Winchester*
BELOW *Saxon window at Boarhunt*

Saxon and Norman churches

Hampshire has some complete late Saxon churches still much the same as when they were built. Boarhunt, Corhampton and Headbourne Worthy are small and simple, and show what many of the larger ones grew from. They mostly have little architectural detailing, and that little is rather clumsy. Breamore, more complex with its Saxon crossing and amazingly with an Anglo Saxon inscription on one arch, is rather overwhelmed by later alterations. The county is rich in late Saxon sculpture (uncommon elsewhere in the country) with roods (representations of Christ on the cross) at Romsey, Headbourne Worthy and Breamore, but all have been defaced so that only the outlines remain. The roods and all the churches mentioned date from very late in the Saxon period – to around 1000. Titchfield porch is earlier, but it is difficult to date precisely.

The churches from after the Norman Conquest are more beautiful than their Saxon predecessors, and they are found in all sizes. Winchester cathedral stands out, but of course much of it is later. Portchester, East Meon, Warnford and Winchfield are virtually complete Norman churches, and Pamber a handsome fragment. The large churches at Romsey and St Cross (Winchester) show the Early English style emerging from the Norman.

The big Norman churches impress with their height and sophisticated decoration, but the fat pillars, round arches and deeply cut patterned decoration of the Norman style are to be seen in the majority of Hampshire's medieval churches.

Saxon ★ ★ ★ *Breamore* ★ ★ *Boarhunt; Corhampton and Head-bourne Worthy.*
Norman ★ ★ ★ ★ *East Meon; Portchester; Romsey Abbey; Cathedral and St Cross Winchester.*
★ ★ ★ *Pamber; Petersfield; Warnford; Winchfield.*

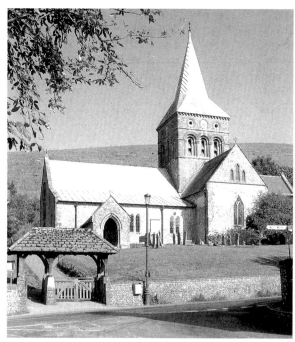

East Meon church

Avington. BELOW *Inside Avington church*

Churches 1540-1800

Nationally there was very little church building in the century after the Reformation of the 1530s turned England from a Catholic to a Protestant country. Hampshire is exceptional in having several simple 16th century towers, mostly built because the earlier ones had fallen down (Bishop's Waltham and Droxford are the best examples) and the church at Southwick which was rebuilt in 1566.

Hampshire has little in the way of church building from the 17th century, with only part of Portsmouth cathedral, but many furnishings. The 18th century is much richer, with three good early churches and two later ones, none of them large. The three earlier ones all date from around 1717. Hale is distinctively classical, and gains from its siting. Wolverton and Abbott's Ann are both brick, Wolverton being the prettier but Abbott's Ann the more famous because of the Maiden's Garlands hung inside the church. Avington is of 1770, complete with all its fittings down to the lavishly bound bible.

Non-conformist chapels are not usually so accessible as churches, but one of the finest in Hampshire (at Ringwood) is now a museum and can be seen. It dates from 1727, and still has most of its distinctive fittings.

★ ★ ★ *Abbot's Ann; Avington; Hale; Ringwood Meeting House; Southwick; and Wolverton.*

Churches: 19th and 20th centuries

The 19th century was a great period for church building, but they are often ignored, which seems silly because they can be as interesting (or as dull) as medieval churches. True they lack age, but often they still present a complete scheme of building and decoration, something now uncommon in medieval churches. The earlier 19th century ones are more light-hearted and flimsier, predating intense study of medieval churches and content to use imitation materials such as plaster instead of stone for vaulting, methods the later Victorians abhorred and called 'carpenter's gothic'. Hampshire has a particularly fine example with plaster vaulting – the Regency nave of Micheldever church of 1808, and several complete small churches in playful unstudied gothic, the best of which are Chilworth (1812) and Ashe (1818), both of which use plaster for vaults, and at Ashe even iron and artificial stone for tracery.

After about 1840 churches become more serious and architects more knowledgeable about medieval architecture. Certain styles were regarded as more suitable than others, and so the churches tend to be more uniform. Andover church (1840) stands between the earlier unstudied Gothic and the later serious styles, being plaster vaulted and consistent in style but not restrained by 'correct' ideas of architecture.

There were many objectors to the later Victorian new churches, especially the larger ones. W. H. Hudson, the naturalist, complained in 1903 of the 'immense churches' built in the Hampshire countryside during the later 19th century thinking them usually the work 'of a new over-rich lord of the manor, who must have all things new, including a new big church' to please 'his own peculiar Stock Exchange God... who is a respecter of wealthy persons'.

Hudson mourned the small churches which had been demolished, but we can appreciate their replacements as fine buildings in their own right. Many were by London architects, but a local man, William White (great-nephew of Gilbert White of Selborne) designed many churches in the county, including my 19th century favourite at Lyndhurst where he used the classic Hampshire building material – brick. This is a building which visitors either love or hate, finding it bright and inventive, or brash and inappropriate. White also built several other smaller and cheaper churches in the county.

Fleet (1861) and Itchen Stoke (1866) are also unusual. Fleet in a simpler style, Itchen Stoke complex and after a French original. Farnborough, technically a mausoleum rather than a church, is also French in style, built in 1887 for the Empress Eugenie of France. The

Altar canopy at St Philip's Cosham

position of the church and abbey, on the only surviving wild area of Farnborough and at the top of the hill, adds greatly to its charm.

Two twentieth century churches must be visited. The chapel at Burghclere was built to house Stanley Spencer's paintings of the First World War, which have to be seen in this setting to be properly appreciated. St Philip's Cosham of 1936-8 is a superb building, gathering features from many styles and combining them to produce one of the best 20th century churches in the country.

★ ★ ★ ★ *Sandham Memorial Chapel, Burghclere;*
★ ★ ★ *St Mary Andover; St Philip, Cosham; The Mausoleum, Farnborough; All Saints, Fleet; St Mary, Itchen Stoke; Micheldever, and St Michael, Lyndhurst. (For other White churches see Hatherden, Linkenholt, Longstock, Smannell, St Mark Woolston (Southampton East), Christ Church Freemantle (Southampton West) and Tangley). (St Faith, Lee-on-Solent, is an interesting 20th century church ★ ★)*

WATERSHIP DOWN (B) (2 miles south-west of Kingsclere) The most famous part of the abrupt chalk scarp which runs for nearly ten miles across north Hampshire from the Wiltshire border to Kingsclere. Much of it is so steep that it cannot be ploughed, and so some downland remains albeit without many flowers. The fields on top have become arable. At Watership Down the road leads steeply up through scrubby woodland and beech trees. From the top the views are wide. This particular part of the scarp was made famous by Richard Adams' *Watership Down* (1983). Footpaths lead along the top, the one west leading to Ladle Hill, a hillfort (see Sydmonton).

WELLINGTON COUNTRY PARK (C) (fee: lists); East of Stratfield Saye, right on the county boundary. Flooded gravel pits, with the National Dairy Museum (not large, but interesting), a small children's animal farm (goats, sheep, pigs, chickens etc), a model steam train (rides: fee), nature trails and deer park with fallow deer. The Thames Valley Time Trail is a few plastic models around the park, extolling the need to extract gravel and stone from the area. Windsurfing and boating available on the lake (fee) and crazy golf.

WELLOWS, THE (H) West Wellow is almost all modern development which spreads from the main road, but **East Wellow** is sparse, mostly farms. An attractive landscape with many small hills and deeply cut roads. Wellow Vineyards, recently established in Tanner's Lane is open to the public (fee:lists).

Florence Nightingale (1820-1910) lived with her family at East Wellow. Her father bought Embley Park in 1826, for the family to spend the winters in, using their main home in Derbyshire for the summer. (The large redbrick house, Elizabethan style was rebuilt in 1895 and can be seen in the north-east part of the parish). Florence lived mostly with them until she finally, against their wishes, managed to take up nursing full time in 1853. After the Crimean War and her heroic efforts there, she mostly lived alone in London, but she was buried at East Wellow, beneath the family monument, which has the simple inscription 'FN 1820-1910'. She wished for no memorial at all: she hated her fame.

The church of St Margaret is on one of the small hills, standing alone with the manor house. Florence Nightingale's

Florence Nightingale's monument, East Wellow

grave is beneath the steeple-shaped monument opposite the porch, standing out from the more usual gravestones. The church is basically 13th century. The porch (and the door) and the south aisle are Tudor, and the dormer windows in the roof are Georgian presumably to light a gallery which has now gone.

Inside the wall-paintings, mostly 13th century, are prominent. The east wall is perhaps the best, with kings' heads and architectural decoration around the three original lancets. On the north wall is St Christopher and opposite painted lines imitating stonework with rosettes. The niche by the door is also decorated. All the wall painting is robust, crudely painted but effective.

Fine Jacobean pulpit with tester and inscription, flat communion rails of the same date and more carved panels reset in the stalls and behind the altar. On one of the roof beams across the chancel is a musket, put there in 1805 as a warning of the dangers of firearms, after someone in the village was killed by accident. Displays on Florence Nightingale at the back of the church and in a window.

★ ★ ★ *Church for the wall-paintings, and association with Florence Nightingale. Good walking country.*

WEST END (J) Only made a parish in 1894, but with the odd Victorian cottage and a school. Mostly post Second World War, including the shopping street, but with a big hospital at Moor Green at the

eastern end, which has grown from the workhouse of 1848. The brick church of St James (1890) is on the main road to the south of the shopping street. This main road from Swaythling to Thorney Hill is mostly well-wooded, with largish Victorian houses and modern infill partly concealed by the trees. To the south is the highest point, with Telegraph Lane a reminder of the station built here in 1806, one of a chain which enabled the Admiralty to signal from London to Plymouth.

West Green House

WEST GREEN (C) A hamlet two miles west of Hartley Wintney: a few nice brick houses and woods with paths through. West Green house is large and of circa 1700-1730 plainish and brick. The modern garden is sometimes opened. Prominent classical column of 1976 at the end of the drive (very visible from the road) with a Latin inscription translating 'this monument was built with a great deal of money which otherwise some day would have been given into the hands of the public revenue'.

WEST MEON (J) A pretty village, rather spoilt by the busy road which runs right through it. Lots of thatched cottages, both brick and timber framed. A good example of timber-framing in the small triangular green in the middle. The road to the east is less busy and runs along close to the river Meon.

The church of St John Evangelist is in superb position overlooking much of the village and the hill beyond. It was rebuilt just up the hill from the old site in 1843-6. George Gilbert Scott was the architect of this early and large-scale Gothic revival building. The walls are made from thousands of small squared flints, which the village women are believed to have knapped for a farthing each. Inside it is huge and high with heavy timber roof.

View from West Meon churchyard

Characteristic fittings of the 1840s include the font and the heraldic windows of the west end, brilliant in the tower, faded elsewhere. Above the screen to the tower a finely carved Royal Coat of Arms, dated 1712, saved from the earlier church.

On display are photographs of the rectors since 1872, and an interesting relief plan of the area. In the churchyard lie buried Thomas Lord, the founder of Lord's Cricket Ground (down the path to the lower churchyard, on the left) and the ashes of Guy Burgess, the Russian agent who died in Russia in 1963 (to the north of the tower). Next door to the church a characteristic mid Victorian school, the first this author attended.

★ ★ *Village and church.*

WESTON PATRICK (F) In 1886 fire destroyed most of the old thatched cottages. The church of St Laurence was rebuilt in 1868, neat and flinty with a complicated bell turret. The Norman doorway from the old church was incorporated in the new building. The western part of the village is called Weston Corbett and has a big redbrick Georgian house.

WEST TISTED (J) A scattered village, with substantial recent cottages near the church and a Victorian Gothic old Vicarage. The other side of the church is the moated site of the manor house of the Tisted family and the path to the church crosses the moat, which looks like a dry ditch. Later the manor was the home of the Tichborne family, and to the south-west of the church is supposedly the oak in which Sir Benjamin Tichborne hid from his enemies after the Battle of Cheriton 1644.

The church of St Mary Magdalene retains its simple Norman doorway (porch 1750), and opposite is another, now blocked. The heavy timber bell frame is exposed at the west end. Plain Norman font, and many finely lettered memorials: two up towards the chancel are of such exotic stone that they are difficult to read. The chancel was added on in Victorian times, and has Dutch panelling.

★ ★ *Church.*

WEST TYTHERLEY (H) A good mixture of timber frame cottages, Victorian cottages and houses and more recent ones, mostly brick. The church is severe brick and flint, and although not built until 1833 looks earlier Georgian. The Victorians altered the windows to make them more 'churchy' and added the stone chancel. Unusual and rather theatrical west gallery, 1833 too, and a complex Purbeck Marble font, early medieval from the earlier church.

WEST WELLOW see WELLOWS

WEST WORLDHAM (F) A small and scattered village, with a small church which was badly burnt and heavily restored in 1888. The Georgian brick farmhouse next door is bigger than the church. On the B3006 south-west of the village is a perfect brick tollhouse, octagonal with stone corners, projecting from a larger house.

WEYHILL (D) Seemingly a very ordinary small roadside settlement, with the church of St Michael dating mostly from 1864 and several stuccoed early 19th century buildings including two pubs. In fact it was the site of one of the greatest fairs of medieval England, which probably started

in Saxon times and retained its importance into the 20th century. In the 1820s the sheep fair at Michaelmas which lasted a week sold 100,000 sheep. The sheep fair was the most important annual fair, but there were several others. Horses, cheese, hops and all sorts of manufactured goods were sold, with the fairground stretching all along the triangle of land to the west of the church, and into the fields beyond. Much of this area is now an industrial estate, but close to the church cob-walled single story booths survive which were used by the hop sellers. The most famous description of the fair is in Thomas Hardy's *Mayor of Casterbridge*, set in the 1850s. The last sale (of cattle) was in 1957. In Andover Museum is a small display about the fair.

WHERWELL (D) The village seems all thatch, and really is so along the picturesque road to the church, with the wide river Test and handsome cottages. There was a nunnery here from the tenth century until the dissolution in the 16th century, just to the south of the church, but nothing remains. The Priory is now a handsome early 19th century house close to the church but best seen from the road to Chilbolton.

The church of St Peter and Holy Cross was rebuilt in 1858 in a lively, individual style. Prominent externally is the unusually elaborate wooden spire with windows in the base. Carved fragments from the old church displayed in the new one, and odd bits in buildings around. Effigy of a nun with lots of robes, and close by a simple tomb chest of 1551. Big Victorian mausoleum in the churchyard with carved heads from the old church.

★ ★ ★ *Village.*

WHITCHURCH (D/E) A handsome small town on the river Test, with many Georgian buildings, either redbrick like the Town Hall (now a bank) or rendered. Occasional timber framed cottages. The White Hart Hotel with its rounded corner is one of the best Georgian buildings, but many smaller ones are attractive. The town grew up on the crossing of two important roads and developed some industries. In 1911 there were two flour mills, a silk mill and a large jam factory. *Whitchurch Silk Mill* still survives, and is open to the public (fee:lists), just to the west of the town centre, on an island in the River Test. The building dates from about 1800, and had the clock added in 1815 to celebrate the victory of

Waterloo. It is a plain brick building with broad windows to give light to the looms. Silk has been woven here since 1830, and still is. Some of the machinery is late 19th century, and the water-wheel still turns. Best to visit during the week or earlier on Saturdays when work is in progress. Small display of silk costumes, video on silk weaving etc. Well worth seeing.

The town continues for quite a distance along the road to Laverstoke, and ¾ mile out is The Gables, a large brick and flint building constructed in 1847 as the Workhouse.

The church of All Hallows is to the north-west of the centre, where the houses are more widely spaced. Outside it is all of 1866, with a shingled broach spire, and parish rooms of 1974 attached. Inside there is much medieval, with 1866 chancel. Lots of interesting memorials and fittings, including a very unusual Saxon gravestone, probably of the 9th century with a figure of Christ on the front, an inscription in Latin over the top and a plant scroll on the back. The inscription translates 'here the body of Frithburga lies in peace'. Presumably she was buried in the churchyard: the stone was found in the walls during a Victorian restoration. On the opposite side are the effigies of Thomas Brooke (died 1612) and his wife, while on the wall close by are brasses to his father and mother, put up in 1603. This family lived in the house opposite the church. Many memorials around the church to the Portal family who founded the paper mills in the area in the late 17th century (see Laverstoke). 15th century stone font, and at the back of the church a very unusual testament board, dated 1602 (or 1682) with lots of little pictures, just like printed broadsheets. In the tower a

15th century free-standing wooden spiral staircase.

Opposite the church is a tiny timber framed brick barn standing on staddle stones.

★ ★ *All Hallows church, especially for the memorials.* ★ ★ ★ *Small town* ★ ★ ★ ★ *Whitchurch Silk Mill, an unusual opportunity to see silk weaving and all of a mill of 1800.*

WHITSBURY (G) Another village moved from Wiltshire in 1895. High chalk with windblown yews on the road from Rockbourne. One long street with some good brick, or brick and timber-framed cottages, but the dominating feature is the horse. The village has a large stud, with notices indicating directions for 'barren and maiden mares' etc. The valley has many paddocks with wooden fences and small coppices. The church is to the west, off the main street and is reached by car along a drive signposted 'visiting mares, stud office and church'. The first part of this drive runs along the ditch and back of Castle Ditches, an Iron Age hillfort. The little church of St Leonard stands on a steep knoll: the present building is a replacement of 1878. Odd brick tower, which thins in the middle. Inside lots of nautical memorials and an apparently flying modern organ at the west end. A steep footpath leads down to the middle of the village, with a huge Georgian rectory in parkland on one side.

Whitsbury Down to the north has a prominent Neolithic Long Barrow right on the county boundary and there is another larger one in trees at Round Clump. These are some of the best in the county, and both are on footpaths.

★ ★ *Village.*

WICKHAM (J) The 'finest village in Hampshire, and one of the best in the South of England' (David Lloyd, in *Buildings of England*) and so it is. The huge Square is lined with brick houses and cottages, still homes, businesses and shops, which makes it busy as well as handsome. The square was laid out in medieval times to accommodate markets and a yearly fair: the latter, now a pleasure fair still fills it on 20th May.

Until 1967 the south end of the square, where the main road passes through, was bounded simply by a brick wall. Now, set back from the road, there are flats. The west side of the square has the larger houses, but a little way up from the south-west corner is one of the earliest buildings – Knockers Wine Bar, a jettied house of about 1500-1550 with many wall-paintings of 1600 surviving inside upstairs. Further along, large pair of houses in characteristic grey and red brick, early Georgian. The corner has the prettiest house in Wickham: Eastwood House grey and red brick again, but with a bay supported on pillars over the entrance. The Old House Restaurant on the east side is large and handsome, but the rest of the eastern buildings are on a rather smaller scale.

The northern end, where the road passes through, has in contrast a small gothic flint house of the early Victorian period. Bridge Street leads on from here, curving down to the river, with houses just as good as those on the Square. Queen Lodge is earlier than most, late 17th century with brick imitation columns on the front. The Barracks have some timber framing, and a 19th century notice warning: 'Vagrants found in or near this Place will be Apprehended and Punished with the utmost Severity the Law will Permit'.

Further down, on the left, Chesapeake Mill, built in 1820 with timber from the American ship *Chesapeake*, taken by the British Navy in 1813 when we were at war with America. The small bridge of 1792, the mill and the brewery buildings opposite (now converted to flats) form a strong group of industrial buildings, with a backdrop of the railway bridge.

Over the river and main Meon Valley road is St Nicholas church, set away from the village but originally with the manor house close by. The flint tower with its spire sits well on the knoll, but apart from the reset Norman doorway surviving in the tower most of the church dates from the late Victorian period. Inside the

Whitchurch Silk Mill

ABOVE *Sir William Uvedale's monument in Wickham church*
TOP RIGHT *Bridge Street, Wickham*
ABOVE RIGHT *Eastwood House*
RIGHT *Early Victorian flint in Bridge Street, Wickham*

church is unusual in having no aisles but big transepts, so that in plan it is a cross. In the south transept is the vast memorial to Sir William Uvedale who died in 1615. Alabaster, with reclining figures of Uvedale and his wife, huge canopy with lions on top, and children below.

Beyond the church are two large Georgian houses, one originally the Rectory.

Just to the north from the Droxford Road, can be seen Rooksbury, now a school. This classical house was built in 1835.

Wickham village ★ ★ ★ ★ for the Square.

WIELD (E) Divides into two quite separate settlements. **Upper Wield** has a large green and randomly arranged thatched cottages on one side of it. A timber-framed cottage makes one side of the graveyard. The church of St James was largely rebuilt in 1884, but the Norman doorway survived as does the chancel arch with a squint either side. The roof and west gallery are painted in effective fairground style. William Wallop's large memorial up by the altar has fine alabaster effigies and an elaborate setting. He died in 1617 aged 87, having been three times Mayor of Southampton. **Lower Wield** has some thatched cottages.

St James church ★ ★ for memorial etc.

WIMPSON see SOUTHAMPTON, WEST

WINCHFIELD (C) A rural village, but cut by the railway and the M3 motorway. The northern part is well-wooded. The church of St Mary is in the south-eastern part of the parish, basically a Norman church with a north aisle added in 1850 and a porch of around 1500. Pevsner describes the main church as 'Norman of singular ferocity'. The tower is peaceful Norman, the top restoration of 1850, which is presumably also the date of the conspicuous decorative 'SM's which mark the ends of the iron rods which tie it together. The entrance doorway is the best ferocious bit, highly decorated on too large a scale for the small arch. The chancel arch inside is of the same style, but has been re-cut, a nasty Victorian habit. The chancel is remarkably complete and Norman, but again all the surfaces have been recut. Tower arch Norman too.

Fine wooden pulpit, much carved and dated 1634. Stout communion rail of similar date. One southern window in the chancel engraved by Laurence Whistler. **Winchfield Hurst** to the east is a hamlet with the larger and classical 1871 workhouse now converted to housing.

★ ★ ★ Church, very complete (if over-restored internally) Norman church.

Winchfield church

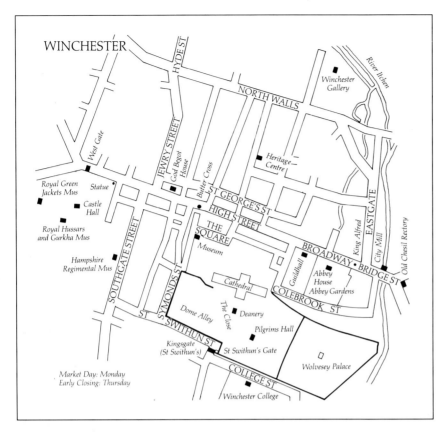

WINCHESTER

Market Day: Monday
Early Closing: Thursday

WINCHESTER (J) Once the capital of England, and still the most interesting place in the county to visit. The Cathedral is well known, but the Castle Hall, Winchester College and St Cross are just as fine, and less crowded..

The Suburbs

History

Winchester has been settled since the Iron Age, and from about 70 AD was a Roman town called Venta Belgarum. By the third century this covered most of the area of the medieval walled town, which re-used the line of the Roman defences. After the Roman withdrawal from Britain the town declined, but a cathedral was built in the 7th century, and there was probably a Royal palace (for Kings of Wessex, not yet England) from about the same time. The town was refounded by King Alfred in the later 9th century and the modern street pattern dates from this refounding. From Alfred onwards the city was the capital of Wessex, and finally from King Egbert (crowned 829) until the Norman Conquest, capital of England. The city reached its greatest extent (before modern times) in the early 12th century when there were probably as many as 8,000 inhabitants in the walled area and the suburbs on the west, south and along the base of St Giles Hill to the east.

Visitors from the 18th century onwards extolled its peace and beauty. The poet Keats stayed in 1819 and considered it 'the pleasantest town I ever was in' with 'not one loom or anything like

manufacturing beyond bread and butter in the whole city'. He found the High Street 'quiet as a lamb' and 'the side streets excessively maiden-lady-like'.

The position of the city was neatly defined by the Duke of Portland in 1662: 'situated in a pleasant bottom by a sweet river running amongst hills'. The hills, still with many trees, provide a scenic backdrop, and along the 'pleasant bottom' and 'sweet river' are superb paths and parks.

The Cathedral is the most beautiful and interesting building in the whole county. The Saxon cathedral was on a slightly different site from the surviving Norman one. The new cathedral was started in 1079, and it seems to have been completed by 1093 when the bones of St Swithun, a 9th century bishop, were moved to the new building. The transepts and crypt are the only parts of the early building to survive in their original state: the central tower fell in 1107 and was rebuilt in a slightly later Norman style. The Lady chapel and the area behind the choir were added around 1200 and in the later 14th century the Norman nave was remodelled to bring it up-to-date. The chancel was rebuilt in 1500-28 with a splendid screen and wooden vaults. The first restoration was 1812-28 when many unfashionable classical fittings (sadly including a screen by Inigo Jones) were removed and replaced by more suitable 'Gothic' styled ones. Another restoration in the 1880s was less drastic but the building was only saved from sinking into the marshy land it was built on in 1906-10 when a diver heroically removed the original wooden foundations and replaced them with concrete.

All the different periods of building are fine, and only personal taste will settle which is best. Superb fittings abound: the cathedral must have the best series of chantry chapels in the country, ranging from the earliest known (Bishop Edington, 1366) to Bishop Gardener's of 1556. The stalls in the Quire are of the highest quality, but are only the best of many wonderful wooden fittings. The whole series of Bishop's memorials is interesting, and Jane Austen and Isaac Walton are buried here.

As this summary suggests, the building and its contents are so rich that really several visits are needed to appreciate it all.

The west front of the cathedral, with the main entrances, is one of the later

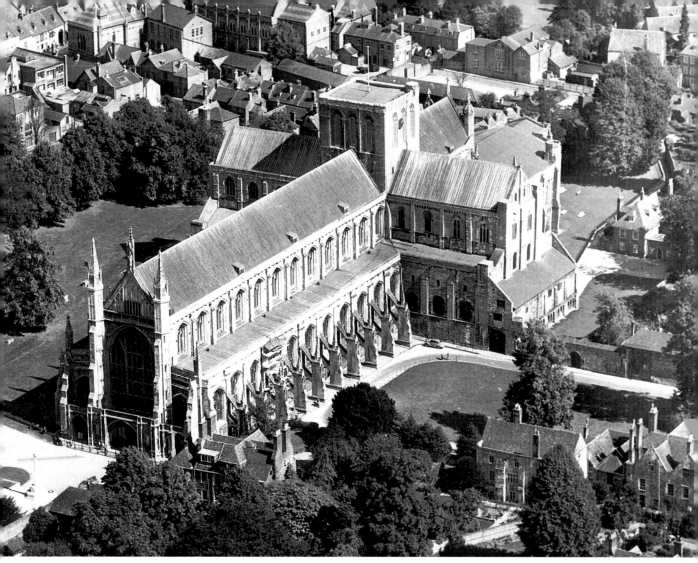

Winchester cathedral from the west

parts of the building, dating from around 1400. The huge window dwarfs the elaborate arches and vaults of the three sets of doors. Once inside the great length of the cathedral is the immediate impression: a famous vista. At 556ft it is the longest cathedral in Europe, with the sole exception of St Peter's, Rome. The Norman nave was heavily remodelled in the late 14th century in the then fashionable Perpendicular style, with groined vaulting and complicated bosses. The adapted pillars between nave and aisles are much heavier than real 15th century ones, but the thickness is disguised by lots of mouldings. Periodically the 16 large bright 1970s banners illustrating the Creation are hung along either side of the nave.

Starting along the north aisle (the left hand side of the building) the huge number of memorials is apparent. Only those which are particularly fine or are to

famous people will be individually mentioned, but many more are worth examining. In the fifth bay along is Jane Austen's grave, marked by a large black floorslab with the usual pious inscription referring to 'the benevolence of her heart, the sweetness of her temper' but no mention of the fact that she was a novelist. The adjacent window of 1900 is a memorial to her, and on the wall is a memorial brass of the same date.

In the next bay is the superb font, made of black marble from Tournai, Belgium, and dating from about 1150. Two sides have doves (or in one case a salamander) in roundels, while the other two have scenes from the life of St Nicholas, a 4th century saint/bishop. Amongst thousands of others, Henry III was baptised at this font in 1207.

The north transept opens out to the left. These transepts are the oldest part of the cathedral surviving above ground,

typical Early Norman with big round-headed arches, heavy and serious with no decoration. The rather good imitation medieval ceiling is of 1820, painted wood. The entrance to the *crypt* (fee:lists) is from the north transept. This is the other surviving part of the early Norman cathedral, plain and large but useless because it floods. Worth seeing as an example of unaltered early Norman. Atmospheric, especially the narrow corridors cut through the Norman east wall to give access to the eastern addition of the early 13th century, in Early English style.

Returning to the north transept, under the Quire is a small chapel, of the Holy Sepulchre, with remarkably complete wall paintings which spread over the vaulted ceiling as well as walls. The chapel dates from about 1200 and the paintings from about 30 years later and in combination give a small-scale but authentic sample of

OPPOSITE *The quire, Winchester Cathedral*
LEFT *Two figures from the Quire stalls, Winchester Cathedral.*
BELOW *Cat & mouse miserichord and mortuary chest on choir screen*

what medieval churches looked like inside. Steps lead up to the choir. All the eastern area is floored with medieval tiles, some patterned, some plain. This is the largest surviving area of medieval tiles in the country, all dating from around 1230.

The Quire and altar area was re-modelled in the early 16th century, and the Quire itself is entered through a fine stone screen dated 1525, with medieval style 'windows' below but a classical frieze above, a typical combination for the date. Balanced on top are theatrical-looking wooden mortuary chests, all of 1525 except the two westernmost ones, containing the bones of Saxon Kings and Bishops, including King Canute. They were collected up from other chests, but in 1642 during the Civil War Par-liamentarians scattered the contents of the two westernmost chests all over the cathedral floor. Later both were replaced and filled with such of the scattered bones as survived.

The dominating features inside the Quire are the wooden fittings. The high bishop's throne is imitation medieval, dating from 1828, but the stalls along the walls are some of the finest medieval woodwork in the country. From letters

we know they were being made in 1308. Plants, animals and human heads all mix together, with the tops of the canopies heavily decorated. They were damaged in the Civil War, but repaired afterwards. There are many misericords, small ledges on the undersides of the seats which the monks leant on during long services. These have less formal carvings, sometimes humorous. A few seats are usually turned up to display them.

The wooden screen across between the quire and nave is of 1874, but based on the patterns of stalls.

The unusually large supports for the Norman crossing tower can be seen either side of the Quire. In 1107 the original Norman tower fell down, less than thirty years after it had been built. The rebuilders took no chances and provided the new short tower with these heavy supports. The wooden vault in the crossing was added in 1634, and the big wooden eagle lectern is of similar date.

Some of the smaller fixed seats in front of the stalls are also 14th century but on either side at the east end are many finely carved rectangular panels of the 1530s-50s including one with HR for Henry VIII. All these seats (apart from the

back stalls) were re-arranged in the 1820s, and more were added. In the centre is the simple Purbeck Marble tomb of William Rufus, King of England, who was killed hunting in the New Forest in 1100. The rather oriental looking pulpit at the east end of the stalls has the inscription 'Thomas Silkstede Prior' and dates from around 1498, although restored and with Victorian stairs and canopy. The wooden vaulting over this area is part of the early 16th century remodelling, as is the stone screen behind the altar. All the statues contained in it are late Victorian. The doors on either side and the heavily carved altar rail are of around 1700.

Returning to the north aisle, attached to the east end of the stone screen is the chapel and tomb of Bishop Gardener who died in 1556. Like the stone screen, it is a combination of medieval and the then new classical style. Gruesome cadaver on the side, a reminder of mortality. This bishop married Mary, Queen of England, to Philip of Spain in this cathedral in 1554.

Behind the altar is the retrochoir, Early English in style, dating from the very early 13th century. Much lighter than the Norman work of the transepts, with

curvaceous arcading all along the side walls, slim Purbeck Marble pillars and lancet windows. The tree-like pillars supporting the groining are obscured by two magnificent chantry chapels. In the aisle is a large wooden chest of around 1300 with external framing on the sides.

Before the first chantry chapel are three medieval effigies, two of 13th century bishops, the other a 14th century knight in armour. Closer to the altar is the medieval-style effigy of Bishop Sumner who died in 1874. The two freestanding chantry chapels here are very fine. The one on the north side is to Bishop Waynflete who died in 1486, with elegant spires, totally decorated. The contrast between the squareness of Bishop Gardiner's chantry attached to the back of the altar this side, and this late medieval one, all flowing decoration, is great. Waynflete's still has its original wooden door and lock.

Three chapels mark the east end of the cathedral. On the left is the Guardian Angels' Chapel, with painted vault of about 1240. The right hand wall is filled by the classical memorial to Lord Portland who died in 1634, with a good bronze effigy. The central Lady chapel was made

longer about 1500, with wall-paintings of that date showing the miracles of the Virgin Mary, now reproduced on boards which cover the originals. The fine wooden screen and stalls inside are also of 1500. The complex wooden altar rail dates from 1662.

Opposite the Lady Chapel is a free-standing metal 'shrine' to St Swithun, dating from 1962, and in front is the simple Purbeck Marble tomb of Bishop Lucy who died in 1204 and who built this area of the cathedral. The chapel in the south-east corner, next to the Lady Chapel, is the chantry of Bishop Langton who died in 1500. Small and full of woodwork. The screen has a fine door (only the right hand side is original) and inside is a big Purbeck Marble tomb. Close to the entrance is a statue of William Walker, the diver whose laborious work early this century saved the cathedral from sinking into the mud beneath it. The arcading behind the main altar with pointed tops is pretty, and dates from around 1320.

The free-standing chantry chapel on this side belongs to Cardinal Beaufort,

RIGHT *Thomas Silkstede's pulpit*

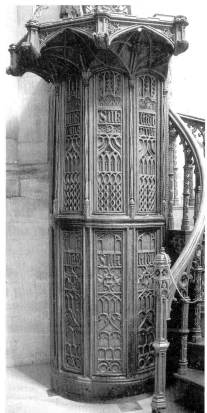

Bishop Waynflete's chantry, Winchester Cathedral

wooden door into it is one of the finest pieces of late medieval woodwork. Close to the steps is the over life size kneeling effigy of Bishop Brownlow North, who died in 1820. The white marble effigy is a real period piece.

The steps lead down to the south transept through the fine ironwork which may be late 13th century. The south transept is early Norman like the north transept, and again has an imitation medieval ceiling of 1820. There are many fine fittings. Towards the Quire are intricately carved swags and drapes of fruit etc, probably from the High Altar and dating from the 1690s. Above is imitation Norman in wood dating from 1820.

In the middle of the transept is the florid memorial to Bishop Wilberforce who died in 1873. Even more twirly than the medieval memorials; his effigy is carried by six angels. Behind, lining the wall, are canopied seats of about 1500 with linenfold panelling. The heavy door through these, with its ironwork, is medieval, probably about 1300.

William Walker's memorial, Winchester Cathedral

Bishop of Winchester, who died in 1447. He was a brother of Henry IV, and his effigy was destroyed during the Civil War and replaced afterwards. Opposite, on the outside wall is the stout figure of John Clobery who died in 1687. He helped restore Charles II to the throne in 1660, but looks ridiculous in his sashes, skirt and wig. To the west an early 13th century doorway, pretty. Attached to the back of the altar on this side is another chantry chapel, to Bishop Fox who died in 1528. He rebuilt the Quire and altar area, and although he used Renaissance or classical detail in his stone screen to the Quire, his chantry chapel is wholly medieval, very fluid but immensely detailed (the statuettes are late 19th century). The

At the end of the south transept is the entrance to the **Library and Triforum Gallery** (fee:lists). A 17th century staircase leads up to the library, which is over the passage between the Cathedral and the chapter house. The bookcases are 1630s, fitted here in the 1660s. Many of the tables are of the same date, and the long thin room lined with ancient books looks a cosy home for the scholar. Two handsome globes dated 1640 complete the furnishings: their representation of the Americas is a little inaccurate. In the room opposite, the treasure of the library is displayed: the Winchester Bible. This was written and illuminated in the scriptorium at Winchester in the years around 1125, and is the finest of all the great illuminated cathedral bibles of the 12th century. The initials are all major paintings, and are the work of several different hands.

A new staircase leads up to the balcony in the south transept, where a recent display holds many of the cathedral treasures, all well laid out in modern cases. There are smaller objects like Bishop's rings and other jewellery; high quality sculpture from the screen behind the altar dating from the late 15th century; superlative fragments from the Purbeck Marble shrine to St Swithun, destroyed at the Reformation; four almost life size painted wooden half-figures of James I and Charles I taken from the 1634 vault in the Quire, the chair Queen Mary sat on when she married in the Cathedral in 1554; and gilded figures from the 1665 organ case. All well worth seeing, and it is interesting simply to be so high in the cathedral, with a good view amongst the Norman architecture of the transept. The museum is highly recommended.

The east side of the transept is cut into two chapels, the left hand side being the Venable chapel which contains an amazing survival – a simple 14th century wooden cupboard. The right hand chapel has the black floor slab of Isaac Walton who wrote *The Compleat Angler* (1653) and lived in the Close for the last part of his life, dying in 1683. The stained glass window of 1914 is also a memorial to him. In the transept are two medieval wooden benches.

Back into the nave, with lots of memorials. On the right is the chantry chapel to Bishop Edington, the earliest chantry chapel in the building and indeed the earliest surviving one in the country. He died in 1366, and the simplicity of his memorial is in contrast to the later ones

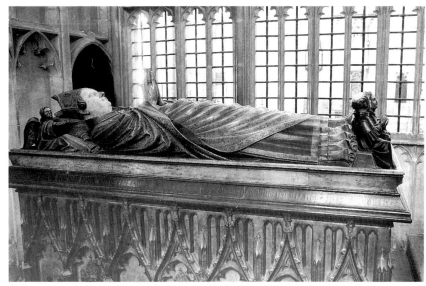
William of Wykeham's effigy, Winchester Cathedral

behind the altar. The alabaster effigy is very human. Further along on the left is the memorial to Bishop Willis who died in 1734, rather silly by contrast with the medieval ones. Willis lies classically on a sarcophagus looking heavenwards, surrounded by marble. Despite the fact that he was 71 when he died, the effigy shows a young man.

The last chantry is to the most famous Bishop of Winchester: William of Wykeham who founded Winchester College and New College, Oxford. He re-modelled this part of the cathedral, and died in 1404. The chantry is much more showy than his predecessor Edington's, but this is perhaps due more to changes in architectural styles than personal choice. The vault of the chapel is so high that it almost doesn't seem part of it. Wykeham lies looking towards the altar, with three small figures of priests or monks at his feet. The statuettes on Wykeham's chantry are Victorian.

Behind the shop, almost at the west end, is the memorial to Joseph Warton, a headmaster of Winchester College who died in 1801. The sculpture of the schoolmaster and pupils is considered to be one of Flaxman's best. On either side of the main entrance door are two bronze figures, one Charles I the other James I, dating from 1638.

The Saxon Cathedral and Palace. The footings of part of the Saxon cathedral, started in the 7th century but rebuilt in the 10th, can be seen to the north of the west entrance, along with a display board explaining the various phases. Some of the finds are on display in the City

Museum in the Square close by. The Saxon kings of Wessex were crowned and buried in this Old Minster, a monastic church which was also one of the most important places of pilgrimage in England.

In 903 another church, also monastic, and called New Minster was completed, just to the north of the Old Minster, so close that the singing of the choir in one church disturbed the singing in the other. The New Minster moved out to Hyde in 1110. The Saxon Royal palace was probably in the area of the green to the north-west of the Old Minster and Alfred and the later kings of Wessex lived there part of the time. Nothing remains above ground of this palace, which was also used by the Norman kings.

A third monastic church was also started in 903, probably where the Abbey gardens are now. Thus a quarter of the walled area of the town consisted of monastic precincts.

The Close really is an enclosure, to the south of the cathedral. There are three gates. One leads from Colebrook Street in the east along a small stream, lined by brick, flint, and stone walls, a picturesque path which gradually gives views of the east end of the cathedral. The more usual entrance to the Close is from the west end of the cathedral, a path created in 1632 to stop people walking straight through the cathedral to reach the other side. The grassy plot just inside the Close was the site of the monastic buildings of the Benedictine Abbey until the 16th century, but now there is no formal arrangement, simply fine buildings scattered about

Cheyney Court, the Close, Winchester

'garnished with grass and shaded with trees' (John Keats) and all happily free of traffic.

The big arches on the far side were the entrance to the early Norman chapter house and form a fine example of that simple, massive style. The arcading on the wall next to the cathedral is of the same date, originally internal.

Most of the monastic buildings, and the later clergy houses, were demolished in the Civil War, and replaced in the 1660s after the Restoration of Charles II. The brick and stone houses opposite the remains of the Norman chapter house date from the 1660s, but the Deanery attached to the other end of the chapter house has some medieval parts. Facing the first green is the 15th century Prior's Hall, and round the corner the stone porch with three arches is 13th century in its lower parts, with vaults inside. Running from this is the brick 17th century long gallery.

On the east (left) side of the second green is The Pilgrim School – the brick house dating from the 1680s, but the north (left) end is a medieval building, called **Pilgrim Hall** because it may have been used by pilgrims to the shrine of St Swithun. It is open to the public when not in use by the school (free). The short hall has two big wooden supports across the roof dating from around 1300, the earliest hammer-beam roof to survive. Crude heads are carved on the ends of three of the 'hammers'. The hall was the common brewhouse for the Close until the 17th century when it became a stable and coachhouse ★ ★.

Leading off to the west is Dome Alley, four redbrick houses built in the 1660s to replace those demolished in the Civil War. Isaac Walton lived here in his old age, with his son-in-law.

The third gate to the Close is St Swithun's Gate, making a picturesque corner with the timber-framed Cheyney's Court, and lots of greenery. Both house and gate are 15th century.

Just outside the Close, through the gateway, is another gate but this time in the city walls. Kingsgate with the church of St Swithun above has been recorded since the 13th century, but the present structure is 14th century, with Georgian brick arches to the pedestrian entrances. The church is worth walking up to: rather like a hall with small domestic windows. Mostly it dates from the 15th and 16th centuries, with a pretty niche in the north wall towards the altar. The font is half in the wall, and close to it a sad memorial to four infants (shown as babies lying on a single tomb) dating from 1612. The whole area is small scale and charming with small amounts of traffic passing under the church, or through the other gate into the Close.

College Street runs east from Kingsgate, with smaller Georgian houses on one side and mostly gardens running up to the city wall marking the Cathedral Close on the other.

8 College Street, with a first-floor bay window, is the house where Jane Austen died in 1817. (Her gravestone is in the cathedral). The house is not open but a slate plaque records her stay.

Further along College Street is

Winchester College, now a public school, but founded by William of Wykeham, the great Bishop of Winchester, in 1382 for seventy 'poor and needy scholars' and only ten fee-paying pupils. The seventy scholars still live in the old buildings, but there are nearly 600 other pupils who live elsewhere in Winchester. The buildings are like an Oxford or Cambridge college, laid out around courtyards.

One can walk through the two main courts to the chapel every day (free:lists), but rather more can be seen in term time. Guided tours (fee) are offered between April and September. Any part in use at the time of a visit will be closed, so school holidays are the best time to visit.

The first building along College Street is the Headmaster's House, neatly squared flint of 1840. Beyond that the medieval walls start, the small windows being the original ones. 1390s gateway, vaulted and with a fine statue of the Virgin outside. A porter, who will explain what is open and when, adds to the feeling of entering a medieval world. The first court (Outer Court) contained the brewhouse, slaughterhouse and stables for the original, self-contained college, but these have steadily been converted to other uses.

Another original gate leads to Chamber Court, still much as it was when built in the 14th century – supremely picturesque with its varied paving and enclosing buildings dominated by the chapel. The scholars still live in this court. The tower in the corner is the original muniment tower still used for storing documents. Fine glass and metal doors of 1966 lead into the chapel, with firstly the school's memorial to the Crimean War of the 1850s. The main chapel is beautiful, all the structure original, with a huge east window. The stained glass glows in

College Street, Winchester: the house where Jane Austen died

vibrant colours, but all the glass except at the west end is a replacement of the 1820s, when the originals had become blackened by corrosion. One original window was rediscovered, restored and replaced in the chantry chapel at the west end, and shows the quality of the original glass, considered to be the best of its date. The other windows in the chantry have glass of 1500. The chantry carries the fine tower which is seen from all over the college. The two large pieces of tapestry displayed are of about 1500, by tradition made for the christening of Henry VII's eldest son in the cathedral. The chantry has a stone vault, but that of the main chapel is of wood, original to the building and in 1952 repainted in its original colours.

The wooden fittings are almost all of this century, but the scrolled fine and foliaged altar rail is of the 1680s (like that in the Cathedral), and the stalls against the walls are 14th century, with misericords. The stone reredos is 15th century, but with Victorian statues.

To the west of the chapel are steps leading up to the first floor hall, also part of the original foundation and still where the seventy scholars are fed. Yet another portrait of William Wykeham, this one a bit closer to his time, dating from 1597. 1540s panelling, and good 1930s stained glass.

In the passage below the stairs is the famous painting of The Trusty Servant, a compendium of all the virtues. In the vaulted cellar beyond is the College Treasury, occasionally open, with displays of silver, Chinese ceramics and so on.

The Cloisters are part of the original buildings, dating from the 1380s, and full of memorials to Old Wykamists. The alleys are atmospheric. Very unusually the garden in the middle is nearly filled in by Fromonde's chantry of 1420, a chapel on the ground floor and library above. The chapel is handsome, with a complicated vault and 1502 stained glass in the east window. The west window has very effective glass of the 1930s.

The free-standing redbrick building is called School, and was built in the 1680s to house the increasing number of pupils. Fine stone garlands decorate it externally, a 1692 statue of William of Wykeham. The interior is one large panelled room, where the teaching was done.

The Meads or school grounds behind School building are ornamented with big old plane trees, and have an uninterrupted view of St Catherine's Hill. The buildings

TOP *Chamber Court, Winchester College.* BOTTOM *The Chapel, Winchester College*

beyond School are mostly later 19th and 20th century, needed as the school expanded. The Memorial Cloisters, commemorating those who died in the First World War, are entered from Kingsgate Street through Commoner Gate (imitation medieval of 1902), not through the college.

★ ★ ★ ★ *Winchester College, for the original buildings, and the medieval atmosphere.*

At the western end of College Street is the **Wolvesey Palace**. The Bishops of Winchester have lived here since 963 when they moved from the Old Minster. The current palace is one wing of the elegant and classical building, built in the 1680s. Attached to the far end is the late medieval chapel, part of the earlier palace but preserved and used for the new one.

A footpath leads along in front of the 1680s palace to the ruins of the large medieval one (fee:lists). The big range on the eastern side (right as you enter) is the ruin of a large hall and subsidiary buildings of about 1135. The southernmost tower is Wymond's Tower, added later the same century, along with

Wolvesey Palace

the big keep to the north, which in fact only housed kitchens despite its war-like appearance. This eastern part was only half the palace: an even larger block of about 1100 existed on the western side of the site, but only the footings of the northern end are exposed as the building extends under the palace and its gardens. Between the two is Woodman's Gate, also 12th century. After centuries of stone robbing, the ruin was finally repaired in the 1920s with the many tile repairs to the arches etc.

From 1302 Royal visitors didn't stay at the Castle because it had been badly damaged by fire that year and never repaired. Instead they usually took over Wolvesey, the Bishop's Palace, and the court had to be lodged in the Close. Dean Ken refused to house Nell Gwynn in the sacred precincts, but Charles II did not take offence and later gave the bishopric of Bath and Wells to 'the little fellow who would not give poor Nelly a lodging'.

★ ★ *Wolvesey Palace, too ruined to be easy to appreciate.*

High Street runs downhill from West Gate and contains buildings from medieval times onwards in the dense mixture which is the essence of English towns, reflecting their growth and functions.

West Gate has been bypassed, but until 1959 all the traffic passed through it. The townward face is 13th century, and the other 14th century with early key-hole shaped gun-ports. The gate is now a museum (fee:lists) and the entrance is up an atmospheric stone staircase. Displays include armour, the Winchester measures, the graffitti of prisoners held here in the 17th and 18th centuries, and a

finely painted ceiling in classical style originally made for Winchester College about 1554. High Street's hill falls away from the Museum windows, but the view from the roof is even more extensive, with the chalk hills all around ringing the city. Worth going in simply for this view from the roof. ★ ★ ★ Gate and museum.

To the south of West Gate is the site of the medieval castle, built after the Norman Conquest to supplement the Saxon Royal Palace down by the cathedral, and as part of the new Norman military system. Most of the Castle has disappeared, replaced by the courts and the other county buildings. Many of these are flint and stone, Jacobean in style but ranging in date from the 1890s to 1930s. Across the road north from Westgate is County Hall itself, neo-Georgian of 1966, and there are other modern buildings, particularly around the rather odd open space, full of steps, on the Westgate side. The long flight of steps marks the Castle defences – a natural slope adapted by the Normans. Beside the lower Victorian building at the upper level the large footings of part of the Norman Castle are exposed. A circular tower is clear: this was the extreme northern point of the castle which extended southwards to include all the area now barracks.

The Great Hall (free:lists) ★ ★ ★ ★ is the only surviving part of the castle, and is part of the rebuilding of 1222 and 1236 by Henry III who was born and baptised in Winchester. By then the Castle was the only Royal residence in the city. Henry's hall is superb: Pevsner described it as 'the finest medieval hall in England after Westminster Hall'.

The big entrance porch is Victorian,

built in 1845 when the hall was used as the county law courts. These didn't leave until 1974, when they moved to the new building just downhill.

The hall is much larger inside than one expects, a fit setting for a King. Tall Purbeck Marble pillars. At the end where the dais would have been is King Arthur's round table, probably made for King Edward in the 1270s and first painted in 1522 for a visit of Henry VIII. The statue of Queen Victoria was made in 1897. At the opposite end Victorian wall paintings surround fine shiny steel doors of 1981.

The castle was badly damaged by fire in 1302, and was not used by Royal visitors after that. It was besieged and taken by Cromwell in 1645, and later destroyed apart from the hall. The southern part was used as the site of King's House (see the Barracks).

Behind the hall is a tiny reconstructed medieval garden, opened in 1986, with an arbour, fountain and so on. Worth seeing. The Barracks which replaced the rest of the castle loom behind.

Below Westgate the street has plain Georgian, Regency with bow windows and fancier Victorian. Just below the county buildings is a fine horse and rider in bronze by Elizabeth Frink (1975).

The County Chronicle office below the junction with Jewry Street seems not to have changed since the paper's foundation in 1772. The firm moved here in 1813, and just inside is the printing press they used from the 1830s. Their weekly newspaper is as traditional, still having small advertisements on the front page. From just below this the street has been closed to traffic. The former Guildhall is marked by the clock held out over the street on a big wooden bracket (both are 1713). Queen Anne's statue is in the centre of the otherwise plain building.

Opposite is the 16th century, timber-framed God Begot House highly restored on this street frontage, but impressive along the side passage, where the upper stories lean out over the ground floor in characteristic fashion. Inside much timber work survives. Below the Guildhall is an unusual house of yellow brick with a large window on the first floor. Several other Georgian houses around, but opposite is a really fine one of red brick, still preserving its original ground floor with delicate plaster across all its seven bays.

OPPOSITE *The Great Hall, Winchester*

The Butter Cross, High Street, Winchester

The street widens at this point, and the dominant feature is the Butter Cross, built early in the 15th century but drastically restored in 1865. Behind is a 14th century timber-framed house. The Norman Royal Palace was in this area, and it has been suggested that the church of St Lawrence-in-the-Square is on the site of the palace chapel. A narrow passage just before the Butter Cross leads past the church, which has been rebuilt several times, and is more interesting for its position, completely enclosed in shops and other buildings, than for its architecture. The narrower part of High Street below the Butter Cross has on the right a sort of arcade, with the first floor of the buildings held up on various types of pillars and the shops set back behind. Medieval and 18th century houses here, all mixed up. The largest house, timber-framed, with figures of bishops on, is largely bogus.

The middle of High Street is the same sort of mixture. The Greek style former Market House on the corner with Market Street dates from 1857, late for that style. The Guildhall on the right is a dominating Victorian mass, a proper municipal building of alien stone, built in 1871 and the more delicate flint extension in the 1890s. Inside the **Guildhall Gallery**

(free:lists) shows temporary art exhibitions in great variety.

Below the Town Hall the street name changes to Broadway. Rather oddly set in a public park, is Abbey House, Georgian brick with little turrets and castellation. Now the official residence of the Mayor of Winchester, its name recalls the nunnery founded by King Alfred on this site, which disappeared after the Dissolution of the Monasteries. One of Winchester's fine series of small parks is behind the house, with the river and another small stream on its boundaries. The little pretend temple was built in 1751 to conceal a mill from the gardens and so improve the view. Fine iron railings between the park and High Street.

Opposite is **The Crusades Experience** (fee:lists) an exhibition housed in St John's House, part of a medieval hospital which provided accommodation for travellers. The front is 18th century and the inside has been adapted to show scenes from the third Crusade of the 1190s. Life size models etc. The 'talking heads' – models which really appear to talk – are amazingly good, but the quality of the rest does not match. ★

In the middle of the road is the massive statue of King Alfred, appropriate since he refounded the town, but only dating from 1901. More of the Hospital of John below the park, this Victorian bit described in 1850 as 'a handsome building in the Tudor style' which formed 'not only an architectural ornament to the town, but a happy and peaceful retreat for decayed worth or declining age'.

Eastgate (the street – the gate itself was demolished in 1768) leads of to the left with a curve of 1840s stuccoed houses whose fronts wave in and out with big bow windows. Tiny balconies between.

Bridge Street leads on over the River Itchen, the fine Portland stone bridge of 1813 being on much the same site as the original built by St Swithun when Bishop in the 9th century. The **City Mill** straddles the river just upstream from the bridge. The brick and tile building dates from 1744. Open to the public in the summer (fee:lists) and occasionally in the winter. The lowest floor inside is dominated by two sluices where the water-wheels were, and some of the machinery remains. Upstairs is a large room, impressive with bare brick walls. ★ ★ *For mill.*

Beyond a small well-stocked garden fills the island between the two mill streams. Worth seeing. From just down

stream the bridge and mill, along with houses lining the bank, form a famously picturesque view.

Over the bridge is the area known as the Soke. Amongst the Georgian and later buildings are several medieval timber-framed ones. By the roundabout is Old Chesil Rectory, 15th century and massively timber framed. The church of St Peter is medieval with a little 13th century tower, but now used by a theatre group. Nice flint and stone chequering.

To the South of High Street Only one important road leads south from the town centre, **Southgate Street** leading towards St Cross with many Georgian brick houses (some large) for a remarkable distance. The curved building on the corner with High Street is early Victorian by Owen Carter (see Jewry Street) and further along Southgate Street on the same side is a big yellow brick and stucco block of four houses, also designed by him.

Set back from the road on the other side a little way along is Serle's house, a

King Alfred at Winchester

sophisticated redbrick building, the centre brought forward with curved sides. It dates from about 1710 and was almost certainly designed by Thomas Archer (see HALE). **The Royal Hampshire Regimental Museum** is housed in two rooms of the house (free:lists), ★.

The large church beyond was built in 1845, early for so faithful an imitation of medieval. Since 1972 it has been the Record Office. The swerve in the street slightly further out was caused by the road in Saxon times avoiding the blocked Roman gate, and then going back to its original line.

The Square is tiny, and best entered from High Street through a narrow passage. The book shop just beyond the passage has a medieval hall surviving inside at the back. The name covers the road running along parallel with the cathedral green. Lots of Georgian brick buildings, mostly large town houses, but with small groups of shops, cafes and an inn. Along Market Street a much earlier house: the Eclipse Inn, timber-framed originally a rectory. **The City Museum** (free: lists) by the main path to the cathedral, was built in 1903 replacing the old market house. Medium size with good displays on archaeology, especially the excavations in the city, Roman villas etc and wonderful reconstructions of chemist and tobacconist shops. Well worth seeing ★★★ (free: lists).

Great Minster Street facing the other side of the green is full of urban Georgian redbrick, as is the area behind it, a warren of small streets running up the hill to Southgate Street. There are shops and cafes scattered about with a little modern infill, but mostly earlier and all attractive. Good individual buildings include a handsome wall with grills and gates once the entrance to a mason's yard in St Thomas Street, and in Symonds Street Christ's Hospital Almshouses, a long block built in 1607 and still in use.

St Swithun Street and the parallel Canon Street leading back to the Cathedral Close are also good. St Swithun Street bounded on the north by the wall of the close. Kingsgate Street south towards St Cross has many Georgian cottages and houses.

To the North of High Street

Jewry Street retains a dense urban mixture. Amongst the Georgian and Regency houses are many old shop fronts and some notable buildings including, on either side of the mid Victorian

Congregational Church, the Old Gaol built in 1805 – elegant in yellow brick with vermiculated corners (stone carved to look like worm tracks). Further along on the other side a severe early 19th century shop front with simple columns. The Elizabethan restaurant really is of that date. The Italianate library with its little tower and big portico was built in 1836 as the Corn Exchange and was designed by the local architect Owen Carter (1806-1859). The rather fancy Theatre Royal a little further along dates from 1912. The Victorian-looking Roman Catholic church of St Peter surprisingly dates from 1926, although there has been a Catholic church on this site since 1792, when one was built for Dr Milner, the great Winchester historian.

The area between North Walls and the High Street used to be filled with streets of Georgian houses, and the western ones still are, although shops are mixed in with houses now. Parchment Street is a good example, and also has three small chapels, the best being the Edwardian castellated Salvation Army Building. The street to the west, St Peters Street, has 17th and 18th century brick too, and at the northern end a huge brick terrace, yellow on the front and red at the back.

Winchester Heritage Centre (fee:lists) halfway along Upper Brook Street has a good exhibition on the history and architecture of Winchester, and a 20 minute film on the same subjects is shown in summer. A good introduction to the city.★★★

The eastern streets have been destroyed by modern large-scale development, and are now part of the shopping centre. The big flinty church of Holy Trinity (1854) survives.

In Park Avenue, north of North Walls is Winchester Art College with its public gallery (**The Winchester Gallery** – free:lists) towards the north end of the college, next to an odd modern building which is surrounded by a moat. The gallery shows a series of exhibitions through the year. Beyond the college is North Walls Park, with two arms of the river passing through it.

Eastern Suburbs: Wharf Hill, St Giles Hill and Winnal

Wharf Hill. From the City Mill at the bottom of the High Street a riverside path leads down towards Wolvesey Palace. As the river turns the path runs alongside the Close Wall now the best surviving part of the city's medieval defences. Some houses

on the other side back onto the river, and others, particularly modern developments, face it. The big brick Wharf Mill (now flats) is dated 1885 and straddles the river. One footpath leads on beside the Close Wall to College Street, but another leads into Wharf Hill, part of a mixed area including 18th century houses and cottages. The right turn at the end of the road leads back to the river at Blackbridge. Beyond the bridge all seems rural, with horses grazing, but in the background is the tower of Winchester College, with Wolvesey Palace to the right beyond the playing field.

Just below Blackbridge was the Itchen Navigation terminus (see entry), and the redbrick house to the left of Blackbridge looking downstream was the manager's house and warehouse built in the 18th century. A large stuccoed house on the other side of the river is romantic in this setting.

Just down Domum Road a footpath leads to the river, across Wharf Bridge, one of the few surviving Navigation bridges. Here also is Winchester College's boathouse. The path leads downstream, with a pair of cottages right on the river, followed by a few modern houses. Otherwise all is rural, the water-meadows to the right being woody, those ahead on the opposite side without trees. St Catherine's Hill is prominent on the left. The path meets a minor road, and turning right along it leads to the more usual footpath to St Cross (see entry).

St Giles Hill. From the bottom of the High Street leads St John Street, running along the side of St Giles Hill, climbing steadily. Mixed 18th and 19th century houses, mostly small but one earlier timber-framed cottage survives. This is an old suburb, and three-quarters of the way along the street is the medieval church of St John the Baptist. In through the 18th century porch. The shape of the building is somehow urban, probably because inside it is square, without the usual emphasis on the east-west axis. The pillars between nave and aisles are fairly simple Norman. In the north wall are two lancet windows, now blocked, but with fine wall paintings in the reveals – one figure clearly a bishop, the others evangelists, all dating from about 1280. A surprising number of late medieval wooden fittings survive: the 14th century screens between chancel and side chapels, and from the 15th century the pulpit, the screen between nave and chancel and two bench-ends with poppy-heads up by the screen. 1774 Royal coat of arms painted on canvas, and a huge brass chandelier in the middle of the nave dated 1791. The organ nearly fills the north chapel.

★ ★ *Church*

Further uphill, along St John's Street, is a green and around it some larger Georgian houses and The Old Blue Boar, a restored timber-framed house dating from the 14th century.

The top of St Giles Hill was laid out as a park and planted with many trees in 1894, preserved from the late Victorian development which quickly spread around the lower slopes. The park gives panoramic views of the whole city, and also provides a romantic woody backdrop when viewed from the other way. This was the site of St Giles Fair, in the 12th century one of the most important fairs in Europe.

Winnal. The northern part over the river is Winnal, with a few old pubs close to the river, but otherwise mostly modern. The water meadows are now a nature reserve, and the southern parts (which are open to the public) have dense and tall vegetation.

Good for birds.

The Northern Suburbs

Hyde is only just outside the north walls of the city, but seems like a separate place, too dense to be a village but certainly not a suburb. Many redbrick Georgian houses and cottages, all sizes and styles. In 1110 the Benedictine nunnery of the New Minster, by the cathedral, moved here but only one monastic building survives. They brought their chief relic, the bones of King Alfred, with them.

The church of St Bartholomew is in King Alfred Place, off Hyde Street (the main road through the area) and was the parish not the abbey church. A rather recut Norman doorway survives at the entrance, but most of the interior is Victorian imitation Norman. Five superlative little capitals from the ruins of the abbey are displayed on the window sills. They probably came from the cloister and date from about 1130.

Opposite the church the 15th century gateway of the abbey sits amongst modern development, with a few older-looking walls around and a small stream close by. The small building adjoining the gateway is also medieval and has its original floor exposed. The rest of the buildings were demolished after the Reformation, and the County

Gaol (now gone) built on the site in 1787.

Leading out of town are several redbrick Georgian houses among the more modern, and one house dated 1835 in a buff coloured brick. In the middle and back towards the city are several buildings and walls with patches or strips of good stone, presumably robbed from the abbey buildings. More Georgian red brick houses here, the largest being Hyde Abbey House. Opposite, with its decorative 17th century gable end on to the street is **Hyde Historic Resources Centre**, a Georgian house and earlier stone buildings behind now used for museum offices and so on, and often with an exhibition on an archaeological theme open to the public (free:lists). On the same side, even closer in, is Marston's Brewery, with buildings ranging from the 1820s onwards.

The North-Western Suburbs

Weeke was a separate village in medieval times, but is now a picturesque part of the continuous development on the road to Stockbridge, with several older cottages, a Georgian redbrick house and a small church. The road curves at Weeke, with lots of trees, and it is very easy to miss the little church of St Matthew. Most of the detail of the building is 17th century, but the narrow doorway and much of the walls is Norman.

Harestock is huge and mostly modern.

The South-Western Suburbs along Romsey Road

The Peninsula Barracks are entered from above Westgate, just up Romsey Road. They fill three-quarters of the site of the medieval castle, which was taken over in 1682 by Charles II as the site for a huge palace. Sir Christopher Wren designed the building, which was intended to have an avenue to the cathedral, and a hunting park behind, leading up the hill to the top of the downs. When the King died in 1685 only the central block was complete, and this was used as a prisoner-of-war camp, and then from 1793 a barracks. The 17th century building burnt down in 1894, and the rebuilding produced the current barracks which continued in use until the late 1980s. They are redbrick around a large square, and the biggest block incorporates some stonework (principally column bases) from the old building. The high position, overlooking the town, is very impressive.

Two of the Barracks buildings now house museums. First is **The Royal Green Jackets Museum** (fee:lists) and the smaller **Light Infantry Museum** (fee:lists). Both have fine modern displays. The Green Jackets museum is large, tracing the history of the parent regiments from the mid 18th century in North America up to the present day, with videos and other modern display techniques. The huge model of the Battle of Waterloo has 22,000 figures. The Light Infantry Museum displays the history and work of the Regiment which was formed in 1968. ★ ★ ★

Another building has **The Royal Hussars Museum** (fee:lists) and **The Gurkha Museum** (fee:lists) illustrating the history of those regiments. These two museums will open soon after this book goes to press.

In 1863 the increasing development up the hill out of Winchester was recorded: 'to the south, and above the barracks, where only a few years ago were only downs and fields, a new town has arisen, which, for pleasantness and health of position, can find few rivals. Pretty and well-arranged villas, and neat terraces' still fill the area, with Clifton Terrace by the railway only the most prominent part. Variegated terraces and other houses fill the hilly area behind, built of brick, flint or stuccoed, ranging in date from the 1820s to the 1870s. A handsome suburb.

The modern Police Headquarters is next door to the stuccoed prison of 1848 with its prominent gate. Opposite, further up the hill, is the County Hospital, a handsome diapered brick building of 1864, now rather masked by modern additions.

Oliver's Battery is a big suburb to the south-west of Winchester, mostly modern. The name comes from a small earthwork well sited on the top of the hill and now covered with trees and surrounded by development. Oliver Cromwell may well have used it for his guns when he besieged Winchester in 1645, but the earthwork is older.

St Cross is virtually a small village a mile south of Winchester, although today development is continuous from one to the other. In 1136 a grandson of William the Conqueror, Henry de Blois, Bishop of Winchester, founded the St Cross Hospital. This was not a hospital in the medical sense, but a provider of hospitality. Thirteen poor men were to be housed, and another hundred fed daily.

There were four other similar institutions in medieval Winchester, but this is the only one to survive in its original form. St Cross suffered badly in the 13th and 14th century from several Masters who robbed it for their own gain, but the worst excesses were in the 18th century. Francis North, a son of the Bishop of Winchester is thought to have gained as much as 250,000 from his fifty years as Master, letting the hospital's property out at cheap rents if large sums were paid to him personally.

Anthony Trollope is supposed to have based his novel *The Warden* (1855) on the hospital, and legal activity forced the Master to resign the same year. The asset-stripping and the court case left the once rich foundation bankrupt, but reformed.

The hospital is in the water meadows. The short drive leads down to the new Master's house of 1899. Opposite is the 15th century outer gateway. In proper medieval fashion the buildings of this outer courtyard lack formal arrangement, but the inner gatehouse ahead certainly impresses. This was part of Cardinal Beaufort's improvements, built in the 1420s. A statue of him survives in the right hand niche. The gate is vaulted, and inside is the porter's hatch. Here one may demand the St Cross dole, the last remnant of original foundation's intention that 100 poor men should be fed daily. The dole is not offered, but given on request. Inside the gate the quadrangle is supremely picturesque, a perfect piece of Old England. The far side is open, with green views of the water meadows, and on the right are the lodgings for the twenty-five brethren. Those who wear

ABOVE *The lodgings (left) at St Cross*
BELOW *The Brother's Hall, St Cross*
RIGHT *St Cross church*

black are of the Norman foundation, whereas the Beaufort foundation brothers wear red, both in an adapted 16th century style.

The lodgings date from Beaufort's time, the mid 15th century, and are in one long neat block dominated by their regular chimneys. The accommodation is like that of an Oxford or Cambridge college, off staircases.

The left hand side has a long covered passage to the church, of timber with brick and stone, added about 1500. Beyond are the gardens, walled and with a lily pond.

The dominating building is the church, tall and solid. It is part of the original foundation, started about 1160. Inside the impression is of height and solidity. The east end is the earliest part, with zig-zag decoration even on the vaulting. The panels of stained glass in the east windows are late medieval. The side walls were altered in the Victorian restoration, but the stone screens below are 15th century. In the chancel and the south chapel are parts of a superb quality wooden screen with heads in roundels etc, dating from the 1540s.

The south chapel is the most intricate part, with zig-zag everywhere. In the nave the change from transitional Norman to Early English comes, with the western part Early English.

Inside St Cross church

Much of the floor is still covered with medieval tiles, with later small insets for memorials, which are otherwise uncommon. The largest brass in the north transept is to a Master of St Cross who died in 1510. Some of the more domestic buildings are open.

Next to the inner gatehouse is the hall, entered through a fine vaulted porch added by Cardinal Beaufort in the 15th century, with the glass over the inner door showing his arms. The hall is atmospheric, with an open hearth in the middle, screens at the entrance end with a gallery on top and the timbers of the roof exposed. The hall is late 14th century, and is still used for meals on special occasions. Quite a lot of old furniture. Behind are the kitchens and store-rooms, with some large old pewter plates etc and a huge fireplace.

St Cross sits in the water meadows, with good low watery views and a higher one of St Catherine's Hill. The only thing to break the peace is the roar of the Winchester bypass. A path along the river leads north back to Winchester, and is a favourite walk. John Keats spent part of 1819 in Winchester, and on September 19th, inspired by his usual daily walk through the Close, down College Street and through the meadows to St Cross, he wrote one of his most famous poems, 'Ode to Autumn':

Season of mists and mellow fruitfulness
Close bosom-friend of the maturing
    sun.

The old village of St Cross is partly along the eastern side of the main road, but a back street entered from close to the meadows also has Georgian houses and earlier cottages, mostly red brick.

★ ★ ★ ★ *For St Cross, the hospital and its church, a remarkable survival from the middle ages, and the water meadows and walk to Winchester.*

St Catherine's Hill is an Iron Age hillfort just to the south of Winchester. The bold hill with its wooded top is a prominent landmark from many parts of the town. Conversely the hilltop gives supremely panoramic views of the city and beyond.

Access is not easy. On foot across the eastern side of the watermeadows an underpass to the Winchester bypass leads directly to the hill, with a good stretch of the Itchen Navigation including a ruined lock close to the underpass. There is a tiny car park, a layby, on the south bound carriageway of the bypass, and a footpath leads to the hill from the minor road to Morestead.

The steep climb to the top is rewarded by the views. From the southern part, where the main path goes up, St Cross with its hospital and church looks like a model across the watermeadows. Modern Winchester spreads along the hill behind, but trees still dominate. Walking northwards along the ramparts the city proper comes into view, with a long strip of the Itchen Navigation in the foreground at the bottom of the hill, and the long low baulk of the cathedral clear behind. Westwards the view is more rural.

The Iron Age hillfort on the top of the hill has a ditch and single bank which is now a warren for innumerable rabbits. In the middle is a clump of beech, successors to those first planted in 1762 by Militia who were camped nearby. From Norman times until the 16th century there was a large (120ft long) chapel to St Catherine inside the hillfort's defences, and from the 16th century the hillfort was used as a playground by the boys of Winchester College, who still all come in procession to the hill on the first day of the Summer and Autumn terms. On the north side of the clump of trees is the labyrinth, a sort of maze where both paths lead to the centre by very winding routes. This is turf cut, and supposed to date from 1710 but is probably much older.

The valley to the south of the hillfort and the down still have their original chalk downland flowers and plants. Alongside the track which leads up the valley are shallow humps and bumps which are supposed to be the communal graves of those who died of the plague in Winchester.

★ ★ ★ ★ *For the downland.*

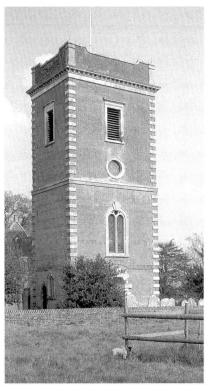

ABOVE *Reading desk, Wolverton*
RIGHT *Wolverton church*
BELOW *Benefactors board, Wonston church*

WINSLADE (E) A hamlet, well wooded with a little Victorian church which looks like a village hall except for the wooden traceried windows.

WOLVERTON (B) In the well-wooded part of north Hampshire off the chalk, still with lots of hedgerows, and with the village scattered about in the style typical of this area. Wolverton House sits in the valley below the church, and is later 18th century.

The church of St Catherine is the best early Georgian church in the county. It was rebuilt in brick in 1716 with a new tower in classical style and the nave of the church cased in brick. The nave looks rather squat because the proportions are still medieval, but the detailing on the transepts and at the east end externally is complex and sophisticated.

Inside the contrast between the 1716 eastern parts and the pretty 15th century wooden roof is charming. The twin reading desks are integrated into the chancel arch and side arches, and the chancel has all its 1716 fittings except the wrought iron screen of which only the end pieces remain. Big wooden reredos, marble floor etc. The elegant font is 1716, as are the box pews. Complicated blank niches etc inside tower.

★ ★ ★ *Church for its date and the completeness of its fittings.*

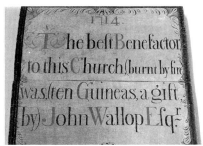

WONSTON (E) A single wandering street with many thatched brick or rendered cottages, well hedged and spread out. The church of Holy Trinity sits down by the river, rather apart from the village. Close to it is the Old House, large but long and low with a Georgian front concealing a medieval house.

The church has twice been damaged by fire – in 1714 and 1908 – but some older parts remain. The tower is of about 1520, and the entrance doorway Norman. Inside are the smooth arches of the 1909 rebuilding of the aisle. The chancel arch is Norman, but the chancel has medieval lower parts with 1909 roof.

WOODCOTT (A) (2 miles north-west of Litchfield) A hamlet high on the chalk, the church of St James and a farm standing alone, with more of the hamlet away to the east at Lower Woodcott, down in the valley. Rural with big farm buildings. The church is 1853, still lit by oil lamps and with 18th century French or Dutch carvings incorporated into the reading desk.

WOODGREEN (G) Big village, denser than most of the western Forest villages. In the middle a tiny triangular green, and off it, beside the modern church of St Boniface, the village hall. It was designed by Herbert Collins, the well-known Southampton architect and decorated inside with fascinating large wallpaintings of 1931, showing the life of the village. Lots of people, including portraits of

Fruit pickers on the wall-paintings in Woodgreen village hall

more than seventy of those living in the village at the time. Well worth seeing (lists : fee) **Castle Hill** to the south has car parks with good views across the Avon Valley and Dorset.

★ ★ ★ *Village hall.*

WOODLANDS (J) (south-east of Bramdean: also called West Meon Woodlands). A scattered hamlet, mostly consisting of later Victorian flint and brick cottages, farmhouse and one large farmyard on the road. At the crossroads, with hardly another building in sight, is the school of similar date, with a tiny wooden spire at the back marking the chapel.

WOODMANCOTE (E) Very rural, and still with woods. A single street which leads nowhere, with the simple church of St James, 1885.

WOOLMER FOREST (F) (2 miles south of Bordon) Cobbet was complaining of the 'infernal Scotch firs and larches' in Woolmer as early as the 1820s, and now much of the area is used by the Army, which has a camp at Longmoor in the middle of the forest. The eastern parts are the most accessible, with many footpaths and some big ponds. Other parts can be walked when there is no firing, and on the A325 just north of Greatham is Woolmer Pond, a large marshy area as well as a large pond, which is home to all twelve English reptiles and amphibians.

Passfield on the north-east is a hamlet just outside the forest with cottages, walls, oasthouses and so on of the local dark brown heathstone. Passfield Common belongs to the National Trust, and is heavily wooded with a great variety of trees. Conford, to the south is similar but wetter, with small greens.

★ ★ ★ *Walking.*

WOOLSTON see **SOUTHAMPTON EAST**

WOOLTON HILL (A) Right on the boundary with Berkshire, on the Greensand with lots of small hills and wriggly roads. A landscape of great variety, good for walking or cycling. Some Georgian brick, but mostly the houses are invisible behind trees and hedges. The church of St Thomas is of 1849, with a stone spire and odd arches inside. Woolton only became a parish in 1850, being split from East Woodhay. To the south-west is Hollington Herb

Garden, a smallish ex-kitchen walled garden filled with all sorts of herbs attached to a nursery (open April-Sept, collecting box). **East End** is a separate part of the village, with 17th century thatched cottages around a triangular green, and several big estate cottages. All brick and flint.

WOOTTON ST LAWRENCE (B/E) Large cottages on large plots informally arranged in the centre, but now with modern infill. There are still several woods, especially to the west, and there used to be more. In 1398 alone the parish supplied 91 cartloads of timber for Winchester cathedral.

The church of St Lawrence is large. The entrance doorway is Norman, as is the north arcade with its rounded arches. The other arcade is 1864, much more exuberant with marble pillars and deeply carved capitals of foliage. The chancel arch has good carvings too on the supports.

In the south aisle is a fine pair of windows engraved by Laurence Whistler. Up by the altar a memorial to Sir Thomas Hooke who died in 1677. The memorial with its superb effigy dates from the 1750s: he had to wait, but they did him proud. Other good monuments too. **Upper Wootton** is high, and a small rural hamlet.

★ ★ *Church for 1864 bits, monument and Whistler windows.*

WORTING (E) Now on the western edge of Basingstoke, but once separate

hamlet. The church of St Thomas of Canterbury is small, of 1848 with a shingled spire. Above the church is the big house, Georgian with a little park. There are other older houses and cottages on the lane to the church and the main road, separated from Basingstoke proper by a bridge under the railway which is long enough to seem like a tunnel.

YATELEY (C) Now very large, with much modern building, but originally a village around the Green. St Peter's church was deliberately set fire to in 1979, gutting the body of the church and damaging the tower. Amazingly the timber porch of 1500 wasn't touched. The tower is unusual – 15th century timber with brick nogging at the bottom and shingles above. Inside the body of the church has been rebuilt as a hall and church, with a separate chapel. Only one wall tablet survives, in the chapel. All plain, with modern fittings. The tower inside has lots of timbers – original arched braces later supplemented with straight scissor braces. The surviving brasses have been re-set in the tower floor.

Yateley Common to the south is the largest surviving area of natural heathland in the north-east of the county, and is now a country park with several car parks off the A30. Birch dominates the woody areas, but there is also oak, rowan, holly, gorse, and lots of heather and bracken. A super area for walking, with several marshy ponds and just hilly enough to give views.

★ ★ ★ ★ *Walking, landscape.* ★ ★ *Church*

A pond on Yately Common

Archaeology

Iron Age House reconstructed at Butser Ancient Farm

In Hampshire it is difficult to produce a complete story of the past from the visible archaeology, not because the settlements and so on aren't there, but because so little can be seen. Successive developments and farming have made the survival of monuments patchy, so there are some areas and periods which have much to show, and others with nothing.

The central chalklands are the best place to see the earliest monuments – the long barrows of the Neolithic and the round barrows of the Bronze Age. A few round barrows are to be found all over the county. All were used for burial, and it is not until the Iron Age that visible settlements occur. The most spectacular are the hillforts, again with the best ones on the chalk. Their high positions give good views, and many still have chalk downland around them. They are the most interesting sites to visit, and the best one of all is Danebury, because excavations over the last twenty years mean that a great deal is known about it. Danebury is also the centrepiece of the fine Museum of the Iron Age at Andover, which should be visited in conjunction with the hillfort.

Butser Ancient Farm has rebuilt Iron Age houses, enclosures and so on, and Iron Age animals and farming. With Danebury, the Museum of the Iron Age and Butser Ancient Farm, Hampshire must be the best place to gain some understanding of the Iron Age.

Martin Down is perhaps the best archaeological landscape in the county, preserving Bokerly Dyke and Grim's Ditch, both ancient boundaries, along with barrows. Old Winchester Hill is also good.

There are two substantial remnants of the Roman occupation of Britain – Silchester with the remains of the town wall, and Portchester with its complete circuit of Roman walls. Portchester is the most spectacular monument in the county, the Roman fort supplemented by a medieval castle in one corner and a church in another.

Martin Down from the air, with (top) Grims Ditch crossing (left to right), Bokerly Dyke more sinuous below, and a trackway cutting across both. Barrows can be seen left below Bokerly and between the track & Grims Ditch.

Netley Abbey

Ruined houses and abbeys somehow fall to archaeology rather than architecture, and the county has several. Netley is a really romantic ruin of an abbey, properly picturesque. Titchfield Abbey and Bishop's Waltham Palace are also worth seeing.

Two odd monuments are difficult to understand. At Breamore and on St Catherine's Hill, Winchester, are mazes – complexes of winding paths cut into the turf. Their date and function are unclear.

★ ★ ★ ★ *Butser Ancient Farm; Danebury; Martin Down; Museum of the Iron Age, Andover; Portchester Castle.*
★ ★ ★ *Bishop's Waltham Palace; Netley Abbey; Silchester Roman Walls; Titchfield Abbey.*

Long Barrows: Martin; Rockborne; and Whitsbury
Round Barrows: Ladle Hill, Sydmonton; Litchfield; Littleton; and Old Winchester Hill.
Hillforts: Beacon Hill; Bury Hill, Anna Valley; Danebury; Ladle Hill, Sydmonton; Old Winchester Hill; Quarley; St Catherine's Hill, Winchester; Stockbridge Down; also Butser Ancient Farm and The Museum of the Iron Age, Andover.
Other enclosures and boundary banks: Abbotstone Down; Castle Hill, Burley; Martin Down; Breamore; Oliver's Battery, Winchester.
Mazes: Breamore and St Catherine's Hill, Winchester.
Roman: Portchester Castle; Rockborne Roman Villa; and Silchester Town Walls.
Medieval ruins: Beaulieu Abbey; Bishop's Waltham Palace; Netley Abbey; Old Basing House; Odiham Castle; Titchfield Abbey; Wolvesey Palace, Winchester. See also Southampton and Winchester for their walls and gatehouses etc.
Museums: many local museums have sections on archaeology (eg Fareham, Portsmouth, Winchester) but only two are devoted entirely to archaeology – Silchester and God's House Tower, Southampton.

Industrial Archaeology

Apart from shipbuilding and other maritime enterprises Hampshire has had few industries, since until this century it was a rural county. Such industry as there was related to agriculture – brewing at places like Horndean, Alton, Winchester and Romsey has left those towns with remnants of the big breweries, and the processing of hops in the east of the county meant that there were many oast houses, particularly prominently at Binstead, Froyle and Kingsley.

Corn mills are another cross between industry and farming, and every village used to have its mill. Many of the buildings survive, Droxford and Horsebridge being good examples, but only a few still work including Botley and Headley. The City mill, Winchester, is the only one formally open to the public, although Botley and Headley can be visited when buying flour.

Surprisingly, considering the large number of rivers in the county offering sites for water mills, there were more than 100 windmills. Only three survive, Langstone and Chalton as part of houses, Bursledon restored to working order and occasionally open to the public. Hampshire has an unusually high number of tide mills because of the many suitable estuary sites and the shelter of the Isle of Wight. Several survive, most notably at Emsworth and Eling. All the machinery survives at Eling, which is open to the public and still produces flour.

Not all mills were for grinding corn. At Whitchurch a big mill used for cloth production survives, still weaving silk and open to the public. Anna Valley near Andover was the home of the Waterloo Iron

In Whitchurch Silk Mill

National Motor Museum, Beaulieu

Works from 1813-1968, and Funtley, near Fareham, was where Henry Cort made his experiments which revolutionised the production of wrought iron. The remains at both places are only slight.

Salt has been produced along the Hampshire coast from medieval times and extensive salterns can still be seen around Lymington in particular.

The large brick industry has left few remains except the many handsome buildings built from its products.

Eastney Pumping Station in Portsmouth is open, and the huge engines are regularly in steam. Twyford Waterworks is also preserved, and occasionally open. The county was important in the development of aeroplanes, especially sea planes and flying boats, and the history of this is well displayed in the Southampton Hall of Aviation. The castle at Calshot has an exhibition on the Schnieder Trophy races, which were based here.

Two museums in the county illustrate the development of motorised transport. The National Motor Museum, Beaulieu has a huge collection of cars, and the Sammy Miller Museum at New Milton is as good for motor cycles.

Canals
Since Hampshire was not an important manufacturing area (and anyway had a long coastline) few canals were built, and those few were not successful. Transport by sea was always more important. The Basingstoke Canal was the longest and most successful, linking the town with the river Wey and thereby London. This has been restored, but there is little left of the other three canals. The Andover-Redbridge has part of its course preserved at Romsey, and there is

one interesting fragment of the Portsmouth canal. The course of the 17th century Titchfield canal and the Itchen Navigation (an improved river rather than a canal) survive. All the interesting remains are described in the Gazeteer. The Basingstoke canal is particularly attractive as it passes through good countryside, with the tow-path providing a winding footpath.

Railways
The county still has a widespread railway system, with many smaller places retaining their original stations.

Early ones include Micheldever, Portchester and Rowlands Castle, with large classical buildings of the 1840s surviving in Southampton (Terminus station) and Gosport, both no longer used by the railways.

Eastleigh was a railway town, created when the locomotive and carriage building works were moved there around 1900. Only the locomotive repairing remains, and this is opened every other year for a popular weekend.

The Watercress line is Hampshire's only preserved railway, running from Alresford to Alton, with steam locomotives. The four stations are well furnished, and the line passes through good countryside, making it a popular attraction.

★ ★ ★ ★ *National Motor Museum, Beaulieu; Sammy Miller Museum, New Milton (motor-cycles); Whitchurch Silk Mill; The Watercress Line.*
★ ★ ★ *Eling Tide Mill; Southampton Hall of Aviation.*
★ ★ *Winchester City Mill; Eastney Industrial Museum, Portsmouth; The Carriage Museum, Breamore.*
Occasionally open: Bursledon Windmill; The Second World War Aircraft Preservation Society, Lasham; Eastleigh Railway works; Twyford Waterworks.
See also *entries for Andover and Redbridge Canal; Basingstoke Canal; and Itchen Navigation. For the Portsmouth Canal see Portsmouth; and for the Titchfield Canal see Hill Head and Titchfield.*

The Watercress Line: Ropley Station

Acknowledgements

Throughout this book I have referred in a rather familiar fashion to several books on Hampshire. The initials VCH are a short reference to a long publication - the *Victoria County History of Hampshire and the Isle of Wight* in five large volumes (1900-1912). This is still one of the most useful historical works on the county, and a good description of Edwardian Hampshire too.

Britton and Bayley produced eighteen volumes on *Beauties of Britain* between 1801-15, a complete description of late Georgian England. Vol 6 includes Hampshire. John Duthy wrote the most interesting of the many topographic books published on Hampshire in the late 18th and early 19th centuries, and I have quoted from his *Sketches of Hampshire* (1839) quite extensively.

Pevsner and Lloyd wrote the Hampshire volume for the Buildings of England series, and readers are referred to them for more detailed information on architecture. I have used the *Guide to the Industrial Archaeology of Hampshire and the Isle of Wight* (ed. Pamela Moore 1984) and *Where to Watch Birds in Dorset, Hampshire and the Isle of Wight* (George Green and Martin Cade 1989), but there is much more information in both books about those subjects.

I have enjoyed all the visiting needed for this book, and all the work in libraries. Working on my native county has been a joy, and I am sorry that the book is finished. I hope I have supplied enough detail for all the places, but I also hope I have not written too much.

Robert Mudie, in the introduction to his three volume *Hampshire* (1838) is conscious of this problem. 'Some may think that I have been rather sparing in the minute details of particular places and objects', but equally the author must try to select. I felt I must try to evaluate as well as describe buildings, villages and landscapes for the intending or actual visitor, and that a colourless un-opinionated description would not do. I apologise to any places I have thereby offended.

Mudie claims 'This description of Hants is an independent work, intended to do equal justice to all the places, features, and interests in the county. For the accomplishment of this object, I have personally collated the documents, and visited the localities; and I have done my best to make the work original, inviting, and useful; though, from its nature it cannot be quite free, either from omissions or mistakes'.

(Mudies' judgement is open to doubt: he was sure the brand new London and Southampton Railway could not compete with the roads or canals, and would anyway cause the county to become infertile because of the reduction in the number of horses kept, and the resultant reduction of the amount of manure available).

With him I apologise for omissions and mistakes, but am grateful to have had the chance to write this book.

I am very grateful to the libraries which have helped me so much during the time I was writing this book. The Dorset County Library (Reference and Lending) have given me their customary cheerful and effective help, and the Local History Library Winchester has also assisted me extensively.

I am also grateful to Christopher Chaplin for his help and encouragement, and the maps; to Mr D B Jeffery for proofing the final version so well and so fast; to Sheena Pearce for her constant word-processing especially in the last frantic weeks of writing; to Pamela Moore for advice on industrial Archaeology; and to all those kind people who answered my enquiries in person or by letters.

The greatest acknowledgement must be to my mother, Betty Draper, who died when this book was virtually complete. She visited many of the places with me, encouraged me with the writing, sorted out all the lists and 'stars', and proofed several versions. I so regret she will not see it complete.

I need hardly express my delight and appreciation of Norman Thomas' photographs, as they are here for all to appreciate. I am very grateful to him for them.

Virtually all of the 400 photographs in the book were taken by Norman Thomas, but there are exceptions, and I am grateful to the following for allowing us to include illustrations for which they hold the copyright: Aerofilms Ltd, 133, top, 205; Basingstoke and Deane Borough Council, 31 top; The Earl of Carnarvon, 35 bottom; The D-Day Museum, 105 bottom; The Duke of Wellington, 105 top right, 182 top; A. F. Kersting, 13, 153, 189, 213; The Mary Rose Trust, 140 top, 140 bottom; The National Motor Museum, 50 centre, 50 bottom; The National Trust, 95 top, 193 top left, 119 bottom; Paultons Park 130 right, 184 top; Lord Romsey, 152 top; The Royal Commission for Historical Monuments, 156, 221 bottom; The Society of British Aerospace Constructors, 75 bottom right; Southampton City Museums, 167 bottom; Whitchurch Silk Mill, 222 bottom right.

Only two of the colour photographs were not taken by Norman Thomas, and I am grateful to the Earl of Carnarvon for allowing the inclusion of the photograph of Highclere Castle and the Captain of *HMS Victory* for the photograph of the *Victory*. John Bartholomew & Son Limited kindly permitted the use of the colour map.

JO DRAPER

The Lists

Contents

These are not lists of what you can see in Hampshire, but lists of the places which have opening times or events which occur at certain times of the year. Further descriptions of most of them can be found under their entry in the Gazetteer, where their map reference letter is also given. Landscapes, villages and towns are not included, but are found in the Gazetteer, and if especially good they are also mentioned in Glorious Hampshire and in the various double page spreads sections on specific subjects. In all cases their map reference letter is given at the start of their entry in the Gazetteer.

Unless otherwise stated the months in the Lists are complete, e.g. March-Sept means March 1st to September 30th. All the information given was correct when this edition of the Guide went to press, but phone numbers are given wherever possible and we would suggest you check opening times in the winter or if you are making a long journey. A lot of work has gone into the Lists, but we have had to rely on advance information, some of which may prove inaccurate. Tourist Information Offices are a good standby and will be happy to help where they can: all of them are shown on the town maps and a list of their addresses is given. We apologise for any mistakes or omissions.

Price Guide: A: 10p-£1, B: £1-£2, C: £2-£3, D: £3-£4, E: over £4. The key gives the price of a single adult ticket, but most places give reductions for children and Old Age Pensioners, some offer family tickets and in some places combined tickets are available for several attractions. Not all of the places charge admission.

Animals, Birds, Butterflies, Fishes

Bird World, south of Farnham on the A325. The best place to see all types of birds. Cafe. 9.30 am-6 pm (earlier in winter) every day except Christmas Day. Price C. (0420) 22140

Butser Ancient Farm: see Archaeology

Finkley Down Farm Park, Andover. Very good for children, lots of farm animals. Cafe. 10.30 am-6 pm, April (or Easter if earlier) to September. Price: B. Andover (0264) 52195

Hawthorns Centre, Southampton Common. Local Natural History. Mon-Fri 10 am-5 pm; weekends in summer 2 pm-5 pm, in winter 1.30 pm-4.30 pm. Free. Southampton (0703)671921

The Hawk Conservancy, Weyhill, near Andover. Superb, especially the displays of birds being flown (not possible when it is raining). Cafe. 10.30 am-4 pm March-October, closing 5 pm in summer. Flying demonstrations 12 noon, 2 pm; 3 pm and 4 pm. Price: C. Weyhill (026477) 2252

Holidays Hill Reptiliary, 2 miles west of Lyndhurst on A35 to Bournemouth. All the New Forest reptiles and amphibians. 8 am-8 pm, April-Sept, but best when sunny. Free.

Longdown Dairy Farm, Ashurst. Modern dairy farm plus farm animals. Best after 2.30 pm when milking starts. 11 am-5 pm daily Easter-October. Price: B. Ashurst (042129) 3326

Marwell Zoological Park, Upham (off B2177 6 miles south of Winchester). Superb zoo, well worth the money. Cafe. 10 am-6 pm every day. Price: E. Owslebury (096274) 407

New Forest Butterfly Farm, Ashurst, Exotic and British Butterflies. Cafe and wagon rides. 10 am-5 pm daily Easter-October. Price: C. Ashurst (04129) 2166

New Forest Owl Sanctuary, Crow, near Ringwood. Very interesting, lots of birds of prey as well as owls. 10 am-5 pm daily, displays at 11 am, 1, 3 and 5 pm. Price: B. Ringwood (0425) 476487

Paulton's Park, for wildfowl, see Miscellaneous

Portsmouth Sea Life Centre, Clarence Esplanade, Southsea. Many types of fish, and octopuses. 10 am-9 pm daily (closing earlier in winter). Cafe. Price: D. Portsmouth (0705) 734461

Sir George Staunton Ornamental Farm, Leigh Park. Very good, with many sorts of animals. 9 am-6 pm daily Easter-October. Price: B (combined tickets with the Sir George Staunton Conservatory available – see gardens) Portsmouth (0705) 453405

Stubbs Farm Trail, Kingsley. Farmland walk. 1 pm-5.30 pm Suns and Bank Hols May-Sept, plus Tues and Wed in August. Teas. Price: B. Borden (04203) 4906

Underwater World, at Birdworld, near Farnham. Tropical aquariums. Open daily Summer 9.30 am-5.30 pm, winter closes 4.30 pm. Price: A. (0420) 22668

Annual Events

Only larger events which happen on the same date every year are listed here: for fetes, flower shows and festivals, Navy Days at Portsmouth, Morris dancing, craft fairs, vehicle or steam rallies, and many other events see the local evening papers, or the weekly *Hampshire County Chronicle*. English Heritatge and The National Trust organise many events at their properties, and all the Country Parks etc have series of guided walks through the year. There are temporary exhibitions at Southampton Art Gallery, The Guildhall Gallery Winchester, John Hansard Gallery, Southampton University and many of the museums.

Late May: New Forest Fair, Brockenhurst; 20 May Wickham Fair.

Mid June: Bishop's Waltham Agricultural Show.

Late June: Fleet Carnival.

Early July: Balloon Festival, Southampton Common; Southsea Carnival; Basingstoke Carnival; Aldershot Army Display.

Mid July: Southampton Carnival; Southampton Show.

Late July: Alton Show; Netley Marsh Steam Rally; Middle Wallop Air Show (every two years: even numbered years); Hampshire Country Fair, Queen Elizabeth Country Park; New Forest Agricultural Show, Brockenhurst; Rushmoor Steam and Vintage Show.

August: Navy Days, Portsmouth; Portsmouth and Southsea Show Southsea Common; Winchester Raft Race, North Walls Park.

September: Southampton Boat Show; Farnborough Air Show (every two years: even numbered years); Alresford Agricultural Show; Romsey Show.

Archaeology and Ruins

Beaulieu Abbey, see houses.

Bishop's Waltham Palace (English Heritage). Big ruins of a big palace. 10 am – 6 pm daily Good Friday-September, rest of year 10 am-4 pm, closed Mons, Tues, Christmas and 1st Jan. Price: B. Bishop's Waltham (04893) 2460

Butser Ancient Farm, see Museums list.

Netley Abbey, Netley (English Heritage). A proper romantic ruin of a medieval Abbey. 10 am-6 pm daily Good Friday-September, weekends in winter 10 am-4 pm. Price: A. Southampton (0703) 453076

Old Basing House, Old Basing. Ruins of the great house, destroyed in the Civil War. 2 pm-6 pm, Wed to Suns, and Bank Hols, April-Sept. Price: A. Basingstoke (0256) 467294

Rockbourne Roman Villa. Footings of the villa and a museum. Good Friday-September weekdays 2 pm-6 pm. Price: A. Rockbourne (07253) 541

Silchester see Museums – walls always open.

Titchfield Abbey (English Heritage) Ruined house converted from abbey. 10 am – 6 pm daily Good Friday-September. Price: A. Titchfield (0329) 43016

Wolvesey Palace, Winchester (English Heritage). Large but very ruined. 10 am-6 pm daily Good Friday-September. Price: A. Winchester (0962) 54766

Castles, Forts

Calshot Castle (English Heritage) Henry VIII fort, with good displays. 10 am-6 pm daily Good Friday – 30 Sept. Price: B. Southampton (0703) 892023

Fort Brockhurst, Gosport. The best of the 1860s forts. 9.30 am-6 pm Mon-Sat, 2-4 pm Suns, April – Sept; 9.30 am-4 pm Tues-Sat, 2-4 pm Suns in Winter. Price: B. Gosport (0705) 581059

Fort Nelson, Ports Down. Palmerstonian Fort, now an outpost of the Royal Armouries, with lots of guns. 12 noon – 4.30pm weekends and Bank Holidays Easter-October. Price: B. Fareham (0329) 233734

Hurst Catle (English Heritage) Henry VIII fort with big later additions. Boats from Keyhaven every half hour. 10 am-6 pm daily Good Friday-September, weekends in winter 10 am-4 pm. Price: B (ferry extra: also B). Milford-on-Sea (05904) 2344

Portchester Castle (English Heritage) One of the best English castles – Roman and medieval. 10 am-6 pm daily Good Friday – September: winter 10 am-4 pm, closed Mons, Xmas period and 1 Jan. Price: B. Portsmouth (0705) 378291

Southsea Castle, Clarence Esplanade. Henry VIII and later, fine position and good displays. 10.30 am-5 pm daily except Xmas period. Price: B. Portsmouth (0705) 827261

Spitbank Fort, off Southsea. Palmerstonian artificial island in the Solent. Cafe. Weekends and school holidays Easter-October, with ferries from Gosport Pontoon and Clarence Pier every 75 minutes, 11 am-5 pm, weather permitting. Price: D (including ferry). Fareham (0329) 664286 or (for ferries) (0983) 64602

Country Parks

(Only those things with opening times eg exhibitions are listed: the parks are open at all times).

Farley Mount Country Park. Free, and free parking.

Itchen Valley Country Park, south-west of Eastleigh. Visitor Centre and teas weekends all year, daily except Mon and Tues in school holidays. Free. Southampton (0703) 466091

Lepe Country Park. Cafe. Car park charge April-Sept. Southampton (0703) 899108

Queen Elizabeth Country Park, 4 miles south of Petersfield. Visitor Centre and Cafe. 12 am-6 pm daily March-Oct, Suns only winter. Butser Hill car park price: A. Visitor centre and Queen Elizabeth Forest car park price: B. Portsmouth (0705) 595040

Royal Victoria Country Park, Netley. Visitor Centre 10.30 am-5 pm Tues-Sun Easter-Oct., Sat and Sun only in winter. Price: A. Cafe all year except Jan. Car park charges. Southampton (0703) 455157

Upper Hamble Country Park. Car Park charges April-Sept. Cafe Easter-Oct at Hampshire Farm Museum, inside park. Botley (04892) 787055

Wellington Country Park, Riseley. 10 am-5.30 pm March-October weekends in winter. Price: C. (0734) 326444

Nature Reserves

Titchfield Haven Guided Walks only available on Fris, Sats and Suns at 9.30 am and 1.30 pm. Price: B. Stubbington (0329) 662145

Gardens

Bohunt Manor, Liphook. Lake with ducks etc. Good trees. 9 am-5 pm or dusk, Mon-Fri, all year. Occasional Sun too. Price: B. Liphook (0428) 722208

Bramdean House, Bramdean. Varied and good garden. Occasional Sunday afternoons through spring and summer (also by appointment). Price: A. Bramdean (096279) 214

Exbury Gardens, 2½ miles south-east of Beaulieu. Huge, with wonderful rhododendrons, azaleas etc, but varied enough to be good at all seasons. Teas. 10 am-5.30 pm early March to early July, early September to late October. Prices: Spring: C; Autumn: B. Southampton (0703) 891203

Furzey Gardens, Minstead. Very varied, good flowering trees and shrubs. Forest cottage open and craft gallery. Daily 10 am-5 pm (or dusk in winter) all year (except Xmas and Boxing day). prices: B Mar-Oct; A Nov-Feb. Southampton (0703) 812464

Gilbert White's garden see The Wakes, Selborne under Museums list.

Greatham Mill, 5 miles north of Petersfield. Cottage style garden, with stream. Interesting. 2-6 pm Suns and Bank Hols mid April-late Sept. (also by appointment). Price: A. Blackmoor (04207) 219

Hackwood Park, The Spring Wood, one mile south of Basingstoke. Good woodlands, spring bulbs etc. Some Sundays late April-May, and October. Price: A. Basingstoke (0256) 23107

Hillier Gardens and Arboretum, Ampfield. Huge, thousands of flowering trees and shrubs, and much more besides. Wonderful value. Teas. Weekends and bank hols, April-Oct. 10.30 am-5 pm Mon-Fri all year. 10.30 am-6 pm weekends and Bank Holidays March-mid November. Open some summer evenings too. Price: B. Romsey (0794) 68787

Houghton Lodge, 1½ miles south of Stockbridge. Interesting garden by the River Test. Hydroponicum. Teas. Easter Sun, Bank Hols. 10 am-12 noon, 1-4 pm daily except Wed and Thurs, March-Sept. Other times by appointment. Price: B, more for hydroponicum. Andover (0264) 810177

Jane Austen's garden see Jane Austen's House, Chawton under Museums list.

Jenkyn Place, Bentley. One of the best. Large. 2-6 pm, Thurs to Suns, plus Bank holiday Mondays, mid April to early Sept. Price: B. Bentley (0420) 23118

Longstock Water Gardens, Longstock, 3 miles north of Stockbridge. Only opened infrequently, on Suns, (see local papers) Price: B. Andover (0264) 810894

MacPennys, Bransgore. Dense woodland garden. 9 am-5 pm Mon-Sat, 2-5 pm Sun, all year except Christmas hols. Price: collecting box. Bransgore (0425) 72348

Mottisfont. Superb when roses out. See Houses list.

Petersfield Physic Garden, High Street, Petersfield. Open daily. Free.

Queen Eleanor's Garden, Castle Hall Winchester. Small medieval recreation. 10 am-5 pm daily except winter weekends close at 4 pm. Free. Winchester (0962) 841841

Sir George Staunton Estate, Leigh Park. The Conservatory with tropical rain-forest flora. Teas. 11 am-5 pm every day except Xmas day. Price: B. Portsmouth (0705) 452110. The Gardens daily, free

Spinners, Boldre. Superb woodland garden. 10 am-5 pm daily except Mon, late April – August, (also by appointment) Price: A. Lymington (0590) 73347

Tudor House Garden, Tudor House, Southampton. Interesting Tudor garden: opening times and other details as Tudor House (see Museums list)

Wyck Place, 3 miles east of Alton. Fine spring garden, 2-5 pm weekends in February and early March. Price: A.

See also Beaulieu, Highclere Castle, Hinton Ampner, Stratfield Saye, and Rotherfield Park in the Houses list. All have gardens worth seeing.

See also the National Gardens scheme annual pamphlet which gives all the gardens open in the county, including smaller ones and those only open briefly which are omitted here.

Houses

Alresford House, Old Alresford. Georgian, built by Admiral Rodney. 2-6 pm Wens-Suns in August, Teas. Price: B. Alresford (096273) 2843

Avington Park, 4 miles north-east of Winchester. Georgian and earlier. Teas. Suns and Bank Hols. 2.30-5 pm Sats, Suns and Bank Hols May-Sept. Price: B. Itchen Abbas (0962 78) 202

Beaulieu House, National Motor Museum, grounds and abbey. Cafe. 10 am-6 pm daily May-Sept, 10 am-5 pm October-May; closed Xmas. Price: E. Beaulieu (0590) 612345

Breamore House. Elizabethan, with Carriage and Countryside Museums. Cafe. Easter and April 2-5.30 pm, Tues, Wed and Sun; May, June, July and Sept. Tues-Thurs, Sat, Sun and Bank Hols; August daily. Price: D Downton (0725) 22468 or 22233

Broadlands, near Romsey. Home of Palmerston and Mountbatten. Cafe. 10 am-4 pm Easter-September daily except Mon (open Bank Hols). Price: D. Romsey (0794) 516878

Charles Dickens' birthplace, Portsmouth, see Museums list.

Gilbert White's house see The Wakes in Museums list.

The Grange, Northington (English Heritage). Ruined Greek style house of 1810. Exterior only. 9.30 am-6.30 pm daily in summer, 9.30 am-4 pm winter. Free. Alresford (096273) 4872

Highclere Castle. Vast Victorian mansion. Cafe. 2-6 pm daily July-Sept. Price: D. Newbury (0635) 253210

Hinton Ampner (National Trust). Recent 'Georgian', with fine furniture and gardens. Gardens open 1.30-5.30 pm Wed to Sun Easter-September, house Tues and Wed only, plus Sats and Suns in August. Price: C for house and gardens. Dorking (0372) 53401

Jane Austen's House, Chawton see Museums list

Medieval Merchant's House, 58 French Street, Southampton (English Heritage). 13th and 14th century townhouse, superbly furnished with reproduction medieval furniture etc. 10 am-6 pm daily Good Fri or 1st April (whichever is earlier) – September. Winter 10 am-4 pm Tues-Sun. price: B. Southampton (0703) 221503

Mottisfont Abbey (National Trust) Superb rose gardens, only two rooms of the house opened. 2-6 pm daily April-September for gardens, rose garden opened 7-9 pm Tues-Thurs and Suns in rose season (phone to check). House Tues, Wed and Thurs only. Price: B. Lockerly (0794) 40757

Rotherfield Park, East Tisted. 19th century house and gardens. 2-5 pm Spring and Summer Bank Hol Suns and Mons, Sun-Thurs in August. Price: C (gardens only A). Tisted (042058) 204

Stratfield Saye. The Duke of Wellington's country house, with good grounds and exhibition. Cafe. 11.30 am-5 pm daily except Fri May-September. Price: D. Basingstoke (0256) 882882

Tudor House, Southampton, see Museums list

The Vyne, 4 miles north of Basingstoke. (National Trust). The most interesting house in the county, early 16th century adapted in the 17th and 18th centuries. Cafe. 1.30-5.30 pm Tues-Thurs, Sat and Sun Easter-mid October; Bank Hol Mon 11 am-5.30 pm, but closed following Tues. Price: C. Basingstoke (0256) 881337

See also: Buckler's Hard and Furzey Gardens, Minstead for cottages; Hampshire Farm Museum, King John's House, Romsey and Fareham Museum for other houses.

Mills

Bursledon Windmill, Bursledon. Opening summer 1990. Contact Eastleigh Museum, The Citadel, 25 High Street, Eastleigh SO5 5LF for times etc.

Eling Tide Mill, Eling Toll Bridge. A working tide mill, well worth seeing. 10 am-4 pm Wed-Sun, all year. Price: A. Check demonstration times by phoning Southampton (0703) 869575

Whitchurch Silk Mill, Winchester Street. 1800 mill still weaving silk. Well worth seeing. Teas. 10.30 am-5 pm Tues-Sat plus Bank Holidays all year, plus summer Sun. Price: B. Whitchurch (0256) 893882

Winchester City Mill, Water Lane. 1.45-4.30 pm Tues-Sat (and Bank Hol Mons) April – 15 Oct. Price: A. Winchester (0962) 53723

Other Industrial Archaeology

Basingstoke Canal, The John Pinkerton canal boat offers trips on the canal, often based at Colt Hill, Odiham May-Sept. Sun afternoons and Bank Hol Mons. Price: C. Farnborough (0252) 549037. Canal Manager: Alderholt (0252) 313810

Twyford Waterworks, Twyford Waterworks Trust, 10 High Firs Gardens, Romsey, Hants SO51 8QA. Currently two open days a year – Sundays in May and Oct, but also parties by arrangement and visitors welcome alternate Sundays when volunteers are working at the restoration. Price: A.

The Watercress Line, preserved steam railway between Alton and Alresford. Trains running Sun most of the year, weekends and some weekdays Easter-October, Christmas school holidays; nearly daily in June and July; daily in August. Return fare from Alton to Alresford: E. Alresford (0962) 733810 or 734200. timetable only Alresford (0962) 734866

See also on Museums list: Buckler's Hard; Eastney Industrial Museum, Portsmouth; Southampton Hall of Aviation.

Museums

Note: all museums closed at Xmas

Aldershot
Aldershot Military Museum, Queen's Avenue. The history of the Army at Aldershot. Good displays. 10 am-5 pm daily March-October; 10 am-4.30 pm Nov-Feb. Closed 24-26 Dec and New Year. Price: A. Aldershot (0252) 314598
Airborne Forces Museum, Browning Barracks. Interesting. 10 am-4.30 pm daily except Mon. Price: A. Aldershot (0252) 24431 extn 4619
Army Physical Training Corps Museum, Queen's Avenue. PT and the Army. 10 am-noon 2-4.30 pm Mon-Fri (not Bank Hols) Free. Aldershot (0252) 24431 extn 2131
Royal Army Dental Corps Museum, Evelyn Woods Road. History of Dentistry. 10 am-noon 2-4 pm Mon-Fri (not Bank Hols). Free. Aldershot (0252) 24431 extn 2782
Royal Corps of Transport Museum, Buller Barracks. Very good displays. 9 am-noon, 2-4 pm Mon-Fri (not Bank Hols) Free. Aldershot (0252) 24431 extn 3834
Queen Alexandra's Royal Army Nursing Corps Museum, Royal Pavilion. Interesting. 9 am-12.30 pm Tues-Thurs, 2-4.30 pm Tues and Wed. By appointment Mon and Fri. Free. Aldershot (0252) 24431 extn 4301
Army Catering Corps, Army Veterinary Corps and Royal Army Medical Corps Museums currently closed.

Alton
The Allen Gallery, Church Street, Alton. Pottery, porcelain and paintings. 10 am-5 pm Tues-Sat. Free. Alton (0420) 82802
The Curtis Museum, High Street. Very good local history and natural history. 10 am-5 pm Tues-Sat. Free. Alton (0420) 82802

Andover

Museum of the Iron Age, superb, heartily recommended. In the same building as Andover Museum and same opening times. Price: A.

Andover Museum, 6 Church Close. Good local museum. 10 am-5 pm Tues-Sat. Free. Andover (0264) 66283

Basingstoke

Willis Museum and Art Gallery, Old Town Hall, Market Place. Clocks, local history etc. 10 am-5 pm Tues-Fri, 10 am-4 pm Sat. Free. Basingstoke (0256) 465902

Beaulieu

National Motor Museum, Beaulieu (see also houses and ruins). The best motor museum anywhere. Cafe. 10 am-6 pm daily Easter-Sept; 10 am-5 pm daily October-Easter. Closed Xmas. Price: E. Expensive but worth it (includes house, grounds and abbey). Beaulieu (0590) 612123

Breamore Countryside Museum and Breamore Carriage Museum see houses list

Bishop's Waltham Museum, Brook Street. Small but good. 2.30-5 pm Suns and Bank Hols April-Oct. Price: A. Bishop's Waltham (04893) 4970 or 2365 or 5500

Buckler's Hard, Maritime Museum and 18th century cottage displays. One of the best. Cafe. 10 am-6 pm daily Easter-Spring Bank Holiday; 10 am-9 pm daily Spring Bank Hol-Sept. 10 am-4.30 pm daily in winter. Price: B. Beaulieu (0590) 612123

Butser Ancient Farm, Nexus House, Gravel Hill, Horndean. PO8 0QE. Currently at Queen Elizabeth Country Park (see entry) but moving south to Windmill Hill. 2-5 pm Mon-Sat, 10 am-6 pm Suns. Price: B. Horndean (0705) 598838

Jane Austen's House, Chawton. Many relics in the house where she lived her last sixteen years. 11 am-4.40 pm daily April-Oct. Wed-Sun Nov, Dec and March, Sat and Sun Jan and Feb. Closed Xmas. Price: A. Alton (0420) 83262

Eastleigh Museum, High Street. Small with modern displays. 10 am-5 pm Tues-Fri, 10 am-4 pm Sat. Free. Southampton (0703) 643026

Emsworth Museum, The Fire Station, North Street. Small but interesting. 10.30 am-4.30 pm Sats and Bank Hols, 2.30-4.30 pm Suns, Easter-Oct. Price: A. Emsworth (0243) 373780

Fareham Museum, Westbury Manor, 84 West Street. Good local history. 10 am-5 pm Mon-Fri, 10 am-4 pm Sat, all year; 12 noon-4 pm Sun May-Sept. Free. Fareham (0392) 824895

Sherings Fordingbridge Museum, off Church Street (no. 53). Good town museum. No fixed opening times: call at office or house opposite, or telephone to check. Price: A. Fordingbridge (0425) 53019 or 52276

Gosport

Gosport Museum, Walpole Road. Good displays. 9.30 am-5.30 pm Tues-Sat, 1-5 pm Sun in May-Sept. Free. Gosport (0705) 588035

Royal Navy Submarine Museum, Haslar. Several submarines, and the history of underwater vessels. Cafe. 10 am-4.30 pm daily April-Oct; 10 am-3 pm Nov-March. Closed 24 Dec-2 Jan. Price: C. Gosport (0705) 52917

Hampshire Farm Museum, Upper Hamble Country Park. Superb, a proper farm with animals, farmhouse and buildings. Cafe. 10 am-6 pm (5 pm in winter) April-Dec. Weekends only Jan/Feb. Price: B. (04892) 87055

Havant Museum, East Street. Interesting. 10 am-5 pm Tues-Sat. Closed Bank Hols. Free. Havant (0705) 451155

Lasham

Second World War Aircraft Preservation Society Museum, Lasham Airfield, near Alton. Several aircraft etc. Sundays. Donation.

Lyndhurst

The New Forest Museum, History and Natural history of the New Forest. 10 am-5 pm, some evening openings in summer. Price: B. Lyndhurst (042128) 3914

The Army Flying Museum, Middle Wallop. Large and interesting. 10 am-4.30 pm daily, closed over Xmas. Price: C. Andover (0264) 62121 extn. 421

Sammy Miller Museum, Gore Road, New Milton. Good motor-cycle museum.

10.30 am-4.30 pm daily April-Oct, Nov-March Sats and Suns only. Price: B. New Milton (0425) 619696

The Teddy Bear Museum (with shop) 38 Dragon Street, Petersfield. Open shop hrs, free. Petersfield (0730) 65108 or 66962

Portsmouth

Combined tickets are available for some of the museums, eg D-Day and the Royal Marines Museum; *Mary Rose, Victory,* and the Royal Navy Museum. Ask at the desk, as these are useful money-savers.

City Museum and Art Gallery, Museum Road. Crafts etc. 10.30 am-5 pm daily except Christmas period. Price: A. Portsmouth (0705) 827261

Charles Dickens Birthplace Museum, 393 Old Commercial Road. Worth seeing both for Dickens and the house. 10.30 am-5 pm daily March-Oct. Price: A. Portsmouth (0705) 827261

Cumberland House, Eastern Parade. Good Natural History and Geological displays. Butterfly house May-Oct as well. 10.30 am-5.30 pm daily except Xmas Day and Boxing Day. Price: A. Portsmouth (0705) 827261

D-Day Museum, Clarence Esplanade. Extremely good. 10.30 am-4.30 pm daily except Christmas period. Price: C. Portsmouth (0705) 827261

Eastney Industrial Museum, Henderson Road, Eastney. Beam engines etc. 1.30-5.30 pm daily April-Sept, first Sun of each month in winter. In steam first Sun in month. Price: A. Portsmouth (0705) 827261

HMS Victory, The Dockyard. Superb. 10.30 am-5.30 pm Mon-Sat, 2-5 pm Sun. Price: C. Portsmouth (0705) 839766 or 750521

HMS Warrior, The Dockyard. Superb. 10.30 am-4.30 pm daily March-Oct. 10.30 am-4 pm Nov-Feb. Closed Christmas Day. Price: C. Portsmouth (0705) 839766

Mary Rose. The Dockyard. The ship and its fine museum. 10 am-5.30 pm summer, 10.30 am-5 pm winter, daily except Christmas Day. Price: C. Portsmouth (0705) 750521

Museum of Dockyard Apprentices, Unicorn Training Centre, Unicorn Road. 10 am-1 pm, Navy Days and April-Sept. occasionally weekdays. Free. Portsmouth (0705) 822571

Old Portsmouth Toy and Doll Museum, Harbour Station Arches. Small. 10 am-5 pm daily. Price: A. Portsmouth (0705) 385995

Royal Marines Museum, Eastney Barracks. Very good. 10 am-5.30 pm daily Easter-Sept; 10 am-4.30 pm Oct-Easter. Price: B. Portsmouth (0705) 819385

Royal Naval Museum, The Dockyard. One of the best. Cafe. 10.30 am-5 pm daily, possibly closed some lunch-times and closed Christmas period. Price: A. Portsmouth (0705) 839766

Southsea Castle, Clarence Esplanade. Worth seeing. 10.30 am-5 pm daily except Christmas period. Price: B. Portsmouth (0705) 827261

Rockborne Roman Villa, with museum. 2-6 pm weekdays. 10.30 am-6 pm Sat and Sun, April-Oct., 10.30 am-6 pm every day July and Aug. Price: A. Rockborne (07253) 541

Silchester (Calleva) Museum, Silchester Common. Daylight hours, every day. Free. (0734) 700362

Selborne
Romany Folklore Museum, Limes End Yard, High Street, Museum and workshop repairing living vans. Good. 10.30 am-5.30 pm most days Easter-Sept. Price: A. Selborne (042 051) 486

The Wakes: Oates Memorial Library and Museum, and The Gilbert White Museum, High Street. Scott's Antarctic expedition, African explorations, and Gilbert White the naturalist. 12 noon-5.30 pm daily except Mon, open Bank Hol Mon. Price: B. Selborne (042 050) 275

Southampton
Bargate. Medieval town gate and folk life. Currently closed, but normally opening times as God's House Tower. Free. Southampton (0703) 224216/632493

City Art Gallery, Civic Centre. Superb gallery. 10 am-5 pm Tues-Fri; 10 am-8 pm Sat; 10 am-4 pm Sun. Free. Southampton (0703) 832769 or 231375

God's House Tower, Winkle Street. Good archaeology and good building. 10 am-noon, 1-5 pm. Sat. Close at 4 pm Sun 2-5 pm. Free. Southampton (0703) 224216/632493

John Hansard Gallery, University, Highfield. Temporary exhibitions. 10 am-6 pm Mon-Sat. Free.

Maritime Museum, Wool House, Bugle Street. Good displays and good building. 10 am-1 pm, 2-5 pm. Sat close at 4 pm.

Sun 2-5 pm. Free. Southampton (0703) 224216/632493

Medieval Merchant's House, French Street see Houses list.

Southampton Hall of Aviation, Albert Road South. Very good. 10 am-5 pm Tues to Sat. 12 noon-5 pm Sun and Mon in school holidays. Price: B. Southampton (0703) 635830

Tudor House Museum, St Michael's Square. House and displays very good. 10 am-1 pm, 2-5 pm Mon-Fri. Sats closes at 4 pm; Suns 2-5 pm Free. Southampton (0703) 224216/632493

Winchester
City Museum, The Square. Archaeology and history of Winchester. Well worth seeing. Times as Westgate Museum. Free. Winchester (0962) 863064

Guildhall Gallery, The Broadway. Temporary Exhibitions. 10 am-5 pm Tues-Sat; 2-5 pm Mons and Suns. Closed Mon Oct-March. Free. Winchester (0962) 852874

Hyde Historic Resources Centre, Hyde. Temporary Exhibitions. 9 am-5 pm Mon-Fri. Free. Winchester (0962) 840222 extn 2269

The Crusades Experience, St John's House, The Broadway. Modern technology of 'Talking heads'. 10 am-5 pm daily. Price: C. Winchester (0962) 856706 or 841598

The Ghurka Museum, Peninsular Barracks. Opening summer 1990. 10 am-5 pm Mon-Sat, 12 noon-4 pm Sun. Price: A or B. Winchester (0962) 842832

The Light Infantry Museum, Peninsular Barracks. The history of the regiment since 1968. times as Royal Green Jackets. Price: A. Winchester (0962) 864176

The Royal Green Jackets Museum, Peninsular Barracks. Good displays. 10 am-5 pm Mon-Sat, 12 – 4 pm Sun. Price: B. Winchester (0962) 863846

The Royal Hampshire Regimental Museum, Serle's House, Southgate Street. Smallish. 10 am-12.30 pm, 2 -4 pm Mon-Fri; 12 – 4 pm Sat, Sun and Bank Hols. Easter-October. Free. Winchester (0962) 86384.

Westgate Museum, High Street. Good for the building, its vies and contents. 10 am-5 pm Mon-Sat, 2-5 pm Sun April-Sept; closed Mons, and Suns closes 4 pm October-March. Price: A. Winchester (0962) 869864

Winchester Cathedral Library and Triforium Gallery, inside the cathedral. Fine new disys, the Winchester Bible and

the library. 10.30 am-1 pm, 2-4.30 pm every day except Suns Easter-Sept, winter Wed and Sat only. Price: A. Winchester (0962) 853137

Winchester Gallery, Winchester Art College, Park Avenue. Temporary exhibitions. 10 am-4.30 pm weekdays all year, Sats in term time 9 am-12 noon. Free. Winchester (0962) 842500

Winchester Heritage Centre, 52/54 Upper Brook Street. Good displays on the history and buildings of the city. 10.30 am-12.30 pm, 2-4 pm Tues-Sat, 2-4 pm Sun. Film shown April-Oct. price: A. Winchester (0962) 864292

For other exhibitions see Stratfield Saye and Broadlands under houses list; Fort Nelson under forts list; Royal Victoria Country Park, Netley.

Miscellaneous

Fawley Power Station, Fawley. Public open day each year at end of July, or book a tour. Fawley (0703) 893051 extn 244

Ordnance Survey, Maybush, Southampton. To see exhibition or a guided tour phone Southampton (0703) 792608 or 792354

Paulton's Park, Ower, Romsey, Southampton. Children's amusement park, with, as well, wildfowl, village life museum, animals, etc. Cafes. 10 am-6.30 pm March-September, closes earlier spring and autumn; October weekends and half-term week. Price: E. Southampton (0703) 814442

Southsea Model Village, Lumps Fort, The Esplanade. 10 am-sunset, March-October. Price: A. Portsmouth (0705) 294706

17th century Village, Howe Road, off Grange Road, Gosport. Reconstructed village, open for a few days May-Sept. each year. Price: C. Information from Fareham or Gosport Tourist Information Offices: Fareham (0329) 824896; Gosport (0705) 522944

Vinyards
Lymington Vinyard, Wainsford Road, Pennington Village, Lymington. Vinyard walk, slide show, herb garden, wine tasting. 10.30 am-4.30 pm daily except Sat, May-Sept. Price: B. Lymington (0590) 672112

Wellow Vinyards, Merryhill Farm, Tanners Lane, East Wellow. Guided tours. Woodland walk. Cafe. 11 am-11 pm Mon-Sat, 12 noon-2.30 pm and 7.30 – 10.30 pm Sun. Price: C. Romsey (0794) 830880

Other Buildings

Portsmouth Garrison Church, Old Portsmouth (English Heritage). Ruined apart from the chancel, which is fine. 10 am-6 pm daily Good Friday-Sept. Price: A.

Ringwood Meeting House, by Furlongs Car Park. Interesting building of 1727 with all its original fittings. Open daily in summer except Sun and Mon. In winter Wed mornings and possibly other days. Price: A

Sandham Memorial Chapel, Burghclere, near Newbury (National Trust). Built to house wallpaintings by Stanley Spencer. 11 am-6 pm (or dusk if earlier) daily all year. Closed Xmas and New Year. Price: A. Burghclere (063527) 394 or 292

Woodgreen Village Hall, Woodgreen near Fordingbridge. Amazing 1931 wallpaintings. No regular opening hours. Price: A. to book or find out when open phone Downton (0725) 22288 or 22221

Winchester
Pilgrim Hall, The Close, Winchester. Small medieval hall with hammer-beam roof. Daily when not in use by the school. Free. Winchester (0962) 854180
St Cross, just outside Winchester. Splendid Norman church and medieval hospital buildings. 9.30 am-12.30 pm. 2-6 pm daily except Sun in summer, 10.30 am-12.30 pm, 2-5.30 pm daily except Suns in winter. price: A. Winchester (0962) 51375

The Great Hall, The Castle, Winchester. The second best medieval hall in the country. 10 am-5 pm daily, but winter weekends 10 am-4 pm. Sometimes closed when used for other purposes. Free. Winchester (0962) 841841
Winchester College. Super medieval buildings. The public may walk through the two courts to the chapel from 10 am-4 pm (6 pm in summer) daily except Sunday. Suns 2-4 pm (6 pm in summer). In term times the Cloisters and Fromond's Chantry may also be seen. Guided tours (Price: B) are offered from April to September every day at 11 am, 2 and 3.15 pm. The Treasury is open some Suns and Bank Holidays 2-4.30 pm. If in doubt as to what is open (rooms in use are not seen) ask the porter at the gate. Winchester (0962) 64242

Tourist Information Centres

Very good for supplying information, by post, telephone or visit.

*Open part of the year, usually summer

Aldershot, Military Museum, Queen's Avenue, GU11 2LG (0252) 20968

Andover, Town Mill car-park, Bridge Street, SP10 1BL (0264) 24320

Basingstoke. Willis Museum, Old Town Hall, Market Square, RG21 1QD (0256) 817618

Beaulieu, National Motor Museum, SO42 7ZN (0590) 612345

Eastleigh, Town Hall, Leigh Road, SO5 4DE (0703) 641261

Fareham, Westbury Manor, West Street, (0392) 824896

Farnborough, The Library, Pinehurst Avenue, GU14 7JZ (0252) 513838

Fleet, Gurkha Square, Fleet Road, GU13 8BX (0252) 811151

Gosport*, Falkland Gardens, PO12 1EJ (0705) 522944

Havant, 1 Park Road South, PO9 1HA (0705) 480024

Hayling Island*, Sea Front, Beachlands, PO11 9QF (0705) 467111

Lymington*, St Thomas Street car-park (0590) 672522

Lyndhurst, New Forest Museum car-park (042 128) 2269

Petersfield, The County Library, 27 The Square, GU32 3HH (0730) 68829

Portsmouth
Portsmouth, The Hard, PO1 3QJ (0705) 826722
Continental Ferry Terminal*, Rudmore Roundabout, PO2 8QN (0705) 698111
Clarence Esplanade, Southsea, PO5 3PE (0705) 832464

Ringwood*, Furlong Lane car-park, BH24 1AZ (0425) 470896

Romsey*, Bus station car-park, Broadwater Road, SO5 8GT (0794) 512987

Rownhams M27 service area (westbound) SO1 8AW (0703) 730345

Southampton, Above Bar Precinct, SO9 4XF (0703) 631437

Winchester, Guildhall, The Broadway, SO23 9LJ (0962) 840500